DONALD EVANS is a member of the Department of Philosophy at the University of Toronto and author of *The Logic of Self-Involvement, Communist Faith and Christian Faith,* and *Struggle and Fulfilment.*

Donald Evans deals with the language and experience of religious faith, the attitudes necessary for authentic human existence, and the fundamental framework for moral decisions. He takes a comprehensive view in which philosophy of religion, philosophical anthropology, and moral philosophy converge as he focuses on certain pervasive attitudes which are the common core of faith, authenticity, and morality.

In setting out his own position Evans outlines and responds to the basic ideas of four influential thinkers: Ian Ramsey, Sam Keen, Gregory Baum, and Paul Ramsey. The book includes revised and extended versions of some articles previously published, reflecting important modifications in Evans's perspectives, and new materials which explain the shift in his thinking from linguistic analysis to existential reflection.

Evans first examines the problem of how religious language can indicate the transcendence of God while being grounded in human experience, contrasting 'objectivist' and 'existentialist' approaches. Moving to a consideration of religious experience, he argues that Keen's 'basic trust' implies belief in God. In dialogue with Baum he then weighs the relative importance of personal and political liberation. In the essays that follow, he turns to issues concerning moral decision-making, ultimately linking religious attitudes and moral virtues by showing their common origin – a receptivity to divine activity in human beings who are becoming more authentically human.

Faith, Authenticity, and Morality is an innovative exploration of some crucial issues in contemporary philosophy and religion by one of the most distinguished commentators on the subject.

DONALD EVANS

Faith, Authenticity, and Morality

UNIVERSITY OF TORONTO PRESS
Toronto Buffalo London

© University of Toronto Press 1980
Toronto Buffalo London
Printed in Canada

Library of Congress Cataloging in Publication Data

Evans, Donald D
  Faith, authenticity, and morality.

  Includes index.
  1. Christian ethics – United Church of Canada authors.
  I. Title.
  BJ1251.E85   241   79-21336
  ISBN 0-8020-5424-2

To Ian Ramsey
an inspiring teacher and a splendid man

Contents

Acknowledgments

The completion of this book was made possible by a Killam Senior Research Scholarship granted by the Canada Council for 1975–7. The book has been published with the help of grants from the Canadian Federation for the Humanities, using funds provided by the Social Sciences and Humanities Research Council of Canada, and from the Publications Fund of University of Toronto Press.

The book involves extensive quotation and/or paraphrase of material in essays which I have previously published. I acknowledge with thanks permission to use, in revised form, material from the following: 'Ian Ramsey on Talk about God,' *Religious Studies* 7:2, 3 (1971); 'Keen on Authentic Man,' *Studies in Religion*, 3:1 (1973); 'Gregory Baum's Theology of Liberation,' *Studies in Religion*, 1:1 (1971); 'Paul Ramsey on Exceptionless Moral Rules,' *The American Journal of Jurisprudence*, 16 (1971); 'Does Religious Faith Conflict with Moral Freedom?' in Gene Outka and John Reeder, eds, *Religion and Morality* (Doubleday, 1974); 'Philosophical Analysis and Religious Faith: Some Retrospective Reflections' in F. Duchesneau, ed, *Faith and the Contemporary Epistemologies* (University of Ottawa Press, 1977).

I also acknowledge with thanks permission to quote from letters which I received from Ian Ramsey (16 November 1970) and Gregory Baum (20 July 1970 and 22 October 1975) in response to my requests for comments on my interpretation of their works.

DE *July 1979*

Abbreviations

for works frequently cited in this book

WORKS BY IAN RAMSEY

AC   'The Authority of the Church Today,' in *Authority and the Church*, ed R.R. Williams (London: SPCK, 1965)

BP   'Biology and Personality: Some Philosophical Reflections,' in *Biology and Personality*, ed I. Ramsey (Oxford: Blackwell, 1965)

BPEM 'Berkeley and the Possibility of an Empirical Metaphysics,' in *New Studies in Berkeley's Philosophy*, ed Warren E. Steinkraus (New York: Holt, Rinehart & Winston, 1966)

BSR   *On Being Sure in Religion* (London: Athlone, 1963)

CD   *Christian Discourse* (London: Oxford University Press, 1965)

CE   'The Concept of the Eternal,' in *The Christian Hope*, no ed, SPCK Theological Collections No. 13 (London: SPCK, 1970)

FI   *Freedom and Immortality* (London: SCM, 1960)

FIR   'Some Further Reflections on *Freedom and Immortality*,' *The Hibbert Journal*, 59 (July 1961)

ICBC 'The Intellectual Crisis of British Christianity,' *Theology*, February 1965

LR   Letter from Ian Ramsey to Donald Evans, 16 November 1970, in response to a request for comments on Evans's 'Ian Ramsey on Talk about God'

MDA *Models for Divine Activity* (London: SCM, 1973)

MELP 'Miracles: an Exercise in Logical Mapwork,' in *The Miracles and the Resurrection*, no ed, SPCK Theological Collections No. 3 (London: SPCK, 1964). This Oxford Inaugural Lecture was first published in 1952 by The Clarendon Press.

MJGC 'Moral Judgments and God's Commands,' in *Christian Ethics and Contemporary Philosophy*, ed Ian Ramsey (London: SCM, 1966)
MM *Models and Mystery* (London: Oxford University Press, 1964)
MMR 'Models and Mystery: A Reply,' *Theoria to Theory*, 1:3 (April 1967)
MT 'On the Possibility and Purpose of a Metaphysical Theology,' in *Prospect for Metaphysics*, ed Ian Ramsey (London: Allen & Unwin, 1961)
PA 'Polanyi and J.L. Austin,' in *Intellect and Hope*, ed Thomas A. Langford and William H. Poteat (Durham, NC: Duke University Press, 1968)
PG 'A Personal God,' in *Prospect for Theology*, ed F.G. Healey (Welwyn, Herts: Nisbet, 1966)
PR 'Paradox in Religion,' *Aristotelian Society Supplementary Volume*, 33 (1959)
RB 'Reply to R.B. Braithwaite's *An Empiricist's View of the Nature of Nature of Religious Belief*,' in *Christian Ethics and Contemporary Philosophy*, ed Ian Ramsey (London: SCM, 1966)
RL *Religious Language* (London: SCM, 1957)
RS *Religion and Science: Conflict and Synthesis* (London: SPCK, 1964)
SEI 'The Systematic Elusiveness of "I",' *The Philosophical Quarterly*, July 1955
TG 'Talking about God: Models, Ancient and Modern,' in *Myth and Symbol*, ed F.W. Dillistone (London: SPCK, 1966)
TL 'Theological Literary,' *The Chicago Theological Seminary Register*, 53:5 (May 1963)

WORKS BY SAM KEEN

AW *Apology for Wonder* (New York: Harper, 1969)
BWE *Beginnings Without End* (New York: Harper, 1975)
TDG *To a Dancing God* (New York: Harper, 1970)
TYS with Anne Valley Fox, *Telling Your Story* (New York: Doubleday, 1973)
VV *Voices and Visions* (New York: Harper, 1974)

WORKS BY GREGORY BAUM

AR 'Alienation and Reconciliation: A Socio-Theological Approach,' in Francis A. Eigo, ed, *From Alienation to At-Oneness* (Villanova, Pa: Villanova University Press, 1977)

J   editor, *Journeys* (New York: Paulist Press, 1975)

LB   Letter from Baum to Donald Evans concerning chapter 4, October 1975; quoted with his permission

MB   *Man Becoming* (New York: Herder, 1970)

NCT 'Toward a New Catholic Theism,' *The Ecumenist*, May–June 1970

RA   *Religion and Alienation: A Theological Reading of Sociology* (New York: Paulist Press, 1975)

WORKS BY PAUL RAMSEY

CCE 'The Case of the Curious Exception,' in Paul Ramsey and Gene Outka, eds, *Norm and Context in Christian Ethics* (New York: Scribner's, 1968)

SR   'Some Rejoinders,' *The Journal of Religious Ethics*, 4:2 (Fall 1976)

SROM 'A Christian Approach to the Question of Sexual Relations Outside of Marriage,' *The Journal of Religion*, 15:2 (April 1965)

FAITH, AUTHENTICITY, AND MORALITY

Introduction

This book turned out to be very different from what I had originally envisaged. My first plan was simply to publish under one cover six essays which had appeared in various journals and books, so as to make them available together to a wider readership. Such a collection would not have been a mere aggregate, for the concluding essay would have dealt with many themes which had been discussed in the previous ones, and the other essays would have been connected in many ways, though implicitly. However, a reader for University of Toronto Press suggested that I undertake to relate the essays explicitly to each other and revise them in response to more recent works by the authors whom I discuss, and I then decided to extend them in response to developments in my own thought. The result is that instead of merely collecting some essays I have written a book. I have omitted one of the essays because it is not intimately connected with the others.[1] The rest appear as chapters in a cumulative argument which shows why I eventually came to have the philosophical approach and convictions which are set forth in the final chapters. And the intellectual autobiography goes beyond the original essays, for I have also included more recent discoveries and changes in my thought. Indeed, the book is roughly twice as long as the five essays were together in their previously published form.

Faith, Authenticity, and Morality is a philosophical study of three areas: the language and experience of religious faith, the personal and political attitudes which constitute authentic human existence, and the fundamental framework for moral decisions. These areas seem to be unrelated, but in my investigations they gradually converge. Philosophy of religion, philosophical anthropology, and moral philosophy can all focus on certain pervasive attitudes or ways-of-being-in-the-world which are the common core of faith, authenticity, and morality.

Only gradually, however, did this common focus become clear to me. At first I tended to consider religious faith, authentic human existence, and moral issues separately. And my ideas developed gradually not only in solitary reflection but also in scholarly dialogue with other thinkers. Four of these thinkers are discussed in the book: Ian Ramsey, Sam Keen, Gregory Baum, and Paul Ramsey. The late Ian Ramsey was a brilliant English philosopher whose account of traditional theories of analogy between man and God in terms of linguistic 'models' and 'qualifiers' is a very significant contribution to contemporary philosophy of religion. Sam Keen focuses not on language but on experience, writing with great sensitivity and depth concerning the inner struggles which are common to religion, psychotherapy, and existentialism as these are actually lived by people. I think that his account of authentic human existence is one of the most important in recent American philosophy. Gregory Baum is an outstanding Canadian theologian whose theology of liberation is in my opinion unmatched in its combination of profound perceptions concerning both the personal and the political dimensions of human life. Baum's understanding of human nature, and of the divine at work in man, is greatly enriched by his intensive studies and involvements in depth psychology and critical sociology. Paul Ramsey is generally acknowledged to be one of the most outstanding Christian ethicists since World War II, even by those who share with me a critical stance towards many of his conservative positions concerning particular moral issues. His reflections concerning the foundations of Christian ethics are tough-minded and challenging, so one learns a great deal by wrestling with his thought. The fifth thinker whom I consider and criticize in this book is myself. I look on myself, not as a pygmy gazing up at four giants, but as a colleague who tries to stand on their shoulders so as to see farther. And, to muddle the metaphor, I also stand on my own shoulders as I reflect retrospectively on what I thought and wrote in previous years.

In chapter 1 I outline the outcome of my own investigations concerning analogy. First I distinguish three kinds of analogy: analogy of activity (divine activity is analogous to human activity), analogy of relation (divine-human relating is analogous to human-human relating), and analogy of attitude (a religious attitude is analogous to a non-religious attitude and God is the appropriate focus of a religious attitude). Then I note that analogies can also differ in their content (the human activity, relation, or attitude used as starting-point) and in their form (the way in which this content is modified so as to be applicable to God). My classification of analogies provides a framework for interpreting the various ways of thinking about God which appear in subsequent chapters. Another framework is provided by a contrast between objectivism and existentialism. For an objectivist, meaning is best expressed in language which can be correctly understood in a neutral, impersonal way and truth is best discovered by a disinterested, detached observer. For an existentialist, meaning and truth are best ascertained from a non-neutral, self-involving stance.

Chapter 2 is the culmination of a series of studies in which I explore the linguistic dimension of religious faith.[2] Ian Ramsey's scattered writings concerning religious language and divine transcendence seem to contain many linguistic insights which need to be brought together and studied carefully. So I have decided to systematize and interpret his thought in a brief but comprehensive survey. I find very illuminating his account of *how* religious people talk and think about God, but not his account of *why* they do so. His account of such expressions as 'infinitely loving,' 'all-trustworthy,' and 'unchanging' shows how God may be thought of as analogous to human beings, that is, similar yet radically different. But his account of the experiential basis for such linguistic expressions is inadequate. For example, I note the need for a depth-psychological investigation of the pervasive trust which is expressed in such affirmations as 'God is all-trustworthy.' Like other analytic philosophers of religion, including myself, Ramsey needs what I call a 'more profound philosophical anthropology.' My conclusion is that 'Ramsey's interpretation of talk about God depends a great deal on what he believes about man, his conceptions of human trust, wonder, hope, commitment, love and integrity.' In the postscript to chapter 2 I consider such topics, and I delve more deeply into them in dialogue with Keen (chapter 3) and Baum (chapter 4).

In chapter 3 we move into normative anthropology. I ask such questions as 'What style of life is most in accord with human nature?' or 'What kind of character is most authentically human?' or 'What basic attitudes are necessary conditions for human fulfilment?' Such questions have to do with *ethics* – not an ethics of *doing*, in which we ponder what kinds of things we should do, but an ethics of *being*, in which we ask what kind of persons we should be. In chapter 3 the normative anthropology and ethics of being lead to religion, for Keen's normative anthropology is one in which a person's life-style and character and fulfilment are founded on basic trust; and I argue that such an attitude, which pervades a person's responses to his whole environment, implies a belief in divine Providence. I propose what I call an 'anthropological-logical' argument for religious belief which involves two contentions: (1) such-and-such an attitude is a necessary condition for human fulfilment and (2) the attitude implies a religious belief. Concerning Keen's anthropology, I note that although he is heavily dependent on Freud, for whom trust in Providence was an infantile illusion and delusion, Keen derives from Erik Erikson a psychoanalytic interpretation of basic trust which is open to a positive evaluation of such trust and of any religious beliefs which it may imply.

Whereas some of the most powerful and memorable passages in Keen's work draw on his experiences in individual psychotherapy, Baum's most moving language in *Man Becoming* (MB) expresses his insights into the process of *group* psychotherapy. In this process a man is confirmed and confronted by others and thereby enabled to let go of his self-deceptive and self-destructive defences, becoming receptive rather than resistant to life. For Baum in MB liberation is 'the passage from fear to trust, from hostility to love, from ignorance to self-knowledge, from passivity to creativity, from self-centeredness to concern for others.'[3] The process in which this change takes place is especially intensive and explicit in group psychotherapy, but it occurs in many situations where people meet face to face. For Baum God is the more-than-human mystery present in human life wherever man is liberated from dehumanizing forces. In MB the forces are mainly within individuals, especially in what may be called the 'familial unconscious': the unacknowledged defences against both love and pain which began in childhood and which continue throughout life. In Baum's more recent book, *Religion and Alienation* (RA), the dehumanizing forces are mainly in the power structures of society which collectively cause widespread injustice and misery. What Baum calls 'structures of domination' not only produce social evil but also produce a 'social unconscious' which is manifested in deceptive ideologies. These ideologies legitimate the structures of domination and sanction the social evil. In RA what Baum calls 'faith-conversion' is mainly politicization. It involves a liberation from the false consciousness so that one can now discern the nature and source of social evil, and it involves an identification with the powerless in their struggle against oppression and towards a more human society. In MB Baum emphasizes personal liberation, therapy, and depth psychology, connecting these with profound traditions of Christian piety. In RA Baum emphasizes political liberation, social action, and critical sociology, connecting these with profound traditions of Christian prophecy. Together, the two books provide a theological anthropology (or anthropological theology) which is very profound and wide-ranging.

The chapter on Paul Ramsey involves a rather abrupt switch from issues concerning religious faith and normative anthropology (with its ethics of *being*) to issues concerning an ethics of *doing*. The central question in the chapter has to do with exceptionless moral rules: Are there some kinds of action which I ought never to perform, whatever the consequences of not doing so? In a major article Ramsey not only defends exceptionless moral rules but also provides a major statement of the theoretical framework which he presupposes in his many writings on specific ethical problems. I found that as I responded to the challenge of his arguments against exceptionism I was forced not only to revise some of my own views so as to move towards exceptionless moral rules but also to recognize the importance of moral vocabulary in moral decision-making. Allegedly exceptionless moral rules usually involve such expressions as 'stealing,' 'slander,' 'lying,' 'adultery,' 'breach of confidence,' 'disloyalty to a friend,' 'torture,' and 'direct killing of the innocent.' Even if someone rejects the claim that one or all of these rules is exceptionless, he should recognize at least the intrinsic moral relevance of the fact that an action is properly described in one of these ways. Not only is moral deliberation a matter of reflecting concerning the consequences of an action; it also involves reflecting concerning the meaning of a moral term in relation to the action: Would this action be an instance of such-and-such? Moral vocabulary shapes our understanding of situations and actions and enters into our decisions concerning what to do. Since moral vocabulary is common to a community with a tradition, one can see that acceptance of a Christian moral vocabulary may be an important element in Christian faith. So Christian faith involves not only language which indicates divine transcendence (chapter 2), basic trust (chapter 3), receptivity to personal liberation and participation in social liberation (chapter 4), but also acceptance of a moral vocabulary.

All these elements and many others appear in chapter 6. Although the chapter has a narrow focus, indicated by its title 'Does Religious Faith Conflict with Moral Freedom?' and by the concrete religious material chosen for study, namely a new creed authorized by the United Church of Canada, it has grandiose aspirations. It is an outline sketch for a whole philosophy of faith and morality. In it I not only draw together many of the linguistic, anthropological, and moral reflections of the earlier essays; I also try to indicate some of the components of an overall view of religious faith, authentic existence, and morality. I link together religion and morality through their common origin: divine activity in authentically human individuals who are receptive. Receptivity is the common necessary condition for religious attitudes such as basic trust and for moral virtues such as love. In a postscript I go beyond this position and suggest that many pervasive stances such as basic trust are both religious attitudes and moral virtues, so that the human constituents of religion and morality are not merely linked to a common necessary condition but are actually identical.

The final chapter deals with two philosophical issues which have arisen in the book as a whole. First, there is a need to explain my shift in philosophical method from an analysis of religious language to an investigation of religious attitudes as these are experienced in a deeply personal way. Secondly, there is a need to clarify my claim that basic attitudes imply religious beliefs, so that if a man has basic trust he will realize in reflection that he is committed to belief in God. In my exploration of both issues I reach the conclusion that in order to understand what is central in religion we need to use language to get at experiences which are prior to language. Philosophical reflection is in this case an attempt to articulate pre-linguistic experience.

Three final notes: 1 / For the benefit of readers who have seen earlier versions of chapters 2 to 6 I outline, early in each chapter, the differences between the earlier and the present versions. The most lengthy additions are the postscript to chapter 2, the latter half of chapter 3, the discussion of Baum's RA in chapter 4, and the postscript to chapter 6. The first and last chapters are new, though they draw extensively on two previously published essays.[4] 2 / Chapter 5 differs from the others in that, whereas I provide a comprehensive survey of Ian Ramsey's philosophy, Sam Keen's philosophy, and Gregory Baum's recent theology, I deal directly with only one major article by Paul Ramsey. I have two reasons for not trying to survey his work in Christian ethics: the task is already being carried out by others,[5] and my own interest here is not in specific moral issues but in the foundations of ethics as these relate to faith. 3 / My writing style in this book does not reflect my acceptance of the feminist critique of traditional philosophical style in which human beings are referred to exclusively in male-gender language. In a book which is a companion volume to this one,[6] where I explore the conflict between human trust and distrust, I was free to follow a consistent policy concerning the need to include the female half of the human race explicitly in talk about human beings, for I was not involved in lengthy expositions of other thinkers whose style is traditional. In this book, however, with its extensive quotation and discussion of excerpts from works written prior to the development of scholarly sensitivity in this matter, I have followed earlier practices. For example, I know that Gregory Baum would not now talk about '*man* becoming' when generalizing about what it means to be human, but he did, and I have not tried to change from this even when I present my own views. Frequent variations in this regard would have been awkward and jarring.

1

Analogies and the Idea of God

In 1963, stimulated by the linguistic analysis of J.L. Austin, I published a book called *The Logic of Self-Involvement*.[1] It has the subtitle 'A philosophical study of everyday language with special reference to the Christian use of language about God as Creator.' Since 1963 my work in philosophy of religion has gradually shifted from Austinian analysis of secular and religious *language* to phenomenological and psychological investigations of secular and religious *attitudes*. This change in philosophical focus arose from reflections concerning the inadequacies of a purely linguistic approach to perennial problems in philosophy of religion, especially those concerning the use of analogies to indicate the transcendence of God. I have found Ian Ramsey illuminating, as we shall see, but I have gradually become convinced that his revised version of traditional 'analogy of being' needs to be supplemented by an 'analogy of attitude' and that the latter analogy requires far more than linguistic analysis for its elucidation. The need for an analogy of attitude has also emerged in my studies of Barth[2] and Preller[3] on analogy. The main impetus, however, has been from my reflections concerning issues which arose from *The Logic of Self-Involvement*. I have summarized some of these in a recent article,[4] which I shall be quoting or paraphrasing in the next few pages.

The most important and most novel item in *The Logic of Self-Involvement* was an analysis of what I have called 'onlooks,' that is, attitudes whose linguistic expression has, or can have, the form 'I look on *x* as *y*.' Here are some examples:

I look on my life as a game (or a struggle, or a search, or a voyage, or a dream, or a drama, or a pilgrimage).

I look on human history as a drama whose crisis is imminent (or a cycle of death and rebirth, or a series of challenges and responses).

I look on nature as an intimate companion (or a vindictive enemy, or a sacred trust, or a resource to be exploited).

I look on God as father (or shepherd, or judge, or liberator, or light, or breath of life, or architect and maker of the universe).

Not all onlooks have the linguistic form 'I look on x as y'; an onlook is an attitude which *can* be expressed in this form. The notion covers much of what has been called 'myth,' 'world-view,' 'ideology,' 'parable,' or 'symbolic framework.'

An analysis of onlooks can be very illuminating in matters of religious faith, as we shall see in chapter 6. But the problem of how to refer to a transcendent God cannot be illuminated in this way. In the formula 'I look on x as y,' if God is the x, the onlook presupposes some *prior* successful reference to Him. Once we have such a reference onlooks can have their very important place in religious language, but not before. So in *The Logic of Self-Involvement* I sketched the beginnings of an approach to the problem of divine transcendence.

I began with a metaphysical account of the human person. Influenced by Martin Buber and by later writings of Austin Farrer, I gave a special technical meaning to the word 'person.' What I meant by 'person' was something 'metaphysical' in the sense that it cannot be explained by reference to observable or introspectible characteristics of human beings, but only by reference to an *attitude* which is appropriate towards human beings as persons. In every human being there is something which, as I said, 'claims my concern, reverence, personal involvement and acknowledgment of value – my "*agapé*", to use the New Testament word. This attitude does not depend on his particular observable qualities. A person is a being *such that* "*agapé*" is the appropriate attitude. A person has something extra which makes this attitude appropriate, but I cannot specify this something extra except in terms of "*agapé*" ... Each human being has particular characteristics to which we respond with various attitudes; but to one attitude ("*agapé*") there is no correlative particular-characteristic. That to which this attitude is a correlative response is the man's "person".'[5]

The term 'person' was thus used to give an indirect or attitudinal description of a metaphysical entity: a person is a being such that *agapé* is appropriate. In a logically similar way God is a being such that *worship* is appropriate. Later on in the book I gave an indirect or attitudinal description of God. God is a transcendent metaphysical entity, and the transcendence is understood by reference to the *unlimited* character of the constituents of worship: unlimited glorification, submission, trust, awe, and openness. These constituents are responses to transcendent personal qualities in God: glory, authority, faithfulness, power, and presence. What these transcendent qualities are in God can only be understood indirectly, by reference to the unlimited attitudes which are the appropriate response or acknowledgment. God is thus a being such that worship is appropriate. God differs from man, not because God is unobservable whereas everything about man is observable, but because, although He resembles the personal-worth metaphysical reality in man, He is worthy of *worship* rather than *agapé*. And worship differs from *agapé* in being an *unlimited* active attitude. And worship differs from other attitudes, for example, trust, in being the *unlimited* version of that attitude. More generally, worship is similar to various human attitudes, yet radically different from them; that is, worship is *analogous* to them.

My approach in *The Logic of Self-Involvement* thus led me to explore what I came to call 'analogy of attitude' which I compared and contrasted with 'analogy of being' or 'analogy of activity.' Concerning the latter, I had come to accept Austin Farrer's view[6] that Thomistic analogy of being is most intelligibly understood as an analogy between human activity and divine activity, where divine activity has an unlimited character. I then began to recognize that Farrer's version of neo-Thomism was only one of many different versions of analogy of activity, which could vary in both *content* and *form*. The *content* of an analogy of activity is a positively-valued human activity which is chosen as a starting-point. Farrer's content is deliberate, free, moral action. Others can begin with different activities: loving someone, making an artefact, being artistically creative, using language to comprehend and communicate, inspiring someone by one's presence. The *form* of an analogy is a procedure whereby the meaning of the content is radically modified, while still retaining some connection with the original. In traditional analogy form is elucidated in terms of three 'ways': eminence (God is perfect or unlimited love), negation (God is not love), and causality (God is cause of love). Concerning analogy of attitude, which increasingly came to predominate in my thought, I found a similar variety based on differences in content and form. Concerning *content*, a variety of human attitudes have been suggested as starting-points for the analogy. Schleiermacher[7] began with dependence, Tillich[8] with concern, Otto[9] with awe, Buber[10] with

I-Thou openness, Keen[11] with trust. Which of the contents should be included? Which of those included should have priority? I found that linguistic analysis provides no answers to these questions. As I shall show in this book, I gradually came to see that these are questions of normative anthropology (which attitudes are constituents of human fulfilment?) and of existentialist epistemology (which attitudes are conditions for discerning the divine?).

Concerning the *form* of the various analogies of attitude, I wondered how to construe the way in which unlimited trust transcends limited trust. How does unlimited trust differ from very, very great trust? Can we actually understand what unlimited trust is or do we know only that it is *not* the same as any trust we can understand and that it lies in the direction of a scale of ever-increasing trust? Or is God to be construed mainly as the *cause* of trust? Concerning such problems I was at first fascinated by the linguistic dimension. For example, how are we to construe the shift in the meaning of the word 'trust' when someone says, 'I trust you, no matter what happens?' Where trust is thus unconditional it differs radically from ordinary trust for it does not presuppose a contrast between kinds of events which would tend to confirm it and kinds of events which would tend to disconfirm it. Another interesting feature of some analogies of attitude was one which I discovered at work in some analogies of activity as well – a fourth 'way' of *pervasiveness* alongside the three traditional ways. God is not only perfect love and not-love and cause of love but also pervasive love. And worship is not only perfect trust and not-trust and caused by God; it is also pervasive trust. In the next chapter I shall show how Ian Ramsey's discussion of analogy in terms of what he calls 'models' and 'qualifiers' helped me to see this: where the qualifier is a word such as 'all' ('all-trustworthy,' 'all-trusting'), the divine activity or human attitude is made all-inclusive or pervasive in scope. Through my study of Ramsey I thus came to see that religious attitudes are *doubly* pervasive: *outwardly* focused on a reality which pervades the whole natural and social environment and *inwardly* influential on all aspects of the personality and on all momentary stances towards particulars in the environment. I also became convinced that the inner pervasiveness is primary. In order to explore it adequately I had to shift from linguistic analysis to a kind of philosophical anthropology which, like Sam Keen's, draws on resources from phenomenology, depth psychology, and existentialism.

One existentialist whom I explored for insights concerning religious attitudes was Martin Buber. For some time I interpreted his conception of divine transcendence in terms of analogy of attitude: God is that towards which an unlimited and pervasive I-Thou attitude is appropriate. Such an interpretation does not totally misrepresent Buber. But neither does an interpretation in terms of analogy of activity: God's I-Thou addressing of us differs from the human in that it is perfectly constant and completely pervasive. Neither interpretation, however, allows us to see what is central in Buber: 'The relation to a human being is the proper metaphor (or real simile) for the relation to God.'[12] My prefabricated classification of analogies as either analogy of attitude or analogy of activity had to be enlarged so as to include a third kind: analogy of relation.[13] This kind, which is not confined to Buber, begins not with a human attitude or a human activity but with a human relation – in Buber's case, an I-Thou encounter. We do not consider divine activity in abstraction from appropriate human attitudes or vice versa; each is in dynamic relation with the other. The main focus is on what happens *between* God and man and *between* man and man, not on what happens '*inside*' each.

Is there a fourth kind of analogy? I do not know. Nor do I claim that the systematic subdividing of these analogies which I am about to present is comprehensive or final. But I have found that my abstract analysis of analogy has been a useful tool in interpreting and comparing a vast variety of philosophical theologies, including those considered in this book. So I am going to set forth my skeletal schema as a background framework for the rest of the book. Flesh and spirit will be added in subsequent chapters. Indeed, the structures of analogy have only emerged clearly for me as I pondered quite specific ways in which thinkers move from the human to the divine. The subsequent pigeon-holing of their thought is often provisional and is no substitute for a detailed exploration.

I have come to distinguish three kinds of analogy:

1 *Analogy of activity* God is activity which is analogous to such-and-such activity (call it A_1) of an individual human being.
2 *Analogy of attitude* God is that towards which an attitude of worship[14] is appropriate; worship is an attitude which is analogous to such-and-such an attitude (call it AT_1) towards another human being.
3 *Analogy of relation* God is that which is related to people in a way which is analogous to such-and-such relation (call it R_1) between two human beings.

Some thinkers such as Ian Ramsey present versions of all three kinds of analogy. Other thinkers restrict themselves entirely or almost entirely to one kind. Each kind of analogy starts with something human and then modifies or qualifies it in a radical way so as to indicate or describe divine transcendence. The human starting-point provides the specific *content* for the analogy (A_1 or AT_1 or R_1) and the kind of radical modification constitutes its *form*. For example, in Austin Farrer's version of analogy of activity the content is a deliberate, free, moral action and the form is a scale of increasingly less imperfect human activities (actual or ideal) which points towards a perfect activity which is divine. In Frederich Schleiermacher's version of analogy of attitude the appropriate stance towards God is an absolute dependence which resembles, but radically differs from, attitudes of dependence on other human beings in that it is pervasive and unlimited. In Martin Buber's version of analogy of relation God, like a human being who enters into personal encounter with us, addresses us in an I-Thou way, but the encounter is radically different in that it is pervasive and perfect.

Differences concerning content

The analogies employed by Farrer, Schleiermacher, and Buber differ because they are of different kinds: analogies of activity, of attitude, and of relation. But two analogies of the same kind may differ – in content or in form. Let us first look at differences in content, which are of two sorts: 1 / differences in the content itself and 2 / differences in the location of the content.

1 / The content itself may vary though the kind of analogy remains the same. In analogy of activity A_1 might be Farrer's deliberate, free, moral action, but it might be Victor Preller's[15] using language to know or some other important kind of human activity such as making artefacts. In analogy of attitude AT_1 might be Schleiermacher's dependence, but it might be Sam Keen's trust (see chapter 3) or some other important kind of human attitude such as obedience or gratitude or devotion. In analogy of relation R_1 might be Buber's I-Thou encounter, but it might be Paul Ramsey's mutual covenant (see chapter 5) or some other important kind of human relation such as that between ruler and subject.

For each kind of analogy the choice of something human to be the only content or the dominant content is of immense importance for the whole philosophical theology.

2 / A second difference concerning content may occur even when there is agreement concerning the *kind* of content selected as starting-point, for

example, the activity of loving or the attitude of trust or the relation of I-Thou encounter. The difference has to do with where this starting-point is to be located. Is it an activity, attitude, or relation which is common to human beings generally or is it uniquely in Jesus Christ, who is the only way to begin to think about God? Some Protestant liberals and some Roman Catholic defenders of natural theology accept the first alternative and some Barthians the second. Other thinkers such as Ian Ramsey take a *via media*. For them the content is present in human beings generally, but the unique and normative instance is in Jesus Christ.

Differences concerning form

I have noted two respects in which analogies which are of the same kind may differ in ways pertaining to content. They may also differ in *form*, in two main respects: 1 / concerning which 'way' of analogizing is emphasized, and 2 / concerning the extent of the transcendence ascribed to the divine beyond the human.

1 WAYS OF ANALOGIZING

I use the term 'way' to indicate my link with traditional analyses of traditional 'analogy of being' in terms of three 'ways': eminence, negation, and causality. My own analysis differs in two respects. First, the distinction into ways is not confined to analogy of activity (my version of analogy of being) but also applies to analogy of relation and analogy of attitude. Secondly, for each kind of analogy I include a way of 'pervasiveness,' so there are four ways, not three:

(i)   perfection (cf eminence)
(ii) negation (i.e. non-limitation)
(iii) pervasiveness (or universality)
(iv) origination (cf causality)

I shall first describe these four ways as they apply in *analogy of activity*. (In what follows, except for some additions concerning the way of origination, I quote from my own earlier study.[16])

(i) *Perfection*[17] We start with some human activity, such as making artefacts, judging wisely, or deciding freely; the activity is regarded as good in some respects and to some extent. We assume, or we claim to know, what counts as a limitation or imperfection in the activity, and we proceed to construct a scale of actual and then of conceivable cases of the activity, a scale in which imperfection gradually decreases. If we extrapolate the scale indefinitely upward, we see that it points towards *perfect* activity, activity than which none more perfect can be conceived. Since all limitation or imperfection is eliminated, it differs from any of the activities which we conceive on the scale, even the most eminent. There must be a shift in the meaning of terms such as 'maker,' 'wise,' or 'free' as applied to God, such that we cannot fully grasp the new meaning.

(ii) *Negation* The negative way insists that God is non-limited, non-finite. This way has three versions. In one version negation is a subordinate element in the way of perfection. As we have seen, limitations and imperfections are negated or denied as the scale in the way of perfection is being constructed. A second version is independent of the way of perfection, and radically qualifies it. Even the non-imperfect elements in human activity (actual or ideal) are not present in the divine activity. God is beyond all human concepts and categories, even the most lofty and abstract. God is neither wise nor non-wise, neither good nor evil, neither active nor inactive, neither existent nor non-existent ... The third version is closely linked with a mystical approach in religion: God is not anything which can be imagined or thought or felt, for a man finds God by emptying his mind of all images, thoughts, and feelings. The way of perfection, as a way of thinking about divine transcendence, must be transcended if God is known mystically.

(iii) *Pervasiveness* An activity which is noticed and understood in a particular situation is thought to be present in the whole of the world which a man experiences. For example, the active, trustworthy benevolence of a human parent is taken as representative of whatever power is pervasively or universally at work in one's whole natural and social environment. Since the meaning of 'trustworthy benevolence' as applied to a parent is understood by us in *contrast* with the untrustworthiness or the malevolence of other beings in the universe, the meaning must shift when the expression is applied to that which is active in *all* beings. According to the way of pervasiveness divine activity transcends human activity in that it somehow pervades the whole universe, not being confined to this or that spatio-temporal locus which can be contrasted with others.

(iv) *Origination* Divine activity transcends human activity by being its origin, source, or cause, not in a sense which eliminates free will, but as a source of power which either sustains human beings as centres of acti-vity in existence or liberates human beings so that an activity goes beyond unaided human powers. There are thus two species of origina-tion, which I shall call *'creation'* and *'grace.'* In both species there is usually an assumption that divine activity as source of human activity resembles what it originates as well as transcending it by being the source; but the resemblance assumed may be either considerable or minimal. In some thinkers any sharp distinction between the two species of origination is rejected, along with any sharp distinction between 'natural' and 'supernatural'; the relation between divine activity and a human activity such as loving is both sustaining and liberating. Where the distinction between creation and grace is maintained, it corresponds roughly to a distinction between contents: activity found in human beings generally versus activity found only in Christ or in those like him. Where origination is grace, God is the periodic liberating source of our 'break-throughs' in our own activity. Here the choice of content is espe-cially important. In what 'break-throughs' is God believed to be most significantly at work? In a religious experience or in a resolution of an Oedipal complex or in a new commitment to the cause of the oppressed?

Analogy of attitude also has four ways. (For (i) and (iii) I quote from my own study.[18])

(i) *Perfection* We start with some human attitude as it occurs when appropriately focused on people or things: trust, hope, courage, grati-tude, awe, humility, dependence, submission, conscientiousness, loyal devotion, rejoicing in another. Considering the attitude, we assume or we claim to know what counts as an imperfection or limitation in it, and we construct a scale of actual and then of conceivable cases of the attitude, a scale in which imperfection gradually decreases. If we think of an indefinite upward extrapolation of the scale, we see that it points towards a perfect attitude (e.g. perfect trust). This perfect attitude would be (true) worship, or an element in (true) worship. God is that towards which such an attitude is appropriate.

(ii) *Negation* The negative way insists that worship is *not* limited in various respects. This way has three versions. In the first version nega-tion is a subordinate element in the way of perfection; as the scale of decreasing imperfection is constructed, imperfections are negated. The second version is independent of the way of perfection and radically qualifies it: true worship transcends even the non-imperfect elements in the attitude which provide the starting-point for the analogy. For example, Rudolph Otto's 'numinous' experiences[19] are extremely different from any awe which might be considered in a scale. In the third version negation is part of a mysticism in which there must be a detachment from all attitudes to spatio-temporal beings: true worship is *not* any of these attitudes, even exalted versions of them.

(iii) *Pervasiveness* I shall outline this analogy by using trust as an example. If a man trusts Jones not to harm him, this attitude involves only a 'part' of him, and it is focused only on one 'part' of the universe. Consider what happens if trust becomes an ongoing basic stance of his whole personality *vis-à-vis* the whole natural and social environment. Then the attitude is pervasive and unrestricted in scope, both within the person and in external range. The man still trusts Jones in one respect and perhaps distrusts Smith in another, but there is an overall trustful stance towards Jones and Smith and everyone, and towards things in nature. This stance unifies the variety of particular attitudes to particular people and things: the man is generally trustful rather than wary, defensive, and anxious. And the world has a unity corresponding to this trust: whatever it is that pervades the whole cosmos, giving it unity, is trustworthy; it is reliably *for* me rather than neutral or against me. Pervasive trust differs radically from ordinary trust in that this or that specific harm (even suffering or death) is not precluded, yet somehow I cannot *really* be harmed. As Wittgenstein said concerning his experience of feeling '*absolutely* safe': 'I am safe, nothing can injure me whatever happens.'[20] This obviously involves some shift in the meaning of 'trust.'

(iv) *Origination* This is similar to origination in analogy of activity, except that here the divine activity is the source of an attitude rather than an activity. There are two species, as before – creation and grace. The version of origination which seems to me to be of most interest is a special version of origination as grace. The attitude with which one starts is neither an obviously non-transcendent attitude such as ordinary trust or hope or courage nor an attitude which surpasses ordinary attitudes solely in that grace is required to supplement human powers or dispositions. Instead, one starts with a transcendent attitude, having already employed one or more of the other three ways. Thus God is first understood by means of one or more of the other ways and then God is understood as being, also, the *source* of that transcendent attitude, e.g. absolute hope (Marcel)[21] or courage in spite of meaninglessness (Tillich).[22] The notion of origin or source is used here, of course, in such a way as not to eliminate human freedom to receive the attitude or to reject it.

Analogy of relation also has four ways.

(i) *Perfection* We start with some human relation, e.g. an I-Thou encounter (Buber) or a covenant (Paul Ramsey, see chapter 5). Considering the relation, we assume or claim to know what counts as an imperfection or limitation on it, and we construct a scale of actual and then of conceivable cases of the relation, a scale in which the imperfection gradually decreases in one of the participants while the other responds accordingly. If we think of an indefinite upward extrapolation of the scale, we see that it points towards a perfect relation between God and an ideally responsive human being.

(ii) *Negation* The negative way insists that the relation between God and man is *not* limited in various respects. As in the case of analogy of activity and analogy of attitude the negative way has three versions which I shall not repeat here.

(iii) *Pervasiveness* A person *A* starts with a relation such as an I-Thou relation with another person *B*. This particular relation with *B* is distinguishable from his I-Thou relations with other persons *C, D, E,* and *F,* for each of these persons has a distinct, contrasting spatio-temporal identity. But *A* may become involved in a pervasive relation if he takes his relation to any of the other persons as representative of a relation which differs from all particular relations in that it is all-inclusive. The pervasive relation is present in all of *A*'s relations with other persons and all of his other dealings with his environment. The pervasive relation is not another relation alongside others; rather, it is the ultimate context for all these relations. *A* knows that with which he is pervasively related only as the Other in that relation; and the relation is known only as that *within* which one sees everything particular as happening or existing.

(iv) *Origination* This is a way in which God transcends the human relation by being somehow its origin or source, though without violating human freedom. God is a hidden influence at work in relations between persons, working either as creation or grace. (In chapter 4 we shall see how Gregory Baum uses the way of origination as grace when he depicts God as the gracious mysterious presence at work in the mutual confirmation and confrontation which occurs in therapeutic groups and elsewhere when people encounter one another in depth.)

We have considered the first respect in which analogies may differ according to their form, namely according to the *way* which is emphasized. The second respect has to do with differing interpretations of the *transcendence* which the analogy involves. How great is the gap between the human and the divine?

2 EXTENT OF TRANSCENDENCE

Some thinkers are very cautious, others very confident, concerning the extent to which analogy involves or provides an understanding of God. Although this difference can sometimes be understood as a matter of the extent to which the negative way is emphasized and the version of that way which is employed, it can also be understood in terms of differing interpretations of one or more of the other three ways. Consider, for example, the way of perfection in analogy of activity. There are differing views concerning the shift in meaning of words applied to God (I quote from my own study.[23]) Some religious thinkers hold that the only thing we know about this meaning is what the *direction* of the scale indicates. For example, concerning wisdom, it is less misleading to think of God's wisdom as being like the highest wisdom I can conceive than to think it is like my own actual wisdom; and certainly it is less misleading to say 'God is wise' than to say 'God is stupid.' Although some thinkers claim not more than this concerning our understanding of divine transcendence, others claim that we have a glimpse, as it were, of that beyond which the scale points. Indeed, some would go beyond this to claim that the glimpse of divine transcendence is what enables us to construct our scale in the proper direction.

Dominance of one kind of analogy

Philosophical theologies differ not only concerning the content and form of analogies but also concerning which kind of analogy is dominant. If analogy of activity is dominant and is interpreted in a confident way with respect to our thereby understanding transcendent divine activity, there is no need to use the other kinds of analogy to determine our relation to God and appropriate attitudes towards God. These can be based directly on what has been already established concerning divine activity. If analogy of attitude is dominant and is interpreted in a confident way, there is no need for analogy of activity or analogy of relation. God is defined as 'that towards which worship is appropriate.' If we understand fairly clearly what worship is, we can see what divine activity must be if worship is to be the appropriate attitude towards it, and we can understand the relation of man to God as that of worshipper to appropriate focus of worship. If, however, analogy of relation is dominant (e.g. in my own thought: see chapter 6), neither divine activity nor appropriate human attitudes can be considered separately, for the meaning of each correlates with that of the other. For example, the pervasiveness of reliable divine activity and the pervasiveness of human trust in response to it are understood in relation to each other, not separately. An analogy of activity and an analogy of attitude are developed in reciprocal dependence, both being subordinated to an analogy of relation. This subordination holds whether the analogy of relation is interpreted in a confident or a cautious way.

We have considered how analogies may differ in content (kind of content and location of content), in form ('way' and extent of transcendence), and in relative dominance. Another way in which analogies differ has to do with the epistemological presuppositions which underlie their use. Thinkers differ concerning what attitudes are best for understanding meaning and for discovering truth. Two rival epistemologies can be distinguished, which I shall call 'objectivist' and 'existentialist.'[24]

Objectivism versus existentialism

For an objectivist, meaning is best expressed in language which can be correctly understood in a neutral, impersonal way, and truth is best discovered by a disinterested, detached observer. Subjective involvement with whatever is being understood and known is something which varies from person to person and which usually distorts one's comprehension and perception (unless set aside or consciously allowed for) so it is an obstacle to attaining universal inter-subjective agreement concerning meaning and truth. An objectivist use of analogy thus insists on minimal self-involvement in understanding both the initial meaning of the content and the subsequent meaning when the analogy shifts to transcendence as the form is applied. Otherwise what each person means by 'transcendence' or 'God' may differ, and the terms cannot have a real, objective reference, since for each person it will be a matter of 'God *for me.*' Hence an objectivist using analogy of activity will typically start with a content which is comprehensible impersonally and neutrally at both the beginning and the end of the process of thought in which the analogy is applied – for example, he will use 'making' as content and apply a way of perfection which points towards divine making such as creation *ex nihilo.* Even if the *degree* to which one understands *ex nihilo* is minimal, the *kind* of understanding should be impersonal and neutral.

What I call an 'existentialist' approach differs from objectivism in that a specific kind of self-involvement is held to be a prerequisite for understanding what is being said and for discovering the truth. Moreover, the quality and extent of one's self-involvement will determine the degree of adequacy of one's understanding and the degree to which one discovers the truth. The species of self-involvement which one existentialist thinker calls for often differs from what another calls for. What they all have in common is that the prerequisite attitude is contrary to the neutral detachment of objectivists. When an existentialist uses analogy, he will insist on some kind of self-involvement in understanding – perhaps in understanding the initial human content, certainly in understanding the transcendent activity, relation, or attitude. For example, Buber's analogy of relation begins with a content (human I-Thou encounters) which requires an I-Thou attitude to be understood, and moves to a transcendent I-Thou relation which cannot be understood in an I-It way. (I-It attitudes include those which I call 'objectivist.')

At first sight my contrast between objectivist and existentialist analogy might seem to coincide with my contrast between analogy of activity on the one hand and analogy of relation and analogy of attitude on the other. This was my own first impression. The initial content of an analogy of activity is typically some human activity which one can understand (or thinks one understands) in an objectivist way – making, deciding, thinking, etc. Indeed, the activity may be one which an objectivist regards as best carried on in an objectivist way. If the initial content itself includes some subjective involvement (e.g. loving), he may nevertheless think he can understand it in an objectivist way; if he can, and only in so far as he can, the analogy can be properly begun. The application of the form to the content in analogy of activity is also typically objectivist, with no new subjective involvement required as one moves in thought from the human to the divine. But analogy of activity *could* be existentialist. The initial content might be a human activity which the thinker believes can only be understood to the extent one is subjectively involved in it, e.g. loving someone or artistically creating something or raising someone's political consciousness. And even if the initial content has no such prerequisite for understanding, there may be one for the process of thought which occurs as the form is applied. For example, someone may claim that the way of perfection in analogy of activity requires personal aspiration; otherwise the movement of thought and words towards perfection is empty of any transcendent meaning.

Analogy of relation and analogy of attitude are typically existentialist. Usually the initial human relation or human attitude cannot be adequately understood unless one is subjectively involved in that kind of relation or attitude. And usually the transcendent relation or attitude has self-involving requirements for understanding which are even more stringent. But it is possible to have versions of each analogy which are objectivist. If one starts with a content which is itself carried on in an objectivist manner, an objectivist way of understanding it is appropriate. For example, the human relation in an analogy of relation might be one in which two people work together, dispassionately and disinterestedly, making an artefact. Or the human attitude in an analogy of attitude might be itself objectivist, for example, impersonal neutrality. If the way of pervasiveness is applied in each case we end up with a divine-human relation of pervasive co-creation or with a kind of worship which is a pervasively objectivist stance (a scientific stoic's contemplative posture). Then the transcendent relation or the transcendent attitude is open to objectivist understanding. If, however, the content for an analogy of relation or an analogy of attitude requires self-involvement to be under-stood properly, an objectivist approach seems inappropriate. There are some subtle and important questions which arise even in this kind of case. But it is time we turned to consider Ian Ramsey.

2

Ian Ramsey on Talk about God

For Ian Ramsey[1] talk about God raises many philosophical problems:

If we are not to use anthropomorphic concepts like love, power, wisdom, we cannot talk about God; but if we *do* use them, how do we manage to talk of God and not man? (MJGC 152*)

Believers wish on the one hand to claim that he (God) is indescribable and ineffable, and yet on the other hand to talk a great deal about him. Nay more, when they speak of God they say that he is transcendent and immanent, impassible yet loving, and so on. But if we speak like this, are we talking significantly at all? Here is the Falsification Problem: What kind of talk can this talk about God be, if it permits us to use such conflicting descriptions of God and to continue to use these descriptions in the face of any and all empirical phenomena? (RL 13–14)

Ramsey holds that we can manage to talk of God while using anthropomorphic concepts, and that talk about God can be significant in spite of apparent contradictions. His philosophy is essentially an account of *how* such talk is significant. He presents his analysis of religious language as an answer to the narrow empiricism of Antony Flew (MM 59–60) and Richard Braithwaite (RB 84) and also as an alternative to the accounts given by Karl Barth (PR 212) or a 'Scholastic doctrine of analogy' (MM 7). His is an important alternative, one of the most important in modern philosophy of religion, but it is difficult to grasp as a whole. Ramsey's philosophy is scattered among many brief occasional pieces, in each of which some old Ramsey ideas are sketched and some new Ramsey ideas

* Abbreviations are identified on pp xi–xii.

are introduced. He provides no comprehensive overall account.[2] Instead, his philosophy emerges like a jigsaw puzzle where each piece overlaps with some of the others and also fills a gap left by all the others. Moreover, even when all the existing pieces are put in place, there are gaps left open; we have only some hints as to how they might eventually be filled.

This essay is an attempt to provide a comprehensive overall picture, an outline sketch of Ramsey's philosophy as I understand it. Since it is only an essay, and since it is not only a summary but also an interpretation of Ramsey's thought, it may be misleading in some respects. Certainly it will not convey the stimulating brilliance and lively wit of Ramsey's writing. But it seems to me important to try to obtain an overall picture. I have found that doing so has forced me to set aside many criticisms of Ramsey which arise from piecemeal studies of his works, since Ramsey often remedies obscurities and defects in one book or article by dealing with them in another. When we can see an overall picture the real weaknesses of his philosophy, as well as the strengths, emerge much more clearly. For this book I have added a postscript in which I indicate what I take to be some of the weaknesses and strengths. I also show how such considerations have influenced my own thought.

This chapter differs from the essay originally published in 1971 not only by the addition of a postscript but also by the addition of new notes and by some changes in the text itself. The revision is designed to explore more fully various issues which are also considered in other chapters of this book. In addition, Ramsey commented on the 1971 version of the essay in a private letter[3] and also referred me to his 1966 Zenos Lectures (MDA) which were not available in print until 1973. In this version of the essay I note and respond to some important new material in his letter and his lectures.

The chapter consists of five sections and a postscript. In the first section we shall consider what Ramsey regarded as his first task: to challenge a narrow form of empiricism in which reality consists solely of what is publicly observable (ICBC 109). If such an empiricism were accepted, any belief in God would obviously be untenable. Ramsey proposes a wider form of empiricism. He holds that whatever is real has some relation to experience, but that what men experience cannot be reduced to public observables, since what men often discern is observables and 'more.' Unless there is 'more' there is no God, though to show that there is 'more' is not in itself to show that there is God.

1 Discernment of 'more'

Ramsey gives a great many different examples of situations where we discern observables and 'more.' Indeed, he provides such a vast variety of examples, useful perhaps in a shot-gun barrage against narrow empiricism, that the reader is bewildered. Ramsey does not sort out his examples clearly, distinguishing them into types each of which has a different kind of 'more.' And his examples are not equally relevant, or in the same way relevant, to the 'more' which is God. My own classification, which covers most of his examples, would be as follows:

1 *Awareness of I*

(a) *I*, as a conscious subject using language, am more than my describable, observable behaviour. For the subject-object distinction presupposes that there is at least one subject, and all language presupposes a subject using language. (BP 180; MM 27; TL 4; RS 39–41)

(b) *I*, as conscious agent, acting in a free or personal or authentic way, in contrast with an involuntary (or conditioned reflex) way, an impersonal (or official) way, or an unauthentic way, am more than my describable, observable behaviour. (FI chs 1, 2; MT 169, RL 22–3)

2 *Personal encounter* The *I* of another human being whom we discern in personal encounter is more than his describable, observable behaviour. (PG 63–8; RL 19–20, 26; RS 14; cf BP 203, AC 71)

3 *Moral claim* A moral claim to which one responds in a situation is more than the situation as described in terms of observables. (FI ch 2; RL 16–18, 29–31; MT 172; MJGC 166–7; RS 42–3; BP 185–6)

4 *Aesthetic wonder* An impressive work of art such as a picture, a poem, or a symphony, which evokes wonder, is more than the describable features of the work of art. (RL 72–3; cf RS 13–14; RL 76)

5 *Whole* A whole is more than the sum of its parts. For example, a Gestalt pattern is more than the sum of its parts. (RL 23–4; MM 10; CD 5; FI 93–4; cf CE 41–3, 47)

6 *Scientific models* What a scientific model is about is more than the observables to which it is applied. For example, electricity as a current is more than what is observed; light as waves or particles is more than what is seen; the opposition of an induced current to a magnet is more than what is observed. (MM 13–14, 19–21; RS 20–2)

7 *Infinite mathematical series* A circle is more than any polygon in an infinite series where each polygon has one more side than the previous polygon. The number 2 is more than any sum in an infinite

series '1 plus ½ plus ¼ plus ⅛ plus ¹⁄₁₆ ...' (RL 69–70; TG 91; PR 206, 208; FIR 354)

8 *Concrete particular* A particular thing in its concrete particularity is more than any list of features on the basis of which we recognize it or identify it. (PA 178, 183; MELP 6–7; cf BP 198)

All these kinds of 'more' will be discussed at various points in the essay. All are important, in different ways, for the overall picture. The central case of the 'more,' however, is 1b. For Ramsey the awareness of *I* is the key to all the other discernments of 'more.' He links it closely to the experience of freedom in human activity. Unfortunately his account of freedom is rather crude and confused. For example, he equates actions which are impersonal or official with behaviour which is merely a reaction to stimuli (FI 29, 33). And although he sometimes restricts freedom to cases of response to moral claim (FI 30, 38), sometimes he does not; instead, he finds freedom wherever an action has the agent's 'personal backing' (FI 21–4). But it is better to ignore such defects in his analysis, and to consider the main thrust of his argument, which is to focus our attention on cases of self-awareness which are paradigms, cases where the experience of *I* is most intense, powerful, and indubitable. 'The paradigm for understanding all disclosures is the disclosure that each of us has of himself in decisive, free, moral action' (FIR 355; cf FIR 350–1). In paradigm cases Ramsey holds that we can have no doubt about 'I' referring to something experienced, yet what the word refers to is something which transcends all descriptions in terms of behaviour. We should note that although the 'more' to which 'I' refers is best discerned in paradigm cases, these cases differ for Ramsey only in degree from others where the self-awareness is minimal. Indeed, Ramsey holds concerning class 1a that *I* is presupposed in *any* experience, since it has a subject-object structure, and in *any* conscious use of language, since any use implies a user; *I* is presupposed even though the subject of experience or the language-user is only minimally aware of *I*. The examples under 1b, however, are needed to elucidate any minimal self-awareness in 1a. Concerning 1b, Ramsey's main points are these:

(i) That to which 'I' refers *transcends description*.
(ii) Nevertheless the word 'I' is *presupposed* by all discourse concerning me (though 'I exist' does *not entail* any statements in this discourse). 'I' thus can be said to 'preside' in a *unifying* way over the discourse.

(iii) The word 'I' refers to a 'more' which is *discernible*, that is, in some way experienceable.

(iv) This 'more' is a form of *activity* rather than a mere happening or movement.

Ramsey links 1b closely with the next three kinds of 'more': with personal encounter (PG 63–4), moral claim (FI 30, 38; RS 42–3; MT 167), and aesthetic wonder (RL 72–3). The paradigm cases of 1b are all *responses*. Maximal self-awareness occurs in responses to another person, a moral claim, or an aesthetic wonder. From this two things follow. First, the paradigm discernments of *I* are correlated with discernments of something *other* than *I*. The other is something 'more' than observables, according to Ramsey. Self-awareness is correlated with awareness of an external other which, like the self, transcends observables. Secondly, the discernment of self and other is associated with a response which is a self-involvement, a commitment, rather than a flat, neutral, disinterested assent. We shall consider Ramsey on commitment more fully later on. We shall also return to examples in classes 5, 6, 7, and 8.

The next step, however, is to outline Ramsey's position concerning the *objectivity* of the 'more.'[4] He distinguishes three senses of 'objectivity.' In one sense *all* experience is objective. That is, it is an experience of something, of an object; it has a subject-object structure (RL 24, 28; MMR 268). In this (to me, dubious) sense Ramsey claims objectivity for dream images (CD 88) and for hallucinations of pink rats (ICBC 109). In a second sense there is the objectivity which characterizes physical objects, an objectivity 'which people only too often take as a paradigm of objectivity' (MDA 61). (This sense is similar to what I called 'objectivism' in chapter 1.) A similar objectivity characterizes human beings when we study them scientifically. We pick out publicly observable features of a physical object or a person in accordance with our own interests and purposes. These features are 'objective' rather than 'subjective' in that their reality can be confirmed by other observations and other observers; in this sense dream images and hallucinations are not objective but subjective. In a third sense, which applies to Ramsey's 'more,' 'the claim for "objectivity" – "objective reference" – is grounded in the sense I have of being confronted, of being acted upon, in the discernment I have of some claim impinging on me' (MDA 61) *via* dream images or physical objects or duty or persons (MDA 62). This kind of objectivity, according to Ramsey, involves a *disclosure* of the 'more,' concerning which he says a great deal

(MM 58; CD 88; PG 66–8; TG 87–8; PA 196; FI 99). We do not discern the 'more' in a wilful way, prying out its secrets on our own initiative; rather, we respond to a disclosure, which occurs when we are actively confronted by another agency or quasi-agency which declares or reveals the 'more' to us. We are aware of an initiative which is like our own but not our own. We are relatively passive in relation to the initiating activity of that to which we respond. (This third sense of 'objective' is the closest to what I have called an 'existentialist' way of discerning reality.)

The notion of disclosure is obviously most immediately applicable to situations of personal encounter (class 2), when we respond to the self-disclosure of another human being. But Ramsey also finds a quasi-personal disclosure when he discerns a moral claim (class 3), where there is something 'which may be usefully compared with the claims another person makes on us in social behaviour' (MJGC 169; cf MT 172). The experience of moral obligation or duty is an experience which is similar to being confronted, challenged, or commanded, even though no other human being need be confronting, challenging, or commanding us. And when we respond to a work of art with aesthetic wonder (class 4), Ramsey says that 'something is exhibited which is characteristically personal,' namely, the genius or inspiration of the creative artist (RL 72).

Ramsey even claims that the notion of disclosure extends to any recognition of concrete particulars (class 8). Particular things disclose their reality to us (PA 183, 196). Here Ramsey's statement seems to be similar to the thought of Martin Buber, who talks about an 'I-Thou' encounter with a tree.[5] Like Buber, Ramsey is not ascribing consciousness or a soul to a tree, but he is emphasizing our sense of being confronted, of an initiative and a reality which is not our own. Ramsey finds *activity* in the particular thing, something remotely analogous to human activity. Similarly in his account of scientific models and invariants (class 6), which abstract from particulars, he also finds something remotely analogous to personal activity (RS 72–4, 82; TG 93; MMR 266). One reason for this is that according to Ramsey many of the most general concepts which we apply to nature (energy, opposition, attraction) have primary application to our own activity as persons (CD 84; cf TG 93). Another reason is that, according to Ramsey, reference to reality is assured to models and invariants, and even to fundamental conceptual schemes (AC 69, 72), by virtue of the disclosure character of the insights from which they arise. A scientific model is authenticated because the universe discloses itself (MM 13, 19). What science is about is always 'disclosure given' (MMR 268; cf MM 20–1).

Ramsey seems to be stressing the element of passivity in our experience of discernment or insight, the sense of an initiative not our own which is at work, remotely resembling in its reality that of another human being who actively reveals himself to us. Thus he finds disclosures even in the mathematical cases (class 7), when we see that the infinite sum points to the number 2 (RL 69–70), and in the moment of Gestalt insight (class 5), when we move from parts to whole (RL 23–4). As he often says, 'The penny drops'; we do not make it drop. Since even the 'more' of mathematics or Gestalt is disclosed to us, all eight classes of 'more' are disclosures. And we see that for Ramsey the notions of 'more,' 'objectivity' (i.e. reality), 'disclosure,' and 'activity' are all closely interrelated, and are all extended in meaning from a paradigm application, namely the experience of freely responsive self-awareness (class 1b).

Ramsey's first step is thus a challenge to any narrow form of empiricism which reduces reality to public observables. His second step is to relate the various kinds of 'more' to disclosures which are 'cosmic.'

2 The 'more' and cosmic disclosures

The first clue concerning the relation between the 'more' and cosmic disclosures is to be found in what Ramsey says about self-involvement or commitment. We have seen that in so far as any discernment of the 'more' includes a response to a disclosure it includes some personal commitment. Ramsey gives most emphasis to the commitment in our responses to moral claims, but he also points out our commitment of trust or loyalty to a friend in personal encounter. Indeed, Ramsey extends the notion of commitment or self-involvement so that it is included in the response to a concrete particular (PA 194), the acceptance of a scientific or common-sense conceptual framework (AC 69–70, 72), and the acceptance of a set of geometrical axioms (RL 32–4). When Ramsey discusses religious commitment first in RL, he says that it differs from non-religious commitment in a twofold way. It is a 'total commitment to the *whole* universe' (RL 37). He notes that a commitment to some geometrical axioms has the whole universe as its scope (RL 32–5); but the commitment is not itself religious, for it is not total, it does not involve the whole man. In contrast with this, a captain's commitment to his ship or a man's commitment to his beloved may be total; but, according to Ramsey in RL, the scope of such commitments is far less than the whole universe and hence they are not in themselves religious. A religious commitment must be both all-inclusive in its scope or reference and total in its personal involvement. It must be cosmic in range and it must subordinate all a man's other commitments, concerns, and inclinations to itself. It is unrestricted and pervasive in scope, both external and internal. (This double pervasiveness of religious commitments will be extremely important in my discussion of faith in chapters 3 and 6. It is also relevant to my account of Ramsey's 'universalizing qualifiers' later in this chapter.)

The cosmic and personal elements come together for Ramsey in our commitment when we respond to an overriding, unconditional moral claim in a particular situation (RL 30–1; FI 40–2; MMR 265). If I acknowledge that I ought, unconditionally, to do X in this particular situation, my commitment has a negative all-inclusiveness; whatever else may be the case in the whole universe, X is my Duty in this situation; I am refraining from responding to anything other than the particular, overriding moral claim. This negative all-inclusiveness is obviously different from the positive all-inclusiveness of some commitments which we shall consider later, for example, 'I trust the universe.' Ramsey nevertheless holds that the negatively all-inclusive commitment to a Duty in a particular situation can be called 'cosmic' (PG 69). Since the personal element is evident in the unconditional, total self-involvement of the response to Duty, the response is for Ramsey a *religious* commitment, fulfilling both the cosmic and the personal conditions for religion.

Although for Ramsey an unconditional moral commitment is religious, and is a response to a cosmic disclosure, it is not by itself a response to *God*. Ramsey says that if the only cosmic disclosure were that of Duty or Absolute Value, there would be no need for the term 'God' (FI 46–7; cf MT 173). 'Duty' or 'Absolute Value' would suffice. The term 'God,' for Ramsey, integrates a *variety* of cosmic disclosures, as we shall see. Here we should note a typical and crucial step which Ramsey has already taken in his argument: he has assumed that the 'more' in *all* cases of overriding moral claim is some *one* reality. We have already noted his basis for ascribing reality to each moral claim: we have a sense of being actively confronted by another. But here a further step is taken: *one* reality, which deserves a metaphysical label such as 'Duty' (or 'God'), is confronting us in each and every instance.

Commitments in response to overriding moral claims are not the only ones which are negatively all-inclusive. Although in RL Ramsey denies that the loyal devotion of captain or lover is cosmic in scope, in later writings he cites 'You are the whole world to me' alongside a statement concerning Duty as an expression of cosmic commitment and disclosure

(MMR 265; cf TG 87, FI 63). This later view is more consistent with his position concerning moral commitments, for the speaker is saying, in effect, 'Nothing else matters except my devotion to you' (cf 'Nothing else matters except doing X, my duty in this situation.') But probably Ramsey is ambivalent about how to classify a total personal commitment which is focused on only a *part* of the universe. On the one hand, the commitment, like a Tillichian ultimate concern focused on one's spouse or one's nation, is religious in its personal pervasiveness. On the other hand, in spite of its negative all-inclusiveness, it is not positively cosmic; indeed it is idolatrous. Ramsey does not say much about idolatry (RB 84–6; TL 7–8), but his position seems to be similar to that of Tillich: a total commitment or ultimate concern should not be focused on any finite observable, or even on the particular 'more' disclosed in a finite observable and considered by itself, but only on God. Concerning idolatry and Duty Ramsey is not clear. On the one hand, he does not seem to allow that an unconditional response to Duty could ever be idolatrous, even though Duty is only negatively all-inclusive. On the other hand, he does insist that, although a particular disclosure of one's Duty in a particular situation may be certain, there should be an openness to new and different disclosures, and a flexibility in any formulation of moral policy (BSR 36, 46–7).

We have been considering the negative all-inclusiveness of duty or devotion. What would a disclosure commitment with positive all-inclusiveness be? The best examples in Ramsey, I think, are those where a 'more' of the whole universe is disclosed in a context of personal encounter or of aesthetic wonder. Let us consider personal encounter (TG 79–81; PG 63–5; RL 26–7; MM 16, 59). First, according to Ramsey, I have personal encounters with other human beings in which their trustworthiness and concern are disclosed and I respond with trust and gratitude, feeling secure and at home. Then there is a disclosure of a somewhat similar trustworthiness and concern in some aspect of nature. Ramsey points to the reliable regularity of the seasons, with their seed-time and harvest (TG 80; MDA 16). He also reminds us of particular occasions when a landscape 'comes alive.' Our surroundings feel familiar and 'this familiarity develops into a feeling of friendship which finally evokes a sense of cosmic kinship' (RL 27). In one passage Ramsey waxes Wordsworthian:

It may be that we are walking in remote, mountainous country, and as night comes on we are filled with all kinds of uncertainties and anxieties. But then we refresh ourselves at a mountain stream, look up to the stars as symbols of stability, and find our path illuminated by the moon. A sense of kinship with nature strikes us; the Universe is reliable after all. (TG 80)

Note the move from a particular situation to the whole Universe. The situation is taken as representative of the whole (CD 7). The quasi-personal 'more' to which Ramsey's traveller feels a kinship and to which he commits himself in trust is disclosed through the stream, the stars, and the moon; but it is also related to everything that has brought them and him together in the particular situation. The disclosure is that the Universe is reliable.

Peter Berger[6] talks about a cosmic disclosure of reliability. He describes how a particular person, 'a face of reassuring love, bending over our terror,' can symbolize a cosmic trustworthiness. A child wakes in the night, alone and frightened. Mother comes, and her presence somehow conveys the message 'Everything is all right.' For Berger this common parental reassurance has such cosmic scope ('not just this particular anxiety, not just this particular pain – but *everything* is all right') that it can be translated as 'Have trust in being.' A similar disclosure is cited by Ramsey from chapter 3 of Joseph Conrad's *Typhoon* (MDA 3–4). A seaman, Jukes, describes his experience as the ship is hit by a typhoon:

The darkness palpitated down upon all this, and the real thing came at last. It was something formidable and swift, like the sudden smashing of a vial of wrath. It seemed to explode all round the ship with an overpowering concussion and a rush of great waters, as if an immense dam had been blown up to windward. In an instant the men lost touch with each other. This is the disintegrating power of a great wind: it isolates one from one's kind. An earthquake, a landslip, an avalanche, overtake a man incidentally, as it were without passion. A furious gale attacks him like a personal enemy, tries to grasp his limbs, fastens upon his mind, seeks to rout his very spirit out of him. Jukes was driven away from his commander. He fancied himself whirled a great distance through the air ...

He poked his head forward, groping for the ear of his commander. His lips touched it – big, fleshy, very wet. He cried in an agitated tone, 'Our boats are going now, sir.'

And again he heard that voice, forced and ringing feebly, but with a penetrating effect of quietness in the enormous discord of noises, as if sent out from some remote spot of peace beyond the black wastes of the gale; again he heard a man's voice – the frail and indomitable sound that can be made to carry an infinity of thought, resolution and purpose, that shall be pronouncing confident words on the last day, when heavens fall, and justice is done – again he heard it, and it was crying to him, as if from very, very far – 'All right.'

To what extent are claims based on cosmic disclosures based on empirical evidence? Obviously if we interpret 'Everything is all right' as an empirical generalization comparable to 'All swans are white' it is false. The claim has to be understood in the context of a disclosure experience which somehow takes account of events which seem contrary to its truth. The conviction of Ramsey's traveller that the universe is reliable does not preclude his perishing under an avalanche a few minutes later, and he knows this. The child and Jukes feel reassured in spite of a darkness and loneliness and terror which do not totally disappear. Yet although cosmic disclosures are not generalizations based inductively on empirical evidence, Ramsey maintains that they do have a measure of empirical support. For example, he holds that patterns in the world resemble the reliable regularity of a trustworthy friend (TG 80; cf MM 16; PG 65). This rational support from empirically observable patterns in the world Ramsey calls 'empirical fit' (MM 17, 21, 58–9). This empirical fit is important:

If the empirical circumstances were such that some threatening frowning state of affairs could rarely, if ever, be seen in the perspective of a world smiling upon us; if Whittier's counsel to take a long look back never showed cares and trials like mountain ranges overpast, never traced undeserved blessings, then providential discourse would be unjustified.   (MDA 20)

Ramsey concedes, however, that empirical fit is not a matter of an argument from analogy such as those which Hume effectively disposed of. There is no straightforward analogy between the way the world goes and the way a reliable friend or benevolent administrator treats us. Providential discourse, such as talk about a divine 'economy,' is justified by a cosmic disclosure which arises from a 'way of looking at the world' (MDA 17). A trustworthy particular is not seen as one item of empirical evidence to add to our store of inductive data; rather we look on it as a representative of the whole.

An aside: It seems to me that Ramsey does not attach enough importance to the perspective or onlook which we have to bring to the world if there is to be a cosmic disclosure of Providence. It seems to me that the disclosure is most closely linked, not with patterns in the world, but with patterns in the *psyche* of the viewer. Patterns in the world are relevant, and help to give some plausibility to claims which, though not based on induction, are not blatantly contrary to inductive evidence. But whether or not the universe seems friendly rather than hostile or neutral or conflictual depends more on the individual's conscious and unconscious view of himself and of other human beings. Indeed, whether or not he sees a universe at all – as Ramsey does – rather than an unintegrated multiverse or even a chaos depends a great deal on the extent to which his own personality is well-integrated. World-views and depth psychology are intimately related. I shall discuss this further in the postscript to this chapter and in the next chapter.

Let us continue Ramsey's account of cosmic disclosures, shifting from personal encounters to responses of aesthetic wonder (RL 72–3). When we are impressed by a work of art, our response of wonder and awe is a response to the creative 'more' in a particular, finite observable. Ramsey claims that we can move from this to a response of wonder which 'has the whole universe as its focus' (RL 73). How? If Ramsey treated this case in a way similar to his treatment of personal encounters, the next step after viewing a work of art would be to respond with wonder to something in nature which is similar to a work of art. Then we would take the particular wonder in nature as representative of the whole, a disclosure of the 'more' of the universe. Ramsey's actual treatment of this case, however, is different, though such a route to a cosmic disclosure would be quite compatible with his philosophy. Ramsey does arrive at a cosmic, all-inclusive disclosure, but by a different route. Using a 'qualified-model' approach (which we shall examine later), he applies the formula 'creator *ex nihilo*.' For Ramsey, 'creator' is the descriptive term, the model, and '*ex nihilo*' is the prescriptive qualifier, the directive concerning what to do with the model. We are to construct a series of real or imagined works of art (creations) in each of which there is less and less dependence on pre-existing material and more and more dependence on the creativity of the artist. Since eventually in the series there is no pre-existing material, the creation then includes *everything*. Hence the disclosure which occurs is cosmic, all-inclusive.

Ramsey maintains that we are responding to the same 'more,' namely God, when we respond to an unconditional moral claim, to a trustworthy cosmic providence, or to a wondrous cosmic creativity. To apply the term 'God' to a cosmic disclosure is to consider it in relation to other cosmic disclosures, claiming that the same single reality is revealed in all of them. Thus when Ramsey considers 'God' and unconditional moral claims, he says that to move from 'Doing X is my Duty' to 'Doing X is God's will' is to provide an alternative account of the same disclosure, but in a more comprehensive context, one which includes non-moral cosmic disclosures (FI 46–55; cf MJGC 167–8; FIR 354–5). The expressions 'God' and 'God's will' include not only the 'Duty' disclosed in situations of moral claim, but also the reassuring cosmic trustworthiness disclosed in seed-time and harvest, and the wondrous cosmic activity disclosed in the sheer existence of created beings. Though Ramsey does not give the latter disclosures labels, let us do so: 'Providence' and 'Creativity.' Ramsey is then saying that to move from talk about 'Duty' to talk about God is to talk about the disclosure of Duty in a more comprehensive context, which includes disclosures of Providence and Creativity. Similarly 'Providence' would be replaceable by 'God' when related to Duty and Creativity; and 'Creativity' would be replaceable by 'God' when related to Duty and Providence. The word 'God' refers to the one 'more' in all three kinds of disclosure, the 'one cosmic individuation' which is the 'objective reference of every cosmic disclosure' (MDA 65).

Ramsey's way of relating Duty to Providence and Creativity is very relevant to issues which will be considered more fully in chapter 6, issues concerning relations between morality and religion. For this reason, as background for chapter 6, I shall here digress briefly from the main flow of my outline of Ramsey's philosophy to consider what he says or implies concerning these issues. It is clear that according to Ramsey one cannot *derive* moral judgments from statements concerning God which depend on *non*-moral cosmic disclosures, statements concerning God as Providence or Creativity. And although Christians may seem to derive moral judgments from statements about God's 'will' or 'command,' this is not so. Ramsey notes that a moral judgment is open to *interpretation* in terms of such talk, since the judgment is a response to an unconditional, overriding moral *claim* (MJGC 165), and responding to such a claim is analogous to responding to a command. But talk about God's command is not logically parallel to talk about, say, the sergeant-major's command. I can discover what the latter is by hearing it, and I can decide whether or not what he commands is moral. But according to Ramsey the only way I can discover what God's commands are is by responding to moral claims which are disclosed as unconditional; thus there would be no sense in asking whether a divine command were moral or whether it were unconditional. Ramsey does not regard a moral claim as unconditional (or as moral) because he believes or knows it to be a divine command. Rather, he regards a moral claim as a divine command (i.e. as a claim disclosing the same cosmic individuation as disclosures of Providence and Creativity) because it is unconditional. Thus on the one hand morality is for Ramsey autonomous from religion, if we mean by 'religion' the non-moral elements in religion. And on the other hand morality is itself religious, it is part of religion, in so far as it is based on moral claims which are unconditional.

Let us return to Ramsey's assumption that in all three kinds of cosmic disclosure – Duty, Providence, and Creativity – there is one 'more,' one 'cosmic individuation,' one single 'objective reference.' Why so? Why not three 'mores'? One reason is that for Ramsey all three disclosures have to do with the same range of observables, namely, the whole universe. I question this, for it seems to me that Duty is merely *negatively* all-inclusive. Indeed, I shall argue later on that an assumption of unity for all disclosures does not arise from their all having to do with the whole universe, but rather from the human need for *personal* unity instead of being split among various total commitments. But let us continue to follow Ramsey's own line of argument here. For him all three disclosures have to do with the whole universe. Why does it follow from this that the same 'more' is disclosed in each? It follows for Ramsey because he is convinced concerning an analogy between *I*-and-my-behaviour and God-and-universe. There is only one 'more,' one '*I*' for all my varied behaviour, and the relation between God and the universe is analogous to the relation between *I* and my behaviour. 'God is other than the Universe ... as he who discloses himself in and through it, something like, though not exactly like, the way we disclose ourselves through our bodily behaviour' (MMR 269). And, of course, we each disclose ourselves in various ways – making moral demands on people, being reliable friends, creating works of art – but it is the same *I* which is disclosed.

This analogy between God as the 'more' of the universe and *I* as the 'more' of my behaviour is a central pivot in Ramsey's philosophy. Before we explore it more fully, we should notice one possible source of confusion concerning it. Ramsey sometimes uses '*I*' to refer, not only to the 'more' of my behaviour, but to all my behaviour and its 'more.' The word '*I*' does not refer to an entity which is separable logically, epistemologically, or ontologically from some expressions in bodily behaviour. The word 'God,' in so far as it resembles '*I*,' is similarly linked to the universe. So Ramsey sometimes uses 'God' to refer, not only to the 'more' of the universe, but to the whole universe and its 'more.' The word 'God,' like '*I*,' may refer to *observables and 'more'* (RL 38; TL 11). Each word may refer to a *whole* (CE 41) which includes both an aggregate of observables and the 'more' which unifies them. Usually, however, it is most appropriate to interpret Ramsey as using 'I' and 'God' to refer to the 'more,' considered as distinct from observables. Thus God is the 'more' of the universe.

In some passages Ramsey is apt to mislead readers because he equates 'God' and 'universe' or 'whole universe.' He says that the word 'God' refers to the whole universe (CD 82), and he uses 'the universe' where one would expect him to use 'God': the universe 'declares itself' (PG 66; MM 58), 'discloses itself' (MM 13, 19), or 'confronts us' (TG 87). Ramsey's language here is puzzling,[7] but it can be interpreted so as to cohere with his main ideas. In these passages he is using 'universe' and 'whole universe' to mean 'all the observables and their "more"' (one of the meanings for 'God'), whereas usually 'universe' means 'all the observables' (or 'cosmos' or 'world'). In these passages the universe is viewed as a whole which includes not only all observables but also the 'more' which unites them all together.

In my exposition of Ramsey I have been using 'universe' as a synonym for 'world' or 'cosmos,' and I shall continue to do so. Thus 'God' refers either to the universe and its 'more' or to the 'more' of the universe. The latter is usually the most appropriate version: God is the 'more' of the universe, its 'single individuation' (TG 87) whose relation to the universe is analogous to the relation between *I* and my behaviour. This analogy is so central in Ramsey's philosophy that it deserves special consideration. Why does it seem to him to be so apt and so illuminating?

3 God and 'I'

The first reason is that, as we have seen, Ramsey thinks that the scope of observables for all cosmic disclosures is the same, namely, the universe. Similarly the scope of observables for disclosure of *I* is the same, namely my bodily behaviour. And as my body is that by means of which men refer to me, the observable basis for identifying me as a distinct individual, so the universe is that by means of which men refer to God, the observable basis for identifying Him as a 'single individuation.' Since the universe is spatially all-inclusive, references to God have two peculiarities. First, it makes no sense to talk about trying to 'locate' God, as one might locate a man, for God is the 'more' of the universe, and it makes no sense to talk about locating the universe (PG 68; cf CD 74–5). Secondly, there is no possibility that the word 'God' might have no reference, as the expression 'planet of the Evening Star' may have no reference. The reference is for Ramsey 'inalienable' (CD 89; cf CD 82), since there can be no problem in referring to the universe, and since 'God' refers to the 'more' of the universe – whatever that more may turn out to be.

We have been thinking of the identification, location, and reference for *I* and God in *spatial* terms. A second reason why the analogy between *I* and God seems apt and important to Ramsey has to do with *time.* According to Ramsey both *I* and God include that which is in temporal succession while also transcending it. The transcendence of time by *I* is for Ramsey closely linked with the free activity of *I*, especially in response to Duty (FI 66, 73; cf FI 23). His argument is that what *I* responds to is spatio-temporal and '*more,*' and that there is an awareness of *I* as being similarly transcendent. Personal activity takes place in a particular place at a particular time, but it does not consist solely of that which can be described in spatial and temporal terms. *I* transcends the finite sequence of observable behaviour, not only in a particular action, but over a whole life-time, unifying it into a whole. God similarly transcends a sequence of observables in which He is active, unifying it into a whole (CE 41), but the sequence is a doubly infinite temporal series, infinite both retrospectively and prospectively. This all-inclusive temporal series, called 'sempiternity,' may be the context or setting for a cosmic disclosure to men, a disclosure of God as eternal (CE 48; cf CE 44, 47; FI 76, 79). If we start in a particular situation with a disclosure of love or vitality and consider it in the setting of sempiternity, the cosmic disclosure is of God as eternal love or eternal life.

A third reason why Ramsey's analogy between God and *I* seems illuminating to him has to do with *activity.* All cosmic disclosures are of a 'more' which is a confronting activity that is somewhat like, though not exactly like, the confronting activity of another human being. The cosmic disclosures all have an objectivity, a reality, which is somewhat like that of another *I* (PG 68).[8] Indeed Ramsey criticizes some theologians in so far as their accounts lack a sense of the objective activity and otherness of God (CD 59, 76). We should note that for Ramsey even Duty is to some extent like *I*. He does speak of Duty as 'non-personal' or 'impersonal' (PG 69; cf CD 83), but he also says (in the same place) that in a disclosure of categorical obligation 'we are aware of an *activity* confronting, engaging our own.' He warns us that we cannot safely talk about Duty as God's 'command' or 'will' unless we realize how vastly different this talk is from talk about a man's 'command' or 'will' (MJGC 169–70; cf FI 51). But he also notes that we experience Duty as a claim which is comparable to the claim of another human being to whom we respond in social behaviour (MJGC 168–9).

A fourth reason for Ramsey to stress his analogy between God and *I* has to do with a contrast which he applies to both, a contrast between certain, incorrigible awareness and uncertain, corrigible description (MT 176; AC 74; cf FIR 355; PR 212; BSR 1, 23; CD 25; TL 5–6; BP 183–4, 187). 'We are as certain of God as we are of ourselves ... But no description is guaranteed' (MT 176). Ramsey considers the statement 'I have a headache' (MT 176) and analyses it into two parts: 'I exist (incorrigible) ... with a headache (corrigible).' Similarly any statements concerning God involve for Ramsey an incorrigible element ('God exists') and a corrigible, descriptive element. 'God exists' is incorrigible *both* because one cannot fail to refer to God (*qua* the 'more,' whatever it is, of the universe), and because one cannot doubt that one is being actively confronted by a real, objective other (PG 68; MDA 61). Whenever my *I* is disclosed to me, I am incorrigibly certain concerning my own existence, but any statement in which I express what is disclosed is corrigible. Similarly when God is disclosed to me, I am certain concerning His existence, but any statement in which I express what is disclosed is corrigible. Both *I* and God transcend description. Both, however, are disclosed in and through describable observables, and what is disclosed is related to those observables (BP 183–4, 187). Both 'I' and 'God' are 'united with verifiably descriptive words, without themselves being verifiably descriptive' (PR 209; cf PR 215).

Fifth, we should notice one way in which Ramsey manages to maintain his key analogy when it is threatened by the possibility of a plurality of cosmic 'mores' or of a self-contradictory cosmic 'more.' The threat comes from traditional religious statements which seem to be grounded in cosmic disclosures that conflict. Ramsey meets the threat by interpreting the statements so that they are all grounded in qualitatively similar situations. For example (PR 208), he claims to reconcile talk about God as 'infinitely loving' and 'impassible' by relating both expressions to the 'same kind of situation' – presumably one which has to do with an unchanging stability or reliability, a providential concern for man. He also brings together God as 'Duty' and as 'all-powerful' by interpreting the latter in terms of the power of a never-failing love, which has a moral claim upon us (FI 56–9). He interprets 'eternal punishment' (BSR 18–19) in relation to a disclosure of a reconciling love which overcomes separation, and 'eternal death' (BSR 20) in relation to a disclosure of 'infinite love' to men who feel 'utterly isolated, forsaken, alone.' Yet 'impassibility,' 'omnipotence,' 'eternal punishment,' and 'eternal death' *can* be linked, respectively, with disclosures of cosmic aloofness, ruthlessness, vindictiveness, and emptiness. Ramsey can plausibly and coherently relate all cosmic disclosures to one divine 'more,' but this is because he selects his disclosures and interprets them on an already assumed basis which provides criteria of selection and principles of interpretation. Some of this basis is provided by his conviction that a cosmic disclosure occurs when we respond to the 'more' disclosed in the life, death, and resurrection of Jesus Christ, which is a 'more' of loving personal activity (CD 25, 59; RB 87; TL 39; RL 166, 173; MDA 40). For Ramsey the love disclosed in Jesus Christ is at work everywhere – in the midst of human suffering, moral inadequacy, and death, and even within the pain and travail of nature. It is true that Ramsey associates talk about God as 'Father' and as 'Holy Spirit' with cosmic disclosures which are somewhat different from those associated with talk about God as 'Son,' disclosed in Jesus Christ (TL 39). But the christological disclosures seem to be the most important. They provide an implicit criterion of selection, for in practice Ramsey does not allow anything contrary to them to *count* as a cosmic disclosure. And Ramsey tends to interpret all traditional religious statements in relation to disclosures of loving personal activity. Thus Ramsey's analogy between God and I is supported by his stress on the self-disclosure of God in loving personal activity, especially that of Jesus Christ.

A sixth support for the analogy is closely related to this. For Ramsey the human behaviour which can be an occasion for cosmic disclosure of divine love is not restricted to that of Jesus Christ. The behaviour of Christians – individually and as a church – should also provide such an occasion for cosmic disclosure. That is, the appropriate response to a cosmic disclosure of divine love is not only a response of *worship* towards God (RL 89, 185; TL 39; FI 58), a worship which is a loving, total commitment (RL 46); it is also a response of *witness* (TL 39; AC 71–80; CD 24–5, 59–60). Witness is behaviour which so expresses love towards other men that it can be for other men an occasion for cosmic disclosure. If Ramsey mentioned only worship, he would be saying that the response of men to God is somewhat like the response of men to another I who actively confronts them. But in his talk about witness he is also saying that God actively discloses Himself *through* some of the activity of men; so for this additional reason God is like the I of men. The bodily behaviour of Jesus, and sometimes that of Christians, discloses not only the activity of men but also (or therein) the activity of God. (How the divine and human activities are related is not adequately clarified by Ramsey, as we shall see.)

The seventh support for Ramsey's analogy between God and *I* is not theological, but metaphysical (MT 173–4; RS 73–4, 79; FI 48; RL 59–60; MELP passim). As a metaphysician Ramsey looks for one ultimate concept by which to find unity in the universe. A metaphysical key-word must, he thinks, be able to unify diverse kinds of language while not being restricted to any one of them. If it belongs only to one, there will be category mix-ups when it is applied to another. Ramsey finds that the word 'I' unifies the diverse kinds of language (gross-behavioural, physiological, chemical, physical, etc) which are used to describe me, while not belonging exclusively to any one of these. All particular descriptions of me presuppose 'I' or 'I exist' or 'I am active,' though 'I exist' or 'I am active' entail no particular descriptions of me. Ramsey finds that the word 'God' works in a similar way. It can integrate the vast variety of kinds of language which are used to describe part or all of the universe. Each and every descriptive assertion presupposes 'God exists' or 'God is active,' but these entail no descriptive assertions.

A metaphysical key-word must fulfil a second requirement for Ramsey. It must unify, not by being more abstract than all other terms, more remote from the reality of concrete particulars, but by referring to this reality (MELP 7). Within Ramsey's philosophy we can see how 'I' does this for language concerning me. But how can 'God' do this for all of language? Ramsey holds that any word, suitably qualified, can lead to the characteristically religious situation of disclosure (RL 80) and that there is no situation which cannot in principle give rise to a cosmic disclosure (TG 87). This is because for Ramsey every disclosure whatsoever, if understood in a wide enough context, can eventually bear the name 'God' (FIR 354–5; cf MT 172, n 2). This is true of a disclosure of the 'more' of a concrete particular. It is also true of the disclosure of the 'more' of a Gestalt, a scientific model, or a mathematical series. In each case the 'more' is an active reality which does the disclosing. For Ramsey, assuming his analogy between *I* and God, the reality in each case is God. Let us consider the analogy again. Suppose that I see Jones moving his little finger. I see the finger moving and 'more' – the 'more' being the *I* of Jones. The same *I* is also sometimes disclosed in a movement of arms or legs. The same *I* is also disclosed sometimes when Jones acts in an intensely personal way; but in such cases the disclosure of *I* is much more profound. Similarly, for Ramsey, any disclosure of 'more,' if set in the comprehensive context of other disclosures of 'more' in the universe, is a disclosure of God. Indeed, the analogy has still further implications. Disclosures of the *I* of Jones vary in the extent to which the reality of *I* is revealed, but all are disclosures of *I*. Similarly all disclosures of reality vary in the extent to which the reality of God is therein revealed, but all are disclosures of God.

Here Ramsey closely resembles William Temple,[9] for whom all events are revelations of God, though not equally revelatory, and for whom the transcendence of God in relation to the world is like the transcendence of *I* in relation to my bodily behaviour. Like Temple, Ramsey is open to two critical questions:

First, what is the relation between the activity, reality, or 'more' of God and that of the particular person, situation, or thing through which God discloses Himself? If the relation between God and observables in the universe is like that between *I* and observable bodily behaviour, what then is the relation between God and *non*-observables such as the 'more' of a man or of a tree? What is the relation between God and *I*, between God's activity and mine?

Secondly, how does God transcend not only the world, but *I*? How does the transcendence of God transcend the transcendence of *I*?

We shall consider these questions in turn.

4 The one 'more' and the many 'more'

The relation between *I* and my bodily behaviour does not provide an apt analogy for the relation between God and *I*, or between God and any of the many particular 'mores' of particular observables. The relation between the one divine 'more' and the many particular 'mores' needs another kind of analogy if it is to be at all intelligible. Ramsey seems to hint at another kind of analogy, another kind of approach to the use of the word 'God' as a unifying key-word:

The word 'God' is a unique and ultimate key-word dominating the whole of a theistic language scheme, an 'irreducible posit' to which the theist appeals as his end-point of explanation. (PR 208)

Concerning the expression 'irreducible posit' (which also occurs alongside 'key-word' in RL 47) he refers us to a page in Quine's 'Two Dogmas of Empiricism,' which in turn refers us to some pages in Quine's 'On What There Is.' The Quine essays[10] also seem relevant to Ramsey's attack on the 'illegitimate supposition that theological words *mirror* and *picture* what they talk about' (PR 217, my italics), for Quine attacks a similar supposition concerning words and statements in general. I shall briefly sketch some of the ideas expressed by Quine in his two essays.

Quine rejects a narrow empiricism in which each word or each statement is related to a particular set of sense experiences for both its reference and its meaning. Quine insists that statements are related to sense
experiences 'not individually but only as a corporate body.'[11] Some statements such as those about physical objects ('The cat is on the mat'),
while not reducible to statements about sense experiences, are very
closely related to them and dependent on them. But other statements
('Hydrogen atoms have one electron') are more remote from sense experiences, so that no particular sense experiences are strictly linked with
them as confirmation or infirmation. For Quine physical objects are
'irreducible posits.'[12] That is, they have a reality of their own, not being
reducible to sense experience, but they are posited by human beings who
create linguistic and conceptual schemes. At a more abstract level we
posit theoretical entities such as electrons. Even more remote from particular sense experience, we posit entities of mathematics and logic. Quine
assumes[13] that there are *entities*, referred to by terms in our statements, at
each stage of remoteness from sense experience. The ontological furniture
of the universe does not consist solely of sense experiences or of physical
objects. Electrons, for example, *exist* even though they are irreducible
posits, not identifiable with any particular set of sense experiences or
physical objects. On the other hand, if we start from some sense experiences, we can talk about them in relation to electrons if we widen the
context beyond those particular sense experiences and shift into electron
talk.

Any interpretation of Ramsey in relation to Quine has to be tentative,
for the evidence is slim. But I think I can see what it is in Quine that
Ramsey finds congenial and useful. For Quine a theoretical word can
have a real reference which is not a reference to some particular sense
experiences or particular physical objects, while nevertheless we can talk
about a sense experience or a physical object in relation to the theoretical
word if we widen the context and shift into the appropriate theoretical
level of language. Thus for Ramsey 'God' can have a real reference which
is not any particular, yet we can talk about a particular in terms of God if
we widen the context cosmically, and shift into religious language.
Ramsey differs from Quine, of course, in that Quine is interested in
scientific theoretical terms rather than in 'God,' and has nothing like
Ramsey's 'more.' Where a Quinean theoretical term is remotely linked to
sense experiences, Ramsey's 'God' is remotely linked to *discernments* of the
'mores' of particular persons and things. These 'mores' are discerned in
experiences which include sense experience but go beyond it, experi-

ences where we are aware of being actively confronted by a particular reality. The word 'God' does not refer to any particular 'more' or to any group of 'mores' as an aggregate. Rather, in this strand of his thought Ramsey seems to be suggesting the following analogy: The word 'God' is related to the particular 'mores' in a way which is somewhat analogous to the way in which a Quinean theoretical term is related to that which is experienced in sense experience.

If Ramsey were to apply this analogy fairly rigorously, there would be no discernment experience of the divine 'more.' Instead, there would be an experience of a particular 'more,' the 'more' of a finite particular, and this 'more' would then be related to the theoretical term 'God' in a complex linguistic scheme which as a whole is applied to the universe. Sometimes Ramsey seems to be thinking in this way, but he also has ideas which tend in an opposite direction. We have seen that he allows for discernment experiences of 'more' when we are using theoretical scientific or mathematical terms; and he seems to allow for a discernment experience of God as such – especially, as we shall see, in the use of model-and-qualifier language. Thus it seems that for Ramsey the term 'God' resembles both a Quinean theoretical term (e.g. 'electron') and a word used to refer to the 'more' of a concrete particular (e.g. 'I'). His main emphasis is on the latter comparison, on the analogy between God/observable universe and I/observable bodily behaviour. This analogy, which we have considered in the previous section, does not elucidate the relation between God and *non*-observables such as I. What is the relation between the activity, reality, or 'more' of God and that of a particular person, situation, or thing through which God discloses Himself? The analogy which Ramsey seems to be deriving and adapting from Quine has the merit of linking divine 'more' and particular 'more' without identifying them. To identify them is *either* to make God the sole reality, eliminating the distinct reality of the many particular 'mores,' *or* to reduce God to being an aggregate of the many particular 'mores.' But the analogy drawn from Quine has the demerit of down-grading and depersonalizing the reality of God. Even if a Quinean theoretical term is thought to have a real reference, the reality is very different from the reality of an active I, and inferior to it. To think of God as if He were like an electron is virtually to reject any thought concerning Him as being like an I – which is the thought from which we start in Ramsey. Surely we are more likely to elucidate the relation between God and an I or quasi-I by comparing it to the relation between two finite Is, the relation where one person inspires, encourages, influences another person. This analogy, too, has its drawbacks. It obscures the relation between God and the observable universe, and it does not indicate how God can unite all realities if He is one particular reality alongside other particular realities. Nevertheless it is a better analogy in this context than Ramsey's favourite analogy is. The analogy between God/observable universe and I/observable behaviour simply does not help at all when we try to understand the relation between God and non-observables such as the 'more' of my behaviour or the 'more' of a tree.[14]

One way of considering the relation is indicated in Ramsey's suggestion that *activity* is a fundamental unifying concept (MELP 16–24; CD 84; PG 69; MT 174). We have seen that for Ramsey God is disclosed as activity in a variety of kinds of activity – primarily in human activity, but also in activity which only remotely resembles human activity. For example, the disclosure of God as Duty is a disclosure of an activity to which we respond, though the activity is only to a limited extent comparable to the activity of a human *I* which makes claims on us. There is also a remote analogy between the activity of *I* and the activity of God as disclosed in that of physical things (CD 84) or of entities in scientific theory – their 'opposition' (RS 21–2) or 'energy' (TG 93). God as activity somehow unites all the varied kinds of activity in the universe. How? One possibility would be that God is activity-as-such, that which the varied kinds and degrees of activity in the universe have in common not as an abstract property, but as a concrete, real universal in which particular activities participate. Such an account requires a metaphysical system in which universals can be in some sense 'real' and 'concrete,' and where particulars can 'participate' in universals. This raises formidable problems, and in any case I find no more than occasional hints of such thinking in the background of Ramsey's writings. When he explains how the word 'activity' can be common to levels of language concerning many different kinds of entities, he does not postulate a real universal, but points us to *I* as the unifier and then to God in analogy with *I*.

In this section we have been considering one problem raised by the analogy between God/observable universe and *I*/observable behaviour: the analogy does not help us to understand the relation between God and non-observables. The second problem which we noted earlier is that the analogy is inadequate in its treatment of divine transcendence. To this problem we now turn.

5 Divine transcendence

We have seen that for Ramsey the transcendence of God is to be understood partly by analogy with the transcendence of *I*. Before we consider some other aspects of divine transcendence, let us examine this central analogy again, focusing on Ramsey's notion of *mystery*. As a prelude for his consideration of the mystery of God Ramsey considers *I*, because *I* is 'the best (and perhaps the only) clue to all genuine mystery' (PR 218; cf MM 28; TL 6). For Ramsey 'mystery' is not a synonym for temporary or permanent ignorance of facts (TL 2). Rather, Ramsey understands 'mystery' in close relation to his account of *I*. As a mystery *I* is disclosed rather than merely observed or perceived. A mystery such as *I* is a 'more' which transcends description itself but which can be indirectly described because it is associated with observables. It 'explains' observables in the sense that it unifies them as their presupposed ultimate reference, but not in the sense of being an entity in an explanatory theory from which statements about observables can be deduced.

These aspects of mystery, which pertain not only to *I* but to God, have already been considered. It is also important to note the ways in which mystery is for Ramsey *paradoxical* (TL 1–6; PR passim). As a mystery *I* (or God) transcends observables and yet is immanent in them; it is indescribable (ineffable) and yet we refer to it and talk about it; it is 'more' than observables, yet not just 'more of the same thing'; it can be known with certainty, yet all descriptions are indirect and corrigible. Thus for Ramsey the central theological paradoxes of transcendence/immanence, ineffability/effability and certainty/corrigibility cease to appear as sheer contradictions and can be recognized as mysteries analogous to the mysteries of *I*.

This does not mean that for Ramsey God is transcendent only in the ways that *I* is transcendent. Already we have considered three ways in which God transcends *I*. First, we saw in the previous section that God not only transcends the observable universe as *I* transcends bodily behaviour, but also transcends all the *I*s and other centres of particular activity in the universe, somehow disclosing Himself through all of them and uniting them all together. Secondly, God transcends *I* in that a total commitment, worship, is appropriate towards God and not towards any *I*. It is inappropriate to focus a total commitment on something less than the 'more' of the whole universe. Indeed, it is idolatry. For Ramsey 'God' differs from 'I' in that part of its meaning is 'worthy of worship' or 'rightly evoking worship.' To refer to God is to refer to what is 'given in worship' (RL 185; cf RL 89; BP 186; TL 39). Thirdly, if the relation between God and the observable universe is like the relation between *I* and observable bodily behaviour, God differs in that the scope of observables through which He is disclosed is all-inclusive – the universe rather than a particular body. Hence, as we have seen, it makes no sense to try to locate God, and there is no possibility that the word 'God' might have no reference.

Something else, which we have not considered, follows from the fact that when we talk about God we refer to an all-inclusive range of observables. God differs from any and every *I* in that He acts in *all* things. Hence, according to Ramsey, if we take a descriptive word (e.g. 'loving') which applies to human beings and apply it to God, it is implicitly modified by 'all,' or some similar word (TL 8; RB 85). If we say 'God is loving,' what we mean is made explicit by 'God is *all*-loving.' Or, so as to indicate temporal all-inclusiveness as well, we might also say 'God is *ever*-loving' (CE 48; cf CE 44). Similarly, in expressing other cosmic disclosures we say 'God is *universally* reliable' or 'God is maker of *all* things.' The descriptive words, such as 'loving,' 'reliable,' or 'maker,' Ramsey calls 'models.' The modifying words, such as 'all,' 'ever,' or 'universally,' he calls 'qualifiers.' He maintains that the meaning of the model must shift when the qualifier is applied. He does not explain why there must be a shift, but the reason is fairly obvious. Almost all descriptive words apply, by virtue of their meaning, to some things and *not* to others. When we learn to use a word such as 'reliable,' we learn to distinguish a reliable person or a reliable climate from one which is not reliable. If the descriptive word is to apply to all things, as it must when it applies to God as the *universe* and its 'more,' then it presumably must change somewhat in meaning. For it is not that the cosmic disclosure has provided some additional information concerning observables; rather they have been discerned in a new way. The change in meaning occurs when a descriptive term is qualified by a word such as 'all.' Such a word, which I shall call a 'universalizing' qualifier, does not function in the same way as such words as 'very,' 'extremely,' or 'wide-ranging.' It functions as a directive, a prescription, to extend the range of observables in space and time so that the descriptive term has all-inclusive scope and hence a new meaning. The shift in meaning produced by a universalizing qualifier is not a feature of language concerning *I* but of language concerning God. It occurs because talk about God is talk about the whole universe and its 'more' rather than about something less inclusive. Universalizing qualifiers indicate an *analogy* between divine activity and human activity; that is, divine activity is similar to human activity, but transcends it by pervading the whole universe. Also (although Ramsey did not note this), universalizing qualifiers indicate an analogy between a religious attitude and a non-religious attitude. We recall that Ramsey describes a religious commitment as a 'total commitment to the *whole* universe' (RL 37), both internally and externally pervasive. Universalizing qualifiers indicate external pervasiveness, which is one way in which a religious attitude transcends a non-religious attitude. (My own analysis of religious attitudes in chapters 3 and 6 is influenced by Ramsey's treatment of them as doubly pervasive and by his analysis of universalizing qualifiers, which I consider to be one of his most significant contributions to philosophy.)

Qualifiers are a distinctive feature of language concerning God, a special indicator of divine transcendence. Ramsey considers not only what I have called 'universalizing' qualifiers but also others, which I shall call 'perfecting' qualifiers. He does not distinguish between the two kinds of qualifiers, but the distinction is important.[15] Consider, for example, the difference between saying 'God is all-loving' and saying 'God is infinitely loving.' Ramsey uses the qualifier 'infinitely' to generate a series which focuses, not on the range of love, but on its quality or intensity or relative perfection (RL 46–7). He generates similar series for 'infinitely wise' and 'infinitely good' (RL 65–7). In each case the 'more' which is disclosed is not inherently cosmic in scope. Rather, it is an absolute perfection towards which the series points – a love or wisdom or goodness beyond which there is none superior. Instead of thinking of God as all-inclusive, *pervasive*, in the range of his activity, one thinks of him as *perfect* in the quality of his activity.

Why does one think in this way? What is Ramsey's basis in experience for this conviction concerning divine perfection? It seems to me that the basis is in human aspiration and idealism. We aspire towards an absolutely perfect love, wisdom, and goodness, an Anselmic ideal than which none superior can be thought. When we reflect on a series which points towards absolute perfection, we may have a glimpse, as it were, of that perfection. Since for Ramsey the experience has the character of a disclosure in which a 'more' actively 'breaks in' on us, he is sure of the objectivity, the reality, of what is disclosed; the ideal is real. And the ideal is God, for Ramsey identifies the 'more' of Anselmic aspiration with the 'more' of cosmic disclosures (Duty, Providence, and Creativity), especially the 'more' disclosed in Jesus Christ.

The distinction between universalizing qualifiers and perfecting qualifiers reflects a distinction between two different approaches in religious experience and reflection, and a distinction between two different ways in which God transcends *I*. They are not incompatible, but they are different. On the one hand, we begin with an experience of a 'more' which is discerned in a particular person and/or a particular natural scene, and we extend the range of the 'more' to include the whole universe. God transcends *I* because His activity is all-inclusive, pervasive. On the other hand, we consider a series of ever-increasing virtue, a series generated not only by observation but also by aspiration, and we discern as a reality the ideal perfection towards which the series points. God transcends *I* because His activity is perfect.

How are these two approaches related? It seems obvious to me that they are broadly compatible; God can be both pervasive and perfect. A more interesting question is whether they are independent or are necessarily connected with each other. For example, need a perfect love be pervasive? Need a pervasive love be perfect? To take the first question first, it seems to me plausible that reflection concerning divine perfection leads to the idea of divine pervasiveness: surely a perfect, unlimited love would be all-inclusive rather than restricted. One can see how this line of thought and feeling might be directed from perfection to pervasiveness. Thus one could come to the idea of pervasiveness, not directly by cosmic disclosure, but indirectly by reflection arising from aspiration. The experiential basis would be in aspiration. Concerning the second question, it seems to me less immediately plausible that reflection concerning pervasive love leads to the idea of perfect love. Couldn't a pervasive love be low-grade ('God loves everybody and everything but not very much')? We can all think of a *human* love which is relatively broad in its range but low in quality. Why not assume a similar possibility in the case of divine love? There is a difference, however. In the case of pervasive, *all*-inclusive love as discerned in a cosmic disclosure, the universalizing qualifier produces a shift in the meaning of 'love' so that divine love can somehow include elements in our experience which seem to be radically non-loving (avalanche, loneliness, darkness, terror). Divine love can include these elements because of some unique quality. It is a love which is perfect, unsurpassable, in one crucial respect; it somehow sustains and reconciles us to *whatever* has happened or might happen. Pervasive love is in this respect perfect. Such an idea of perfection, however, is only one of the various ideas which might arise if one began with the way of aspiration. The other ideas are not implied by the way of cosmic disclosure. So there is a difference between a set of religious convictions arising solely from cosmic disclosures and one arising solely from the way of aspiration. The latter set might well include all convictions in the former; but not vice versa. (In chapter 6 my account of divine activity includes little concerning divine perfection beyond what is implied by divine pervasiveness.) Often, however, both ways arise from a *common* experiential basis: a highly valued particular, e.g. a good man, is taken as *representative* of that which pervades the universe and also as a *pointer* towards perfection. Also, it seems to me that there is a human drive to unite the two ways wherever they occur in the same person, for both involve commitments of the whole person, and thus need to be united within the person; the alternative is a radical split and a less than total commitment to each. In my view it is mainly the drive to unity within oneself that necessitates and makes possible an authentic conviction concerning a unity for what would otherwise be the various 'mores' in the cosmos – pervasive Providence, pervasive Creativity, Duty, and Perfection. (I shall pursue this further in the postscript.)

I have digressed somewhat from my exposition of Ramsey. So far I have only roughly indicated his ideas concerning perfecting qualifiers. He actually has a good deal to say about them which deserves careful study (RL 65–79; FI 92–100; TL 6–12; cf TG 94–5; MM 60–1). His favourite perfecting qualifier is 'infinite' or 'infinitely.' He compares its use in religious language with its use in mathematics. For example, there is the infinite sum: '1 plus ½ plus ¼ plus ⅛ plus 1/16 plus ...' The word 'infinite' is a directive to continue the series indefinitely, without limit. At some point, perhaps when we get to 1/32 or perhaps later when we get to 1/8192 we suddenly have a disclosure: '2!' Similarly, in the expression 'infinite-sided polygon' the word 'infinite' is a directive to generate a series (triangle, square, pentagon, hexagon, etc). At some point we have a disclosure: 'Circle!' As each series proceeds, it comes closer and closer to 2 or to a circle. When the sum adds on 1/8192 it is closer than when it added on 1/64. A polygon with 1008 sides is a better approximation of a circle than is a polygon with 3 sides. But no matter how many terms we add to the sum, it is not 2. And no matter how many sides the polygon is given, it is not a circle. No finite number of terms or finite number of sides, however large, will suffice. Only an infinite sum or an infinite polygon is equivalent to 2 or a circle.

Ramsey applies all this to such religious expressions as 'infinitely good.' To say that God is 'infinitely good' is not the same as saying that He is 'very, very good.' The qualifier 'infinitely' is a directive to generate a series of increasing goodness and to continue it indefinitely, without limit. At some point there is a disclosure of that towards which the series points, but which it never reaches: God. No finite goodness – that is, no describable, conceivable goodness – is the same as God. Yet that which is very good is a better approximation than that which is scarcely good at all.

There is one obvious difference between the mathematical series and the religious series. The mathematical disclosure is not a disclosure of 2 or of a circle, but of the *relation* between a series and 2 or a circle. We already understand and know 2 and a circle. Indeed, we have to use 2 to generate the infinite sum! But the religious series is supposed to help us come to understand what 'God' means and what 'loving' means when applied to God. We do not already understand what 'God' means. Hence in a later article Ramsey suggests a revision of the polygon analogy (TG 91). Let us suppose that we do not already know what a circle is, and that when the series of polygons generates a disclosure, we can only use the symbol x to refer to what is disclosed. Then talk about many-sided polygons would be a reasonable approximation to x, if we sought to talk about x, for the series of polygons gave rise to the disclosure of x. But x would not itself be describable or conceivable. We would realize that x is *not* a polygon, even a many-sided polygon. But we could talk about x as a polygon if we always – implicitly or explicitly – applied the qualifier 'infinite.' This would remind us that x was disclosed, not described, and that no finite polygon is an x. The mathematical case, thus revised, is very similar to the religious case. To say 'God is infinitely good' is to refer us to what may be disclosed as we generate indefinitely a series of increasing goodness. Infinite goodness cannot be described, only disclosed. No describable goodness, however great, is the infinite goodness of God. Yet to speak of God as very good is a better approximation than to speak of Him as scarcely good; and it is a reasonable approximation because a series of ever-better goodness, pointing in the direction of infinite goodness, gave rise to the disclosure. Nevertheless 'God is infinitely good' does not entail 'God is good,'[16] just as 'A circle is an infinite polygon' does not entail 'A circle is a polygon.' The qualifier 'infinitely' or 'infinite' produces a shift of meaning in 'good' and 'polygon.'

I have already alluded to a similarity between Ramsey's perfecting qualifiers and Anselm's 'that than which none greater can be thought,' which functions (I think) as an operator or directive rather than as a description, and which thus resembles a qualifier. Ramsey's use of a mathematical notion of infinity is explicitly related by him to another medieval thinker, Nicholas of Cusa (FIR 354, n 1). In James Collins's[17] exposition of Nicholas, to which Ramsey refers, an infinite series can orient us 'in the direction of God.' Nicholas, however, seems more agnostic than Ramsey, for Ramsey claims a *disclosure* of the infinite. Actually, Ramsey is much closer to Austin Farrer. It is true that Farrer's *Finite and Infinite*[18] does not explicitly use a mathematical analogy, does

not stress linguistic matters, and does not make clear the role of qualifiers. Yet Farrer calls for an '*indefinite* upward extrapolation' of a scale
of activities which yields for him an 'idea,' but not a concept, of an
unlimited, perfect, divine activity.[19] Farrer's great book is a form of
Thomism, radically revised to meet the challenges of Hume and Kant.
Ramsey's connections with Aquinas are less direct, but not negligible. He
sees himself as doing 'in principle' what Aquinas was doing. Though he
is not committed to Aquinas's ontology and system, he is offering a 'possible *generalization* of Thomism.' I am not sure what Ramsey means here
(RL 185), but my impression is that he regards some of Aquinas's reflections concerning talk about God as having a significance and truth
independent of Aquinas's ontology and system. Certainly Ramsey's perfecting and negating qualifiers are twentieth-century descendants of
Aquinas's 'way of eminence' and 'way of negation.' (There is also a similarity, though more remote, between Ramsey's cosmic disclosures of
activity and Aquinas's way of causality.) My point is that Ramsey's stress
on disclosure experiences and on language uses should not blind us to
his affinities with Farrer and even with Aquinas.

This brief digression was meant to show that Ramsey's qualifiers are a
way of thinking about some very traditional problems concerning divine
transcendence. This point should be kept in mind as we turn from his
perfecting qualifiers to his negating qualifiers. These are exemplified in
the words 'immutable' and 'impassible' (RL 50–3). In each case the prefix
'im' is equivalent to 'not,' and works as a qualifier on a model – 'mutable'
or 'passible.' We are directed to start with the models, fixing on mutable or
passible features of perceptual situations, and then to apply the qualifier
'not,' progressively obliterating these features. The words 'immutable'
and 'impassible' are not descriptions of God; rather they are designed 'to
give a kind of technique for meditation,' so as to 'bring about that
discernment which is the basis for talking about God' (RL 53). Ramsey
says that their main merit is 'evocative' (RL 53). Ramsey often stresses
the 'evocative' function of religious language, contrasting this with the
'descriptive' function which others have attributed to it. This has naturally provoked considerable criticism, even though he explicitly disclaims
any verbal magic (RL 79), denying that we have power over God so as to
bring about disclosures at will. It would perhaps be better to stress the
theme of 'technique for meditation.' In some traditional mystical contemplation all perceptual features, not only the mutable and passible
features, are progressively obliterated from consciousness. Then, when
the mind is empty and receptive, a mystical experience may occur. It

cannot be produced at will, but the meditative technique facilitates it. If it occurs, what is discerned is strictly indescribable, since all describable features have been eliminated from the mind. Yet the indescribable is positive and real; it is God. It seems clear to me that Ramsey's negating qualifiers operate in such a meditative context. Their main function is to 'evoke a discernment,' but in the sense that they direct meditation so as to facilitate a discernment. (The other kinds of qualifier are also 'evocative' in a similar sense – not the sense in which someone shouting 'Booh!' evokes fright, but in the sense of instructions for meditation which, if followed, may give rise to insight.[20])

A second function of negating qualifiers is linguistic. The statements 'God is immutable' and 'God is impassible' function as second-order commentaries or rules concerning first-order talk about God. As Ramsey says, 'If anything is "mutable" it will not be exact currency for God; ... if anything is "passible" it will not be exact currency for God' (RL 53). I am not sure what he means by 'not exact currency.' No descriptive language whatsoever is 'exact currency' for God, in the sense of being applicable without qualifiers. Ramsey seems to mean something much stronger than this concerning 'passible' and 'mutable.' In one passage (RL 89) he contrasts 'God is impassible' with 'God is infinitely loving.'

Each assertion evokes the suitably odd situation, each claims an odd positioning for the word 'God,' a position away from the straightforward language of passibility or love; but the second assertion is more positive in claiming that this special positioning can nevertheless be reached from ordinary language, to which words like 'love' belong, once this ordinary language has been appropriately qualified, as by the word 'infinite.'

Presumably the special positioning cannot be reached if we start from 'passible' or 'mutable.' Ramsey is denying that they are applicable to God at all. The statements 'God is not mutable' and 'God is not passible' thus seem to be logically similar to such statements as 'Thoughts are not spatial,' 'Numbers are not temporal,' or 'Electrons are not coloured,' which express second-order rules of language. For Ramsey all first-order talk about God must be understood in accordance with second-order rules, 'rules for our consistent talking' (RL 84) about God. And often, as in the case of 'immutable' and 'impassible,' what may look like a first-order description at first sight is actually a second-order rule. A great deal of theology is for Ramsey formal-mode discourse: it is not talk about God, but talk about talk about God (TL 38–9; RL 173, 179).

We have been considering negating qualifiers. How are they to be compared with perfecting qualifiers and universalizing qualifiers? They can be contrasted with perfecting qualifiers in that they deny that such-and-such an imperfection (e.g. mutability) is present in God, whereas perfecting qualifiers imply that such-and-such a relative perfection (e.g. love) is an approximation of what is present in God. But in Ramsey's thought there is a more obvious contrast between negating qualifiers and universalizing qualifiers. A universalizing qualifier *includes* everything observable in relation to what has been discerned (e.g. reliability), whereas a negating qualifier *excludes* everything observable, since all things are mutable or passible or otherwise imperfect in some way. A negating qualifier directs us to a 'more' which is not the universe, whereas a universalizing qualifier directs us to the universe and its 'more.' For Ramsey, however, the 'more' disclosed by the negating qualifier is the same as the 'more' disclosed by the universalizing qualifier. That is, the God disclosed to the mystics is the same as the cosmic God disclosed through persons and nature.

The contrast between negating and universalizing qualifiers and the assumption that they both lead to the same destination are evident in Ramsey's treatment of the qualifier 'eternal' (FI 94–6; cf CE 48; BSR 17). He says that it can work either negatively, by exclusion, or positively, by inclusion. Negatively, 'eternal life' is understood as '*not* ending-life,' '*not* temporal'; it directs us beyond all temporal features until there is a disclosure. Positively, it is understood as 'temporally all-inclusive life,' 'sempiternal life'; it directs us to extend the temporal range of life indefinitely until there is a disclosure. Where 'eternal' operates as a negating qualifier, nothing temporal is ascribed to God. Where 'eternal' operates as a universalizing qualifier, everything temporal is ascribed to God, who is 'more' than all, but includes all. (Incidentally, we should note here that, although sempiternity involves a doubly *infinite* series, it is not a *qualitative* series as is the infinite series of a perfecting qualifier. Some writers, but apparently not Ramsey, would interpret 'eternal' as a perfecting qualifier as well.) Ramsey also gives both a negating (exclusive) and a positive (inclusive) use of the qualifier 'necessary' as applied to the model 'being' (TL 7–8). Negatively, 'necessary' is understood as '*not* contingent,' and directs us to exclude things which might not have been, continuing the exclusion until there is a disclosure. Positively, 'necessary' directs us to construct a series of things which are presupposed for the existence of other things: 'dining-hall, college, city, state ...' We continue towards that which is presupposed for any and all things, until there is a cosmic disclosure.

There is an important difference between negating qualifiers on the one hand and universalizing and perfecting qualifiers on the other. When a negating qualifier is applied, the word to which it is applied is rendered totally inapplicable to God. Whatever it describes in the world provides no clue whatsoever as to the nature of God. When, however, a universalizing or perfecting qualifier is applied, the word to which it is applied (e.g. 'loving') undergoes a shift in meaning, and is only an approximation of what is true of God, but it does provide some clue as to the nature of God. Consider, for example, the two uses of 'necessary' as a qualifier for 'being.' It is one thing to say that God is unlike anything in the world, since everything is contingent; it is another thing to find in the relative necessity of something in the world (which many other things presuppose for their existence) a clue to the nature of God.

In this section we have seen how Ramsey indicates divine transcendence by applying universalizing, perfecting, or negating qualifiers to models. There is another way in which models may be qualified – by other models. If, for example, God is 'my loving father,' 'my shepherd,' 'my potter,' and 'my strong tower' (MM 59–60; TL 10; TG 89), then *none* of these descriptions can apply to Him with their ordinary meanings. The application of each restricts what inferences can be legitimately made by the others, so the meaning of each is shifted. If we add a few hundred more descriptive expressions, using the widest possible range of models (TG 84, 92), the mutual qualification of models will be very great. Obviously whatever all the models apply to cannot be any particular observable in the universe. Indeed – though Ramsey does not make this clear – the effect on meaning will be rather similar to that produced by a *universalizing* qualifier. Any description associated with a disclosure of God in one situation will be modified by descriptions associated with disclosures of God in *all* other situations. Thus Ramsey argues that conflicts between models are not a difficulty or defect in religious language, but an intrinsic feature, another way of indicating divine transcendence.

Although a haphazard piling up of models, each qualifying the other, is useful in indicating divine transcendence, Ramsey thinks it is also possible and useful to relate models in an orderly, coherent way, subordinating some models to others (TG 84–9; cf CD 57–60, 83–6; TL 9–10; PG 69). He is fairly clear as to *which* models are for him 'super models' or 'dominant models,' but not as to *why* they are so. 'Activity' seems to be the most dominant model,[21] though 'person' is also very high in the hierarchy, and 'love' comes close after it. He says that 'person' dominates 'power,' 'wisdom,' and 'love.' 'Love' dominates 'suffering servant,' 'remnant,' and 'life-given-as-ransom' (in christology). 'Love' also dominates 'protector,' which in turn dominates 'shepherd.' 'Protector' dominates 'King,' 'Judge,' and 'Tower.' We can see that in each case a dominant model is more comprehensive than its subordinates, and binds them together.[22] But does it do this by abstraction, by limiting the subordinate models to whatever they have in common, and thus making discourse concerning God more 'reliable' in relation to the transcendence of God?[23] Or does it do this by enrichment, by drawing together all the varied implications of the subordinate models, so that discourse concerning God becomes more 'fertile' in its 'articulation possibilities'? Ramsey seems to hold that dominant models work in both ways, though he sometimes mixes them. But perhaps the two approaches in the ordering of models are compatible if they are clearly separated. On the one hand, we seek models which need minimal qualification, either by qualifiers or by other models, so as to indicate the transcendence of God. On the other hand, we seek models which have maximal richness of meaning, including at least implicitly the meanings of many terms which have been associated with disclosures. We do this because God is immanent, related to the empirical world. The same model, viewed in different ways, may be used in the two approaches. 'Activity,' for example, as that which all particular realities have in common, is a concept which needs minimal qualification in order to be applied to God. But if we consider 'activity' in explicit relation to a host of subordinate models, and regard their meanings as somehow implicit in, and gathered together in, 'activity,' then we have a super-model with maximal richness of meaning.

Ramsey's account of how models may be related in an orderly, coherent way is very sketchy and not very clear. But I have suggested some ways in which it can be interpreted which might make it fairly acceptable. Even so, however, it does not by itself provide adequate ground for rational preferences concerning models. Ramsey may have succeeded in his attempt 'to clarify Christian controversies by elucidating the logical placings of traditional Christian phrases' (RL 185), but what about *other* phrases? Why talk about God in the ways which Ramsey has chosen for analysis?

The issue of rational preference arises throughout Ramsey's philosophy, though he rarely deals with it. We recall that his cosmic disclosures are disclosures where something in a person or in nature (or in

both) seems to be true of the whole universe – trustworthiness or creativity or love. Whatever seems to conflict with each disclosure is not
allowed to overthrow it. Models drawn from experiences of hostility or
neutrality or arbitrariness in persons or nature are subordinated to the
trustworthiness model, which is 'dominant' over them, not in the sense
considered above, but in the sense of having an overriding priority. But
why shouldn't a cosmic disclosure of hostility or indifference or arbitrariness (or ruthlessness or emptiness or chaos) have overriding priority over Ramsey's cosmic disclosure of trustworthiness? As we have
seen, Ramsey claims a kind of 'empirical fit' for his disclosures, but many
features of our experience provide an 'empirical fit' for very different
disclosures. It seems to me that Ramsey does not sufficiently acknowledge that there is a *choice* to be made concerning which items (e.g.
friendly or hostile) in the universe are taken as representative of the
whole, as models to receive universalizing qualifiers. There is a choice
between putative cosmic disclosures (e.g. cosmic trustworthiness versus
cosmic hostility) and between the corresponding pervasive attitudes
within oneself (basic trust versus basic distrust). Which disclosure and
attitude do I accept as dominant in my life? Ramsey's criterion of
'empirical fit,' while relevant to the choice, is inadequate, even if we supplement it with his formal or metaphysical criteria of coherence, com-
prehensiveness, consistency, and simplicity.[24] Rather, it seems to me that
a major reason for preferring a disclosure of cosmic trustworthiness is
that a person who commits himself to it and to whatever pervasive trust
is within himself tends to become more authentically human, more
fulfilled as a human being. Appeal to such a reason presupposes convictions derived from reflections concerning a broad range of human
experience. It presupposes a philosophical anthropology which Ramsey
does not provide.

The issue of rational preference also arises in Ramsey's presentation of
negating and perfecting qualifiers. We may well ask for his basis for
judging one human trait or activity as an imperfection, not to be ascribed
to God at all, and another as a relative perfection, which can point
towards God. For example, on what basis does he set aside some kinds of
punishment as inappropriate, and select a punishment which expresses a
reconciling love which overcomes separation? Or when he considers
'God is impassible' and sets aside anything that changes, on what basis
does he assume that change is an imperfection? Why not, as in much
modern theology, a changing God as the ideal for changing man? Or
when he applies 'infinitely' to loving, and tells us to 'think away any

imperfect, finite, limited features' (PR 208), how does he know what counts as an imperfection in love? For example, is *need* for the loved one an imperfection or a relative perfection? More generally, if the use of perfecting qualifiers arises from what I call the 'way of aspiration,' how do we decide among aspirations? How do we decide what counts as a constituent in human perfection or human fulfilment and hence as a model to which a perfecting qualifier is to be applied? A philosophical anthropology seems to be required.

When Ramsey talks about 'specifying an "ultimate" understanding of the universe in terms of our most significant insights' (FL 47) we want to know how he selects the insights which are most significant. Also, we want to know why he assumes that there is an ultimate understanding, a *unity*. This is his most basic assumption. Why not a multiverse or even a chaos? On what grounds does he assume that all our insights – all our disclosures whether of duty or Providence or creativity or perfection or mystic negation or Jesus – are of one and the same 'more'? In answer to this question Ramsey (in LR) said he would appeal to one of his formal metaphysical criteria: simplicity. This kind of reply does not reckon sufficiently with the profoundly personal nature of the question. The extent to which a person sees an ultimate unity depends mainly on the extent to which he himself is a unity. Indeed, there is an element of choice here, which is most obvious in a person who alternates between times when the world and himself are unities and times when both are split. He chooses whether or not to struggle in such a way that unity comes to predominate. Especially if there are several disclosures, each of which call for a total commitment, he must assume an ultimate unity for the disclosures; otherwise he will be split among several commitments none of which can be total except at the expense of the others. Requirements of human nature are more important here than formal metaphysical criteria. Once again I feel the lack of an adequate philosophical anthropology in Ramsey.

Ramsey's answers to all the various questions of rational preference which I have raised depend on an appeal to three different authorities, with an overdependence on the first two: Christian tradition, metaphysical criteria, and human experience. His third source of criteria is inadequately explored in that there is little reflection concerning human nature. Issues concerning rational preference (and indeed a great deal else in Ramsey's account of religious language) would be illuminated if his account of human experience were deepened by focusing explicitly on the question, 'What are our most significant insights concerning *man*?' For Ramsey's interpretation of talk about God depends a great deal on what he believes about man, his conception of human trust, wonder, hope, commitment, love, and integrity. Ramsey's philosophical theology needs a more profound philosophical anthropology. Nevertheless his account of talk about God is a major contribution to contemporary philosophy of religion.

Postscript

As I have noted in chapter 1, my exploration of different kinds of analogy in thinking about God has been influenced and illuminated by Ramsey's writings. It is clear that versions of all three kinds of analogy are used by him:

1 / God's *activity* in the universe is analogous to an individual human being's activity in his observable behaviour. God's activity differs in being perfect and/or pervasive. This difference is indicated when a human activity is taken as a model and then perfecting and/or universalizing qualifiers are applied. Ramsey also uses two versions of the way of negation. In one negation is subordinate to the way of perfection and expresses a second-order rule of language concerning the inapplicability of some words (e.g. 'mutable') to God. In the other negation is linked with mystical contemplation as an approach to God.

2 / God's *relation* to a human being is analogous to some relations between two human beings in that in each case there are two activities, one initiating and one responding. In each case the responder becomes aware of himself or herself as active in response to the activity of the other. The relation to the divine activity differs in that it somehow *includes* all the relations with the other human beings; it also includes analogous relations with all other particulars. Thus the divine-human relation differs from the human-human relation in its pervasiveness.

3 / Worship is a commitment which differs from other commitments in two ways: the *whole* human being is involved, and the commitment is *unconditional*. The first differentiating feature clearly follows the way of pervasiveness. The second is less easy to place. An unconditional commitment (I am committed no matter what happens) is negatively all-inclusive. The all-inclusiveness links it to the way of pervasiveness. The negation links it to the way of negation.

I have indicated the form of each kind of analogy in Ramsey without indicating the various *contents* which he gives in each case. The content involves a choice of something human (activity, relation, attitude) to be the starting-point for constructing the analogy. For example, in 1 Ramsey starts with human activity which is friendly or loving or creative; in 2 he starts with one human being revealing himself to another; and in 3 he starts with human attitudes of trust and devotion. Since his philosophical anthropology is sketchy, the content of all three kinds of analogy is not adequately investigated or presented. This defect seems specially evident to me in the content of his analogy of attitude. I have already criticized Ramsey's account of trust. Later on in this postscript I shall amplify some of my criticisms. Ramsey's strongest point, it seems to me, is his account of the form of analogy of activity. There his model-and-qualifier analysis sheds new light on issues arising in traditional Thomistic analogy of being. Indeed, Ramsey sometimes seems to be not very far from the position of some neo-Thomists in which what I call 'analogy of activity' is dominant and other analogies redundant. But his analogy of activity is on the whole less confident than theirs, so he has a subordinate place for analogy of relation and analogy of attitude. Indeed, he sometimes seems rather remote from Thomism (and from an analogy of activity influenced by Berkeley) and closer to an existentialist personalism where analogy of relation is dominant. It seems to me that this second position is more compatible with the role which he often gives to *attitudes* as he works an analogy of activity. It also seems more compatible with his stress on the *responsive* character of the activities which he selects as content for analogical thinking. But although analogy of relation is thus crucial for his thought, his account of it is inadequate. Let us consider this defect first, before turning to criticize his analogy of attitude.

My main criticism of Ramsey's analogy of relation is that the content is interpreted mainly in terms of a Berkeleian empiricism and only secondarily, and sketchily, in terms of personalistic existentialism, which is what Ramsey needs. In Berkeley there is a dichotomy between an awareness of sense impressions or mental images and an awareness of the free activity of one's own self. The existence and nature of other centres of activity, whether human or divine, involve an inference (or at least a judgment) based on an argument from analogy: I know my own activity and I seem to be acted upon by an agency similar to my own. On this approach, with its Cartesian starting-point, I am aware of the existence and nature of my own activity independently of any relation to other centres of activity. And there is no special self-involvement (commitment or receptivity) required in order to come to know the other centres of activity, or their nature. The nature of other human centres can be understood as being the same as my own, and the nature of divine activity can be understood by means of an analogy of activity. There is no need for an analogy of relation and no place for one except in complete subordination to analogy of activity.

The influence of Berkeley, which is explicitly acknowledged and, indeed, stressed by Ramsey (LR, BPEM, SEI), is in conflict with a personalistic existentialism which can also be discerned in his thought, though the historical influences are far less clear.[25] Whether or not such existentialists as Buber and Marcel influenced Ramsey, he does resemble them in many respects. I shall sketch some of Buber's ideas here, in a way which reflects Buber's similarity with Marcel, though Marcel uses different terminology. According to Buber I discover the existence and nature of my own personal activity only in I-Thou relation to another active personal being, human and/or divine. My awareness of other Thous requires a special I-Thou stance of commitment and receptivity which is radically different from the I-It stance in which I perceive observables and sometimes make inferences to unobservables. On such an approach analogy of relation is basic and there is no independent analogy of activity; I can think of God only in the divine-human relation, not by analogy with the activity of an isolated individual human being. The fundamental ontology and epistemology are based on interpersonal relations; I-It experience of observables and inferences to unobservables is secondary and dependent. (I-It includes many of the attitudes I have called 'objectivist.')

Although Ramsey sometimes starts, in Cartesian-Berkleian style, with an (I-It) awareness of the activity of an isolated *I*, he at times resembles Buber, in two ways: (a) For Ramsey the paradigm discernment of *I* is correlated with discernment of another centre of activity to which one responds. (b) For Ramsey discernment of the 'more' (i.e. the activity) of another requires and involves a stance which is in response to the claim of the 'more' as this is actively disclosed to us; this responsive stance is different from that of a disinterested observer. Both (a) and (b) are in conflict with the modified empiricism which Ramsey has adapted from Berkeley. A modification of empiricism, in which Berkeley modifies Locke and Ramsey modifies Ayer, is not what is needed, for it merely adds an awareness of the subject in subject-object knowing.[26] What is needed is a philosophy which *replaces* subject-object knowing by subject-subject (I-Thou) knowing as the epistemological starting-point, and which locates its fundamental ontology in I-Thou relations rather than in whatever can be known in an I-It way. It seems to me that (a) and (b) could have been presented much more clearly and consistently within a philosophy which was explicitly and dominantly personalistic – Ramsey's modification of Buber or Marcel rather than of Berkeley. Then the fundamental ontology and epistemology and use of language would be located in interpersonal relations, rather than these relations being a secondary, puzzling, and 'logically odd' addition to a fundamentally subject-object world. Thus there would have been a clear starting-point for an analogy of relation which can give an adequate place for Ramsey's stress on the responsive attitudes which are inherently involved in any discernments of divine activity.[27]

When I wrote the 1971 version of this essay on Ramsey I was still not sufficiently free of the modified empiricism which characterized *The Logic of Self-Involvement*[28] to be fully aware of the conflict within Ramsey's thought between modified empiricism and existentialism. But I was moving vigorously away from modified empiricism, and some of my new directions are evident in chapters 3, 4, and 6. Indeed, some new directions were already evident in my criticisms of Ramsey for not deeply probing the *attitudes* which people bring to the world when cosmic disclosures occur. I now turn to amplify some of these criticisms as I consider Ramsey's version of analogy of attitude.

Let us consider again the attitude of *trust*, which I have discussed several times during my outline of Ramsey's philosophy. I argued that whether or not the universe seems to be pervasively friendly or hostile depends mainly on the dominant pervasive attitude which one brings to the universe: trust or distrust. What Ramsey calls 'empirical fit' is relevant, for the broad range of one's experience should not be utterly contrary to one's cosmic conviction. Extremes such as pollyanna Leibnizeanism or paranoid conspiratorialism do not meet such a test. But the main test, I contend, is a practical one: which pervasive attitude (and which world-view that goes with it) ought to be dominant in one's life?

The more profoundly a person is aware of the struggle within himself between these pervasive attitudes the more clearly he is likely to see the issue of rival world-views in relation to this struggle rather than in relation to estimates concerning empirical evidence. For this reason I have included here the example of Conrad's *Typhoon*. Ramsey's choice of it indicated to me a move in the direction of a more profound investigation of trust. If Ramsey had continued in this direction he would have become less concerned about whether or not a disclosure of cosmic reliabiility has 'empirical fit' and more concerned about the depth-psychological dimensions of the pervasive trust and distrust which underlie cosmic disclosures.

Jukes's response to the commander's strong presence occurs in spite of an external situation which has produced overwhelming impulses towards distrust. In spite of his loneliness, helplessness, and terror he hears the commander's 'All right' as a guarantee of ultimate cosmic reliability.

The external struggle between commander and typhoon for Jukes's self is partly a symbolic way of depicting a struggle which goes on in every human being and which is merely accentuated by external factors. This is an internal struggle between two pervasive attitudes, trust and distrust. The internal elements in this struggle are more directly described in a true story, made famous by R.D. Laing,[29] which I remembered as I read the extract from *Typhoon*: Jesse Watkins's 'ten day voyage.' Watkins ventures forth on an inner trip into his hidden psychic past, opening himself to the full onslaught of previously repressed feelings. These almost overwhelm him with fear, but they also put him in touch with his own resources of trust. It is interesting that when Watkins tries to describe the climax of his dramatic inner struggle he changes from direct description to an analogy which is drawn from his experience in an external crisis similar to that of Jukes. He tells of his first week at sea as a boy, when he was terrified and undone by a storm, and he says that he found confidence and assurance because the calm presence of veteran sailors somehow enabled him to find his own inner resources of trust.[30] Conrad's story reminds me not only of Watkins but also of the incident which I quoted earlier from Peter Berger – the child waking in lonely panic who is reassured by the trust-grounded presence of his mother and by the assurance conveyed in the words, 'Everything is all right.' Berger's incident is presented mainly as a parable of *adult* faith, but it is also a true account of what happens in childhood. The inner struggle between trust and distrust begins in infancy. Indeed, Erik Erikson[31] provides a classic psychoanalytical account of how fundamental conflict begins during a crisis which we all go through in early infancy and how our ways of trying to cope with that crisis persist, though open to some change, throughout the rest of our lives. Alongside the insights of such depth psychology we can also place those of some existentialist philosophers, for example Gabriel Marcel's[32] account of the conflict between hope and despair (cf trust and distrust) and Søren Kierkegaard's[33] account of the conflict between faith and despair (cf trust and distrust). The conflict between trust and distrust is also central in some theologians, e.g. H. Richard Niebuhr.[34] For Niebuhr faith has to do with 'that trust or distrust which is said by some psychologists to be the basic element in the development of personality in a child's first year and to which theologians, notably Luther, have pointed as the fundamental element in religion.' Faith has to do with 'the attitude of the self in its existence toward all the existences that surround it, as beings to be relied upon or to be suspected,' an attitude which is 'fundamentally trust or distrust of being itself.' This basic attitude of trust or distrust 'accompanies all our encounters with others and qualifies all our responses,' and it is the 'chief ingredient in our interpretation of the radical act or agency by which we are selves.' In matters of religious faith cosmological convictions are secondary, for they 'express rather than found' the fundamental attitudinal interpretation in its trust or distrust of 'the alien and inscrutable power that elects us and all things into existence.'

Thus Ramsey's investigation of trust[35] would have been much enriched, in my opinion, by a combination of insights from depth psychology, existentialist philosophy, and Niebuhrian-Lutheran theology. (The influence of this combination on Sam Keen and on myself will be discernible in chapters 3 and 6.) If Ramsey had moved more in this direction, each of these three resources would have emphasized the subjective involvement of the individual as the main factor in his cosmic convictions. Thus Ramsey would have moved even more in a direction which some of his critics were already deploring. According to Brian Hebblethwaite,

The most serious criticism leveled against Ramsey's philosophical theology is that it fails to guarantee objectivity ... that this analysis, even for the believer, deprives religion of its object. Now the accusation of atheism is patently absurd ... But the fact that Ramsey's philosophical theology is susceptible of a subjectivist interpretation, should make us suspicious of its adequacy as an account of religious language.[36]

Personally, I would be more concerned if a philosophical theology were open to an *objectivist* interpretation, for this would mean that it is remote from authentic religious faith, which requires self-involvement in its understanding of meaning and its ascertaining of truth. I would not call Ramsey an 'objectivist,' though he does veer in that direction when his analogy of activity is dominant. And in so far as for him subjective involvement is a necessary but variable element in understanding and coming to know God, there are existentialist elements in his thought which are bound to seem 'subjectivist' to any objectivist, for such elements undermine the objective meaning and objective truth which the objectivist requires. So my suggested revisions of Ramsey, with their emphasis on a dominant existentialist analogy of relation and a depth analysis of such attitudes as trust, would have made him even more open to objectivist criticism.

A further non-objectivist development has also been recommended earlier in my discussion of the basis for choice between competing world-views. I contend that the choice is to a great extent a choice between pervasive attitudes: which attitudes promote authentic, fulfilled human being? Instead of first asking 'Does God exist?' one first asks 'Ought I to try to live so as to cultivate and express pervasive trust?' Instead of first somehow establishing in an objective way the existence of God as Providence, perfect and pervasive in reliability, and then somehow showing that pervasive trust is appropriate towards such a God, one first somehow establishes that pervasive trust is a condition or constituent of authentic, fulfilled human life and then somehow shows a connection between pervasive trust and the conviction that God exists. The connection is alleged to be a *logical* one: in expressing such-and-such an attitude a speaker implies that he has such-and-such a conviction.[37] This type of connection can be clearly seen in the case of expressions of gratitude. In saying 'I am grateful' I imply that I believe that some personal agent has voluntarily done something for my benefit. A similar kind of logical connection is alleged in the case of trust: in saying 'I have pervasive trust' I imply that I believe in Providence. Whether or not there is such a logical connection in this case is a matter of dispute, as I shall indicate in chapters 3 and 6. In the final chapter I shall present my conclusions concerning the character of the connection. This will involve considerable revision of what I present here and elsewhere in the book. Here I will present my earliest version of the argument.

The argument has a form in which there are two distinguishable contentions:

1 / *Normative Anthropological* Human nature is such that attitude X is necessary for human authenticity or fulfilment or personality; therefore one ought to cultivate and live by attitude X.

2 / *Logical* Expressions of attitude X imply belief in God; therefore if one does have the attitude one would be logically inconsistent if one denied that one believes in God.

In one version of this anthropological-logical argument attitude X is pervasive trust. In other versions it is respect for the moral law (Kant) or absolute dependence (Schleiermacher). Kant's anthropological contention is that 'the predisposition to *personality* is the capacity for respect for the moral law as in itself a sufficient incentive for the will.'[38] In order to be a person, a responsible individual acting according to the inner law of one's free nature, one must respect the moral law; to reject it is to forfeit personal fulfilment.[39] Schleiermacher's anthropological contention is that absolute dependence is 'the highest grade of human self-consciousness' and 'an essential element in human nature.'[40] Kant's logical contention is that belief in God as Providence is presupposed[41] by respect for the moral law. This 'presupposition' is claimed on the basis of an analysis of alleged elements in the moral law, so Kant's logical argument is more complex and indirect than the one I have mentioned which moves from pervasive trust to Providence. Schleiermacher's logical contention is that 'the *Whence* of our receptive and active self-consciousness as implied in this consciousness (absolute dependence) is to be designated by the term "God".'[42] Sometimes a logical contention is made without a prior normative anthropological claim. John Cook Wilson,[43] for example, notes simply that some people do have an attitude of reverence. If someone happens to have such an attitude, belief in God is implied. Wilson does not claim that if someone lacks such an attitude he is failing to fulfil his human nature, so the question whether one *ought* to have or cultivate the attitude is left open.

In chapter 3 a form of the anthropological-logical argument will be considered, so I have prepared the way for this by an initial sketch. It is also helpful at this stage to note four important points concerning such an argument. First, the alleged logical connection between attitude and conviction is not disproved by pointing out someone who has the attitude (e.g. pervasive trust) and who acknowledges no belief in God; people can be illogical. Secondly, the logical connection which this argument claims to find is very different from a *psychological* connection which some thinkers claim to find – an empirical connection between having a kind of attitude (consciously or unconsciously) and having a kind of conviction (consciously or unconsciously). For example, a religious thinker may allege that, if one has an attitude of pervasive trust, then one will also, as a matter of psychological fact, have some theistic convictions, though these may well be unconscious. Instead of saying that professed atheist John Smith who has pervasive trust is rationally committed to theistic convictions, the claim is that John Smith really *is* a theist at an unconscious level. (In chapter 7 I shall challenge the stark logical/psychological dichotomy as it is applied to connections between attitudes and beliefs, but it is a useful starting-point in analysis.)

A third feature of anthropological-logical arguments has to do with the anthropological contention. Usually the attitude which is cited as necessary for human fulfilment is one which we can understand only to the extent that we have it and experience it within ourselves. And only to the extent that we understand it can we appraise its importance and significance for our own lives. On this existentialist approach meaning and truth seem to be limited to meaning and truth *for me*, the individual. But there then seems to be a gap between the existentialist data and the *universal* claims concerning human nature which are made on the basis of the data. For example, how can one move legitimately from saying 'Pervasive trust is something which *I* understand and value and believe to be necessary for my authentic humanity' to saying 'Pervasive trust is similarly essential for *all* human beings'? Indeed, is there not some element of objectivism in even making such a claim? Or is there somehow a valid route from the deepest and most personal experience of the individual to truths which apply to all persons? This tension between individual and universal claims will be evident in the thought of Sam Keen when we examine it in chapter 3.

A fourth feature of anthropological-logical arguments is that they can be closely related to analogy of attitude. In analogy of attitude one tries to discover what worship is. One can then allegedly conceive, or at least minimally understand, what the appropriate focus for this attitude would be, if it existed. One does not thereby show that it is rational to believe that such a focus exists. At most one shows that to express the attitude is to imply a conviction that such-and-such a focus for the attitude exists – the logical contention in the anthropological-logical argument. Analogy of attitude thus needs the anthropological contention of that argument if there is to be a rational basis for belief in God. If that contention is rejected, if, for example, it is maintained that pervasive distrust is necessary for authenticity, then an atheistic belief would be implied. But if we agree that trust is necessary and that it implies belief in God, we do then have a rational basis for belief in God. The anthropological-logical argument is not, of course, a proof of God's existence. It is at most an argument supporting the rationality of belief in God's existence: such belief is implied by an attitude which one rationally ought to cultivate because it is necessary for human fulfilment. The argument does not rule out the possibility that beliefs implied by the attitudes required for human fulfilment are actually false. But if the truth or falsity of such beliefs cannot be directly established, it seems rational to opt for attitudes which promote fulfilment and to acknowledge the beliefs which are then implied.

The anthropological-logical argument takes place in the context of an epistemology which can be called 'neo-Kantian,' for it resembles Kant in moving from a normative anthropology to belief in God.[44] In such an epistemology, though there may be (and perhaps must be) an existential-ist access to truths concerning human nature, there is no such access to metaphysical truth, which must be inferred. The epistemology involved in a typical existentialist analogy of relation is very different: Trust is superior to distrust, not because it is necessary for human fulfilment (though it might be), but because it enables one to discern God in rela-tion with oneself. More generally, in an existentialist metaphysical epis-temology such-and-such a non-neutral pervasive attitude is allegedly superior because it is a necessary (and perhaps sufficient) condition for discerning ultimate truth. As I have pointed out in a recent article,[45] dif-ferent thinkers suggest different attitudes: 'not only trust and distrust but also courage in spite of meaninglessness, '*angst*' in the face of free-dom, heroic defiance of death and other human limitations, absolute dependence, respect for the moral law, "I-Thou" openness, and mystical contemplation.' But although the content of the claims differs, the form is the same: (If and) only if you have such-and-such an attitude, you will have access to metaphysical truth. Depending on the attitude, the alleged truth is theistic or atheistic. If, for example, the attitude is I-Thou open-ness, there is allegedly an awareness of God in I-Thou encounter with oneself. In such theistic personalism an existentialist analogy of relation is at work. One does not first have an attitude and then ask what would be the appropriate focus of the attitude, what metaphysical beliefs are implied by the attitude. Rather, because one has the attitude one is able to discern its focus. The metaphysical belief is then an articulation of what one discerns.

Such existentialist experiences are impressive, but not conclusive. There are many possible non-neutral stances from which one can view the world, and each of them can seem to bring an impressive meta-physical discernment. Indeed, the very same person can have conflicting discernments if, for example, he shifts from trust to distrust. Which apparent discernment is veridical? Is ultimate reality positive or negative in relation to human aspirations? Here the existentialist epistemology in metaphysics needs to be supplemented by a neo-Kantian one, which can provide an additional reason for favouring trust and the belief which it implies. We have seen, however, that both the anthropological and the logical contentions of the neo-Kantian argument can be challenged, and that even if both contentions are conceded, we cannot be *sure* that we are not involved in *false* beliefs when we cultivate attitudes which fulfil us. Thus the neo-Kantian argument needs to be supplemented by an appeal to existential discernment, where we seem actually to experience the metaphysical reality in question. Both arguments together, even when they coincide, are not conclusive; there is still a place for judgment and decision. In this respect, however, theism is in no worse a position than atheism (unless we assume that there is some objectivist way to decide between the two alternatives). For example, we shall see in the next chapter that Freud's atheism is open to question in the same way as theism. Freud claims that distrust is the stance required of mature human beings, and he assumes the atheism which this stance implies, reinforced by his distrustful metaphysical discernment of mother nature as malevolent. But we can challenge his trust in distrust as the way to authenticity and metaphysical truth.

I have noted some of the differences between a neo-Kantian use of analogy of attitude and an existentialist use of analogy of relation in proposing a rational basis for belief in God. Another difference can be clarified if we note the element of *abstraction* which analogy of attitude involves. Although the attitude – e.g. worship as pervasive trust – is an attitude towards an *X*, in relation to an *X*, we first set aside its intentional focus and deal with the attitude solely as a psychological state of the individual. And although the state is to be understood existentially, by reflecting on one's own pervasive trust or lack of it, its metaphysical focus has been set aside, so that no existential access to that focus is in view. We then ask what *would be* the appropriate focus of this attitude, what convictions are *implied*. But actually the attitude as experienced by the individual himself often also involves an awareness of the focus; the individual experiences himself in *personal relation* to the focus as a *reality*; he is aware of being receptive to a transcendent other which is a liberating presence.

There is a subtle difference between this existentialist analogy of relation as found in, say, Buber, and the way of origination as grace in analogy of activity which we shall find in Keen (chapter 3). In both there is an experience of being liberated, but in the former this experience includes some awareness of the Liberator revealing His *presence* and personal relation with us in His liberating activity. This awareness is not part of the experience in the latter, where all one is aware of is the *effect* in oneself of the Liberator's activity; this activity cannot be described except as being liberating and being not the same as one's own activity. In both analogies a person identifies the source of one liberating experience with the source in others and calls the one common source 'God,' but the liberating experiences differ in the two analogies. In originating-grace analogy of activity far less is revealed concerning the Liberator; the outcome is more 'agnostic,' as Keen would say. In chapter 4 a similar agnostic caution will be seen in Gregory Baum's use of originating-grace analogy of relation. Unless we assume that the Originator resembles what He brings about, we are very limited in what we know or believe concerning Him. In chapter 6 I shall break from this 'agnosticism' and use an existentialist analogy of relation. We have seen that Ramsey is also sometimes close to such an analogy. Often, however, he is more aptly construed as working an analogy of activity, using a way of origination as both creation and grace while not distinguishing these sharply. For Ramsey divine activity is affecting us whenever we have a 'breakthrough' to the 'more,' whenever our activity becomes a discernment commitment of other activity. It would be interesting to pursue this line of interpretation further in Ramsey, as we did the other three ways in analogy of activity. It helps to explain why he collected instances of the 'more' in such a casual, unsystematic way, somehow relating them all to God: any instance is as good as any other since all equally show us as much and as little concerning God as Originator. But it is time we turned to Keen, whose use of the fourth way is more explicit, and whose 'breakthroughs' are less purely epistemological and more deeply personal.

3

Sam Keen on Authentic Man

What style of life is authentic? What style of life is most in accord with human nature? How is man best defined? These three questions can be regarded as different versions of the same fundamental question. An important recent answer is given by Sam Keen in his major work, *Apology for Wonder* (AW), in which he brings together insights from phenomenology, existentialism, history of religion, contemporary literature, psychoanalysis, psychedelic experience, and theology. The synthesis of ideas which he produces is clear, comprehensive, and creative. Keen draws on some thinkers who are in my view more original and more profound, for example, Gabriel Marcel, H. Richard Niebuhr, and Erik Erikson.[1] But Keen's account of human nature is unusually interesting because of the wide variety of intellectual perspectives and personal involvements which he brings together. Also, as we shall see, Keen's philosophical anthropology is specially significant for philosophical theology.

One of Keen's suggestions in AW is that authentic man is *timely* man, sometimes Apollonian and sometimes Dionysian, whichever is more appropriate to the occasion. This suggestion is reflected in the style of AW, for Keen can be either Apollonian or Dionysian: he can be precise, analytic, and orderly, imposing an abstract architectonic structure on his material; and he can be passionate, poetic, and spontaneous, vividly expressing his immediate concrete experience. His medium fits his message. This is true of his concluding message in AW, that authentic man is *graceful* man, neither purely Apollonian nor purely Dionysian at any one time, however timely, but combining some of the best features of both life-styles by being grounded in basic trust. The final chapter, in which he writes a 'quasi-theological postscript' concerning graceful man, is a superbly graceful essay.

In this chapter I shall be quoting Keen extensively, for the changing styles of life which he describes are reflected in changing styles of writing. By the end of AW Keen is moving towards a new life-style and writing style in which he rejects his earlier Apollonian attempt at a systematic philosophical anthropology organized in abstraction from his own personal experience. Thus it is no surprise to find that in his next work, *To a Dancing God* (TDG), Keen presents a series of impressionistic autobiographical confessions and ponderings concerning his own struggles towards a more authentic existence. By probing his own pilgrimage and sketching the ways which he has found to be blind alleys or fruitful paths he hopes to illumine the paths of others. His hope is supported, as we shall see, by the conviction that the psychoanalytic depths of any individual's story reveal a great deal concerning everyone's story. Because of Freud Keen's explorations of his own nature can lead to truths concerning human nature generally. And, quite apart from Freud, the Keen of TDG has existentialist reasons for starting with himself. Like Kierkegaard and Marcel, he finds it phoney to write impersonally, as if he were 'the voice of Philosophy, or Theology, Or Modern Man' (TDG 2) rather than an existing historical individual using his intellect to reflect on how his own life-style can become authentic.

Keen's intensely personal writing in TDG arises not only from his Freudian conviction and his existentialist stance but also from a Dionysian influence on his intellect. He articulates this later in *Voices and Visions* (VV):

If eros was to warm my flesh I would have to let it soften the concepts I used to think about the world. My driving mind would have to learn tenderness. Instead of making ideas march goose-step, I would have to allow them to tumble over each other like kittens. (VV 7–8)

The ideas in TDG often do tumble over each other in delightful ways. I do not want to make them march goose-step, but I shall try to sort them out in relation to AW. In this chapter, even more than in my 1973 version of the essay, I shall use material from TDG extensively to fill in the brief sketch of authentic graceful man with which Keen ends AW.

Keen's three most recent works, which were not available at the time I was writing the 1973 version, have not led me to make extensive revisions or additions. *Telling Your Story* (TYS) is a how-to-do-it book written in the spirit of Esalen and the human potential movement. A practical guide to growth in self-awareness, it is good of its kind, but it contains little that sheds further light on what I take to be the main elements in Keen's account of human nature. VV is an excellent collection of interviews which Keen conducted with nine thinkers for *Psychology Today*. The common topic is human nature, and there are alternatives drawn from Marxism, mythology, psychotherapy, the occult, and mysticism. Keen expresses his own views only in his brief introduction and in occasional statements during interviews, but he says enough to indicate a few new developments in his thought. These will be considered in the latter half of this chapter. *Beginnings Without End* (BWE)[2] is similar to TDG in style and substance, though it is less explicitly religious. It contains some new variations on old themes and also some new themes. I shall note some of these as the occasion arises.

This chapter contains five sections. Section 1 is an outline of Keen's contrast between *homo admirans* (wondering man) and *homo faber* (fabricating, technological man). In section 2 I summarize Keen's investigations of Apollonian and Dionysian life-styles as alternative ways to authenticity. The first two sections are virtually the same as in my 1973 essay on Keen. In section 3 I consider Keen's own proposal for authenticity: trusting, graceful man, who has basic attitudes of gratitude, wonder, decisiveness, and fidelity. This section includes a few new insertions from VV and BWE and a more extensive discussion of how basic trust is presupposed in Keen's account of decisiveness and fidelity. Section 4 is a substantial revision. I interpret Keen's philosophical theology in relation to my analysis of analogies. I find an analogy of activity (way of originating grace) and an analogy of attitude (way of pervasiveness). The latter analogy is linked to an anthropological-logical argument in which the logical part of the argument is not explicit. In the last section, which is almost entirely new, I explore the anthropological part of this argument. I note that Keen both accepts and rejects elements in Freudian thought. Like Freud, he insists on an inherent human need for pervasive trust. Unlike Freud, he draws positive theological conclusions from this. In the last section I also consider what I believe to be defects in Keen's anthropology, above all his excessive individualism.

1 'Homo admirans' versus 'homo faber'

The opening chapter of AW is a phenomenology of wonder. Keen finds two elements in a healthy response to something that is wonderful. First, there is a puzzlement which evokes curiosity and which initiates a search for an intellectual and practical grasp of the object. Secondly, there is an admiration which develops into an appreciative contemplation and grateful celebration of the object, its uniqueness, value, and mystery. This second element is what we usually call 'wonder.' Keen goes on in the next chapter to consider wonder in children, referring to studies by Piaget, and he shows that the two elements in response to something wonderful are not inherently incompatible. A growing ability to reason and to control one's environment does not conflict with spontaneous appreciation and delight. Fabrication and admiration develop together. The loss of childhood wonder comes from the influence of parents and other adults who are anxious about anything which cannot be mastered and controlled. 'The explanation for the loss does not lie in a genetic approach to the experience of children,' but 'in a study of the pathology of adult experience' (AW 59). As Keen explains later, the modern adult represses wonder because he feels threatened by whatever he cannot grasp and manipulate, either with his tools or with his technical reason. He is *homo faber*, man the fabricator. His external and internal world is for him a meaningless or hostile chaos apart from the orderly limits which he imposes on it. Whatever is spontaneous, mysterious, and strange is a menace to his security. *Homo faber* constructs an intellectual house of steel so as to feel secure, but it is a house without wonder; indeed, it is a prison.

Keen's wonder is like Rudolph Otto's 'the holy' in being what Otto calls '*mysterium, tremendum et fascinans.*'[3] These Latin labels indicate a mystery towards which we ambivalently feel both fear and attraction. Otto would insist on a sharp difference between the secular wondrous and the religious holy, a difference which many modern western men perceive. But Keen argues that the distinction is a cultural product arising from a dubious dichotomy within a dominant strand of Christian thought. On the one hand, there is the Wholly Other God, who has revealed Himself in the sacred history of Israel and of Jesus Christ. On the other hand, there is the secular world: nature, everyday life, art, the body, sexuality. This dichotomy has fostered the assumption that nothing in the secular world is capable of being revelatory or holy. Keen goes on:

That alteration in Western self-understanding which has lately emerged under the banner of the 'death of God' is largely a result of the dichotomy of which I have spoken. When God becomes segregated from the times, spaces, and activities in which the majority of life is lived – when a wedge is driven between the holy and the quotidian – the concept of God becomes either insignificant or positively repressive and must be rejected if the integrity of human life is to be retained ... Since man is a totality, faith cannot be separated from reason, spirit from body, history from nature, or the unique from the quotidian without paying the price of schizophrenia. And before man will accept schizophrenia as his permanent condition, he will kill off any god who prevents his reunion with himself. (AW 89–90)

In this passage there are indications of an underlying theme, made fully explicit later in the book. For Keen views of man, his world, and his God should receive a primarily psychoanalytic appraisal. An authentic style of life is a healthy style, which fosters an integrity, a comprehensive unity, in the personality. An inauthentic style of life is an illness, tending towards schizophrenia. Thus Keen's criteria for authenticity come partly from psychoanalysis. But this is not his only source. He respects the wisdom of men in the past, and relies on evidence from the religious history of mankind. 'Pivotal myths of archaic man, philosophical expressions of the Greek mind, and theological doctrines of the Hebrew-Christian tradition agree in considering wonder a necessary ingredient of authentic life' (AW 61). Keen's third chapter is a brilliant and subtle account of pre-modern 'traditional' man. Keen does not exaggerate the similarities between the diverse mythological, philosophical, and theological symbols. Indeed, he often displays distinctive elements of a world-view with great insight, for example, in his exposition of the Hebrew-Christian ideas of man as image of God and as creature of God. But he finds a common world-view as well, one which is conducive to wonder. Compared to modern man, pre-modern men look very much alike.

Primal man, Greek man, and Judeo-Christian man are but three species within a single genus which may be called *homo admirans* (wondering man), teleological man, or idealistic man. They share the assumption that the cosmos is a teleologically ordered system, governed by a rational mind or minds comprehensible to the human mind. Their major differences concern the questions of whether the mind ordering the cosmos is immanent or transcendent and whether evidence for this mind is found primarily in the recurring sequences of nature or in the unique events of human history. As we shall see in a later chapter, the irreconcilable conflict is not between the primal-Greek and the Hebrew-Christian views of man but between the traditional notion that man lives in wonder in a cosmos already partially informed by patterns of meaning and value, and the modern view that man lives in constant anxiety in a chaos which he alone must shape and make meaningful. (AW 80)

If nature and human life are not already informed by a 'given' meaning and value which men can discern by mythological imagination or cosmic reason or religious faith, then wonder is not a response to reality but a sentimental indulgence; for wonder is an appreciative contemplation and celebration of meaning and value which is already there in things and people. Instead of the wonderful world of *homo admirans* there is the wonderless world of *homo faber* and his technical reason.

Keen's next two chapters are devoted to *homo faber*. His conclusion is that *homo faber* does not have an authentic style of life. To understand oneself as *homo faber* and to live accordingly is to encourage and invite various forms of schizophrenia. *Homo faber* oscillates between fantasies of omnipotence and nightmares of impotence. He is the godlike creator of all meaning and value, yet he has no value within himself. He tries to master everything, but he is the victim not only of death but of his own technology. He is also split in his attitude to nature. He feels hostile and fearful towards what he cannot control, but becomes contemptuous once he can control it. He cannot bear the idea of limitations on his operations, an ecology of nature, but he discovers that these limitations are inescapable. He is obsessed with clarity, 'the scrubbing compulsion of the mind – a defence mechanism against the threat of the chaotic mystery of life' (AW 130), yet ultimate questions keep coming up and he feels helpless in his inability to begin to think about them. 'He cannot get any purchase on them with his prehensile tool-using mind. *Homo faber* has become all thumbs' (AW 130). His technical progress brings increased leisure for play and for intimate personal relations, but his life-style turns play into organized competitive work and turns sex into an anxious concern about 'making out.' His vision of a technological utopia a few decades hence, in which full human control will allegedly be achieved, alienates him from his present existence, with its abundant evidence of human limitation and impotence. Keen sums up the inauthenticity, the illness, of *homo faber* as follows:

At the root of the neurotic self-understanding of *homo faber* lies the failure to come to terms with the connected notions of *limit* and *gift*, hence with that mode of perceiving and celebrating which we have been calling wonder. To be is to be something: to accept oneself and the world is to accept limits which are prior to and unalterable by individual decision. The world into which any existing person emerges is already richly informed with meaning and value. Before I begin to choose, I am already shaped by being male, white, middle-class American, and having a certain range of available energy and intelligence, tastes, opinions, aspirations, and so on. To accept myself is to accept the limits as gifts – not as unalterable, but as the specific shape my existence bears at the moment when it first becomes conscious of the responsibility for deciding and defining new limits for itself. The resentment against all a priori limits (the necessity of death or the givenness of value) by *homo faber* reflects a hostility toward the givenness of human existence which is merely the reverse side of the refusal to admire, to wonder, and to be grateful. (AW 149)

The central portion of Keen's book is thus an apology or defence of wonder, the life-style of traditional *homo admirans*, and an attack on the life-style of his opposite, modern technological man, *homo faber*.

2 Authenticity: Dionysian or Apollonian?

In the next chapter of AW, however, the focus widens from wonder to authenticity, and in this broader context Keen links his contrast between *homo admirans* and *homo faber* to a more inclusive contrast between Dionysian man and Apollonian man. Since wonder is an important element in Dionysian existence, we are not surprised to find that Keen calls for a more Dionysian life-style in modern life. But the chapter on childhood wonder has prepared us for an account of authenticity in which *both* Dionysian wonder *and* Apollonian mastery have a place. Indeed, Keen's central argument is that a purely Dionysian life, like a purely Apollonian life, is inauthentic to the point of madness. The man who is authentic or healthy is *homo tempestivus*, the timely man, who gracefully oscillates between Dionysian and Apollonian modes of being in the world, celebrating or cerebrating in relation to the changing moments, seasons, and crises of life. Keen is himself a timely man when he chooses a contrast between Dionysus and Apollo rather than some other typology:

I have chosen this typology (which was used with great power by Nietzsche) because it reflects the radical alternatives that *seem* to confront the young: either repressive order or undirected violence, either conformity or rebellion, either surrender to the system or turning on, tuning in, and dropping out; either work or ecstasy, either discipline or freedom, either abiding commitments or spontaneity, either the ego or the id, either the past and the future or the present. (AW 152)

What could be more 'timely,' 'relevant,' and 'with-it' in 1969? Yet Keen's chapter also has profound and perennial significance.

His own summary of his contrast between Dionysian and Apollonian styles of life cannot be bettered (AW 193–4):

DIONYSIAN	APOLLONIAN
Man-the-dancer responds to experience as it is given in its multiplicity. *Homo ludens* is oriented toward play, levity, fantasy, spontaneity: he is libidinal, erotic, living primarily in feeling and sensation, destroying boundaries and exploring diversity.	Man-the-maker fabricates an environment from the raw material of nature. *Homo faber* is oriented toward work, seriousness, realism, regularity; he is governed by a strong ego, living primarily by thinking and willing, by erecting boundaries, giving form, intellectual and material possession.
Without wonder there is no knowledge of the *world*. Thus, one axis of knowledge is: intuition, silence, welcoming receptivity, relaxation in the presence of the other. In wonder man attends to the kaleidoscopic plurality of the world; he juxtaposes and savors particulars. Wondering knowledge is immediate, sensuous, enthusiastic, a matter of participation and union, an overcoming of the estrangement between subject and object.	Without action there is no *knowledge* of the world. Thus, one axis of knowledge is: judgment, abstraction, categorization, synthesis. Laboring reason goes beyond immediacy in a search for understanding. Intelligence acting upon the world to reduce the chaos of plurality to terms that are manageable ... The knowledge which results from laboring reason is pragmatic, objective, universal, and verifiable.
In wonder, value and meaning are discovered as given in the encounter. Authentic life involves the 'feminine' moment of opening to, welcoming, nurturing the meanings which are given in the immediacy of sensation, relationship, environment, personality; it involves letting things happen ...	In acting, man creates values and meanings by his vows, covenants, contracts, projects. Authentic life involves the 'masculine' element of aggressive control, of projecting and realizing a world; it involves making things happen ...
Personality begins with the gift of relationship. In the beginning is the breast, the world of total succor. The world of primal experience is a matrix of gift and limitation.	Identity begins with decision and action. To separate the self from the matrix one must pass from what is imposed to what is chosen. In the world of mature experience chosen and given limits are in harmony.

Appropriate responses to the world as given in wonder are: admiration, gratitude, appreciation, celebration, contemplation.

Appropriate responses to the world which must be created by human action are: problematic questioning, searching for explanations, solutions, causes.

The contrast, as worked out in detail by Keen, is fascinating. For example, he has an extensive discussion of the Dionysian style as advocated in Norman O. Brown's psychoanalytic body-mysticism and as exemplified in some forms of psychedelic experience. But what is perhaps most interesting is his way of appraising each style. He claims that not only individuals and societies can be relatively healthy or sick, but also views of man, models of self-understanding. Individuals may be psychopathic and societies sociopathic, but it is also true that ideas concerning man and his place in the world can be *ideopathic*. Therefore when Keen looks at a model of man with its associated world-view, he asks how it functions, what attitudes, feelings, actions, and aspirations it renders appropriate, and whether these promote health or sickness. He recognizes that each model is an artificial construct which no particular individual is likely to instantiate in its purity, unmixed with other elements. In someone for whom one model is dominant there are elements from the other model as well. But he proposes a method for showing the inadequacy of a model by considering a relatively unmixed case, tracing the process in which the model becomes increasingly dominant, until it gains complete control of a personality. Each model, he claims, has a psychopathology, a continuum of ever-increasing sickness. The continuum culminates for each in a form of psychotic schizophrenia.

Keen first considers the Apollonian style of life. It becomes pathological 'when the vision of the necessary destroys the vision of the possible – when law denies novelty, when reason eclipses enthusiasm, when compulsion prevents spontaneity, or when the regular ceases to be wonderful' (AW 164). The psychopathology continuum here begins with the claustrophobic fantasies and dreams of normal persons, who may feel limitations of space to be repressive and frightening, as if they are trapped, with no way out. Then there is neurotic depression, a feeling of being weighed down, a decline of freedom, hope, buoyancy, wonder, and enjoyment. The neurotic's life seems to consist of a 'feelingless repetition of routine acts' (AW 165). Inside there is an emptiness, a vacuum. The next stage away from health is neurotic obsessions and compulsions, the sense that one is in the power of an alien force or law. 'Better a victim than a vacuum' (AW 166). Finally there is a paranoid form of psychotic schizophrenia, in which a 'fantasy kingdom is constructed which is inhabited by a hierarchy of authorities, demons and gods, who conspire to create a world of total compulsion' (AW 166). This psychopathology is fostered by an Apollonian model of man if its concern for law and order becomes too dominant. An Apollonian man may be so concerned to limit and control his environment and himself by imposing on them a structure of law and order that he denies his own freedom and hope. Apollonian philosophies stress determinism, so that man is impotent in spite of his dreams of omnipotent rational control; and they stress a relentless regularity in the universe, which makes genuine hope irrational. The structure created by reason weighs man down. Anything spontaneous in nature or in himself, which he cannot grasp and control, must be repressed from consciousness. 'Apollonian pathology also destroys the intuition (which lies at the heart of the experience of wonder) that finite existence, with all its limited and tragic character, is nevertheless a gift. *When all is necessary, the given is equivalent to the imposed, and man is not a recipient but a victim*' (AW 173). Keen does not claim that Apollonian ideas always or typically lead all the way to psychosis. 'It frequently happens that a mild form of illness seems to innoculate the sufferer against a more severe form of the same illness: neurosis is often a protection against psychosis' (AW 164).

Dionysian pathology begins 'when the vision of possibility destroys awareness of the necessities and limits that govern existence as it is presently known. In Dionysian madness all limits, boundaries, and laws are dissolved in the endless flux of existence, and the world is reduced to chaos and absolute contingency. The world becomes a wilderness which cannot be domesticated by thought, will, or action' (AW 176). The psychopathology continuum begins with the fantasies or dreams of normal persons in which space is felt to be limitless, immense, empty, and terrifying. One is lost in space, falling endlessly, without any limits or landmarks to give a sense of direction. The next stage is 'anomie,' a drifting through life without much sense of limits accepted or decided upon. Like a weightless astronaut adrift in space, one has nothing solid to push against to establish one's own sense of personal identity. Then there is a neurotic regression. A man begins to live partly in his childhood, when he 'commanded in imagination a kingdom of absolute possibility' (AW 179). These delusions of infantile omnipotence then increase to a point where dream and fantasy take over, the self is lost, and the continuum ends with a form of psychotic schizophrenia. This psychopathology is fostered by a Dionysian model of man if it is the dominating model, for there is an excessive stress on participatory union rather than individual identity, passivity rather than decision, unlimited openness rather than rational limitation, imaginative possibility rather than real actuality. Keen's decisive argument, indeed, is that exclusively Dionysian models of man which have been propounded (for example, by Norman Brown) are in themselves indistinguishable from psychoses. Nevertheless we need Dionysian elements in our lives. Thus for Keen the crucial task is to 'distinguish between that touch of madness which is the essence of wisdom and sanctity, and pure madness in which human responsibility and dignity are destroyed. To distinguish between divine and demonic madness is to discover when Dionysus is the god of grace and when he is the bringer of destruction and pathology' (AW 181).[4]

Where Apollo dominates there is repression. Where Dionysus dominates there is regression. Each model of man, by itself, leads towards schizophrenia. Each is a rejection of the other. Yet each feeds on the threat posed by the other. Fearful of extreme Apollonian repression, men turn to an extreme Dionysian life-style. Fearful of Dionysian regression, men turn to an extreme Apollonian life-style. Each fear can operate in the same person, impelling him towards conflicting extremes. Yet men need elements from both life-styles for a healthy, whole existence. How can this be done? One suggestion in Keen is an oscillation between the two modes of being, responding appropriately to the changing moments, seasons, and crises of life. But this suggestion, which Keen connects to the model of man as *homo tempestivus*, does not seem very sensible. To alternate between Apollo and Dionysus could be to alternate between two forms of madness – not an authentic style of life but a manic-depressive form of illness. Somehow we must be Apollonian without much repression and Dionysian without much regression. How? One way would be to dilute each element, trying to reduce the intensity of both reason and emotion, both work and play, both curiosity and wonder, both will and sensation. But this would be a drab compromise, a half-life. Keen has a different solution: a model of authentic man as *graceful* man.

3 Authenticity: graceful man

Although Keen also gives this new model the label '*homo tempestivus*,' it is a very different model from the one to which that label appropriately applies. Instead of oscillating in a timely way between Apollo and Dionysus, graceful man exemplifies a selection of elements from both models, revising, combining, and reconciling them in relation to a new dominant style of life. At any one time elements from both models will be present. Graceful man goes behind the modern dichotomy between Apollonian man and Dionysian man to regain some of the attitudes which traditional man had before the modern schizophrenia set in. Since these attitudes are religious, graceful man is religious; but, unlike traditional man, he is agnostic. (Later I shall query this alleged agnosticism.)

Keen moves from timely man to graceful man by means of an image which links them together: man as dancer. When someone begins dancing with others, his sense of timing is linked with his having 'learned to trust himself to be appropriately moved by the music and the motion' (AW 198). We recall that Keen first introduced man as dancer in his account of the Dionysian style, contrasting him with Apollonian man as maker. Here, however, man as dancer is an image of graceful man, who is not simply Dionysian. Keen looks at graceful action not only in a dance but also in sport or in social intercourse or in man's overall response to his natural and social environment. He finds that graceful action presupposes two attitudes:

The foundations of gracefulness are: *trust* in the context within which action must take place and *confidence* in the ability of the self to undertake appropriate action. Grace involves a casual rather than aggressive stance, a nonthreatened acceptance of the self and the world. In the deepest sense, relaxation is possible only when the context within which action must take place is perceived as friendly to the actor. Indeed, we might describe graceful action as at once relaxed and vigorous. (AW 203)

Keen does not explicitly relate the model of graceful man to his contrast between Dionysus and Apollo, but there is a fairly obvious implicit relation. Trustful, receptive relaxation combined with confident, vigorous action gives us Dionysus with minimal regression or passivity and Apollo with minimal repression or compulsiveness. The action of graceful man has a pattern which is neither a boundaryless fantasy in which the self is lost nor a rigid fabrication which imposes alien order on self and world. The pattern is like the free, creative response of a dancer to the pattern already given by the music and the motion of other dancers. And unlike dominantly Dionysian or Apollonian man, graceful man is not moving along a psychopathological continuum which leads to schizophrenia. The more he trusts his environment and the more confident he is in his own ability to respond appropriately to it, the more integrated he becomes. Graceful man is inwardly harmonious.

Trust in one's context is a prerequisite for confidence in one's ability. The need for a quite specific trust is obvious in the case of dancing or athletics. For example, in order to learn how to swim, one must trust the support of the water. But the interrelation between trust and confidence can be much more general, involving a total style of life. I once heard a Buddhist monk explain 'faith' in terms of an analogy with what happens when we learn to swim. And Keen points out that according to Erik Erikson a 'basic trust' is necessary for a healthy personality. Keen notes a continuity between this basic trust and the language of religious faith. 'For the religious man, God-language functions to affirm that the ultimate context into which human existence is inserted is trustworthy' (AW 205). It is trustworthy rather than hostile or neutral. Whether or not a man uses God-language, he must have this basic trust if he is to be mature, according to Keen. 'This is the source of the ability to relax and act gracefully' (AW 206). Keen's mature, authentic man thus differs from what he finds in Camus. 'The alternative to such trust is the heroic masochism of Sisyphus which revels in alienation and considers despair the badge of human courage and authenticity' (AW 206). Instead of revelling in his alienation from the world graceful man celebrates his at-homeness in the world.

We have seen that graceful man's basic trust enables him to be relaxed, unanxious, and confidently creative. He is also *grateful*. Since the ultimate context of his life is trustworthy, since it 'intends the fulfillment rather than the frustration of those values we hold to be fundamental for human dignity' (AW 205), he is grateful for his existence – even for the limitations, deformities, and graceless elements which are part of him. As Keen said earlier: 'To accept myself is to accept the limits as gifts – not as unalterable, but as the specific shape my existence bears' (AW 149). Graceful man also accepts environmental limits as gifts, for he trusts their ultimate context. He is grateful for the gift of being – his own being and that of his environment. Quite apart from his own efforts there is already a trustworthy source of meaning and value on which he can rely. So he is grateful.

Graceful man has also an element in his style of life which is even more distinctively Dionysian: he *wonders*. He rejoices in the presence of things, immersing himself in the 'primal simplicities of the world which are given in sense and feeling' (AW 210). He is filled with admiration, enjoyment, and appreciation in the presence of 'objects and events and persons that are luminous with meaning' (AW 210). Like traditional man he responds with wonder to the holy, but he finds the holy in the depths of everyday life: 'The sacred is incarnate in flesh, things and events' (AW 210). For graceful man the sacred is within the secular, the mysterious is within the familiar, the awesome unknown is within the known. But before this can happen, 'the sham of rationality, the illusion of control, the cultural compromise of false sanity must be shattered' (BWE 70). The security provided by a purely Apollonian life-style must be abandoned – and that requires a good deal of trust in oneself and one's environment.

Graceful man, then, can be defined in terms of his basic attitudes: a *trust* which enables him to have confidence in his immediate and ultimate life-context and so to act with relaxed vigour; a *gratitude* for the gift of being, including the gift of external and internal limits on his life and the gift of meaning and value which is already there; and a *wonder* which exuberantly celebrates the mysteries of immediate sensuous awareness. Graceful man trusts, is grateful, and wonders. But these three attitudes are not equally important. Trust is the necessary condition and context for the gratitude and wonder which Keen depicts.

Trust has a similarly crucial place in Keen's understanding of two other attitudes which he includes in his model of authentic man: *decisiveness* and *commitment*. These are revised versions of stances which Keen mentions as parts of the modern Apollonian life-style in the passage which I have quoted at length. Some parts of that life-style are not included in Keen's model: in general, those which have to do with the technical intellect of *homo faber* as he arranges an orderly world in his mind and in his environment. But Apollonian man is not only technological (*homo faber*); he is also Sartrean (wilful man, *homo volens*, as I shall call him). And Keen includes revised versions of Sartrean attitudes. The Sartrean element in a purely Apollonian man is the autonomous, separated will of *homo volens*, which he exercises in two different ways (I quote again from AW 194):

Identity begins with decision and action. To separate the self from the matrix one must pass from what is imposed to what is chosen.

In acting, man creates values and meanings by his vows, covenants, contracts, projects.

The first is a Sartrean kind of decisiveness, the second a Sartrean kind of commitment. In each case wilful Apollonian man exercises his will in lonely isolation from both the external world on which he acts and his own internal attitudes and feelings. In Keen's revised version of decision and commitment, however, the will is exercised in the context of a trustful stance which pervades the whole person. This means that, although authentic man is a distinct individual, taking responsibility for what he does with his life in his decisions, he expresses his creative decisiveness as someone who trustfully, gratefully, accepts the individuality which he has been given, with all its limitations and imperfections. And although Keen sees commitment as active and creative, it has for him the form of fidelity. That is, commitment is a matter of being trustworthy in response to a pervasive trustworthiness in one's environment.

I shall consider Keen on individual decisiveness first, and rather extensively. (Concerning fidelity I shall be brief.) Decisiveness is for Keen an acceptance of full responsibility for one's own life-style, limiting oneself in some directions, projecting oneself in others. Although Keen is obviously influenced to some extent by Sartre, this is clearly not a Sartrean self-creation *ex nihilo*. Rather, it is an active response to that which is 'given' in oneself and one's environment, which one accepts in trust and gratitude and wonder.

To accept myself is to accept the limits as gifts – not as unalterable, but as the specific shape my existence bears at the moment when it first becomes conscious of the responsibility for deciding and defining new limits for itself. (AW 149)

The life of authentic man has a shape or pattern which combines acceptance of what is given and decisiveness in what is created. Keen feels the 'pain of limitation' (TDG 112), the tragic restriction to one self, one path, one life. But he resists the impulse to flee into unbounded Dionysian fantasy and he rejects a self-enslavement in Apollonian law and order. Instead he chooses his limits. Some limits he chooses by deciding to create himself in this shape rather than that. But other limits he chooses by deciding to accept them as given rather than resenting them, rejecting them, or trying to eliminate them. He comes to accept many external restrictions and internal imperfections. Either he *can* not remove them or, in his judgment, he *need* not remove them.

Keen is thus very wary of perfectionism:[5]

Perfection in love?
Love imperfection. (BWE 99)

If we are most authentically human when we are able to perceive and love all that is faulted, lame, and imperfect, then both education and therapy should beware of the rhetoric of triumph – becoming whole, realizing the full human potential. (VV 84)

The human-potential movement in education and therapy can become perfectionist. So also can western adaptations of eastern mystical disciplines, where sometimes an 'antiseptic spiritual obsessionality' so persistently works on the psyche that it destroys the 'casual acceptance of the imperfect actuality of life which is the essence of grace' (VV 18). Decisiveness is too wilful when it is perfectionist, for it lacks the patient relaxation and receptivity of trustful decisiveness.

Keen also finds the heroic, embattled decisiveness of Carlos Castaneda too wilful, and rejects it for similar reasons (VV 15–16). Castaneda links decisiveness with death:

When there is no way of knowing whether I have one more minute of life, I must live as if this is my last moment. Each act is the warrior's last battle. So everything must be done *impeccably*. Nothing can be left pending ... When death stands to your left, you must create your world by a series of decisions. (VV 121–2, my italics)

Castaneda commends what he calls 'gestures': 'A gesture is a deliberate act which is undertaken for the power that comes from making a decision' (VV 123). The content of the decision need not be significant. In general, decisiveness is for him a means to the accumulation of personal power. Keen rejects this warrior life-style, which 'defines the world in terms of danger and conflict and therefore requires the accumulation of armor and power' (VV 16). For Keen, since the ultimate context of one's life is trustworthy, decisiveness in creating one's self need not be belligerent. Death may stand on his left but life stands on his right, giving him both his limitations and the power to go beyond them.[6]

Keen's revised version of Apollonian commitment is *fidelity*. (His account shows the influence of Gabriel Marcel.[7]) According to Keen, 'the ability to bind ourselves over a period of time by contracts, promises, and vows is the source of that continuity which is essential to a sense of selfhood' (AW 190). This point by itself could be made by a Sartrean Apollonian who sees commitments as a device for wilful self-creation along with other projects of the isolated individual who must create his own security and meaning and identity. But Keen sets commitments in a context of trust:

We were nurtured and given existence by the web of concern and commitment which was early woven around us by parents and friends, and we continue to give birth to ourselves only to the degree that we have the courage to define and limit ourselves by the making and keeping of promises. (AW 190)

Such fidelity has basic trust as a prerequisite, for it is a response to the trustworthiness of others. This trustworthiness is only discerned in others to the extent that we can trust. Moreover, it is only valued and emulated to the extent that we have the experience of benefiting from it, an experience which depends on our trust in others.

The major obstacle to trust is paranoia:

Jogging on a pier in San Francisco. A fisherman starts a long cast. As his pole comes back, the lure with three-pronged hooks whips dangerously close to my eye. My brain registers DANGER. I veer aside with my best broken-field running step. My mind immediately translates the impulse DANGER into the paranoid judgment: He intends to do me evil. Immediately I catch my paranoia and correct my judgment: There is danger here but he intends me no evil. The transition from alienation to trust takes place in a milisecond. Paranoia must be countered with trust a hundred times a day. (BWE 17–18)

The opposite of paranoia is the assumption that the 'other' is a friend. I may enter the darkness and mystery of the other (man, woman, world, God) without armoring my body with tension or anesthetizing it by fear. That which is strange is approached in friendship, not alienation. We are in this thing together. (BWE 18)

4 Authenticity and God

Authentic man trusts, and this enables him to be a man of gratitude, wonder, decisiveness, and fidelity, resisting paranoia. In matters religious Keen recommends what he calls a 'trustful agnosticism' (TDG 139). He says: 'We may not claim to have *knowledge* of God. An honest theology is necessarily agnostic' (TDG 156). At the beginning of TDG Keen tells us that 'The dancing god to whom the title of this book refers is neither Apollo nor Dionysus. Indeed, he is nameless and, perhaps, must remain so' (TDG 5). Keen's conclusion in AW was similar. He told how a total stranger once gave him a very unusual knife and then disappeared. 'For weeks after this event I lived with a pervasive sense of gratitude to the stranger and with a wondering expectancy created by the realization that such a strange and wonderful happening could occur' (AW 211). Keen asks: 'How important is it to know the name of the stranger and thank him for his gift?' His answer is that it is not very important. Similarly, he says, it is not very important to know the name of God (that is, to be able to describe God) or to thank him in *worship* for the gift of existence, though we may *celebrate* this gift with a sense of gratitude and wonder. What matters for psychological and spiritual health, that is, for authenticity, is our basic attitudes such as trust and gratitude and wonder. Earlier Keen had said that talk about God can have a function, for it can 'nourish and restore the sense of basic trust by affirming in symbolic language that the ultimate context of life is succoring and trustworthy' (AW 204). But what matters first of all is authentic life and the basic attitudes which it requires and includes. Talk about God has only a secondary, functional role.

As Keen portrays this role, it is in principle dispensable. Presumably if someone has a very strong basic trust he will not need God-talk to nourish it, let alone to restore it. He will have no need to affirm religious convictions, whether in symbolic language or in Keen's language. But I question Keen's assumption that he can separate basic attitudes and religious convictions in this way. Earlier he claimed to show an intrinsic connection between world-views and dominant attitudes in Apollonian and Dionysian life-styles; presumably there is a similar kind of connection in the case of graceful man. We may agree with him (at any rate I do) that the encouragement of basic trust, gratitude, and wonder is more important than the use of talk about God to affirm religious convictions. But we cannot fail to notice that when Keen himself describes basic trust, his description includes an articulation of religious convictions, for example, 'that the ultimate context of life is succoring and trustworthy.' Perhaps someone else might be able to describe a kind of basic trust which does not include or imply religious convictions (that is a possibility which I shall consider later), but Keen does not. What Keen means by 'basic trust' cannot be fully understood without the various affirmations of religious conviction or elucidations of the word 'God' which he provides:

We may use the word 'God' to signify the unity and trustworthiness of the unknowable source and end of all mundane reality ... The word 'God' serves an indispensable function for the man who wishes to make a consistent affirmation of the trustworthiness of the mystery which surrounds his existence. (TDG 156)

In prayer I feel my words going out to the unknown mystery which I trust is the caring context of my existence. (TDG 124)

To say 'God is' with the total self ... is functionally equivalent to affirming the following with the mind and the guts ... The ultimate significance, meaning, security, value, dignity of my life is not dependent upon anything I can do, make or accomplish. Therefore, my action may spring out of what I am rather than arising out of a desperate need to establish myself. I am already founded, rooted, grounded in (depth metaphors) or contexted and encompassed by (metaphors of inclusion) that which guarantees my integrity. (TDG 130–1)

Any language is authentically theological which points to what is experienced as holy ... We may now define the holy as 'that irreducible principle, power, or presence which is the source and guarantor of unity, dignity, meaning, value, and wholeness. (TDG 103)

Keen says that none of this involves '*knowledge* of God' (TDG 156). But his basic trust does involve *belief* in God, whether he uses the word 'God' or other expressions such as 'the unknown mystery which is the caring context of my existence' or 'that which grounds and guarantees my integrity' or 'the source and guarantor of unity, dignity, meaning, values and wholeness.' Yet Keen denies that the idea of God has content (TDG 156), and, as we have seen, he says that we cannot 'name' God, presumably in the sense of describing Him by ascribing attributes to Him. These claims seem to me to be inconsistent with his actual procedure. The various alternative expressions which he suggests as substitutes for 'God' do give the term descriptive content. It is true that this content has to do with God understood as the focus of the human attitude of basic trust, not with God as understood in Himself apart from self-involving attitudes. The content is only understood indirectly *via* basic trust, and basic trust is only understood to the extent that one has it. Thus the meaning of the description or definition of God does not meet objectivist standards. But Keen is employing an existentialist analogy of attitude in which 'God' means that towards which an attitude of basic trust is appropriate.

Keen uses the way of pervasiveness in his analogy of attitude. Basic trust, in contrast with ordinary trust, is pervasive. Its scope is any and every situation, and its focus is whatever reality unifies the cosmos. Its opposite is a basic distrust, a pervasive stance of 'suspicion, hostility and eternal vigilance' (AW 204). Basic trust can persist even when nothing particular remains in which one can trust. Indeed, one of Keen's routes to basic trust is through an experience of the void, in which all that one has relied on for security and meaning vanishes (TDG 20–1). In the realization that there is nothing he *can* do to give his life security and meaning there is a sudden leap to the realization that there is nothing he *must* do, since these come as a gift with life itself. In contrast with such pervasive trust, ordinary trust is not all-inclusive in scope; it does not even include the storms of life, let alone the void. Keen's basic pervasive trust is an assurance that one is already grounded in, and contexted by, that which is the trustworthy source and guarantor of one's integrity. Keen's elucidation of basic trust by the way of pervasiveness leads immediately to an expression of the religious conviction which it implies or includes.

Earlier I have raised the question whether someone might describe a kind of basic trust which does not include or imply religious convictions. In order to answer this question I shall here introduce a distinction between 'cosmic' and 'religious' convictions. A cosmic conviction is a belief that some reality pervades the whole of one's environment as a unifying constant. A religious conviction is a cosmic conviction in which this reality is further designated in ways similar to what is held in traditional religions. The convictions which I find in Keen are not only cosmic but religious.

Basic trust includes or implies a cosmic conviction if it is doubly pervasive and doubly unifying. Consider *pervasiveness* first. In so far as any attitude is internally pervasive, that is, an influence on a person's way of dealing with any and every situation, it is also externally pervasive; the total person is related to everything in the cosmos in accordance with the attitude. But some doubly pervasive attitudes such as anxiety tend to disintegrate both the person and his experienced world. In contrast with this Keen advocates doubly pervasive attitudes which are also doubly *unifying*, integrating both the person and his experienced world. Instead of falling apart in a pervasive chaos or multiverse, one relates as a whole person to a unified universe. So if a basic attitude is one which is both doubly pervasive and doubly unifying it includes or implies a conviction concerning an X which is a unifying cosmic constant. But this conviction is not necessarily religious.

Keen's description of basic trust includes various references to the conviction that the cosmic constant is 'trustworthy.' What he means by this, however, is very different from what someone else might mean. Consider, for example, the minimal trust which I or anyone must have in order to live at all in the world. Without it a person lets himself die, or commits suicide, or falls into deep psychosis. I must be able to feel that I can rely on there being a minimal regularity and order in my environment, even if this affects me harmfully more frequently than it affects me helpfully. Without such minimal trust I literally cannot take a step lest the earth cave in on me. Such a trust is doubly pervasive and doubly unifying, yet the cosmic conviction which it includes or implies is minimal: my environment is not completely chaotic, but is unified by some constant reality (e.g. matter?) which is orderly and regular. Some religious apologists like to call such a conviction 'religious' and then claim that all men must be religious. This seems to me misleading, for it obscures the enormous differences between such a conviction and a clearly religious conviction such as that implied by Keen's kind of basic trust. For Keen the cosmic reality is 'trustworthy' in the sense that it can be relied on for the security and meaning and integrity of human life. This is a cosmic conviction which is very close to traditional religious belief in divine Providence. Thus whether or not basic trust includes or implies convictions which are appropriately called 'religious' depends on the character of the basic trust.

Is it possible that there is a kind of trust which is neither doubly pervasive nor doubly unifying but which has a very important influence on human life? Such an attitude would not include or imply any cosmic conviction. Anyone is free to call such a trust 'basic,' but if he does he will mean something very different from what I mean in this book. The sense in which a basic attitude 'includes' or 'implies' a cosmic conviction is something which I shall explore in chapter 7. There we will see that the issue is more complex, more fascinating, and more fundamental than might appear at first glance.

Let us return to Keen, however. What I have found in his writing is an analogy of attitude, way of pervasiveness, in which the religious convictions which are included in, or implied by, basic trust are affirmed without acknowledgment of the *logical* connections between attitude and conviction. Instead, Keen speaks of the *function* of such affirmations in nourishing and restoring trust. But the reason why talk about God nourishes and restores basic trust is that it expresses the convictions which basic trust includes or implies. Keen even postulates a 'nonreligious affirmation of basic trust' (AW 206), but he immediately contradicts this notion (as he must, in my view) by explaining it in terms of religious conviction:

The mature man, whether religious or non-religious, chooses to credit the context that nourishes and creates him as being worthy of trust. (AW 206)

Actually in this quotation we have a conflated expression of what I see as Keen's implicit anthropological-logical argument for rational belief in God. The normative anthropological claim is explicit: 'mature' man has basic trust. The logical claim, though not acknowledged, is implicit: basic trust includes or implies the religious conviction that the context which nourishes and creates us is trustworthy.[8]

The relation between authenticity and religious conviction in Keen has two main elements. One we have considered: analogy of attitude, way of pervasiveness, where an attitude which is a condition of authenticity implies or includes religious convictions. The other we shall now consider: analogy of activity, way of originating grace. Here God is regarded as the source of the grace which fosters authenticity.

According to Keen theology may be 'highly knowledgeable about the sacred' (TDG 157), and the sacred is whatever, in one's environment or in oneself, in general or on particular occasions, fosters authentic life. In TDG Keen tells us a great deal about the sacred, since the book is an intensely personal exploration of the route to authentic life, with its 'dignity, meaning, value and wholeness' (TDG 103). Keen also links the sacred with 'grace': 'There are moments when we find ourselves gratuitously liberated from hurts, habits and hang-ups which shaped our past and recent present' (TDG 145). He also gives a more formal definition of grace:

Let me define grace as 'a sudden reorganization, in a more economical manner, of perceptions, attitudes, and dispositions which results in a relaxation of inner and outer conflicts and in liberation of previously bound energies for projects and relationships which are satisfying to the maturing self.' In the contemporary idiom, grace is a happening rather than an achievement, a gift rather than a reward. By lessening the alienation between self and self, self and others, self and world, it creates the possibility of action which is integral and responsible. It sets the self free from compulsive reaction to the past for a present and a future containing genuine novelty. (TDG 145)

Grace is thus a species of the sacred in which the sacred occurs momentarily and dramatically. The sacred is whatever fosters authentic life. And the word 'God' refers to the source of the sacred. God is the activity beyond ourselves which fosters our authenticity.

Keen claims that the view which he is commending is 'agnostic' concerning God, though highly knowledgeable concerning the sacred. But if, as I have argued, Keen is committed to belief in God and God is believed to be source of the sacred, then it would seem that the more we know concerning the sacred the more we believe concerning God. The content of this belief does not meet objectivist criteria of meaning, of course, for it can only be understood to the extent that one trusts. Keen 'trusts' that the unknown mystery is the caring context of his existence and as such is the source of the sacred, the origin of grace, liberating us into authentic life. Keen's approach is clearly existentialist concerning the content of religious belief. It is also existentialist in another respect, for we can only come to understand what human authenticity is to the extent that we are becoming authentic. To an objectivist all this may seem indistinguishable from agnosticism. Certainly Keen is remote from the position of thinkers who confidently use the way of perfection in analogy of activity to establish the nature of God as He is in Himself and then confidently use a cosmological argument to establish His existence. But Keen's position is also remote from what is usually called 'agnosticism' in religion, for his authentic man is committed to a basic belief of the religious person: there is a divine Providence everywhere at work in human life as the grace which enables us to live authentically.

Beyond this belief, however, Keen is in a sense 'agnostic.' The content of his theology is not as rich as might first appear. Though his rich phenomenology of the sacred occurs in the context of belief in God as source, it is not the case that each new item in the phenomenology adds another item to the theology, an additional characterization of God. Though for Keen God is the ultimate caring context of human life and the source of each instance of the sacred, it is not clear that for him the sacred reveals or resembles the source. In this respect Keen's thought differs from a personalism which uses an existentialist analogy of relation. In such a personalism there is an awareness of the Liberator revealing His presence and His personal relation with us in His liberating activity. Although Keen's basic trust implies various convictions which personalize God as trustworthy, benevolent, caring, etc, it does not involve a personal-encounter relation with God. He experiences the sacred, but not the source. He celebrates the gift, but does not worship the Giver. He employs an analogy of activity, way of originating grace.

In his more recent writings Keen shows a radical reluctance and reticence concerning expressions of religious conviction. This may indicate a further change in his own personal perspective. It is certainly different from much of what he says in TDG, where there is an abundance of such expressions, even though he often avoids the word 'God.' But in TDG there were strands of thought which could lead naturally to his later silence concerning God. What matters most is the phenomenology of the sacred, not the theology of the source. What matters most is the basic attitudes, not the convictions which are implied and which, after all, can only be properly understood in relation to the attitudes. What matters most is reverent wonder, not abortive attempts to describe mystery, attempts which tend to destroy wonder:

It would be interesting to see what would happen if theologians would recover the essential reverence of the tradition of negative theology and would understand their role not as 'service to the word' (a Barthian concept) but as guardians of silence. In the modern world, we desperately need to discover appropriate ways to say 'Take off your shoes – you are on holy ground; allow silence, you are in the presence of sacred mystery!' (TDG 139)

Here Keen seems to be calling for what I have called the second version of the negative way which applies to *any* attempts to describe God, however arrived at. That species, you will recall, is not a subordinate element in the way of perfection but radically qualifies it, challenging *any* transfer of terms from the human to the divine. For Keen wonder and silence go together in authentic life: 'The more I am struck with the poignancy and wonder of being alive, the less I want to talk about God or about theology' (TDG 139).

Thus Keen's view of trust has become increasingly 'agnostic' and silent. Another trend which began in TDG and can be seen in his later writings links trust and the *body*.[9] On this point a variety of sources converge to influence Keen – Marcelian existentialism, hatha yoga, encounter-group experience, and psychoanalysis of early childhood. All of these can be seen in the last chapter of TDG, where Keen coins two aphorisms:

As a man is in his body so he will be in the world.   (TDG 148)

As a man is in the world, so will he be in the mystery that founds, sustains and engulfs the known world.   (TDG 155)

To trust one's body, to identify oneself with it so that one becomes 'fully incarnate' (TDG 149), is to trust that which cannot be fully *controlled*. The rejection of a mistrustful Apollonian urge to dominate begins with the body. And 'as I trust or mistrust the rhythm of my body, so I trust or mistrust my total world' (TDG 150). As I enjoy my body or seek to use it as an instrument, so I will either enjoy or utilize the world. Keen tells how his breathing becomes measured and slow and his body relaxes (through hatha yoga?), and he says: 'I yield myself to the mystery that is my abiding place with cool trust' (TDG 141). Keen is willing to use the word 'God' to refer to this mystery, though he is reluctant to do so:

If, however, we wish to use the word 'God,' it should signify that the mystery that is the ultimate context of human existence is to be trusted in the same manner as the body and the world are to be trusted. A stance of openness, expectancy, and what Erikson calls 'basic trust' is to be adopted toward all those dimensions of reality that impinge upon the individual but are beyond his ultimate control.   (TDG 155–6)

In Keen's view religious faith depends on, and is inextricably connected with, an attitude of trust towards one's own body: relaxed rather than rigid, receptive rather than wary. In this respect Keen's stress on the bodily dimension of faith is similar to that of Alexander Lowen in his work *Depression and the Body*,[10] which explores that dimension in great detail, using the insights of bioenergetics. Few contemporary theologians have an adequate awareness of what Keen discerns concerning trust in the body and trust in God. Indeed, I shall later be criticizing both Baum's anthropology (chapter 3) and my own earlier anthropology (chapter 6) for this very reason.

I have pointed out two trends in Keen's recent thought – *silent* trust and *bodily* trust. A third trend is an increasingly explicit tension and alternation between two stances: heroic man and graceful, trustful man. On his 'hard days' Keen cultivates a stoic courage so as to be able to 'look straight at the wintry smile on the face of truth' (VV 190). On such days he agrees with Ernst Becker (and with Freud, as we shall see) that we must heroically eliminate 'all consolations that are not empirically based,' pursuing truth irrespective of what we need or want. In this heroic mood he finds an affinity with Becker's call to defy death by leaving behind something that 'heightens life and testifies to the worthiness of existence' (VV 183). This commitment to a model of authentic man as heroic is in tension with Keen's commitment to graceful, trusting man:

On those soft days when I am permeable to everything around me, anything seems possible and I know that the courageous way is the one with greater trust and greater openness to what is strange.   (VV 190)

It is clear that Keen regards the stance of his soft days as superior. And we have seen that he rejects Castaneda's version of heroic man. But there are indications that Keen's earlier ideas of graceful, trusting man are in tension with an increasing fascination with heroic man. He even defends his soft days by describing them as 'the courageous way'; that is, it is more genuinely heroic to be trustful and open. And in his positive reactions to Joseph Campbell's version of heroic man (VV 10–11) we find hints of a possible synthesis: in order to become receptive, wondering, graceful man, one must first heroically descend into the hell of ego-death; then one will receive the miraculous gift of rebirth 'into the wonder of ordinary life' (VV 11). Keen seems to be saying that one first heroically faces the worst and then gracefully receives the best. The path to plenitude lies through the void. The courage which is required to travel the *via negativa* becomes a trust which opens up a transfigured world.

Nothing is so important as nothing.
Accept emptiness and you may be filled. (BWE 57)

In BWE Keen reveals an increasing awareness that there is a sham form of heroism which is linked with a paranoid narcissism and which is not a way to trust but rather the most fundamental obstacle to trust:

What are the building blocks of which the prison of the ego is constructed? I, I, I. One is one and all alone and evermore shall be so. No one to trust except me. And I am untrustworthy. I am afraid to stay in here by myself and afraid to lower my drawbridge and let the world come in. I circle endlessly in solitary confinement looking within myself for the bedrock of my security and excitement. Yet the more I look the deeper I fall in obsessive self-consciousness. I bore downward into my already troubled psyche and watch myself carefully. Isolated in the circle of my own consciousness. It is painful and safe in here. No one can take the tragic glory of my self-inflicted wounds from me. I am the mock hero in this war between me, myself and I. And you are outside; a stranger; an alien, an enemy. I command the San Simeon of my imagination; a castle set on a hill. The logical end of the modern individual is: destructive self-consciousness (I am watching me) or paranoia (they are watching me). (BWE 13)

Keen goes on to identify much of his own heroic individualism with this narcissism:

Even to contemplate a nonalienated form of consciousness threatens the red badge of courage I was awarded by the Existentialist Philosophers Association for manfully stomaching my nausea and accepting the truth of my ontological aloneness. The modern intellectual's masculinity has been certified by his nihilism. Our dignity comes from the wounds we have suffered in our metaphysical isolation. But what if these wounds are self-inflicted? Then the courage of individualism begins to look like masochism ... If we were not alone in the depths of our consciousness, who would we be? Without our wounds would we have our dignity? And why are we so terrified of 'homecoming'? Of contentment? Of the communion of all consciousness? (BWE 14)

Yet we have seen that there is also for Keen a kind of heroic individualism which is realistic and genuine, a negative way through solitude and the void which leads to a new life of trust and openness and wonder. If he accepts his aloneness and emptiness he can eventually come close to others in a fullness of life. But narcissism and the negative way are similar in that they both involve a withdrawal into oneself. The distinction between them is crucial, for one leads farthest away from trust and the other leads to the firmest form of trust, a trust which has endured an ultimate test.

5 Keen's normative anthropology: starting with the individual

Keen finds, in the depths of his own life-story, truths concerning human nature and concerning God. Events which might seem to have only individual significance have universal significance and theological significance. The most striking example of this is in chapter 3 of TDG: 'Reflections on a Peach-Seed Monkey.' When Keen was a child, his father made a promise to him and yet never kept it, though what was promised meant the world to Keen. Years later, visiting his dying father, Keen brought himself to say: 'In all that is important you have never failed me. With one exception you kept the promises you made to me – you never carved me that peach-seed monkey' (TDG 101). Two weeks before his father died Keen received the monkey in the mail:

For me, a peach-seed monkey has become a symbol of all the promises which were made to me and the energy and care which nourished and created me as a human being. And, even more fundamentally, it is a symbol of that which is the foundation of all human personality and dignity. Each of us is redeemed from shallow and hostile life only by the sacrificial love and civility which we have gratuitously received. As Erik Erikson has pointed out in *Identity and the Life*

Cycle, a secure and healthy identity is founded upon a sense of *basic trust* which is first mediated to a child by the trustworthiness of his parents. Identity has its roots in the dependability, orderliness, and nurturing responsiveness of the world of primal experience ... I uncover the promises made and kept which are the hidden root of my sense of the basic trustworthiness of the world and my consequent freedom to commit myself to action.   (TDG 101)

For Keen the story of the peach-seed monkey has both universal and theological significance. The universal significance is that not only Sam Keen but everyone needs basic trust in order to find a secure and healthy identity. The theological significance is that basic trust involves belief in the holy, the 'irreducible principle, power, or presence which is the source and guarantor of unity, dignity, meaning, value and wholeness' (TDG 103). Though Keen is reluctant to use the word 'God,' we have seen that his convictions are clearly theological. Basic trust involves belief in God, particularly what religious believers call 'belief in Providence.'

When Keen asks himself for a justification for his first move, from individual to *universal* significance, his answer is an appeal to 'two major discoveries of Freud' (TDG 102). The first is that 'the crucial history the individual must recover to be whole is familial rather than communal' (TDG 102). This is because each individual has repressed many fidelities and infidelities, gifts and wounds, in his own early family history; he cannot become whole unless these are de-repressed and dealt with as parts of himself for which he takes responsibility in the present (TDG 102, 31–4). The second Freudian discovery concerning human nature is this:

Once the individual recovers his own history, he finds it is the story of every man. For example, when shame and fear dissolve and I am able to confess that I hated as well as loved (or vice versa) the father who nurtured me, I discover that I am one with Oedipus ... The more I know of myself, the more I recognize that nothing human is foreign to me ... When the individual goes to the heart of his own biography unhampered by shame or repression, he finds there a universality of experience that binds him to all men.   (TDG 103)

Presumably if an individual does not undergo psychoanalysis or some analogous process of de-repression, he does not find the hidden love and hate, trust and distrust, and other elements in the kind of universality of experience to which Keen refers. Keen is claiming not only that there is a way to the most fundamental truths concerning human nature *via* the depth-history of the individual, but that this way is the only way. In

Keen's presentation of the two Freudian 'discoveries' their verification ultimately depends on the experience of individuals during de-repression. The two Freudian claims do not meet objectivist criteria of meaning and truth, for the extent to which one understands and accepts them depends on the extent of one's self-involvement in a process of de-repression. In my own view (and, I think, in Keen's) this process goes on not only in psychoanalytic sessions but also in many non-clinical, everyday contexts, so that what Keen appeals to is to a considerable extent intelligible and testable for readers in relation to their own experience. But where readers disagree with Keen or with me we can always claim that they have not had the requisite kind of experience of de-repression. This makes the appeal to a non-objectivist Freudianism impregnable at the cost of rendering it implausible to the outsider. On the other hand an objectivist 'scientific' version of Freudianism is in my own view implausible. It is difficult to justify universal claims on the basis of psychoanalytic evidence. An adequate exploration of this difficulty would require another book. I will not attempt it here. Instead, I will simply state my own general agreement with Keen concerning the Freudian discoveries, except for one reservation concerning his expression of the first: 'The crucial history ... is familial *rather than* communal' (TDG 102, my italics). I agree that the most important history is familial, but communal history is almost as important. Probably the Keen of VV, who as we shall see gives much more emphasis to the communal, would accept this reservation.

Having appealed to Freud, Keen says to the reader: 'The peach-seed monkey, then, belongs as much to you as to me' (TDG 103); Keen's need for basic trust is an example of everyone's need. Keen's use of Freud to move from the individual to the universal is not surprising, though the move itself is obviously open to criticism, as I have indicated. What is surprising is that Keen then moves from the need for basic trust to make *theological* claims which are the opposite of Freud's. Freud said that the human need for trust in parental figures is one of the sources of religious beliefs, and he saw this human origin as a reason for discrediting such beliefs. Keen, as we have seen, uses an implicit anthropological-logical argument for the rationality of religious convictions: human authenticity (integrity, wholeness, maturity, health, dignity, etc) requires basic trust; basic trust is elucidated in ways which involve expressions of religious conviction. Yet Keen starts with an anthropology which he explicitly attributes mainly to Freud. How is it that Freud and Keen can come to such opposite conclusions concerning religious conviction?

Let us have a brief look at Freud's position concerning religion as it appears in *The Future of an Illusion* (hereafter referred to as F).[11] There Freud interprets both psychoanalytic experience and religion by bringing to them a questionable philosophical framework. The framework, which can be rejected by someone who accepts the two general Freudian discoveries mentioned by Keen, has three main elements. I shall call these 'positivism,' 'heroism,' and 'geneticism.'

Freud's positivism is explicit:

To many questions science can as yet give no answer; but scientific work is our only way to knowledge of external reality. (F 55)

What he means by 'scientific work' he has already explained as a process of reasoning on the basis of observations (F 43). When he applies scientific work to the dogmas of religion and to the various arguments used to support these dogmas, Freud finds that the dogmas are either false or untestable. They are false in the sense of being so incompatible with everything we have discovered about reality as to be comparable with delusions. They are untestable in that their reality-value can be neither proved nor refuted – like the religious and metaphysical propositions ridiculed as 'meaningless' by modern positivists such as the early Ayer.[12] And if religious people appeal to 'intuition' or 'trance' rather than to observation and reasoning, Freud insists that all they get is particulars concerning their own 'mental life' (F 55), not information concerning God. It seems to me that, given Freud's positivism, his conclusions concerning the truth-value of religion are inescapable. But for a thinker who is not positivistic, religious beliefs which are untestable by science may nevertheless have a non-scientific rational basis. For example, this possibility is left open in the psychoanalytical thought of Erik Erikson.[13] Also, it is affirmed in Kant's anthropological-logical argument and in the personalist existentialism of Buber and Marcel. For Freud, however, religious convictions such as belief in divine Providence are clearly irrational. This means that for him the attitude of trust which is associated with such a belief is also irrational, regardless of whether or not such an attitude is *needed* by human beings.

Freud's 'heroism' is a conviction that man's mature overall stance should be one of distrustful, vigilant defensiveness against a hostile world, which he wilfully dominates as much as possible by means of science. This conviction is closely associated in Freud's mind with his positivism, and in F he does not seem to see it as a distinct element in his own philosophy. But it is actually separable from his positivism, which is an epistemological doctrine concerning how we get to know reality, rather than a doctrine of normative anthropology concerning what human attitudes are most mature, authentic, etc. Indeed, in so far as positivism encourages any anthropology, it has most affinity with one in which an attitude of impersonal neutrality is paradigmatic for authentic human life. Such an attitude is very different from Freud's. He personalizes nature and radically distrusts her. Unlike our parents and our culture generally, 'nature does not ask us to restrain our instincts, she lets us do as we like; but she has her peculiarly effective mode of restricting us: she destroys us, coldly, cruelly, callously, as it seems to us, and possibly just through what caused our satisfaction' (F 22). It seems obvious to me that such a conviction is just as unscientific as is a belief in divine Providence. Indeed, if the latter is open to psychoanalytic explanation as a projection of infantile hopes and wishes, the former is just as open to psychoanalytic explanation as a projection of infantile fears of the Bad Mother who deprives and destroys even when she provides satisfaction. Freud, however, does not give such an explanation of his own attitudes and convictions in relation to Mother Nature as he does for religious belief and trust in a Father-God (F 39–40, 51). Rather, he sees basic mistrust ('aa permanent condition of anxious suspense and a severe injury to his innate narcissism' (F 24) as the rational result of the way nature actually treats us – depriving and destroying us rather than providing for us and nurturing us. But obviously Freud here is as mistaken as a religious believer who thinks that basic trust can be justified by an appeal to the empirical facts: there is much in nature that helps us, and much that harms us. The question is which to *regard* as dominant. The choice is between basic attitudes of trust and distrust which are brought *to* the facts, not derived *from* them. In its theoretical expression this choice is one between normative anthropologies of *heroism* and of *grace*. According to Freud, to believe oneself to be the object of the tender care of a benevolent Providence is to 'remain a child' rather than to 'venture into the hostile world' in order to be 'educated to reality' (F 88–9). Letting go of the consolations of religion takes courage, for one finds oneself 'like a child who has left the home where he was so warm and comfortable.' To live as a stranger in the real, hostile world is to live heroically.

Freud explicitly maintains that nothing that he says against the truth-value of religion needs the support of psychoanalysis (F 65). That is, his positivist attack stands on its own. This is also true, I think, of his attack on religion from his stance of heroism. Various thinkers have attacked religion as childish and cowardly without explaining its origins by reference to repressed infantile feelings. And Freud's view of the world as pervasively and personally hostile is just as open to psychoanalytic explanation as is a religious view of the world as pervasively and personally friendly. Underlying the difference in world-view is a different choice of basic attitudes as normative for human nature. That choice is not dictated by Freud's psychoanalytic evidence. Indeed, Erik Erikson uses psychoanalytic evidence as his justification for advocating a supremacy of trust over distrust as normative for human nature in both infants and adults. Erikson's normative anthropology also differs more generally from Freud's in that the kind of 'ego' which Erikson values and encourages is far less Apollonian than Freud's. Instead of the ego as intellect and/or will dominating the internal passions and external chaos, Erikson's ego is the whole personality learning mutual adjustment with its environment, an adjustment which involves both giving and receiving.

What I call Freud's 'geneticism' is his reference to the infantile genesis or origins of a belief as a way of discrediting that belief. Freud is not crude in his geneticism. He insists that a belief can be 'illusory' in the sense that 'wish-fulfilment is a prominent factor in its motivation' (F 54) without necessarily thereby being 'delusory' in the sense of being in conflict with reality. A psychoanalytic explanation of the origins of a belief does not for Freud by itself discredit the belief's truth. But he does hold that if a belief has been shown to be irrational on non-psychological grounds, these grounds are given additional support by such an explanation (F 57, 63). It is as if an already mortally wounded belief can be given the *coup de grâce*. Whether or not Freud's qualified geneticism is tenable, it is clearly inapplicable if one's philosophy is neither positivistic nor heroic, so that belief in Providence is neither obviously false nor obviously immature. Then psychoanalytic explanations have no inherent discrediting force at all. Indeed, some such explanations can be used to give *support* to religious beliefs and attitudes, as can be seen in Erikson's thought and in Keen's implicit anthropological argument which is greatly influenced by Erikson: the need for a supremacy of basic trust over basic distrust emerges in early infancy and continues throughout life as the indispensable basis for successfully meeting subsequent crises during infancy and childhood and adulthood; and basic trust implies belief in Providence.

I have contrasted Freud and Erikson on the matter of Freud's positivism, heroism, and geneticism, for Keen relies on Erikson, and Erikson shows us how a psychoanalyst who is firmly within the Freudian tradition can start from similar psychological data and move to a very different position concerning religious convictions. Erikson's data also differ from Freud's, but in ways which are too subtle and too complex to try to discuss here. But the differences in data do not suffice to justify the differences in conclusions. These depend on the differences in the philosophies which are brought to the data. Thus, when Keen, more explicitly than Erikson, brings an existentialist philosophy (in which questions concerning world-view and questions concerning authentic human life are inseparable and the latter are dominant), it becomes clear how Keen can appeal to Freud's two 'discoveries' concerning man while rejecting Freud's denials concerning God.

In the first part of this section I have considered Keen's anthropology in relation to psychoanalysis, Freudian and Eriksonian. The problem has been how Keen could move from his individualistic starting-point to draw conclusions concerning human nature and concerning God. I am in general agreement with the moves which Keen makes. In the rest of this section, however, I shall point out what I take to be some inadequacies in Keen's anthropology, most of which arise from his excessive individualism. One defect is the very narrow focus of his thought: basic trust and decisive acceptance of limits. Although Keen is influenced by Erikson in his overall approach to religion through psychoanalysis, he focuses almost entirely on the first two of Erikson's eight crises and their resolution, giving little attention to the other crises. According to Erikson there are eight stages in human life, each with its typical crisis: early infancy, mid-infancy, late infancy, childhood, adolescence, young adulthood, middle age, and old age. The way in which one deals with each crisis tends to persist throughout the rest of one's life unless the original crisis is re-lived and dealt with in a new way. If an earlier crisis is not resolved fairly satisfactorily, a person finds it difficult to resolve the next crisis well; and this in turn affects his strength to deal with the crisis which follows. So the first crisis, which initiates the conflict between trust and distrust, is the most crucial, and the second, which initiates the conflict between decisiveness and self-doubt, is almost as important. Keen explicitly links the conflict between trust and distrust with early infancy and cites Erikson on this point, as we have seen. He does not, however, explicitly link the second conflict with mid-infancy, when a child discovers new power in relation to others and new limitations imposed by others. In self-doubt he may either try to deny his own powers, becoming passive and fatalistic, or try to deny his limitations by manipulating and dominating his limiters. Whether or not Keen links the problem with mid-infancy, he sees it in terms similar to Erikson's and his resolution is similar to Erikson's – a combination of unhumiliated acceptance of limits and creative, decisive use of the powers one actually has.[14] Keen's graceful man is understood mainly in terms of the two virtues which help to resolve positively the conflicts which begin in the first two stages of human life. Such resolution is important, for it profoundly affects the rest of one's life and the way in which one deals with subsequent crises. Basic trust and decisive acceptance of limits are necessary conditions for, and constituents of, authentic life. But some of the later constituents are equally important, though in a different way. They are not mainly *conditions* in relation to other constituents, but rather *goals*. I am thinking particularly of I-Thou love and social concern. It is true that although a rudimentary version of each of these virtues may appear relatively early in life, the mature version requires a satisfactory resolution of all the earlier crises. But it seems to me that, although we are never entirely free of problems relating to the earlier crises, our wrestling with them should be primarily for the purpose of greater freedom for love and for concern. A preoccupation with acquiring a secure sense of one's own identity can become narcissistic unless it is viewed as a stage in a movement towards an expansive, outgoing mode of life. Keen overemphasizes the intrapersonal conditions for authentic interpersonal and communal existence, as if these conditions were themselves the goal. In fairness to Keen I should insist that he does not omit the interpersonal, for he includes Marcelian fidelity as a major virtue. Also (a point I have not mentioned before), although he views the process of de-repression mainly as a means to liberation of the individual, he also sees it as a means of removing inner blocks which we have placed in the way of seeing other persons as they really are and relating to them accordingly (TDG 30, 34). And, as I shall soon be showing, Keen does give considerable weight to the communal or political in VV. But his main focus is intrapersonal. This affects his view of *grace*, which happens mainly *within* oneself rather than *between* oneself and other people. Both the main focus of personal attention and the location of grace tend to be in oneself: one's own trust and decisiveness, one's own liberation from hurts, habits, and hangups, one's own liberation from schizophrenia towards integrity, one's own wondrous enjoyment of the world. All this is very important, but by itself a preoccupation with grace as a help in dealing with early Eriksonian crises is excessively individualistic. There is little stress on grace as an individual liberation which comes *via* other people, let alone a stress on grace as a liberation which occurs for an *us* rather than only for a *me*. (Both these ideas are important in Gregory Baum's view of grace, which we shall consider in chapter 4.) And since Keen focuses mainly on what grace does for and in me rather than on my relation with the Giver of grace, it is not surprising that he thinks of God by means of analogy of activity, way of originating grace, rather than by means of an analogy of relation. Keen's essential starting-point for analogy in man is the individual – the 'break-throughs' in his activity and the attitudes needed for his authenticity – rather than a relation between persons. Therefore Keen uses analogy of activity and analogy of attitude.

I have criticized Keen's narrow focus on the first two Eriksonian crises. A second criticism, which I have already indicated earlier in this essay, is that Keen fails to find any place for elements of *homo faber* in his portrayal of authentic man. This seems to me to be connected with a neglect of the fourth Eriksonian stage (roughly ages 6–12), in which a child needs to acquire competence and discipline in learning the language, customs, and technology of his culture. If the first three crises were not resolved well (especially the third crisis, concerning guilt and initiative), this stage can be disastrous. Instead of the *homo faber* element in personality developing as part of a larger whole, a child may go on identifying himself with his unresolved relations with his parents, so that coping with the world becomes an irrelevant bore and a distressing burden. Or he may become exclusively *homo faber*, completely identifying himself with his ability to make things work, thus evading direct confrontation with the repressed and unresolved crises of infancy. I have seen how in either case work therapy can later be a help as a reliving of this childhood crisis so as to resolve it in a more constructive way. A fairly satisfactory resolution of the earlier crises is a precondition of this, but exclusive focus on these crises will not by itself enable a person to use tools as an expression of competence, co-operating with other people and with nature so as to arrange and change the environment in creative ways. To acquire such competence is a further human task. Competence is important because it is a constituent in one's own individual authenticity and fulfilment. Also, since each person is part of a community which is profoundly affected by technology for good and ill, the social concern of authentic man should move him to gain enough competence to be able to contribute his own small creative influence in relation to technology. He need not, and should not, exercise his competence in the defensive, dominating style of *homo faber*. But the skills, curiosity, and discipline of *homo faber* can and should become part of his personality.[15] To opt out is to be deprived of something intrinsically human for himself and to evade a responsibility to society.

My third, and final, criticism of Keen has to do with something to which I have already alluded: his neglect of *political* or *communal* man as part of his model for authentic life. Except in VV and BWE there is little recognition of this ideal of social concern. Political man identifies himself with the struggles of the oppressed, not only 'in his guts,' but also in practical reformist or revolutionary activity, dealing in largely impersonal ways with the impersonal institutions and power structures of society. I concluded my 1973 version of this essay, which was written before I had read any of VV or BWE, with this complaint against Keen:

Concerning politics, he offers only a hope that an authenticity in inner individual life and in face-to-face relations may somehow change the institutional structures of society – a new version of fundamentalist piety. He rightly finds something sacred in his gut-reaction of outrage when a Vietnamese is tortured, but seems to find nothing sacred in the Apollonian search for hard-headed strategies by which to stop the war.

Even more radically, we may question the primacy of a search for authentic life in a world where so many lack the elementary necessities for life itself, where men need food from any source, whether it be authentic or inauthentic. Is the modern search for personal authenticity, like the earlier concern for personal salvation, a 'spiritual' luxury? Is an ethic of 'being,' of life-style, a luxury in a world which needs an ethic of 'doing,' of practical improvements in the material well-being of the poor? Or can the two somehow be combined? This is a personal and theological question which is perhaps even more important than the question about Dionysus and Apollo concerning which Keen has shed so much light. Authenticity or bread?

My criticism did not take into account the politicization of Keen's consciousness which is expressed in VV:[16]

Since every individual consciousness is in constant resonance with the surrounding society, no person can be free so long as any person is enslaved. The same nerve endings with which we feel private passions register our compassion toward the public world beyond the psyche. I and we are one. There is no separation of the body and the body politic. Since personal and public liberation are linked and we live within the tragedies of actual history rather than the ideal utopia, partial liberation is the best we can hope for. The fullest path for the individual is to be responsible for his personal transformation and for some action that may allow society to move in a more just and erotic direction. (VV 9–10)

If reality is socially defined, then the structure of the individual is determined by the economic, political, and ideological structures of his time. And if we want to change the person we must change the society. Man has no inside that is unrelated to the outside, no psyche that is uncolored by the polis. (vv 160)

But Keen still insists that authentic life for the individual is possible without a rebirth of society (vv 9) and he agrees with Joseph Campbell's rejection of the Marxist claim that we cannot have a harmonized psyche until we have a harmonized society (vv 82). How can this position be reconciled with the remarks which I have just quoted? Perhaps it cannot be fully reconciled, but one important factor is Keen's insistence on authentic man's graceful acceptance of imperfection in the world and in himself. Even if the self is greatly influenced by society, and cannot be perfect unless society is perfect, authenticity is possible since authenticity is not perfection but a way of living with imperfection. Thus, although, as Keen says, 'partial liberation is the best we can hope for' (vv 10), complete liberation is not required for authentic living.

Both the personal and the political are included in Keen's later account of authentic man. One element in authenticity is a trustful *acceptance* of imperfections in self and society. But Keen also discerns another element: an active commitment to the *transformation* of the self and of society. These two elements do not fit comfortably together. There is a tension between feeling at home in a trustworthy world and feeling alienated and indignant in a world which must be changed.[17] As Gregory Baum has said: 'God is not only the life of our life but also the abiding pain we experience in the face of a suffering, oppressed and hungry humanity.'[18] Some such tension is to be found in any anthropology and theology which is profoundly influenced by the Bible. Biblical faith in God is both a trusting acceptance of God as provider for all men and an active commitment to God as righteous liberator of the oppressed. What is not clear in Keen is whether he, like the Bible, finds divine grace not only in intrapersonal liberation (and perhaps interpersonal liberation) but also in political liberation. This is an issue which will be central in the next chapter as we consider Baum's theology of liberation.

4

Gregory Baum's Theology of Liberation

Gregory Baum's understanding of religious faith and divine grace is focused on both personal liberation and political liberation. The personal dimension (intrapersonal and interpersonal) is explored in *Man Becoming* (MB), and the political dimension in *Religion and Alienation* (RA). In 1971 I published an essay on MB. One of my criticisms was that Baum neglected the political dimension of faith and grace, but this criticism is no longer appropriate in view of RA. This chapter consists of a revised version of my essay on MB and an original study of RA. The tension created by the divergent emphases of the two books is creative and illuminating. It seems to me that together they provide an unusually profound and wide-ranging understanding of human nature as seen in the religious perspective.

1 Man becoming

1 GOD AND MAN DEFINED TOGETHER

In MB Baum interprets Christian theology in relation to experience of personal liberation. These experiences are a central concern both of the Gospel and of many modern men, both Christian and non-Christian. Baum interprets them theologically because for him God is the mystery present in human life, liberating men to become more truly human. God is the more than human redemptive presence, enabling man to become man. For Baum man enters into the very definition of God, and vice versa. All talk about God (theology) and all talk about authentic human life (anthropology) are talk about the divine liberation of man. Theology and anthropology are inextricably intertwined. God cannot be understood as man's 'over-against,' separable from man, for every statement about God is a declaration about the humanization of man. Yet man cannot be understood in separation from God, for to be authentically human is to be liberated by God. Unlike some secular or humanistic theologians Baum does not reduce the divine to the human. He does not translate talk about God into talk about man without God. When Baum thinks about 'man becoming' he thinks about man being liberated by God.

Thus for Baum God is defined in relation to man, and man in relation to God, and the focus of both theology and anthropology is on the process in which man is liberated to become more truly human. But what is this process? What counts as becoming more truly human? Many modern theologians might accept Baum's formal principle concerning theology, anthropology, and human liberation, while differing from him concerning the concrete process of humanization. In terms of my analysis of analogies, Baum's formal principle has the form of a way of originating grace; such a form is open to a variety of contents, for thinkers differ concerning what constitute the crucial 'breakthroughs' in the process of becoming more truly human. In MB these occur when a person who is struggling against destructive forces within himself is liberated. This happens as he responds to other persons who confirm and confront him. (In RA, as we shall see, the formal principle is the same but the breakthroughs are political.) Baum begins MB with a picture of human life as 'highly dramatic, a field of conflict between forces of self-destruction and powers – unexpected powers – of creativity and new life' (MB xiii). His understanding of human life is derived mainly from three sources: psychoanalysis, existentialist phenomenology, and Christian tradition (including the scriptures).

Concerning psychoanalysis, he notes that his account is based on long association with Communication Therapy (more recently called 'Therafields'). This is a therapeutic community in Toronto which stresses mutual confrontation and confirmation within groups as an important part of the psychoanalytic process. Thus Baum's insights concerning human liberation are specially illuminated by the therapeutic experiences of people undergoing analysis, especially in groups. What he says, however, is not restricted to this narrow context, for analogous experiences occur in everyday life; wherever people are open to radical removal of self-deceptive and self-destructive elements within themselves. For Baum the word 'therapeutic' refers to a broad range of processes and experiences in which human being are liberated from these elements so as to respond to a call to become well and whole and truly human. In this broad sense his own work in MB can be aptly called a 'theology of the therapeutic' (MB 126).

In his account of liberation Baum draws not only on psychoanalysis, but also on existentialist phenomenology (e.g. Heidegger *via* Rahner) which is concerned with profound and universal human experiences: We are summoned to move from a life of bondage and emptiness to a life of freedom and fullness, and somehow we find ourselves able to respond.[1]

Christian tradition is also important in Baum's account of liberation, though experiences of liberation occur not only within the Christian community but also outside it, just as they occur both within 'therapy' (in the narrow sense of the word) and outside it. Christian tradition has a twofold function in relation to these universal experiences of liberation. First, it functions implicitly in Baum's *selection* of experiences which are in his view 'liberating.' Secondly, it functions explicitly in his *theological interpretation* of these experiences. For Baum Christian tradition provides a uniquely illuminating way in which to affirm the reality and the ever-present possibility of human liberation by that which transcends the human. The Gospel is the 'clarification and specification of the transcendent mystery of humanization' (MB 20) which is going on in human beings everywhere. The church, in a narrow sense of the word, is the community which proclaims the Gospel, explicitly acknowledging the 'universal mystery of redemption' (MB 64). In a broader sense of the word the church is the human community wherever the mystery occurs, even though not explicitly acknowledged as such. But since for Baum the acknowledgment matters, so does the Christian tradition, focused on the Gospel.

2 THE PROCESS OF PERSONAL LIBERATION

What is Baum's understanding of liberation in MB? He provides several brief and broad descriptions with which we can begin. It is 'the passage from fear to trust, from hostility to love, from ignorance to self-knowledge, from passivity to creativity, from self-centredness to concern for others' (MB 134). It is 'the forward movement of man to greater maturity, to wider responsibility, to a growing capacity for truth and love' (MB 39–40). It is growth and reconciliation: 'Man grows when he becomes more conscious of who he is ... Men are reconciled when communication among them leads all of them towards growth' (MB 240).

Liberation can occur in many different ways, but in all of them Baum finds a common pattern: a person responds to others, who both confront him and confirm him, enabling him to grow in self-knowledge. This process goes on from infancy to old age and in all the varied contexts of human life. Indeed, before Baum began to learn from psychoanalysis, he had discovered in *ecumenical* dialogue a powerful process which changes self-awareness. In an essay of intellectual autobiography in *Journeys* (J) he says: 'We realized that we cannot come to self-knowledge by looking at ourselves: only as we are engaged in conversation with others and reflect on their reactions to us, are we able to gain greater insight into who we are' (J 9). But Baum's most concrete and powerful accounts of the process of liberation are mainly derived from what goes on in psychoanalysis. We see this when Baum asks what must happen to a man before he can detect 'how much his life is determined by unavowed hostility or narcissistic fantasies or concealed guilt feelings or even the hidden love of death itself' (MB 157). Baum insists that a man cannot detect any of these by himself, for each man has spent his life thus far in constructing defences against such self-knowledge. Indeed, each one of us is deeply afraid of the truth. 'Many of our attitudes and actions are screens, frantically put up, preventing us from knowing what we really feel' (MB 156). Hence, 'a man cannot come to know who he is unless he is told by another' (MB 157). The word of another 'pierces the screen we have erected between ourselves and reality' (MB 43) – unless the screen is too tough. This qualification has to be added, for we may not really listen to the word, refusing to allow ourselves to be open to it. Instead, we may 'flee from this word and hide more effectively behind our defenses' (MB 43).

We tend to feel that if we listen to it, we may not survive the judgment contained in it. We vaguely sense the area in us where we crumble to pieces, yet we feel that we can just make it if we do not look at it too closely. If this area were to be spelled out to us and if we were to face the emptiness, the self-hatred, or the destructiveness that is in us, we might not be able to survive. In order to listen to the special word, therefore, a special strength is required. Something marvelous has already happened within us if we are able to listen to this special word and respond to it with courage. (MB 49)

What has happened? How can a man bear to listen, dare to respond, to the word of confrontation? It exposes unreality and evil within him, and his bondage to his own past: and it summons him to take responsibility for living in new, unknown directions. He can only respond to the word if somehow he already has a sense of reality and worth within him, and a basic trust in himself and in others. If he has this basis for courage, he has received it as a gift from others, from their recognition and confirmation of him as a person. The gift has come gratuitously, beyond his control. With this loving support from others he has the strength to respond rather than run. And as he responds, his own strength will grow so that he is 'carried forward by his own vitality to love others' (MB 53). 'The man who is free to leave himself and abandon his preoccupations with his own little problems, to be present to others and to share with them, enters more fully into his own humanity' (MB 53). Yet the response to the word of confrontation is always painful and difficult. There is much inner resistance. Even a man who has received strength both by being loved and by loving will feel a temptation to flee:

There is in it an element of letting go, of falling into darkness, of wondering whether destruction awaits us; and yet there is also an element of hope that we are not totally alone, that protection is available, that something new will emerge in us, and as we fall into the darkness there will be a safe place to stand, safer than the one we had before. Entry into self-knowledge changes man's self-consciousness and hence transforms his entire life ... Entry into self-knowledge is always conversion.   (MB 156–7)

One conversion is never enough. Man tends not only towards life and truth but also towards self-destruction and self-deception. Man is not only receptive but also resistant to the life-giving word. One conversion is never enough, for 'being human does not come naturally to man; he must be transformed many times' (MB 158). Liberation to authentic life comes by grace.

3 LIBERATION AND GRACE

When Baum says that being human does not come naturally to man he does not mean simply that being human does not come easily, spontaneously, and smoothly. He means that divine grace is needed to enable man to become man. The Christian Gospel proclaims the Good News that this help is not only needed but available:

Since the life of a man in this world is profoundly threatened from all sides, it is Good News that a transcendent dynamism offers him liberation from his inner obstacles to put him in touch with reality and empower him to respond to it with courage and creativity. To be well, in Scholastic terminology, is not the work of nature but of grace. (MB 159)

Divine grace liberates a person so that he can become responsive to reality and realize himself as a human being. When Baum speaks of 'being well' or of 'holiness' he refers to this self-realization, which occurs in a process of successive conversions into deeper self-knowledge, a process in which the inner obstacles to a life of love and creativity are exposed and overcome.

According to Baum's central conviction, his formal principle for theology and anthropology, God is the mystery in human life which liberates persons to be more authentically human. We thus expect him to interpret any genuine process of human liberation in relation to divine grace. But Baum's formal principle is not merely an arbitrary *a priori*; it is related to his experience. What is it about the process of human liberation that links it with Baum's formal principle? As I have presented his account of liberation in subsection 2, all that is shown is that each individual man needs the confrontation and confirmation which come from other men in order to become authentically human. Why does Baum go beyond this and claim that all men need that which is more than human? For example, he says: 'Man comes to be through a process in which the human community is involved, and yet which is not wholly reducible to human resources' (MB 184). Baum does not try to prove that his claim is true, but part of its basis in human experience can be seen when he presents it in the context of a phenomenological account of the special 'freedom' into which men are liberated:

In this description of human life, we have used the word 'freedom' in a special sense. We have said that freedom is a gift granted to men, which enables them to respond to the summons addressed to them. Freedom here is not simply the ability to choose between inconsequential alternatives. This sort of free choice is built into the human equipment. It belongs to man and is not a special gift to him. But whenever man is challenged, whenever man is threatened by his own passive and destructive tendencies, whenever man is called to love other people or open himself to the truth, then the power to respond is not something that can be taken for granted, something that belongs to his human equipment, something over which he has power. On the contrary, a man finds present in himself a hundred hesitations to respond, to act, and to be in a new way. The freedom to enter into this dialogue or to accept the love extended to him is a power a man finds in himself at certain moments, a power over which he has no control, a power he experiences as a gift. We have suggested that this freedom is created ... by the love he has received. (MB 54)

Here Baum is outlining a distinction which is crucial to his position, a distinction between two kinds of freedom.[2] (This distinction will also be crucial in my own position as outlined in chapter 6.) I propose to call the two kinds of freedom 'wilful' and 'responsive.' Wilful freedom is the power an individual has over capacities which are his own to exercise at will. He is free to move this finger rather than that one, to drive a car, to construct an argument, or to apply 'information research, systematic presentation, techniques of communication etc.' (MB 135) as a teacher. Responsive freedom, on the contrary, is a gift from others, a power to go beyond one's autonomous individual capacities in response to the enabling actions of another, actions which are beyond one's own control, actions of summons or of love. Responsive freedom, such as the freedom of a teacher to the 'truly present to others' (MB 136), is not within his wilful control. Responsive freedom is a gift. Responsive freedom is that by which man becomes truly man.

Baum goes on to locate divine grace in the realm of responsive freedom rather than wilful freedom. 'The freedom to become human is God's gift to man ... This dimension is not only gratuitous by definition but also radically transcends the powers of man' (MB 55). But surely it is one thing to experience one's freedom on various occasions as a gift from other men, a gift which transcends one's individual powers, and another thing to experience it as a gift which transcends human powers as such. Baum's central conviction needs a further phenomenological basis. This is to be found in two passages which I shall quote in full. He himself does not emphasize them, but they seem to me to be the most important in his book. Without them it is not only difficult to see what *basis* he has in experience for claiming that man needs God in order to become man; it is also difficult to understand what he *means* by this. Without these passages his phenomenology seems to show only that each man needs other men in order to become truly human.

The special word available in human dialogue and resounding in conscience does not appear as man's own creation. It is uttered by men but it transcends them. It stands over against them and judges them ... The word of truth that saves us from self-deception may be uttered by a friend or an adversary. In either case the word does not belong to the person who pronounces it. For he, too, is in need of it. He is a faithful communicator of this word only if he acknowledges that he, too, is judged, summoned, and possibly healed by the word he addresses to us. A voice which transcends the human seems to enter into the conversation of men. (MB 45–6)

When people come together to share and be friends, each mediates to the other what he does not totally possess, and their mutual enrichment exceeds by far what each member was able to put into it. The multiplication of power towards the building up of life available in communion reveals the transcendent character of the gift by which men enter into their humanity. There is a gift-dimension in human life that is not reducible to the human. If I reflect only on myself, I might possibly persuade myself that I receive the gift which creates my freedom from the people who have come close to me; but when I reflect on the community of men, made up by people like me, involved in ambiguity and wounded by self-centeredness, then it becomes extremely difficult to suppose that the gift creating their freedom is a purely human reality, under the control of the people involved. This gift is offered from beyond man's sinfulness. The Christian believing that God has involved himself in human history discerns in this gift the saving presence of God to his people. The gift that creates our freedom is the love that God extends to every man and that engenders new power in him to grow in his humanity. (MB 56–7)

In these passages Baum is appealing to an experience which is shared, he assumes, by non-Christians as well as Christians; and he is interpreting the experience in relation to the Gospel as he understands it. The allegedly common experience is one in which there is a gift-dimension on *both* sides of the human encounter. That is, when John responds to Mary's word of confirmation and confrontation, he feels that his freedom to respond is a gift, beyond his own capacities, and Mary feels that her word is a gift, beyond her own capacities. Now Baum would have to admit that some people, including some participants in group therapy, would deny having had such an experience. Many, however, would not deny it. The individual powers of John and Mary do seem to be transcended. But instead of bringing in God, the more than human power, why not interpret the experience in purely human terms – in terms of the unconscious and group dynamics? If, along with Baum, we assume that unconscious forces are real, then we shall find it more, not less, difficult to take at face value an immediate experience of a power which seems to transcend oneself. What seems to be a more than human power, beyond one's control, often turns out to be a release of energy (creative or destructive) from the unconscious. And if we assume the reality of group dynamics, this means that interactions within a group can release forces (both creative and destructive) which are not fully within the control of the people involved and which go beyond their individual capacities in isolation. Where Baum claims there is a power which transcends all human powers, others will refer us to the unconscious and to group dynamics. It is true that Baum is not trying to *prove* that divine grace is required, and he is not claiming that he can distinguish clearly between instances of divine grace and instances of purely human processes. Nor is his interpretation irrational. But he does not seem to acknowledge any challenge from a non-theological interpretation, especially one which involves psychoanalysis. Who can tell what are the limits of human creativity, once someone challenges the repressive defensive structures of personality which foster self-deception and self-destruction? Why not assume that the new trust and love and self-knowledge and creativity which emerge in a man when he is liberated are purely human resources, hitherto untapped? Baum's answer, it seems, is that individual men are too deeply enmeshed in self-deception and self-destruction to liberate each other. Baum's view leads me to imagine two men caught in a quicksand, each struggling to survive and succeeding for a while, but neither able to pull the other one out. For Baum the gift of liberation is offered 'from beyond man's sinfulness.' Baum's conviction here obviously depends on the Christian tradition. But it also depends on his version of Freud's death-instinct theory. According to traditional theology there is original sin, inescapably, in each man. For Baum in MB[3] there is a 'death impulse' (MB 145).

Depth psychology has helped us to discover that much of the trouble we have in our lives – though not all of it – is in some sense self-chosen. The misery that afflicts us is often secretly provoked by our hidden self-hatred. We may destroy the good things that happen to us by skepticism and mistrust, we may attach ourselves to certain people because we are impelled by an unconscious desire to be betrayed or badly treated, we may set the authorities against us and be subject to unjust treatment because unbeknown to ourselves, we feel the need of punishment – the list of self-inflicted miseries that people choose is unending. The unconscious wish to be unhappy or to be punished is as universal as the more conscious wish to be happy or rewarded. Man does not simply love life; he also desires death. This is the ambiguity of human life, in which all men are born. (MB 147)

Not all psychoanalytic theorists would agree with Baum. For example, Wilhelm Reich finds no inherent impulse towards destruction and death.[4] For Reich, the only inherent impulse is towards life. The masochist does not desire pain and punishment as such; he inflicts specific forms of pain and punishment on himself in order to *avoid* a greater pain and punishment which, he fears, would come. What Baum calls a 'death impulse' Reich regards as the result of social repression, from which men can be released. Reich's theory, unlike Baum's Freudian theory, does not provide a basis for a doctrine of original sin which is the basis for a companion doctrine concerning salvation: no liberation except by divine grace. Baum, however, holds that 'without divine grace man cannot become fully human' (MB 60) and that 'without divine transcendence human life cannot be free' (MB 234).

4 BAUM'S USE OF ANALOGY

But Baum's convictions concerning grace do not depend primarily on an argument from premises concerning original sin. Rather, they arise from a pervasive stance of *active receptivity* which he expresses and encourages as he writes MB. It is not only that authentic man experiences responsive freedom in relation to this or that person who gives of himself to him. He has a pervasive attitude of active receptivity towards a liberating power which is pervasively present in all situations, though characteristically working *via* other persons. In any activity which is authentically humanizing there is a sense of being empowered by a mystery beyond oneself: paradoxically, 'I act, yet not I, but the mystery in me.' This pervasive Pauline stance is the existential context for Baum's convictions concerning grace and God. God is that towards which such an active receptivity is appropriate when it is pervasive. God is the pervasive mystery which transcends and unifies the particulars to which one responds in particular active-receptive ways.

But although Baum can thus be interpreted in terms of analogy of attitude, way of pervasiveness, where the attitude is active receptivity, he makes more obvious and explicit use of analogy of relation. The very idea of God as Liberator is based on an analogy with what goes on in human relations. God is not *a* person, according to Baum, but *man's relation to God is personal*:

Man is related to God not impersonally as the effect is to the cause or the waves to the stream, but personally as a listener to the one who speaks and as the recipient of gifts to the giver. Man's relationship to God cannot be reified; it cannot be reduced to categories that apply to the relationship of things. We have shown more than once that God is present in human life as summons evoking man's response and as gift freeing man to create his future. (MB 191)

In this passage Baum is claiming that the relation between God and a man is analogous to the relation between one man and another man. God, like Joe, 'speaks' to John and 'gives' to him so as to free him. (Note also, however, the rather different language which Baum employs in the last sentence of the quotation: God is 'present as summons' and 'present as gift.' Later I shall argue that this language indicates something other than an analogy of relation.) And God speaks and gives to John *via* Joe's words of confrontation and confirmation. What happens when Joe speaks to John and John responds is both the *analogy* and the *medium* for God's presence to John.

In view of all this we would expect that Baum would speak of God as being 'over-against' man. John discerns God's presence in another man, Joe. Not that John equates God with Joe, reducing the divine to the human. And not that John separates God from Joe as a super-person 'behind' or 'beside' Joe. But if we ask John *where* he thinks God is, he will point 'out there' to Joe (and others) where God is present. For John, Joe is 'over-against' him, and so is God, confronting and confirming him.

According to Baum, however, God is *not* 'over-against' man. When I wrote the 1971 version of this essay I thought his denial arose from a confusion concerning two meanings of the word 'man': 'an individual man' and 'mankind collectively.' God can be 'over-against' each individual man without being 'over-against' mankind as a whole. For Baum God cannot be 'over-against' the whole of mankind; God is not separable from all men. According to his formal principle all thought or talk or experience of God is about the transcendent liberating presence *in human life*. Imagine all mankind lined up in a row stretching from west to east, each person looking north, so that no person sees any other person. From Baum's formal principle it seems to follow that no one would be able to discern God's redemptive presence unless this were possible by looking within oneself. This is a possibility which I shall soon consider, but here I set it aside. If a man cannot find God by looking away from human life and cannot discern God at work in human life except in human relations, no one in the west-east row of persons would be able to discern God. For similar reasons Baum rejects a kind of prayer in which John tries to think of God as an invisible person 'out there' and separable from Joe, James, Jim, and all other men. God cannot be in this sense 'over-against' John or any other man. To pray is to respond to the divine grace which comes *via* other people. The divine grace is 'over-against' each individual man since it comes *via* other men; for that very reason it cannot be 'over-against' mankind as a whole.

On this interpretation of Baum, then, theology has two main contentions: (a) an insistence that divine grace comes only *via* other persons, and (b) a use of analogy of relation, way of pervasiveness. There is some textual warrant for such an interpretation, but both (a) and (b) need to be challenged if we are to understand Baum correctly. I did not challenge (b) in the 1971 version of this essay, but I did challenge (a), for Baum does not in fact rule out the possibility that divine grace might come from within oneself. Baum's formal principle does not entail that divine grace comes only *via* other men, although I have thus far given an impression that it does. Divine grace might also come to a man from *within* himself. The formal principle only requires us to look for God in human life: 'Man is alive by a principle that transcends him, over which he has no power, which summons him to surpass himself and frees him to be creative' (MB 185). This statement does not entail that the medium of divine presence to one man must always be other men. Baum considers this possibility, briefly but eloquently, near the end of MB:

To pray is to be in touch with oneself in a new way: to listen to the melody, not made by ourselves, that sounds at the core of our being and, from beyond the sickness that deafens us, summons us to be alive. Since God is redemptively present in man's coming to be, prayer is a way of holding or possessing oneself. This kind of prayer is not a moving away from oneself and reaching out for another, but rather a being in communion with oneself across many obstacles, and a laying hold of oneself in and through the gift dimension that is constitutive of one's being.   (MB 264)

Here Baum is talking about God 'within' an individual in a way which goes beyond the main line of thought in MB. He is not thinking of a case where God is 'within' John in that He has enabled John to confront and confirm Joe. Nor is he thinking of God 'within' Joe only in that the divine strength which has come *via* John has persisted within Joe. What John has done may have helped to make possible Joe's now being in touch with himself in a new way; but the point is that now Joe is in touch with God '*via*' himself. The context of divine presence is here not interpersonal but intrapersonal. Presumably Baum has in mind such a divine presence within a man when he cites the case of someone who is on his way to being exterminated in a gas chamber. If there is no word of summons or care from anyone else to function as the medium for divine grace, then the medium must be the man himself.

In 1971 I did not challenge (b), Baum's apparent use of analogy of relation, way of pervasiveness. Indeed I stressed it, and noted how it made Baum more similar to Buber than he has acknowledged. Subsequent reflection and discussion with him lead me to withdraw (b) now. The very quotation which gave rise to (b) ends, as I have noted, with a different language concerning God, who is 'present as summons' and 'present as gift.' This language need not imply that God is summoner or giver. Rather, another human being summons and gives but God is present when this occurs, present as transcendent power active in that human being or in the relation between him and the person who receives summons and gift. That is, Baum's basic analogy is a *way of originating grace* in an analogy of activity and/or an analogy of relation. Baum's insistence that God is not 'over-against' man is not merely an insistence that God is not 'over-against' mankind. Baum really means to insist that God is not 'over-against' any particular person, say John, in a way analogous to Joe's being 'over-against' John. Baum is thus different from Buber in the form of his analogy, though their contents for analogizing are broadly similar – profound mutual encounters between human beings. For Buber John is in an 'I-Thou' relation with God as Absolute Person, pervasively (and perfectly) saying 'Thou' to John – in this instance *via* Joe. For Baum God is actively present in Joe's act of summons and giving to John, and in John's act of responding to Joe; or God is actively present in the mutual relation of encounter between John and Joe.[5] When I try to understand Baum in a pictorial way, I think of John and Joe in eyeball-to-eyeball mutual encounter while beside them another hidden person encourages them in this by his very presence, though neither John nor Joe is encountering this third person – they are only aware of an empowering presence. This picture, however, has the defect of depicting God as *a* person. In a letter written in 1975 (LB) Baum rejects this image:

The image is beautiful. It does not present my theology however. After all, I emphasize that we should *not* think of God first as a being of some kind and then of the action of this being in human life. God, I insist, cannot be objectified in any way; and hence we should think of God rather as acting, speaking, summoning, etc. without imagining that these actions are residing in a subject, however elevated. The mystery of God is our wherefrom, the summons in our lives, our horizon, etc. and this God ceases to be the true God as soon as we objectify the mystery into a being, a substance, a noun, a subject.

For Baum God is understood by a way of originating grace where the divine activity is personal rather than impersonal, yet not personal in a way which brings a human being into 'over-against' encounter with God, or in a way which depicts God as *a* person. The way of originating grace is used primarily in an interpersonal context – either an analogy of relation or an analogy of activity where the human activities considered are those of two individuals in a depth encounter. But the way of originating grace is also used, as we have seen, in a secondary context – in an analogy of activity where the locus of grace is not interpersonal but intrapersonal.

In all this the originating grace is discerned and is influential in persons who have a pervasive attitude of active receptivity. Hence the way of originating grace is correlated in Baum's thought with an analogy of *attitude*, way of pervasiveness, which I have noted earlier. And for Baum in MB grace is ultimately operative in *individuals*, liberating them 'from fear to trust, from hostility to love, from ignorance to self-knowledge, from passivity to creativity, from self-centeredness to concern for others' (MB 134). Grace works to change personal character, gradually replacing vices by virtues in a process of individual transformation. The change occurs mainly in an interpersonal context. Sin is for Baum a pathological *resistance* to growing up, preferring the defensive and destructive self-deceptions of the past to the creative possibilities for new life in the present. And conversion is for Baum a movement into holiness, from destructive self-deception to creative self-knowledge; it occurs as one is *receptive* to grace. The most crucial conflict which goes on within every person, both consciously and unconsciously, is between resistance and receptivity towards the gifts of truth and life. (In chapter 6 I shall focus on this conflict as I try to plumb the depth-origins of religion and morality.)

I should sum up Baum's use of analogy in MB. He makes use of two interrelated analogies. First, he applies a way of originating grace to an analogy of relation or analogy of activity. Here the context is interpersonal or (to a lesser extent) intrapersonal, and the outcome is a liberation of the individual from personal obstacles to truth and life. Secondly, he applies an analogy of attitude, way of pervasiveness, where the crucial attitude is receptivity as contrasted with resistance. When I discuss RA in the second part of this chapter we shall see that the context for the way of originating grace shifts radically from the personal to the political, with corresponding shifts in the conceptions of liberation, grace, sin, conversion, and faith. I shall argue, however, that part of the outcome of grace is still a change in the individual (though in this case his politicization) and that the stress on receptivity remains at the core of his account of faith. But before we turn to RA there is much to discuss in MB.

5 A CRITICAL DISCUSSION OF BAUM

Concerning MB it seems to me that Baum is correct in making personal liberation the central focus of his theology and in understanding personal liberation in a predominantly psychotherapeutic context. So Baum's theology in MB seems to me to be an excellent, central starting-point for a theology. A starting-point, however, is not enough. There are other necessary elements, close to the centre, which need to be included and illumined, especially the natural, the demonic, the christological, and the political. Baum's theology in MB gives inadequate answers to questions concerning these four areas, questions which we shall consider briefly in the rest of this section: (i) How is God related to the realm of the 'natural' as contrasted with the realm of grace and responsive freedom? That is, how is God related to human bodies, to man's natural capacities for wilful freedom, and to the natural environment? (ii) If experiences of liberation give rise to faith in God, do experiences of bondage and destructiveness warrant belief in a devil? (iii) What role has Christology as a norm in anthropology and theology? (iv) How is God related to the impersonal political dimension of human life? These are all vast and fundamental questions, to which any answers are bound to be inadequate. But it seems to me that Baum's theology needs and deserves some further probing in relation to each of them.

(i) *God and the realm of the 'natural'*
Baum insists that theological language has to be understood as 'a declaration about human life, the faithful acknowledgment of which saves man and establishes him on the way of redemption, and not as information about a supreme uncreated being nor an explanation of the genesis of the world' (MB 218). This is his reason, he says, for completely avoiding any cosmological reference when he interprets the doctrine of God as creator. 'We have not said a word about God's relationship to matter, to the physical world, to the cosmos as a whole. This has been consistent with our method' (MB 218). Later, however, he makes an important concession: 'The doctrine that God is creator of matter may indeed have a salvational meaning. But this has hardly been worked out. We may eventually see that this doctrine discloses unto man his relationship to his

own body, to his sexuality, to his voice, to his ear' (MB 221). It seems clear to me, though perhaps it is not clear to Baum, that he *must* work out this doctrine if he is to be consistent with his own theological method and his own theological concern with liberation. The issue concerning God as creator is whether the transcendent presence which summons and enables me to become more human operates only in the realm of responsive freedom, or is somehow related also to my 'natural' capacities for wilful freedom, to my body, and to the total 'natural' (i.e. non-human) environment. If God is only the source of a supernatural power which He gives me, then He is not related to *me*; He does not liberate *me*, the whole human being. Theology and anthropology, then, hover on the brink of a natural/supernatural dualism, in which there is a natural man and a natural world, neither of which God has anything to do with, and a supernatural addition to man, which God creates. Since such a dualism would be utterly alien to Baum's theological and anthropological intent, it has to be rejected explicitly, and an alternative sought. Baum's procedure is to start from the liberation experience of man, the grace of God as redeemer, while being largely agnostic at first about everything else. I agree with this procedure, but it seems to me that we must go on to ponder the relation between redemption and creation, between the gift of responsive freedom and the 'given' raw material of human life – our bodies, our 'natural' capacities or skills, and the natural environment in which we are immersed. Such pondering is not an optional, non-theological flight into speculative philosophy. It is required by a theology of liberation, especially one which emphasizes psychotherapy. Baum's theology-anthropology needs to consider human bodies, human skills, and human attitudes to the natural environment.

I have found in MB only two references to the *body* (221, 268). Yet unless the personal transformation and self-knowledge which Baum talks about actually involve bodily changes they are incomplete. In chapter 3 we have seen that a man's attitude towards his own body is crucial for his attitude towards other people, towards his natural environment, and towards God as the 'source' and 'ultimate context' of his existence. As Keen points out, basic trust and basic distrust have a bodily dimension. Grace works in the body and the mind together. For example, as Alexander Lowen has noted, a person who is liberated to love undergoes a 'change of heart' not only metaphorically but also literally, for rigid musculature around the heart relaxes. Also, I have seen how a person who is liberated from holding down repressed rage against people and the cosmos becomes less 'stiff-necked' not only metaphorically but also literally. A so-called liberation which is purely psychical is not a real liberation but a splitting of man into a redeemable mind and an ignorable body. Such a split is alien to Baum's intentions, but he does not indicate how it can be avoided, how the body can belong in the realm of grace.

Concerning *skills,* Baum refers to teaching and says: 'There is an aspect of teaching that has to do with information, research, systematic presentation, techniques of communication, etc., and hence can be considered apart from the supernatural order' (MB 135). In contrast with teaching skills there is an aspect of teaching which cannot be separated from the supernatural order, from grace:

If a teacher is able to be truly present to his class, if he can communicate his wisdom to his students without making them feel that it is his own, if he can refrain from using his superior knowledge as a means of dominating them, if he can listen to them without fear and be open to the truth that they utter, even if this demands the modification of his own conclusions, then divine grace is present in his teaching. (MB 135)

On the previous page Baum has attacked a dichotomy which people often make between the supernatural 'religious' realm and the natural 'secular' realm. For Baum, 'Divine grace is present not only in the specifically religious aspect of human life; it is offered in the entire process by which men grow, become themselves, and by doing so create the human world' (MB 134). Man's secular life – the interpersonal relationships through which the human world is created – is supernatural, the locus of divine grace. But what about another aspect of secular life, the exercise of skills? What about man as competent agent, rational-technological man? Baum leaves obscure the anthropological and theological significance of skills, which can be exercised in wilful freedom in a purely 'natural' way. As Baum says, there is a kind of free choice which depends on that which is 'built into the human equipment,' which 'belongs to man and is not a special gift to him' (MB 54). What is it for skills to be exercised in a supernatural, grace-inspired way, within a context of responsive freedom? It is clear that Baum does not want another supernatural/natural dichotomy, this time within the secular itself. But he does not provide a theoretical framework for avoiding this. Here he could well be supplemented by material discussed in chapter 3: Keen's revision of the wilful decisiveness of *homo volens* so it becomes the trustful decisiveness of graceful man, and my own revision of Keen's *homo faber* so as to include him in a model of trustful, graceful man. Both revisions tend to overcome the split between a realm of nature (will and intellect) and a realm of grace (attitudes of responsive trust) by placing the former in the overall context of the latter. Decisiveness and competence can be exercised, it is true, in non-responsive ways. Often they are, and then the contrast with responsive activity is most evident. But they can also be exercised in responsive ways. Grace can liberate the natural powers of man from bondage to a purely Apollonian existence.

We have seen that Baum is relatively unilluminating concerning human bodies and human 'natural' skills. He is also inadequate concerning the theological-anthropological significance of human attitudes towards the *natural environment.* According to MB the process by which man becomes more truly man does not include any change in attitude towards nature. Baum here needs to be supplemented by Keen, whose authentic man is liberated to see nature neither as a mere utensil nor as an enemy, but with a basic trust which involves appreciate wonder and gratitude for existence. Such a stance presupposes convictions concerning divine activity in, or on, nature. This raises again the agonizing problems of theodicy which Baum can easily set aside in MB by relating God, explicitly, only to the realm of response freedom in man. But we can avoid the problems concerning divine responsibility for earthquakes or cancer only if we restrict the scope of divine activity in some such way as Baum does. Such a restriction, however, tends to split man into two unrelated or antagonistic parts, only one of which is related to God – that which is 'liberated' or 'supernatural' or 'spiritual.' Since the wholeness and integrity of man matters greatly to Baum, it is not surprising to find that Baum sometimes seems to fall back on a traditional account of creation, not equating it with redemption: 'The ultimate ground of reality is love. The principle of the *total reality* man faces in himself and in the world is not hostile to him but on his side' (MB 194, my italics). But he qualifies and revises this a few lines later:

Since the world is still being constituted, the principle of reality is its *destiny.* To declare, therefore, that the principle of reality is for man, is love, is Father refers *not so much* to the origin of man and his world as it does to his marvelous destiny. We need not be afraid of the *human* reality because it is involved ... in the never-ending and ever-to-be-renewed process of divine humanization.' (MB 194, my italics)

But what about natural reality? Is Baum's phrase 'not so much' merely evasive? Baum celebrates being liberated; he also needs to celebrate being.

(ii) *God and the realm of the demonic*
One of the interesting features of MB is that it considers not only the
divine but also the demonic. Baum not only finds the divine liberating
power at work in men, a power beyond the control of any individual
men and beyond the sum of their individual powers; he also finds a
demonic realm or dimension in human life, transcending man individually and collectively. This similarity between divine and demonic might
seem to put God and Devil on a par. Each would transcend man in the
same way, though one would be good and creative, the other evil and
destructive. This would be a Zoroastrian dualism – not a supernatural/
natural dualism such as the one we have considered in the previous
section, but a dualism between a good supernatural and an evil supernatural. The idea that human life is a battleground between two *equal*
transcendent powers is contrary both to the Gospel and to Eriksonian
psychoanalysis, with its stress on a 'basic trust' in one's total environment. Baum does not accept such a dualism either. But since he seems to
hold that the divine and the demonic transcend man in the same sort of
way, his position concerning this issue requires special consideration
and clarification. I find two ways in which he avoids such a dualism.
First, in his account of the doctrines of eschatology, Providence, and
divine 'omnipotence' he affirms his faith that divine grace is offered and
available to men in every situation. No matter how powerful the destructive forces which are at work, God can enable man to become, in
some way, more truly human. Even a man on his way to an extermina-
tion chamber can receive new insight, new life. The demonic powers are
not destroyed, but they cannot prevent God from offering his humanizing summons and love in every situation. 'On a deep level that escapes
the judgement of the observer, men make decisions about the newness
that is being offered them; and it may well be that a person who is
gravely ill may say Yes to the divine call and be saved by God every day
from collapsing into total despair and the destruction of life, and that
another man who shares in the universal illness only slightly may say
No to the divine offer of new life and live out some dreadful idolatry and
unspeakable hatred in situations where release from these would have
been available to him' (MB 126). Baum thus affirms that the demonic
never quite gains complete control of any situation. Moreover, although
Baum does not hold that divine power ensures an inevitable human progress, a gradual diminution in the powers of evil during the years to
come, he does not rule out the possibility. God not only cannot lose, He
might win!

A second way in which Baum avoids putting God and Devil on a par is by not talking about a Devil at all. For Baum there is one God, but there are many demonic forces. Baum assumes that wherever man is being liberated, the same divine presence is at work. Why not a great many liberating transcendent powers, corresponding to the diverse ways in which men grow more human? Baum's assumption, that there is one God, is a matter of faith. Obviously one source for his assumption is the Gospel. Another possible source could be psychoanalysis. If the integrity of the human personality requires religious faith, it seems to require faith in one God rather than in many. Baum's position, at any rate, is that the divine is one and the demonic are many. Thus he ascribes to God the power of unity and order, and to the demonic the weakness of plurality and chaos. But all this needs further exploration.

In addition to the two ways in which Baum himself avoids putting God and Devil on a par, I would propose a third: an explicit shift from an objectivist to an existentialist stance towards the question. If one's approach is objectivist, the empirical basis for inferring a Devil may well seem to be as strong (or as weak) as that for inferring a God; as speculative hypotheses they may seem to be equally plausible or equally dubious. But when viewed in an existentialist way the question of a Devil appears differently. To believe in a Devil is either to evade responsibility for the evil in myself by blaming it on a power outside my control which is manipulating me or to seek a realization of some of my fantasies of omnipotence by manipulating a supernatural power to achieve my own ends. In either case I am opting for a life in the realm of the *wilful* – being manipulated or manipulating – rather than in the realm of responsive freedom, being open to confirmation and confrontation so as to discern and to become one's true self. The issue involves a practical life-choice, a decision concerning one's fundamental style of life, whether it is to be alienating or humanizing.

But if we view the issue again in a more objectivist way, it seems that the very notion of a transcendent demonic dimension warrants scepticism. I wonder whether Baum's anthropology really requires this notion. His Freudian version of original sin, plus his account of how evil can be multiplied unwittingly in institutions, seems to me to suffice. In one of his descriptions of *sin* Baum himself seems to imply that sin is sufficient to account for all the destructiveness in human life:

It is man's pathological resistance to growing up. This sin finds expression in man's social life; it is never simply his own. Sin is man's conscious and unconscious unwillingness to enter into new life, expressed and disguised in a multitude of ways, both personal and social; it opposes God's gracious gift of himself and thus prevents man from entering into his destiny. It is this sin that inevitably causes the havoc of which we have spoken. (MB 228)

(iii) Christ as norm in anthropology

Thus far, my discussion of Baum's theology of liberation would leave the reader with a misleading impression, for I have indicated only a few ways in which Baum interprets various traditional Christian doctrines. I have not even noted his account of the divine Word active in human words of confrontation, or his account of the divine Spirit active in human love, strengthening men to respond to the Word. Baum on Word and Spirit is very illuminating, and deserves careful study. His interpretation of God as Father – which for Baum is God as man's destiny – is less satisfactory. We considered it indirectly when we examined a passage where divine creation is interpreted in relation to man's destiny rather than (or more than) in relation to his origins. But it seems to me that what deserves the most critical scrutiny is Baum's Christology.

According to Baum what God has revealed in Christ is that 'the way of God's presence is incarnation. God acts through the human. It is in ordinary words and gestures, in interpersonal relations, that God communicates himself to men ... What is revealed in Christ is that human life is the locus of the divine' (MB 90). Is this *all* that is revealed? If so, then the Gospel concerning Christ is the same thing as Baum's formal principle for theology-anthropology: 'Human life is the locus of the divine' or 'God liberates man to become man.' If Baum's formal principle sums up all that the Gospel proclaims, then statements about Christ, like statements about God, should be translatable without loss into statements about the transcendent redemptive power which is universally active in human life. At the end of MB Baum says: 'It is possible to proclaim the Gospel without mentioning God by name' (MB 284). Does he also hold that it is possible without mentioning Jesus Christ? No. For Baum the Gospel includes the declaration that 'the hidden involvement of God in the humanization of man has become fully, definitively, and unconditionally manifest in Jesus Christ, the Word made flesh' (MB 63). 'While the divine Word summons every man to do the will of the Father and to enter into his destiny, it is only Jesus Christ who ever obeyed this call fully and completely ... He was without sin' (MB 92). Baum thus views Jesus Christ as the one true man, who alone has fully responded to the divine presence, and who is the definitive instance of humanization by divine grace. Such a Christology is in line with much in Christian tradition, but there is a problem concerning what it means.

What does Baum mean when he claims that Jesus Christ is the definitive instance of God's humanization of man? Consider this passage:

Christianity may be called a humanism, to be precise a christological humanism. For in Christ is revealed to us who man shall be or, more carefully, who the transcendent dynamism is by which, gratuitously, all men are summoned and freed to become more fully human. Divine grace recreates in men the perfect humanity revealed in Christ. Christianity is humanistic in the sense that it reveals, celebrates, and promotes the entry of all men into greater likeness to Jesus Christ. (MB 137–8)

If we ignore the clause beginning 'or, more carefully,' this passage seems to set forth Jesus Christ as the one norm for humanization. But in Baum's actual presentation of concrete ways in which divine grace is at work, the New Testament account of Jesus Christ is only one criterion among many. Other criteria come from psychoanalysis and existentialist phenomenology and from other modern views of man. Where criteria conflict, modern ideas sometimes prevail. (It seems to me that this happens in Baum's discussion of the doctrine of divine punishment.) Indeed, Baum is quite open in claiming an independent theological significance for insights of contemporary man. In a definitive article 'Toward a New Catholic Theism' (NCT) he is quite explicit: 'While the traditional theologians simply sought to draw out the wisdom implicit in Scripture and the Church's past teaching, the new theologians think of theology as establishing some kind of correlation (the word is Tillich's) between the normative revelation of the past and the ongoing revelation present in human experience, personal and social' (NCT 54). What is not clear to me is the *way* in which for Baum the revelation of the past is 'normative.' In his Christology the Gospel is clearly normative as a proclamation of God's redemptive presence in human life everywhere. Also, in the passage quoted above, the Gospel locates in Christ 'who the transcendent dynamism is' by which men are liberated. This links the power at work in Jesus with the power at work in us. But what is not clear is how the Gospel and contemporary experience are interrelated as *selective norms* by which we pick out instances of humanization-redemption. Although I usually find myself agreeing with Baum's selections, it is not clear how the New Testament account of Jesus Christ (or Roman Catholic tradition concerning Jesus Christ) functions as a norm alongside modern insights concerning what it is to become more truly human. The most important assumption here, it seems to me, is that there is an 'ongoing *revelation* present in human experience, personal and social' (MB 54), a revelation not only of God but of Jesus Christ. But this still does not clarify how the selective norms operate in practice in Baum's thought.

In so far as Baum's theology is *therapeutic*, it is critical of a good deal in Christian tradition. In his later work, RA, Baum gives the following account of MB:

Theologians should no longer reflect on the teaching and practice of the Christian religion without asking themselves the question to what extent the inherited symbols initiate people into dependencies, guilt and blindness, and to what extent these same symbols, read out of different presuppositions, deliver man from dependencies, guilt and blindness. In a book called *Man Becoming*, I have tried to show that the gospel is in fact a healing message and that to remain faithful to this gospel it is necessary to submit the teaching and the practice of the Christian church to an ongoing therapeutic critique. (RA 99)

In RA Baum is explicit concerning what a socio-political critique of traditional christology would be. Any therapeutic critique of traditional christology in MB is implicit. In general, it is not clear how Baum relates his norms from the past to his norms from the present.

(iv) *God and the realm of the political*
Earlier we saw that Baum does not believe that God's power ensures inevitable progress for mankind. He distinguishes between 'evolution' and 'humanization':

Evolution signifies mankind's entry into higher consciousness and the transformation of the human environment through God's presence in history. Humanization, on the other hand, need not involve the whole of mankind nor the transformation of the environment. *Humanization signifies man's entry into greater faith, hope and love through God's presence in his personal history.* Man may grow in his humanity even if he is exposed to a dehumanizing community and the breakdown of his cultural environment. Jesus' entry into his passion and his death was for him humanization. (MB 117, my italics)

For Baum in MB humanization and divine grace are primarily located in the *personal* history of men. Each man may grow in humanity even if political institutions become demonic. The central focus of Baum's theology of liberation is on how God enables individual persons to become more human. This liberation occurs primarily in the context of face-to-face personal encounters and also in the context of deeper communion with oneself. The focus is on personal salvation, integrally linked to an intimate fellowship of challenge and communion. This kind of central focus, it seems to me, is in accord with that of the New Testament and of most Christian theology. Yet it has a serious drawback. By itself it leaves the whole realm of impersonal, institutional human life outside theology-anthropology, in a limbo. Political activity, the importance of which is so obvious to morally sensitive people today, is not seen to be an integral part of human liberation, an essential locus of divine action.

Baum does not ignore the political dimension in MB. This is part of what he says:

In order to realize himself, man must face the evil on two fronts, in himself and in the society to which he belongs, and unless he wrestles with evil on both these fronts, he cannot move far on the way to growth and reconciliation. If he confines his struggle to the evil within himself, he will not be able to *discern* how much his own spiritual values and his ideals for the community are hidden ways of protecting his social and political privileges. *In order to become himself,* a man must be politicized. In order to *discern* how he profits from the order of society – and here I include the Church – and how this profit creates a bias in his own understanding of life and its meaning, a man must face the destructive and exploitive trends in his own society. He must be willing to submit his life, his ideals, his religion, to what I have called the Marxian critique. (MB 160, my italics)

In this passage Baum explicitly includes politics within humanization; 'In order to become himself, a man must be politicized.' But the emphasis is on self-realization through growing discernment, humanization through growing self-knowledge, rather than on political activity. Indeed, when earlier in MB Baum outlined the Marxist critique, he did so alongside an outline of the Freudian critique, finding in both critiques a divine summons to painful new self-knowledge which breaks down our self-deception and exposes our real motives. The Marxist critique thus is mainly important for personal growth, for new insights into one's own pathology. But what significance has political activity, the attempt to bring about change in the impersonal, institutional relations among men? What significance do these relations have? Is God present in any way as liberator in these relations?

Although Baum neglects such questions in MB, he more than amply treats them in RA, which deals mainly with political liberation.[7] There are some allusions to personal liberation, but in my presentation of RA I shall ignore these until near the end. Then I shall note that there is still an important, though subordinate, place for personal liberation in RA, and I shall discuss the relation between political and personal liberation.

2 Religion and alienation

In RA Baum's formal principle is unchanged: God is still the hidden mystery present in all human life, exposing human sin and enabling human beings to become truly human. Baum shifts his main focus, however, from the personal to the political. This shift means that he draws on different resources in both Christian tradition and secular thought. In MB he mainly interprets Christian piety in relation to depth psychology and he refers to his contact with Therafields. In RA he mainly interprets Christian prophecy in relation to continental sociology and he refers to his studies at the New School for Social Research. By 'piety' I mean a focus on divine grace as judgment on personal sin and hope for personal liberation. By 'prophecy' I mean a focus on divine grace as judgment on social sin and hope for socio-political liberation.

The message of the prophets, including Jesus, was critical and innovative. It was critical of the sacred community for its blindness to collective injustice, the domination of the powerless by the powerful. And it was innovative in that it provided an image of the future which inspired a creative change of social conduct in the present. Baum interprets the prophetic message in relation to what he calls the 'sociological tradition': early Hegel, early Marx, Tocqueville, Toennies, Durkheim, Mannheim, Weber, and Bloch. The outcome is a theology which he calls 'transformist.'[8] God is the mystery present in human life, exposing social sin and revealing a future of justice and reconciliation which is already to some extent a present possibility. Transformist theology exposes structures of domination in church and society and reveals a vision of a better society which inspires social change. Baum contrasts transformist theology with 'ideological' theology, which legitimizes the structures of domination and acquiesces in social evil.

My discussion of RA will be in two parts. First, I shall outline five sociological insights which Baum uses in his transformist theology as he reinterprets the Christian prophetic tradition. Secondly, I shall outline the understanding of religious faith which then emerges and discuss some of its implications.

1 SOCIOLOGICAL INSIGHTS AND TRANSFORMIST THEOLOGY

I shall first summarize the five sociological insights and their implications for theology: (i) The dehumanizing elements in human life include structures of domination in society which cause great evil and which most people are not aware of. Theology should be 'political'; that is, it should make this social sin a central concern. (ii) Ideas are deeply influenced by the institutional structures of society. Theology should be aware of such influences on itself, for its own thought may be to some extent a product of the structures of domination. Theology should be 'non-ideological'; that is, it should not legitimize those structures. (iii) Yet ideas are not only influenced by society; they themselves also influence society, for good or ill. Ideas have social consequences. Theology should accept responsibility for the social consequences of Christian teaching and revise that teaching accordingly; theology should be 'critical.' (iv) Some symbol systems are 'utopian'; that is, they provide a vision of the future which criticizes present structures and inspires men to create a more human society. Theology should be 'utopian.' (v) Human society is an ongoing process in which human beings both are shaped by their past and shape their own future. Such 'historical consciousness' indicates an 'immanental' theology in which God is the mystery present within this very process.

(i) *Structures of domination, social sin, and political theology*
Baum acknowledges that there are many different ways of viewing the sociological tradition, but he himself finds a common humanism: a normative anthropology concerning what is authentically human which gives rise to a moral passion and sensitivity concerning the 'alienating or dehumanizing aspects of society' (RA 2) especially in the institutional power structures which form its fabric. Baum cites Hegel (RA 15), Marx (RA 32), and Toennies (RA 50–1) concerning the structures of domination in relations between societal groups. These oppressive structures produce injustices and sufferings far beyond what wicked individuals cause by their deliberate actions. He gives some examples: economic domination in monopoly capitalism, bureaucratic centralization, institutionalized racism, and subjugation of women, the negation of Jewish existence, the hegemony of developed nations over the third world (RA 190, 216, 218–19). It takes a long time before these structures of domination are recognized as such and before various social evils are discerned and seen to be the effects of these structures. People who belong to the dominant group are least likely to be aware of what is actually going on. Mean-

while human life is profoundly alienated, remote from what it could and should be. Both the oppressor and the oppressed lose touch with what is authentically human.

Baum interprets this sociological analysis of evil in relation to the theological concept of sin. He distinguishes between two kinds of sin: (a) individuals, whether privately or in conspiracy, consciously and deliberately harm the life of society as a whole; (b) society, because of its impersonal structures of domination, harms individuals (as well as subgroups and its own collective life). He says that, although (a) is an 'aspect of social sin' (RA 200), it is a relatively superficial one; and at times he seems to include (a) under 'personal sin.' What he has mainly in mind when he speaks of 'social sin' is (b): the *subject* (rather than the object) of sin is society, and the workings of sin are largely unconscious. Such sin is what the prophets denounced:

The prophets of Israel addressed the people as if they were involved in collective sin and suffered from communal blindness: the prophetic message was meant to raise their common consciousness, to make them aware of what they refused to look at and open them to the summons of the divine word.   (RA 73)

Social sin is more especially the topic of the prophetic preaching. There we hear of collective blindness, group-egotism, and the pursuit of a national life that betrays authentic values and violates the divine command. Peculiar to this collective sin is that it is accompanied by so much self-delusion and self-flattery that the people involved in it are not aware of their transgression.   (RA 198)

How is it that social sin is largely unconscious, a collective self-deception, a communal blindness? Much light on this is shed by sociological analyses of the influence of social institutions on human consciousness, to which we now turn. Such issues, of course, will not even be of interest to theology unless it is already *political* theology, that is, a theology in which social sin is a central category and a major concern.

(ii) *The influence of society on consciousness: non-ideological theology*
According to Baum all sociologists acknowledge that consciousness is socially grounded: 'Society (the institutions in which we live) affects our consciousness (the way we perceive reality and think about it)' (RA 1; cf 247). The collective interests of any group exert a secret and powerful

influence on the symbols through which its members view themselves, others, and the world. Hence theology, as a system of religious symbols, is partly a social product, a reflection of collective interests of church and society. Thus, 'religious symbols must be understood in the context of the society in which they are proclaimed and celebrated and hence vary in meaning and power in accordance with this historical context' (RA 248–9). Theologians need to reflect on the hidden group interests which secretly influence the formation and understanding of their own works. Also, theologians need to choose which groups in their historical context to identify themselves with – dominant classes or countervailing movements. Their theologies will be profoundly affected by that identification.

Although sociologists are in broad agreement that consciousness is socially grounded, they differ concerning the extent and the way in which this happens. One account is given in the Marxist concept of 'ideology':

In the Marxian terminology, ideology is always something false, a distortion of the truth for the sake of social interest, a symbolic framework of the mind that legitimates the power and privileges of the dominant groups and sanctions the social evils inflicted on the people without access to power. According to Marx, every community of men generates through a largely unconscious process a set of symbols that protects its position of power, affirms its identity over against its competitors, and makes it easier for the government to rule. For Marx, then, religion as well as culture are largely ideological in character. Even philosophy, at least the dominant philosophy, is a subtle defense of the dominant class.   (RA 34)

For Marx the crucial structure of domination is *economic*. Baum accepts a modified version of the Marxist theory which differs in that ideology legitimates not only economic power but other forms of institutional power as well, sanctioning the social evils caused by a great variety of structures of domination which are not necessarily dependent on economic factors. In both orthodox and revised Marxism, ideology is by definition false and evil, for it suppresses or distorts the truth so as to support dehumanizing power structures. Ideology is not the result of deliberate plotting by individuals who decide to deceive others. It is a collective self-deception, a false consciousness, from which individuals cannot liberate themselves merely by moral idealism. A radical conversion, involving a radical change of consciousness and a new commitment, is required.

According to Marx, religion is always 'false consciousness, reflecting and protecting the injustices of the present social order ... the supreme legitimation of the structures of domination in human society' (RA 33). Baum holds that this is often the case. He also holds that the structures of domination include non-economic institutions which Marx did not adequately acknowledge. There are often ideological trends in the way in which the Christian message is proclaimed, 'trends that distort the truth for the sake of strengthening the church against its competitors, legitimating the dominant social and economic values of society, and promoting obedience to secular and ecclesiastical authorities' (RA 35). Baum goes on:

The most startling example of ideological deformation in the history of Christian teaching, an example in no way derived from economic pressures but from purely religious sources, is the persistent anti-Jewish bias. ... Because of the church's conflict with the synagogue and because of the church's need continually to justify its messianic reading of the scriptures, Christian preachers and teachers accompanied the proclamation of the Christian gospel with a refutation of Jewish religion and the negation of Jewish existence before God.   (RA 35)

In J Baum reveals that it was his study of Jewish-Christian relations which first brought him into contact with the social unconscious: 'So deeply was the anti-Jewish trend inscribed in Christian culture that the ordinary men of intelligence and good will were unable to discover it. It was woven right into their consciousness' (J 16). Having thus first recognized that Christian anti-Semitism arose as a largely unconscious self-deception which reflected the collective interests of Christians, Baum began to see more clearly the social unconscious at work in other ways and in other groups. In particular, he began to appreciate more deeply Marx's recognition of the social unconscious at work in legitimating the *economic* power of dominant classes. Eventually he came to agree with Marx to the extent of holding that in some historical situations the most important structures of domination are economic and the most important sources of ideology are economic; but he believes that in other historical situations this is not the case.

The concept of ideology is illuminating for Baum as he tries to understand Christian blindness concerning not only the Jews but also the church itself (RA 75–6). In the scriptures there are many clear denunciations of various elements of religious pathology (idolatry, superstition, hypocrisy, legalism, and collective blindness). But the church as a whole has not applied this critique to itself. Idolatry and superstition are denounced in pagans, but their presence within the church goes unnoticed. The Jews are denounced for hypocrisy and legalism and blindness, but these sins remain undetected within the church. Since these pathological elements are tendencies in any religious group, it is not surprising to find them in the church. What is surprising is the way in which the church ignores its own prophetic insights concerning religious pathology when it contemplates itself. For example, the church knows that idolatry is an absolutizing of *any* finite reality – not only a statue or a human being but also a community. Why does the church fail to apply that insight to itself, exposing its own self-idolatry? Baum finds an answer in terms of ideology, the deformation of the truth by a collectivity which *unconsciously* inflates and defends its own powers and privileges against any dangerous scrutiny.

(iii) *The influence of consciousness on society: critical theology*
In the sociological tradition symbolic systems are not only products or reflections of society; they are also powerful influences on society and on individuals. Consciousness is grounded in social reality but social reality is to a great extent created by consciousness. There is a dialectical, two-directional relation between symbolic structures and power structures. Also, not all symbolic structures are ideological, legitimating the existing power structures; some are critical. But whether legitimating or critical, they have power, for they really help to support or to undermine the social *status quo*. Sociologists differ concerning the extent and the mode of this influence of ideas on social reality. Marx saw it as clearly subordinate to the influence in the reverse direction, but he nevertheless allowed it some place. Baum draws on Durkheim and Hegel as he presents his own analysis of the power of symbols.

Durkheim originally contrasted traditional society, bound together by a system of symbols of which people were aware, and modern society, in which there is no such system. But his investigations, especially concerning suicide, led him to believe that modern society must have a hidden symbolic system which affects the consciousness of individuals. This 'collective consciousness' (RA 125) operates as a hidden force. Individuals are not usually aware of it. To become conscious of hidden symbols is to realize what is already at work in the depths of human life, for 'people's self-symbolization enters into the creation of their history, their culture and their society' (RA 129). Baum also notes that Freud's psychological approach has given rise to broadly similar conclusions concerning the power of the symbolic, which reveals hidden unconscious depths within individuals. Though Freud stressed the familial unconscious, which is built up in the infant's relations with his parents, he also allowed for a collective unconscious, built up in the evolutionary history of humanity (RA 118).

Symbols have power in human life not only as expressions of hidden forces at work within human beings but also as *that through which* human beings view reality. Baum adopts the expression 'that through which' from Ricoeur (RA 243) and draws heavily on Hegel, who held that 'the symbolic structure of the mind makes people see the world in a particular way, orient their lives and act in it in a particular direction' (RA 19).

A reading of Hegel more in line with the sociological tradition recognizes him as a social thinker who clearly saw that the human world is not fixed, that it has been produced by people, and that the symbols dominating their imagination had a profound effect on the world they created. The patterns governing the imagination make people select what they regard as significant aspects of reality, combine them into meaningful wholes of one sort or another, connect them with values and relate them to a vision of the future. In this perspective, human experience itself is not a datum presented to the mind but a phenomenon created by the mind. (RA 242)

Baum thus holds that religious symbols have power because they are both revelations of hidden depths within human life and imaginative frameworks through which human life is viewed. But his main stress is on the way in which all symbolic systems, especially religious ones, are *political.* Symbolic structures have a powerful influence on socio-political structures. This is true even when the symbolic structure professes to be strictly non-political: 'No matter how spiritual and private a religious concern may be, it always has a political implication, it is never socially neutral' (RA 104). Religious symbols, as presented in a particular socio-political context, either legitimate the existing system or criticize it, though they may do either of these implicitly rather than explicitly. Since so much of religion is legitimating, theologians have a responsibility to scrutinize and revise Christian teaching and practice so as to minimize ideology. Otherwise the church is supporting social sin rather than being true to its own prophetic tradition. So Baum calls for a *'critical theology,'* which 'enables the church to assume theological responsibility for its own social reality' (RA 195). This is not an area of theology (e.g. a theology of society) but rather a mode of theological reflection which applies to every area of theology – moral, dogmatic, ascetic, etc. It is 'critical' in a twofold sense: first, it is self-critical, scrutinizing the social consequences of its own message so as to be socially responsible; secondly, it is 'critical' in the sense of attacking rather than legitimating social evil in church and society. When Baum speaks of 'critical theology' he means it in the first sense but he also assumes it in the second. (Presumably a politically conservative theologian might regard himself as 'critical' in the first sense although not in the second.)

In its sensitivity to the political implications of Christian teaching Baum's critical theology is similar to contemporary German 'political theology' and Latin American 'liberation theology.' Like both of these it calls for a 'deprivatizing' of Christian teaching:

The preaching of personal conversion to Jesus, understood in an individualistic way, as it has been in many Christian churches, represses one side of the gospel and hence has strongly defensive or even reactionary political implications. For the stress on private conversion makes people blind to the structures of evil in society. People are made to think that the inequities of their society are due to personal sins and can be removed only through the personal conversion of the sinners. What people who stress the conversion to Jesus as their personal saviour fail to see is that the evil in society has a twofold root, in the sinful hearts of men and in institutionalized injustices, and that this evil can only be overcome by a movement that includes social change. The stress on Jesus as personal saviour is always linked, therefore, to the defense of the political *status quo*. The individualistic religion of traditional evangelical and fundamentalist Christians legitimates the individualism of our economic system, and while they present their message as non-political, it has significant political consequences. (RA 209)

Baum gives other examples of how critical theology should operate:

The traditional formulation of christology, while dealing with God's saving act in Jesus, actually had profound, unrecognized and totally unintended structural effects: it has inferiorized the Jews and prepared their social exclusion, and it has led to a church-centred understanding of history and legitimated the white man's colonial invasions of the world. It is the task of critical theology to bring to light the hidden human consequences of doctrine, to raise the consciousness of the believing community in this regard, and to find a manner of proclaiming the church's teaching that has structural consequences in keeping with the gospel. In the case of christology this means that a way of announcing God's Word in Jesus must be found which does not devour other religions but actually makes room for the multiple manifestation of God's grace. There is not a single doctrine of the church, nor a single aspect of spirituality, worship or church life that may be exempted from a critique that distinguishes between intention and structural consequences and evaluates the latter in terms of the gospel. (RA 195)

Baum insists that 'critical theology ... is not the submission of dogma to an anthropological norm as if the human were the measure of the divine; critical theology is rather the submission of the structural consequences of dogma to the revealed norm of the gospel' (RA 196). Baum understands the Gospel as 'God's judgment on, and deliverance from, the destructive and sinful trends prevalent in contemporary society' (RA 190). Unlike some reinterpretations of doctrine, critical theology is not merely an assimilation to dominant cultural trends in society, for it is characteristically opposed to these. Indeed, it is more effectively opposed than are those conservative theologies which refuse to reinterpret doctrine out of fear of assimilation and which thereby refuse to correct any ideological elements, thus assimilating in secret ways. Critical theology is responsive to the changing face of evil in human history, revising the Christian message so as to help Christians to recognize and combat social evil in obedience to the prophetic Gospel. The alternative to a critical theology is a blindly ideological theology which retains the Christian message in a form which helps Christians to ignore social evil or to acquiesce in it.

But what counts as evil? Whatever is dehumanizing. How can Baum then deny that critical theology is the submission of dogma to an *anthropological* norm? The point is rather, I think, that the 'anthropological norm' which determines what counts as dehumanizing or humanizing comes from both Christian tradition (prophecy) and contemporary thought (sociology). And of course for Baum the human is not the measure of the divine, for the human cannot be liberated from social evil without divine grace. The human is the *locus* of the divine.

Baum subjects not only theological doctrines but also sociological theories to pragmatic test. He considers positions taken by Berger (that alienation is anthropologically necessary, RA 109–11) and by Weber (that bureaucratization of life inevitably crushes countervailing trends in society, RA 174–6), and he rejects these positions because of their crippling, legitimating social consequences. Such sociological contentions, like religious doctrines, cannot be conclusively proven or falsified by empirical evidence, and so one can choose to accept or reject them on socially pragmatic grounds. It seems to me that a similar pragmatism is operative in Baum's selection and formulation of theological doctrines. Indeed, this seems to be at the core of critical theology. It is interesting to ask, therefore, whether Baum's choice of a theological rather than a non-theological position in his interpretation of human life is similarly pragmatic. Do we have faith in God because this helps us to work effectively against alienation and towards a more authentic human life in society? Baum argues that some kinds of religious faith do in fact have this influence, in contrast with other religious and non-religious stances. They have this influence because they express and foster attitudes which are conducive to socio-political reform or revolution.

It seems clear to me that Baum is not providing a pragmatic socio-logical-anthropological argument for religious faith analogous to Keen's psychological-anthropological claim that religious language has a useful function in promoting human fulfilment.[9] Baum simply believes in a divine liberating mystery present in human life. This belief is for him true and also useful to humanity, but it is not held to be true because it is useful. It is based in part, as we shall see, on what Baum calls 'religious experience.' Nevertheless it is interesting to compare Baum's treatment of Marx with Keen's treatment of Freud. In each case a critic of religion denounces religion as alienating and explains it away in a reductive scientific manner by showing how it functions, and in each case the response is to point to a kind of religion which is de-alienating and humanizing in function and to commend it for that very reason.

So far I have shown how Baum's theology draws on sociology so as to be political (concerned with structures of domination and social sin), minimally ideological (not legitimizing those structures), and critical (responsible for the social consequences of its teachings). These ideas are obviously interrelated, though they draw on different elements in socio-logy. The same is true of the fourth element, which begins with a famous sociological distinction between 'ideology' and 'utopia.'

(iv) *Utopian symbols and utopian religion: critical, concrete,*
committed, and charismatic
In previous sections I have mentioned that symbols, including religious symbols, can sometimes be non-ideological and that as such they can have a powerful influence on society. But I have said little concerning such symbols and their innovative power. Baum notes that as a Christian theologian he trusts that 'the mystery of God operative in human life

again and again produces creative religion' (RA 163); but he also claims that there is good sociological evidence that religion can have creative, innovative power. This is of course evidence concerning the power of religion rather than the power of God, but it does provide an anthropology which is open to theological interpretation.

Mannheim distinguished between ideological and utopian symbols:

> Religion (or any symbolic language) is ideological if it legitimates the existing social order, defends the dominant values, enhances the authority of the dominant class, and creates an imagination suggesting that society is stable and perdures. By contrast, religion is utopian if it reveals the ills of the present social order, inverts the dominant values of society, undermines the authority of the ruling groups, and makes people expect the downfall of the present system. (RA 102–3)

Here utopian symbolism is revolutionary (radical) but it can also be evolutionary (reformist).[10] In either case it is a 'vision of a new society that evokes criticism of the present order and releases energy for social change' (RA 103). Note that it is thus not only critical of the present but also creative in relation to the future. For this to be the case the vision of the future must be what Bloch called a 'concrete' rather than an 'abstract' utopia (RA 171, 283). That is, the picture of future fulfilment is not only in critical contrast with the alienations of present society, but in realistic touch with possibilities in present society so as to summon forth new ways of thinking and acting which can lead to actual social change. And such a concrete utopia should involve practical commitment. Baum agrees with Latin American 'liberation theology' in its insistence on an active identification with 'the existing movement for emancipation and justice' (RA 289), choosing the side of the exploited and the countervailing movement. Not to choose it and work in solidarity with it is to remain identified in practice with the interests of the ruling class.

Thus for Baum a genuinely utopian religion is critical, concrete, and committed. He also holds that it is 'charismatic.' Though Baum begins with Weber's famous but sketchy concept of the 'charismatic' individual who is a major innovative force in religion, he goes on to give his own illuminating account of why such an individual has extraordinary power and authority over people: 'he touches them where they suffer' (RA 170). The charismatic individual is intuitively aware of what disturbs, wounds, and exasperates people and he can put into words their hidden oppression, articulating the alienation of the community. Hence, as he speaks, 'they verify his words through their own experiences' (RA 170). In his utopian vision he not only opens up the hurts of people; he also provides a heartening hint of how these can be overcome. A charismatic figure may be an unscrupulous demagogue, manipulating people for his own purposes to their destruction. But if he is a prophet, he 'summons people to greater self-knowledge, releases new energy in them, and inspires them to recreate society according to higher ideals of justice and equality' (RA 170).

Baum sees the periodic emergence of utopian religion as an instance of a more universal pattern in human history. The dominant system produces not only ideology but also countervailing movements 'by way of critical response and passing through the creativity of certain personalities' (RA 173). The dominant system produces alienation, to which the sensitive sensibility of the creative charismatic person responds with indignation and a vision of a more humane way of life. This pattern is not a law, for the responses of everyone, including charismatic persons, involve an element of freedom. But the pattern provides a sociological basis for hope that human life in any society will eventually be renewed.

Baum interprets this hope in relation to Christian eschatological symbolism, especially 'Thy Kingdom come.' In his interpretation of this symbolism Baum sees it as utopian: critical, concrete, committed, and charismatic. It is also paradoxical:

History is destined for redemption, yet undetermined; it is alive by a divine drift toward humanization, yet remains locus of catastrophic sins; it is ever open to the unexpected new. (RA 286)

Christians believe that the orientation of history toward renewed life is unalterable, yet the certainty they derive from this is often only the trust that after the great catastrophes produced by human sin we shall again begin to move forward. God is the forward movement *in* history, but not necessarily the forward movement *of* history. (RA 287)

(v) *Historical consciousness and immanental theology*
For Baum God is the forward movement *in* history but not *of* history; God is immanent in history yet transcends history. Baum's immanental theology is related by him to the sociological concept of 'historical consciousness,' which refers to a new human self-understanding which emerged during the nineteenth century:

While at one time the human reality was a *given* for people, which they tried to understand and into which they wanted to fit their lives, in the new age, society was experienced by people as unfinished, as something that still had to be built, as social process, the past of which was a given but the future of which still depended on people's choices ... They began to realize that subject and object are inseparably interrelated, that they have been produced by a common history of interaction, and that men and women, unfinished as they are, constitute themselves as subjects precisely by continuing to build the world as object. People thus began to feel responsible for their future ... People began to feel themselves as having been produced by an historical process and being responsible for creating their future by a similar process passing through their collective decisions. This is the historical consciousness.   (RA 186)

This new consciousness has influenced religious experience and theology:

Christians began to experience God, not as the voice from above that called them away from this world to a higher level, but as a transcendent mystery present in life itself, which summoned people to greater self-knowledge, enabled them to assume responsibility for their world, and moved them forward into the future.   (RA 188)

Baum says that although this immanental theology could not have appeared until historical consciousness appeared, Catholics can see it as being in continuity with very ancient doctrinal trends: 'the encounter of the Logos in human life and the divine destiny of the whole of mankind' (RA 182). (He says that in Protestantism it is 'in continuity with Hegel rather than the original Reformers' (RA 182).) Baum's formal principle is, as we have seen, immanental in a way which is incarnational and universal: God is the mystery present in all of human life, liberating men to become more truly human.

2 RELIGIOUS FAITH, TRANSFORMIST THEOLOGY, AND THERAPEUTIC THEOLOGY

We have seen that in RA Baum retains the formal principle of MB, but instead of interpreting Christian piety in relation to psychology he interprets Christian prophecy in relation to sociology. Instead of a therapeutic theology of personal liberation we have a transformist theology of political liberation. Instead of, in the extreme case, undergoing psychoanalysis, one undergoes politicization.

This contrast between RA and MB is too stark to be true. We have already seen that Baum does allow a place for the political in MB. And in subsection ii below I shall discuss the place which Baum has for the personal in RA. Nevertheless the difference in emphasis between the two books is undeniable, and it involves an important difference in emphasis in the conception of religious faith. So I shall first outline the contrast concerning religious faith.

(i) *Differences between MB and RA concerning religious faith*
In each book there is a set of basic theological concepts which together form a conception of religious faith. The books differ concerning each concept. For example, although the basic form of analogy in both books is analogy of originating grace, what this term means is different in each case. In MB the breakthrough of originating grace in human life takes place in individuals, overcoming dehumanizing elements within them. In RA 'breakthrough religion is always related to, and reacting against, the de-humanizing trends in the *community*' (RA 189, my italics). In MB *liberation* or salvation is personal. In RA it is mainly political: 'the deliverance of people from all the enemies of life, including the oppression and alienation inflicted on them by the social structures of domination' (RA 210). In MB *sin* is an individual's pathological resistance to growing up, so that he prefers the defensive and destructive deceptions of the past to the creative possibilities in the present. In RA sin is social sin: the social structures of domination and the legitimating symbolic structures which in dialectical interaction dehumanize human life. In MB *conversion* involves three interrelated elements: (a) recognizing and turning away from the defensive and destructive deceptions within oneself; (b) identifying oneself with the authentically human possibilities for love and creativity and self-realization which emerge; and (c) acknowledging divine grace at work in this personal liberation. In RA conversion involves three different interrelated elements. Conversion comes to people who (a) 'become aware of, and turn away from, the taken-for-granted injustices built into their society' (RA 202), (b) choose 'an identification with the poor, the dispossessed, the disfavoured and with the movements toward their emancipation' (RA 220), and (c) acknowledge divine grace at work in political liberation.

In RA Baum links conversion and faith so closely that he even speaks of 'faith-conversion' (RA 220). We should examine more carefully what he means by this central theological category. Let us consider the three elements in turn. (a) There is a change of consciousness, or raising of consciousness (RA 208–9), or correcting of false consciousness, in which one becomes aware of the structures of domination and the evil and ideology which these produce. This is a *societal-* rather than a *self*-knowledge, though it does include a new awareness of the ways in which one's own view of society has been distorted and how one's own powers and privileges depend on the oppression of others. Since *not* being aware of social sin has been to one's own benefit, there is much resistance against seeing the truth. The 'painful remaking of consciousness' (RA 213) which is involved is so drastic that Baum interprets it in terms of the Cross. (b) There is also an active identification with the oppressed, a practical commitment to social action towards their liberation. This, too, Baum relates to the Cross, for society punishes those who walk with the poor, hunger and thirst after justice, and struggle against the stuctures of domination (RA 212–13). While expounding the thought of the revolutionary reformer Thomas Muenzer, Baum says that faith consists in 'the conversion away from egotism, domination and alliance with the ruling class, and in the trusting identification with the poor, the exploited, the oppressed in whom God's reign will appear' (RA 279). Such identification precedes critical reflection concerning policy and strategy, including the choice between radical and reformist social action:

Faith precedes calculation, conversion to Christ precedes the mapping out of the converted life, solidarity with the least of Christ's brothers and sisters precedes the search for an adequate plan of joining them in their struggle. (RA 220)

(c) The third element has already been indicated in some of the language which appears above: 'in whom God's reign will appear' or 'the least of Christ's brothers and sisters.' But it is possible for someone to be converted in ways (a) and (b) without being conscious of any such explicitly religious element. For Baum the difference between a purely secular commitment and a transformist religious faith lies in what he calls 'contemplation': a 'contemplation of the divine mystery as source, orientation and horizon of common action' (RA 183) or as 'matrix and enabler in human life and as forward movement in history' (RA 291). Such contemplation is linked with what Baum calls 'religious experience': 'There are movements in people's lives when they are in touch with a reality that transcends the proportions of their day-to-day existence, and made to look at the world from a new perspective' (RA 256). When Baum finds in Bloch's writings a powerful religious quality, one element is 'the paradoxical conviction that in their vigorous actions people are simultaneously being carried forward' (RA 280). This paradox is vividly expressed by Baum himself as he explains what contemplation involves:

In the Christian perspective, action equals passion. While we see, we are being enlightened, while we act, we are being carried forward, while we love, we are being saved from selfishness, and while we embrace all people in solidarity we are being freed inwardly to cross one boundary after another. Every step towards greater humanization is due to the expansion of new and gracious life in us. We are alive by a power that transcends us. (RA 291–2)

It seems to me that this passage expresses a deeply personal awareness of the Pauline paradox of grace which I have claimed to be fundamental in MB. Faith-conversion, whether it be therapeutic or political, involves a pervasive stance of active receptivity or responsiveness. Without this stance a man may have a purely intellectual recognition of destructive trends within himself or in social structures and he may try to be more personally creative or to work for the oppressed, but no radical conversion of the whole personality will occur.

Since faith-conversion, whether therapeutic or political, is an inner change in the *individual*, not in social structures as such, it does seem that there is in this respect some priority for the personal. Political faith-conversion is a change in a person which may or may not actually help to bring political liberation; success is not guaranteed. But the relation between the personal and the socio-political is actually more complex than might first appear. There are in fact a number of different relations, which need to be distinguished.

(ii) *Relations between personal and socio-political liberation*
In his discussion of sin Baum makes several quite different distinctions, each of which can be referred to in terms of a contrast between the 'personal' and the 'social' (or 'political'):

(a) 'There is personal sin knowingly and freely chosen and there is social sin accompanied by collective blindness' (RA 193). As we have seen earlier, social sin is sin where the subject is society, its structures of domination, not the individual; also it affects the ideas and actions of individuals who are largely unconscious of it, rather than being a conscious wrongdoing. Let us call this contrast personal/social$_1$. In it social$_1$ sin includes both the structures of domination and the ideologies and false consciousness produced by them.

(b) But in MB what is known as personal sin is not knowingly and freely chosen. It is largely unconscious, like $social_1$ sin, yet the source of the blindness is not communal but familial, not structures of domination between groups but distortions in relations between parents and children. Baum explicitly distinguishes between these two kinds of unconscious, 'inherited' sin (RA 199). Both of them occur in the individual, and both differ on the one hand from $personal_1$ sin, which is conscious and deliberate wrongdoing by an individual, and on the other hand from social structures of domination, which occur in groups. Let us call them $personal_2$ sin and $social_2$ sin. $Personal_2$ sin is an individual's largely unconscious clinging to defensive and destructive deceptions from his familial past, instead of responding to the creative possibilities for authentic self-realization in the present. $Social_2$ sin is an individual's largely unconscious clinging to deceptive ideologies which disguise the plight of the oppressed and legitimate the interests of dominant groups to which he belongs, rather than responding to the needs of the oppressed in social action. In the case of both $personal_2$ sin and $social_2$ sin the opposite is a faith-conversion which occurs in the individual by divine grace.

(c) In the third contrast $personal_3$ sin includes *both* $personal_2$ and $social_2$ sin, for it includes all self-deceptive distortions in the minds of people, whether these occur individually or collectively. Where $personal_3$ sin has to do with the realm of the mental, $social_3$ sin has to do with the realm of power structures in social institutions. Liberation from $personal_3$ sin would involve both kinds of faith-conversion, whereas liberation from $social_3$ sin would involve a subversion and destruction of unjust power relations between groups in society. Since for Baum there is a dialectical interaction between the realm of the mental and the realm of power structures, neither $personal_3$ nor $social_3$ sin can be ignored.

Although Baum stresses socio-political liberation in RA, he frequently insists that liberation must be both personal and social. (See, for example, RA 199, 205, 208, 210, 272.) What he means by his stress on the social varies, however, according to which personal/social distinction he has in mind:

(a) It is no use simply appealing to people to live more virtuously, 'to live up to their moral ideals' (RA 196), for there is also $social_1$ sin, which consists of impersonal power structures in society and distortions of consciousness produced by these.

(b) It is no use simply helping people therapeutically to find $personal_2$ liberation from false consciousness. They must also find $social_2$ liberation from false consciousness, which involves a focus on social$_3$ liberation in society.

(c) It is no use focusing entirely on changes in the minds of people, even liberation from various kinds of false consciousness. There must also be changes in the power structures of society, social$_3$ liberation, for there is a dialectical relation between consciousness and society; each influences the other and is influenced by it.

All three contentions seem correct to me. The interesting issue in each case is how the two kinds of sin are interrelated and how much relative weight should be given to each, in theory and in practice. Baum says little concerning personal$_1$ sin and social$_1$ sin, that is, concerning their interrelation and their interdependence. The issues here are interesting and important, but I do not criticize Baum for not dealing with them, for they might well have occupied another book. Baum does, however, have something to say in the case of the other distinctions.

In RA personal$_2$ liberation is obviously subordinate to social$_2$ liberation; therapy is subordinate to politicization. In chapter 10 of RA Baum urges that psychotherapy be deprivatized. He criticizes orthodox psychoanalytic theory and practice for legitimating existing power structures in six different ways. In contrast, he applauds left-wing Freudianism for successfully minimizing these ideological elements and for providing an additional critical perspective on social evil. His choice between rival therapies seems to depend more on their social consequences than on their help to the individual. This perspective is also apparent in a recent article, 'Alienation and Reconciliation: A Socio-Theological Approach' (AR), in which he contrasts conservative and radical readings of Freud. Although radical therapy for Baum is superior as therapy, this consideration seems subordinate in what he says. Indeed, there is little in RA to suggest that personal$_2$ liberation is very valuable *in itself*, apart from its possible effects in delegitimating ideologies.

From conversation with Baum, however, it is clear that such an impression of RA is not true to his intent, for he does still regard personal$_2$ liberation as very important in itself. He does not retract MB, but in RA he is more aware of the need for a social critique of psychotherapy. He holds that it needs to be deprivatized along with individualistic religious piety and individualistic existentialism. In AR he criticizes both conservative psychoanalysis and Heideggerian existentialism (especially in its influence on Bultmann, Reinhold Niebuhr, and Tillich) for being ideological in not adequately acknowledging what I call social$_2$ sin and social$_3$ sin. And whereas he only hints at the possibility of a non-ideological existentialism, he presents a non-ideological reading of Freud. Thus, although there has been a shift away from Heideggerian existentialism since MB, psycho-analysis still has a place in Baum's thought, partly because it can apparently be purged of ideology.

But whereas Baum subjects therapeutic theory and practice to a systematic social critique, he does not subject social action (theory and practice) to a systematic therapeutic critique. One striking exception to this occurs when he is trying to understand the 'unrelenting Christian hatred and contempt for the Jews' (RA 82). Having given an outline of a sociological analysis, he says that this alone will not do. He goes on to describe various pathological religious trends in psychoanalytic terms: daughter-parent love/hate, projections of one's own repressed destructive side, transference of hostile feelings, etc. But there is no general contention that the sociological tradition as applied in reformist or radical social action today is in need of a therapeutic critique and that choices between alternative sociological positions might depend at least partly on their consequences for personal$_2$ liberation. It seems to me that just as some therapy needs to be deprivatized so as not to reinforce social repression through failure to acknowledge ideology and the social unconscious, so some social action needs to be 'decollectivized' so as not to reinforce inner repression through failure to acknowledge neurosis and the familial unconscious. Baum would seem to agree with much of this. For example, he says that Christian theologians ought to make a double analysis, social and personal. If they omit social analysis, they encourage the privatizing trend, but if they omit the personal analysis, 'they under-estimate personal freedom and in this way also distort the image of human life' (RA 205). Also, as we have seen, he holds that theology should be consciously 'critical' with reference not only to the social consequences but also the therapeutic consequences of its teaching. But which analysis or critique should predominate? Should we seek mainly personal$_2$ liberation or social$_2$ liberation?

My own position is that there is no simple answer to this question, for it is a matter of both the social context and the personal context. In some societies the *social* context is such that the most basic physiological needs of most people (food, shelter, clothing, medical help) are not being met, and a change in the political power structure could do much to remedy the situation. It seems to me that in such a situation concern for personal$_2$ liberation should generally be subordinate to concern for social$_2$ (and social$_3$) liberation. Here I find Abraham Maslow's typology of 'basic human needs'[11] very relevant. First there are physiological needs, then psychological deficiency-needs (which arise mainly in early familial relations and need some form of therapy), and finally psychological growth-needs (including the need to feel and express social concern). Needs at the physiological level must be to some extent satisfied if those at the psychological deficiency-need level are to be met at all, and deficiency-needs must be to some extent satisfied if growth-needs are to be met at all. Hence the most basic needs, the physiological, have a natural priority. But if the social context[12] is not one of widespread physiological deprivation, I do not think that either kind of liberation should in general predominate. It is then more a matter of *personal* context. What I mean by 'personal context' is the stage which a person is at in his personal development. One person may be sufficiently free from strident psychological deficiency-needs, having sufficiently resolved the three Eriksonian crises of infancy and also the crises of childhood and adolescence, to move with integrity into the realms of the interpersonal and the socio-political. If so, he can focus mainly on social$_2$ liberation. If not, he should focus mainly on personal$_2$ liberation. When I criticized Keen's individualistic focus on early Eriksonian crises, especially the initial struggle between trust and distrust, I said that in general Keen overemphasizes intrapersonal conditions of authentic life at the expense of interpersonal and communal goals. But for each person the relative emphasis should depend on where he, personally, is at. I am not suggesting that everyone who has unresolved psychological problems should undergo deep psychotherapy before venturing into any social action. Nor am I suggesting that some people are so free of such problems that they can sensibly focus their lives entirely on social$_2$ and social$_3$ liberation, without a thought concerning personal$_2$ liberation. It is a matter of relative emphasis.

But the issue of predominance is even more complex than I have indicated. Social$_2$ liberation involves a recognition of the need for social$_3$ liberation, whereas personal$_2$ liberation does not. And, as Baum insists, because of the dialectical causal relation between society and consciousness, it is futile to work solely for a changing of consciousness. Though social$_2$ liberation is itself a change of consciousness it recognizes this fact. Social$_2$ liberation issues in efforts to politicize people, changing their consciousness, but also in attempts to subvert the structures of domination. These attempts do not depend entirely for their success on how many people undergo social$_2$ liberation. Politicization and subversion are each goals which are important in themselves; and each also indirectly helps to bring about the other. In contrast with $social_2$ liberation, $personal_2$ liberation is deficient in that it is by itself oblivious to the need for $social_3$ liberation. Of course, as I have pointed out, $social_2$ liberation is deficient in that by itself it fails to recognize the familial unconscious. But there is an asymmetry in the two deficiencies, for $personal_2$ liberation does not, as I have depicted it, involve a commitment to undermine the familial structures which tend to produce pathology. There could be, of course, a concept of $personal_2$ liberation which includes this element; indeed, some radical therapists work towards such liberation. But we should note that such liberation moves in the direction of $social_2$ liberation. There is a shift from concern about one's own personal hang-ups and one's own personal realization to a concern about other people's; this can naturally broaden to a concern about non-psychological problems which other people have and so move towards $social_2$ liberation or politicization. Also, a radical form of $personal_2$ liberation could involve a shift from focusing entirely on changes of consciousness to a concern about changes in social structures. Although familial structures are between individuals rather than between groups, a concern about the pathological effects of familial structures can broaden into a concern about the pathological effects of group power structures. My main point, however, is that if we take $social_3$ liberation at all seriously, it presents a special challenge to any emphasis on $personal_2$ liberation in the non-radical, privatized form which I have depicted.

Another complication in the issue concerning predominance has appeared above (p 149): faith-conversion, whether therapeutic ($personal_2$) or political ($social_2$), is an inner change in the *individual*, not in social structures as such. The work of divine grace is located in the individual, changing his consciousness and his commitment. Faith-conversion belongs to $personal_3$ liberation rather than to $social_3$ liberation, and grace is discerned in the process of faith-conversion. And presumably the locus of divine grace is the most important locus in human life. But does not $social_2$ faith-conversion include discernment of divine grace at work in the processes of human history when the oppressed are liberated? According to Baum it does, but to me it seems obvious that a person will not see divine grace 'out there' in human history unless he first has experienced some form of $personal_3$ liberation. This is a private, inner happening, however broad the range of its perspective. I quote Baum's presentation again:

While we see, we are being enlightened, while we act, we are being carried forward, while we love, we are being saved from selfishness, and while we embrace all people in solidarity we are being freed inwardly to cross one boundary after another. (RA 291)

This experience of the paradox of grace is specially related to personal$_2$ liberation, for it requires a stance of active receptivity which is closely linked to a pervasive basic trust, a trust which personal$_2$ liberation both fosters and presupposes. Baum's statement that 'We are alive by a power that transcends us' only rings true to the experience of people who have known a considerable degree of personal$_2$ liberation, open to their own unconscious, to others, and to God. It seems to me that RA ends with the same religious core around which MB grew: a pervasive stance of active receptivity and responsive freedom.

There is one crucial addition in RA, however, which is expressed in Baum's very last sentence: 'God is not only the life of our life but also the abiding pain we experience in the face of a suffering, oppressed and hungry humanity' (RA 292). Here religious significance is discerned not only in liberation, whether personal or social, but also in the face of human need. The divine mystery is present not only as grace, as 'life of our life,' but also as unconditional moral claim. God is known not only as summons to self-realization but also as summons to self-commitment. Religious faith is not only Paul's 'I, yet not I, but Christ liveth in me' (Gal 2:20); it is also the discernment of Christ in the need of any of the least of his brothers and sisters (Matt 25:30).

How are the two kinds of faith and the two ideas of God related together? It seems to me that Ian Ramsey sheds light on this question, though my application of Ramsey to Baum is tentative. Baum's acknowledgment of the gift-dimension in life, the enabling grace which encompasses human life, is pervasive and therefore transcendent. And his acknowledgment of the moral claim of the oppressed is unconditional, overriding other considerations, and therefore also transcendent. For Baum, as for Ramsey, there is a crucial move in identifying the two transcendent mysteries as one mystery. For Baum this is not easy. I quote him more fully:

In today's world, it has often become difficult to worship this transcendent mystery since God is not only the life of our life but also the abiding pain we experience in the face of a suffering, oppressed and hungry humanity. (RA 292)

Baum's main theological emphasis in RA, however, is on the grace of God at work in social$_2$ and social$_3$ liberation, politicizing persons and subverting structures of domination. This emphasis leads me to make two criticisms of his transformist theology, both concerning his account of social$_3$ liberation. One concerns structures of domination and humanizing social structures and the other concerns the alleged discernment of God in social$_3$ liberation.

(iii) *Criticisms of Baum's transformist theology*

Structures of domination and other social structures
Are all institutional power structures structures of domination? Is all legitimating of existing power structures wrong? If not, what kinds of structures are good? In MB, as I noted in my 1971 version of this essay, Baum says that 'healthy institutions multiply good' (MB 119) and that 'the beneficial effects are comparatively independent of the generosity, or the lack of it, of the men involved' (MB 120). Baum briefly suggests in MB that there are social processes whereby pathological trends within institutions are checked and health is promoted. Presumably these processes enable man to become more truly man in the sense that the impersonal relations within institutions become 'healthier' or more 'humanizing.' But is this possible? And if so, what processes promote it? What kinds of institutional power structures should countervailing movements try to establish as they gain power?

Baum does not say much concerning such questions in RA. Indeed, by the end of the book a reader might well have the impression that for Baum *all* power structures between groups are structures of domination which ought to be eliminated. RA is to some extent a polemical work, an attack on theologies which blandly and blindly support structures of domination and the ideologies which legitimate such structures. Baum does not soften the impact of his onslaught on theological false consciousness by dealing extensively with issues which could become tangential, defensive evasions. So he is open to misunderstanding. For example, one might mistakenly conclude that his political stance is that of an individualistic anarchist, opposed to all power relations among people and to all institutions that are dominant in any society. This is not his view, and he is actually very interested in issues concerning how power structures and institutions can be humanized – e.g. in the Roman Catholic Church. Concerning many of these, his practical stance would lead to comments which are *both* legitimizing and critical. This means that a transformist theology would be both legitimating and critical in relation to many social structures. But as to how this works out in detail Baum is not clear. I hope that as he continues his work in sociology he will shed light on many of the questions I have noted.

God and social$_3$ liberation

Earlier I expressed doubt whether someone will be able to discern divine grace as social$_3$ liberation in human history unless he has already discerned it within his own life. I want to make a further criticism: Is it wise to try to discern divine activity as social$_3$ liberation in human history at all? Is it actually possible to identify what God is doing politically in the world and then join with him? If one thinks it possible, does not this often lead to fanaticism? It is one thing to come to recognize structures of domination and ideologies and to identify oneself with the dominated, convinced that God has been at work in this process of politicization. It is a further step to decide what to do politically, for example, which countervailing movement to support. Can one be sure that God supports movement A rather than movement B?

Baum is aware of the dangers of fanaticism. Indeed, he differs from Marx in saying that all groups, including the oppressed class and those who seek its liberation, distort the truth to serve their own collective interest and must be open to criticism (RA 34). So the countervailing movement with which one identifies oneself must be open to criticism, though only from a standpoint of solidarity with it (RA 289). But he does hold that God is at work in social liberation$_3$. It seems to me that it would be both wiser and more consistent with his overall position to locate the historical work of divine grace in the minds of people who are being politicized, rather than in impersonal processes of subversion which bring about social liberation$_3$. In his own account of social$_2$ faith-conversion the decision concerning strategy (reformist or radical) is a further step, not in itself part of what God inspires. By grace one becomes aware of social sin and the call to be identified with the powerless, but the choice of a countervailing movement is left open. Indeed, even before the choice between a radical and a reformist movement arises there may be error in one's judgment concerning what counts as social sin and concerning who are the oppressed. And as Baum himself points out (RA 136–7), it is sometimes not at all obvious whether or not a contemporary set of ideas is ideological or utopian, for example, ideas concerning the need to limit economic growth.

I should concede, of course, that even in the fundamental change of personality which political faith-conversion involves there will be sin as well as grace. One's indignation against structures of domination may be coloured by infantile rage against any personal restrictions, and one's identification with the sufferings of the oppressed may be coloured by a need to enlarge one's own self-pity by drawing in others as examples of the same human pain. Locating divine grace in social$_2$ (or personal$_2$) liberation is not an insurance against self-deception and fanaticism. But it seems to me that there is less risk of fanaticism if we do not go on to locate divine grace as well in social$_3$ liberation.

In RA there are two additional considerations which might lead Baum to move away from the position I have been criticizing. First, I noted earlier his sociological account of a pattern in human history which provides a basis for hoping that human society can be renewed even though at present it is oppressive. The most important element in the pattern is a kind of social$_2$ liberation: the free and inspired response of charismatic figures and others to the dehumanizing effects of the current structures of domination, a response which involves a new critical awareness of social evil and an identification with the oppressed. Secondly, I noted earlier Baum's final words in RA, in which the divine presence is discerned, not in social$_3$ liberation, but in an unconditional moral claim in the face of needy humanity.

I am not proposing that Baum *deny* that God is *somehow* at work in social$_3$ liberation. As part of a pervasive faith in divine Providence one can hold that God is somehow at work in ways which do not depend on human receptivity, whether conscious or unconscious, just as God is somehow at work in nature. Having criticized MB for the restriction of divine grace to the realm of responsive freedom in stark contrast with a purely 'natural' realm, I cannot consistently propose that RA restrict divine grace in a similar way in stark contrast with a realm of impersonal social structures. What I propose is that in both cases what divine liberation brings is a change of consciousness which should include new attitudes towards that which lies *outside* the realm of responsive freedom (in which God brings faith-conversion to those who are open to receive it). Personal$_2$ liberation should bring new attitudes towards nature, and social$_2$ liberation should bring new attitudes towards impersonal social structures. In both cases the attitudes involve a recognition of the religious significance of the total context within which faith-conversion occurs.[13]

In chapter 6 issues concerning 'God at work in history' will arise again. In the next chapter, however, our attention shifts not only from such issues but from most of what we have been considering in the first four chapters, where religious *faith* has been our overall focus. In the course of the presentation I have linked theology closely with normative anthropology, however, so that questions concerning religious faith and questions concerning *authentic human life* are inseparable. In Baum's thought, for example, personal$_2$ and social$_2$ liberation both involve a conversion from sin, from a *dehumanized* way of living, and the conversion is a *faith*-conversion. Questions concerning a 'human' or an 'inhuman' life-style are *moral* questions within what is often called an 'ethics of being' in contrast with an 'ethics of doing.' An ethics of being is concerned with what kind of a person I ought to *be*, whereas an ethic of doing is concerned with what kinds of things I ought to *do*. Obviously the two kinds of ethic are not completely separable. Indeed, in chapter 6 I shall try to bring together religious faith, an ethic of being, and an ethic of doing as one coherent, overall religious viewpoint. But in the next chapter I shall prepare the way for this by exploring some important issues in an ethic of doing. In one way we shall be moving back to a kind of reflection which characterized chapter 1, for I shall be once again stressing the importance of *language*. In chapter 5, however, the emphasis will be on the language of morality rather than the language of religion.

5

Paul Ramsey on
Exceptionless Moral Rules

In 1968 I published an article entitled 'Love, Situations and Rules,'[1] in which my concluding section was an attack on the claim that there are exceptionless moral rules. In the same volume there appeared a long article by Paul Ramsey which he devoted to their defence: 'The Case of the Curious Exception' (CCE). I decided to write a reply as a way of continuing scholarly debate concerning this important issue. As I pondered my reply, however, it became apparent that there were other, more important reasons for undertaking a thorough investigation of Ramsey's article. First of all, Ramsey is one of the most important contemporary Christian ethicists,[2] and CCE is a major statement of the theoretical framework which he presupposes in his many writings on specific ethical problems. As such it deserves very careful consideration. Since the article is very complex and difficult, I tried to extract what I took to be its essence, its main lines of argument. A second reason for studying the article in depth was that, although Ramsey focuses it on exceptionless moral rules, he does so in a way which raises, implicitly or explicitly, many of the most fundamental issues in ethics. As I responded to the challenge of his arguments against exceptionism, I found myself not only refining and revising my own arguments and claims concerning exceptionless moral rules but also venturing into what was for me new ethical territory. For example, I began serious exploration of a mode of moral reflection which is central in much non-utilitarian ethics, both secular and Christian. Instead of calculating consequences, the moral agent explores the *meaning* of a moral term in the context of the moral tradition from which it comes as he explores a particular situation of moral choice. A third reason for probing Ramsey's essay was my uneasiness concerning what seemed to be authoritarian and legalistic elements in his way of depicting the relation between Christian faith and moral decision-making. Since CCE makes use of my own analysis of divine action and human response as 'correlative performatives' and is rather similar to some of my own earlier theological views as expressed in *The Logic of Self-Involvement*,[3] I felt a special need to clarify my criticisms and to begin a search for a better account.

This chapter is the same as the resulting essay which I first published in 1971[4] except for a few updating revisions and a postscript. In the postscript I criticize the foundation of Ramsey's theological ethics (love conceived as covenant-fidelity) in a way which relates my discussion of Ramsey to issues which have arisen in previous chapters. The chapter as a whole deals with subtleties and complexities of an 'ethic of doing' which may be of little interest to some readers who are mainly interested in matters of religious faith and an 'ethic of being.' The chapter does provide a useful background for the section in chapter 6 entitled 'moral vocabulary and authority,' which summarizes many of its conclusions. It is possible, however, to skip or to skim this chapter without seriously jeopardizing one's understanding of chapter 6.

Ramsey supports his position concerning exceptionless moral rules by a series of complex arguments. In what follows I try to show that some of his arguments are dubious, whereas others, though not conclusive, are powerful and illuminating. Indeed, he forces me to concede that some moral rules are 'virtually' exceptionless. I have selected seven of his main arguments for consideration.

I

His first main argument depends on a distinction between *singular* exceptions to moral rules and *universal* exceptions, so our first step is to clarify this distinction. Suppose that 'Never do X' is a moral rule.[5] (X is a *kind* of action such as lying, adultery, stealing, etc.) A singular or particular exception to the rule has the form '... except in *this* situation S 1.' A universal exception has the form '... except in this *kind* of situation S.' A singular exception is a violation of a moral rule. A universal exception is a revision of a moral rule. Hence, if someone talks about an 'exceptionless' moral rule, he may mean one of two very different things. He may mean a rule which cannot be violated, or he may mean a rule which cannot be revised.

Another distinction which needs to be noted immediately is one between two senses of 'can': the logical and the moral (or, more generally, the normative). The question 'Can there be an exceptionless moral rule?' may mean 'Is it logically possible for there to be an exceptionless moral rule?' Or the question may mean 'Assuming that it is logically possible for there to be an exceptionless moral rule, can there ever be an adequate moral justification (or, more generally, an adequate normative justification) for holding that any moral rule is exceptionless?

Ramsey's first attack is on two forms of singular exceptionism which some theologians espouse. These may be called 'calculative' exceptionism and 'creative' exceptionism. The calculative exceptionist holds that a calculation of the beneficial consequences of violating a moral rule in situation $S1$ may morally justify a violation. What counts as 'beneficial' depends directly on an ultimate moral norm: happiness, love, self-realization, or whatever it my be. 'Creative' exceptionists, according to Ramsey, 'seem to speak in more intuitive terms of actions that are "unique" and in their uniqueness "creative" of new moral departures. They seem to regard moral action as an unrepeatable spiritual venture that alone can be truly sensitive to the demands of the hour and fully open to the needs of other persons' (CCE 68). Hence a creative exceptionist will violate a moral rule in a particular situation $S1$ on the ground that $S1$ is unique and unrepeatable and that his own moral insight into $S1$ leads him to do something which happens to violate the rule.

Ramsey's attack on calculative and creative exceptionists involves two steps. The first step, which I go along with, is to show that any moral exception to a moral rule must be, in principle, universal rather than merely singular. This step depends on a definition of the word 'moral' such that any moral judgment must, as a logically necessary condition, be universalizable. That is, if a man judges that he ought to do X in situation $S1$, he implies that anyone (that is, anyone similar in the morally relevant respects)[6] ought to do X in situations which are similar to $S1$ in the morally relevant respects – that is, in situations of kind S. Thus no judgment can be a moral judgment unless it implies a moral rule. And no judgment concerning an exception to a moral rule can be moral unless it implies that the exception applies in all similar cases. Any singular exception to a moral rule, if moral, must imply a universal exception. Thus if moral judgments are by definition universalizable, singular exceptionism involves a logical contradiction: a moral exception which is merely singular and hence not moral.

If a calculative or creative exceptionist is committed to singular exceptionism, he is involved in logical contradiction unless he rejects the universalizability requirement for moral judgments – a requirement which seems to me to be part of morality as conceived in Judaeo-Christian and western secular moral traditions. But a calculative or creative exceptionist can retain the substance of his position without being committed to singular exceptionism. He can concede that any moral exception to a moral rule has to be universal, and hold his ground against the second step in Ramsey's attack, which we shall now consider.

According to Ramsey, 'A principle or moral rule cannot be challenged without confirming its validity – *"except ..."* – then must follow good moral reasons for the exception. Without these, no exception; with these, a class of right actions will have been defined within or beside the rule' (CCE 72). That is, an exception to a moral rule is not morally justified unless the agent is able to 'characterize' (CCE 68) the action, stating what features of situation S1 constitute the reason for the exception. The calculative and creative exceptionists thus fail to justify their exceptions. The calculative exceptionist merely states that a *quantity* of benefits will result from violation of the rule; he does not refer to special qualitative *features* of situation and of consequences. The creative exceptionist merely claims that situation S1 is unique, and refuses to state a list of features which, if repeated, would justify an exception again; perhaps God or an Ideal Observer could state the list, but it would be a useless labour, for the situation is repeatable only in theory, not in reality.

According to Ramsey, neither form of exceptionism can morally justify its exceptions. Let us consider calculative exceptionism first. Ramsey draws a legitimate distinction between two broad kinds of universal exception: (a) where we give a description of the exception-making features of the situation and of the consequences of the exceptional action; (b) where we give a quantitative estimate of the beneficial consequences of the exceptional action. Consider these two examples:

(a) Never lie except to save life, as is the case in situation S1.
(b) Never lie except when lying, as compared with not lying, will promote at least quantity Q of benefit, as it does in this situation S1. (If the comparative benefit of lying is less than Q, don't lie.)

Note that the exception in (b) is not singular but universal, The calculative exceptionist need not deny that if any agent were in a situation similar in morally relevant respects, the exception would apply.[7] Where he differs from Ramsey is in his designation of morally relevant respects. The universal reason which he gives for making an exception is not expressed as a description of qualitative features of the action in the situation as it is in (a), 'to save life'; rather, it is expressed in a quantitative estimate of comparative benefits. The term 'benefits' is used to refer to a balance of non-moral good over evil. In some cases the main good consists in the prevention of an evil or harm. In such cases (b) could be revised so as to read: 'Never lie except when lying, as compared with not lying, will prevent as much harm as lying does in this situation $S1$.'

Example (b), then, involves a universal exception. It designates a class of situations in which an exception is morally justified. In showing that singular exceptionism is self-contradictory if any moral judgment is by definition universalizable, Ramsey has not shown that a universal exception must be stated in terms of qualitative features rather than quantitative benefits. As we shall see, there are serious problems raised by quantitative-benefit (QB) exception clauses: whether the benefits are always morally relevant, how we weigh quantity in relation to qualitative features, etc. But QB clauses cannot be prohibited merely by an appeal to the universalizability requirement.

What about creative exceptionism? As Ramsey presents it for consideration, it is not an 'exceptionism' at all, for there are no explicit moral rules, and thus no exceptions are logically possible. But in order to have a creative exceptionism to consider, let us consider the following position: There are some moral rules, for example, rules concerning lying. Any particular moral judgment, *qua* moral – including a judgment concerning an exception to a moral rule – implies a universal judgment. But this universal judgment need not be formulated, for the universalizability requirement is purely *formal*.[8] The creative exceptionist concedes that if any agent and situation were to be similar in all the morally relevant respects, then the same kind of action ought to be done; but these respects are too complex or too elusive to be stated in a formulated rule; and even if they could be formulated, the rule would in fact apply only to this one case. Though repeatable in theory, the case is unrepeatable in practice. Hence an exception to a moral rule, though formally or theoretically universal, is morally justifiable even though the universal exception is not *stated* (and cannot be stated, except by an Ideal Observer). Hence our creative exceptionist might hold the following, for example:

(c)   Never tell a lie except when in a situation $S1$ or in any situation S which resembles this situation $S1$ in all the morally relevant respects. And don't ask me to state specifically what these respects are, or expect that any such situation will ever occur again!

The universalizability requirement for moral judgments does not commit us to stating in each case a universal rule or universal exception to a rule. Perhaps we should do this sometimes, but on other occasions we would surely be wiser to follow the advice of a creative exceptionist and refuse to do so. On the one hand, there is the problem of sheer *complexity*. What I have in mind here is not merely the number and variety of the moral considerations which are weighed, but also the fact that their *relative weight* cannot be schematized so as to have a rule which would apply with precision to any situation other than S1. On the other hand, there is the *elusiveness* of many of the elements in some situations of moral choice, especially those which involve intimate human relations and personal life-style. Especially here there are elements which elude definite conceptualization: feelings and attitudes and influences and idiosyncratic ways of viewing oneself and others. Even a very articulate and sensitive novelist or poet can only sketch and suggest some of these, and they are often unrepeatable in practice; yet they rightly enter into the heart of some moral decision-making. Along these lines Iris Murdoch in her novel *The Bell*[9] vividly (and, I think, deliberately) illustrates the sheer irrelevance of a formulated-rule morality in much of our moral life.

To sum up: Ramsey has shown that there can be no singular exceptions to moral rules. But he has failed to show that there can be no universal quantity-of-benefit exceptions or that there can be no universal unformulated unrepeatable-in-practice exceptions. Now let us consider a new point. If such exceptions are made, they weaken or undermine the moral rules. Ramsey rightly holds that universal exceptions do not weaken or undermine moral rules, but he has in mind cases where the rule revision is formulated in qualitative-feature descriptions, for example, 'Never lie *except to save life*.' But if a moral rule is open to exception whenever a similar quantity of benefit would result, or whenever a creative moral agent judges in favour of an exception, the rule is less firm and strong.

II

Indeed, Ramsey's next claim is that a calculative exceptionism *destroys* any moral rule to which it is applied by turning the moral rule into a mere maxim or summary concerning past cases. Each case is then to be decided as it arises by direct appeal to an ultimate norm such as utility. For example, Ramsey claims (CCE 84–5) that if a moral rule is modified in the following way, it is destroyed:

(d)   We should not commit adultery except when it would do more good on the whole to do so.

I agree with Ramsey that the most plausible way to interpret this is as the replacement of a moral rule ('We should not commit adultery') by a maxim. The maxim would be elaborated as follows:

(d)*A*   Usually adultery results in less good than non-adultery (since it usually causes considerable evil), so usually it is wrong to commit adultery; but in each and every case we have to decide solely on the basis of which alternative will, in the particular case, produce more overall good.

I have called the example '(d)*A*)' because it interprets (d) in an *act*-utilitarian way. An act-utilitarian appeals only to his ultimate norm in each particular case. His maxim is merely a guide, based on a summary of judgments concerning previous cases. The maxim does not provide a distinct and independent consideration alongside the application of the ultimate norm.

But we have seen that a calculative exceptionist could say something very different:

(e)   We should not commit adultery except when adultery, as compared with non-adultery, will promote at least quantity Q of benefit, as it does in this situation $S1$.

This is best elaborated in a rule-utilitarian way:

(e)*R*   The rule 'We ought not to commit adultery', is a good moral rule, whose general observance produces great overall good in society. Therefore the rule should be followed except when breaking it will promote at least quantity Q of benefit, when compared with the benefit of not breaking it. Anything less than quantity Q is insufficient to outweigh the fact that one is breaking this good rule.

Here the rule provides a moral consideration which is distinct from, and independent of, any calculation of the good and evil consequences of following or breaking the rule in a particular case. The rule is weakened, of course; but it is not destroyed. In (d)*A*, as Ramsey rightly claims, a quantitative-benefit (QB) exception clause destroys a moral rule, turning it into an act-utilitarian maxim. But if a moral rule is understood in a rule-utilitarian way as in (e)R (or, indeed, in a deontological way), it is not turned into an act-utilitarian maxim. It still has an independent weight, so that an agent follows it in some cases where breaking it would produce more benefit than following it – that is, in cases where the comparative benefit of breaking the rule is less than quantity Q.

The position set forth in (e)R involves various difficulties, some of which I shall soon note. Here I want merely to refute Ramsey's objection. If Ramsey were correct, a rule-utilitarian could never appeal directly to his ultimate norm to justify a universal exception to a moral rule, for he would thereby have changed the moral rule into an act-utilitarian maxim. If Ramsey were correct, any such direct appeal to an ultimate norm would destroy the moral rule; that is, it would be logically impossible for a moral rule to have a QB exception clause. Thus, if Ramsey were correct, one of the main arguments against exceptionless moral rules would have been disqualified before it could enter the fray, namely the argument that we should add a QB exception clause to many moral rules, '... except when following the rule would cause great harm to others.' But Ramsey is not correct. His argument only holds if any QB exception has to be like (d)A rather than (e)R. When we consider (e)R we see that it is logically possible for a moral rule to have a QB exception clause. Of course, we still have to ask, '*Should* all moral rules have a QB exception clause?' for perhaps some moral rules should not. This is a normative issue, which we shall consider later in relation to some of Ramsey's later normative arguments.

An exception clause to a rule-utilitarian rule or to a deontological rule often refers not to quantitative benefits but to definite qualitative features, for example, '... except to save life.' Such a qualitative exemption condition is sometimes preferred because of the notorious difficulties involved in trying to calculate quantitative benefits. I merely note these difficulties here, without pursuing them. Instead, I want to draw attention to a further difficulty which arises for (e)R, even if quantitative benefits can be calculated satisfactorily. According to (e)R, we judge that the rule can outweigh a quantity of benefit (namely, any less than Q) which might be produced by breaking it. On what basis do we decide that the rule has *this* weight, no more, no less? One way of deciding avoids the problem of weighing incommensurables, though the procedure suggested is sometimes difficult to use. On this procedure a QB exception clause is itself appraised in a rule-utilitarian way. That is, we estimate that the general observance of the modified rule (with its specific QB exception clause) will produce more overall good in society than the general observance of the unmodified rule, or of a modified rule in which the quantity is greater or less than Q. An alternative way of deciding involves a weighing of incommensurables, yet the procedure is somehow frequently used in practice. On this procedure the QB exception clause is appraised in an act-utilitarian way (without asking 'What if most people observed the modified rule?'), while the unmodified rule is appraised in a rule-utilitarian way. Somehow, due weight is given to both approaches and a compromise decision is made. Similarly, there is sometimes a compromise worked out between the moral weight of deontological rule and the moral weight of an act-utilitarian concern to avoid serious harm where this would be caused by following the rule in some situations. Such compromises are part of everyday morality, but they raise serious problems for ethical theory, for their logic or rationale is obscure. I should note that these problems exist, without trying to solve them here.

Perhaps I should also draw attention to an assumption which is crucial in my distinction between (d)A and (e)R, the assumption that rule-utilitarianism is not reducible to act-utilitarianism, the assumption that moral rules can have independent weight for a utilitarian. It has been challenged by some able philosophers[10], but I am not convinced by their arguments.

In this section I have attacked Ramsey's claim that a calculative exceptionist's QB exception clause destroys any moral rule to which it is attached. In the next section I shall support his attack on one position which, if tenable, would exclude the possibility of any exceptionless moral rules.

III

Ramsey's argument is directed against the following position:

There *cannot* by any exceptionless moral rules because, so far as human moral judgment alone is concerned, we cannot know and we cannot formulate rules of conduct that are both certain in their determination of wrongfulness or praiseworthiness and certain as to the description of the actions to which these verdicts apply. This point of view holds that if we are certain that a sort of action is wrong we are uncertain about the actions to which to apply this judgment, and if we are certain about the action we are talking about we remain uncertain whether it should be judged to be wrong or praiseworthy. (CCE, my italics; Ramsey's italics omitted)

A philosopher or theologian who supports such a position may point to the fact that, for many moral agents, the only exceptionless moral rules are those which are 'elastic' in the meaning of their descriptive terms, so that the agent is free to make a moral judgment as to whether or not the description applies. Thus a moral agent may agree that cruelty or murder is always wrong, but he has to judge what is to count as cruelty or murder. Not all infliction of pain is cruelty, and not all killing is murder. For such a moral agent there might be a moral rule which describes a prohibited kind of action in a neutral and definite way so that there is no doubt as to what the rule applies to, but such a rule would probably have some exceptions built into it and, more important, it should be held open to further exceptions. Such a moral agent might agree that it is wrong to tell someone something which one believes to be false, intending to get him to believe this, except in such-and-such kinds of situation; but the rule would have to be revisable in relation to new or unmentioned kinds of situations.

It is a fact, then, that for some moral agents moral rules must be either elastic in meaning or open to further exceptions. But this fact does not prove that there *cannot* be an exceptionless definite-action moral rule. As Ramsey points out, the description of a prohibited kind of action can be as definite as any other descriptions which we give of things or events; the only element of judgment which is necessary is one which is involved in *any* application of universals to particulars. And the description can be expressed in morally neutral terms so that the identification of an action as one which falls under the description does not depend on one's moral stance at all. What counts as 'cruelty' depends on one's moral stance, but what counts as 'telling someone something which one believes to be false, intending to get him to believe this' does not depend on one's moral stance.

There *can* be an exceptionless definite-action moral rule. Indeed, the position which Ramsey attacks, though it sometimes seems to imply that such a rule is logically impossible, is mainly concerned with denying that such a rule would be prudent or moral in view of the limitations of our human wisdom. So the real question is '*Should* anyone accept such a rule?' We shall be in a better position to consider this question later, when we have considered a fourth argument in Ramsey.

IV

This argument is best understood in terms of the distinction, which we have just been considering, between two kinds of moral rule. The rules differ in the type of description given of the kind of action which is prohibited. One rule has a neutral and relatively definite description, the other a non-neutral and relatively indefinite description. A traditional moral rule, such as the prohibition of adultery, can be interpreted in either of these two ways. On the one hand, 'adultery' may be defined as 'sexual intercourse between two people, one or both of whom is married to someone else.' The expression 'sexual intercourse' can be more precisely defined in bodily and physiological terms, and a more precise definition can also be given to the expression 'married.' Then whether or not anyone approves or disapproves of an action to which the definite description, he has no room for doubt as to whether or not it does apply. On the other hand, 'adultery' may be understood as 'unfaithfulness to the marriage bond' or 'marital infidelity.' This is a far less definite description of a species of action, and it is non-neutral. It does not necessarily exclude every case of 'adultery' in the neutral, precise sense of the word. Rather, it excludes whatever violates the mutual fidelity which is intrinsic to marriage. In order to understand what adultery is, one has to understand what marriage is. The meaning of 'adultery,' though not completely vague, is elastic, open to interpretation on the basis of insight. Though marital infidelity is not the same as infidelity in general, what *counts* as marital infidelity cannot always be determined in advance.

Similarly, 'lying' may be defined as 'telling someone something which one believes to be false, intending to get him to believe it' or, in an elastic way, as 'withholding the truth from someone to whom truth is *due*.' And 'stealing' may be defined as 'taking something which by positive law belongs to someone else, without his permission,' or, in an elastic way, as 'taking, without permission, something which by positive law belongs to someone else, and to which one has no *moral* right in relation to the purposes of the institution of private property.'

Ramsey notes that the way in which putative exceptions are considered varies in accordance with whether the key descriptive term – 'adultery,' 'lying,' 'stealing' – is understood in a precise or in an elastic way. On the one hand, there may be a universal exemption because of *exempting conditions* (which I shall call an 'E-approach'). On the other hand, there may be no exception at all, but, instead, a qualification or explication or extension of the *meaning* of the rule in relation to a new or unmentioned kind of situation (I shall call this an 'M-approach'). With reference to the rule against adultery, Ramsey asks us to consider roughly the following alternatives as possible justifications of the action of a Mrs Bergmeier (in a case made famous by Joseph Fletcher):[11]

(f)*E*   We should not commit adultery (i.e. sexual intercourse where one or both parties are married to another) unless a married woman is in a concentration camp whose regulations are that only pregnant women are let go, where her husband and family imperatively need her, and where there is no other recourse. (*exempting-condition exception*)

(f)*M*   We should not commit adultery (i.e. marital infidelity). The implicit meaning of marital 'fidelity' and 'infidelity,' understood more explicitly, and qualified in relation to the woman in the concentration camp, shows us that her action was not adulterous, for it expressed and reinforced her fidelity to her husband and family. (qualified-*meaning*)

Ramsey prefers (f)M to (f)*E* as a justification. Similarly he prefers an *M*-version to an *E*-version in the following examples:

(g)*E*   Lying is telling someone something one believes to be false, intending to get him to believe it. We should not lie, except when this would gravely endanger life, for example, revealing the whereabouts of a Jew to the Gestapo.

(g)*M*   Lying is withholding the truth from someone to whom the truth is due. We should not lie. The meaning of 'lying' does not, on reflection, exclude saying something false so as not to endanger life, for example, saying something false to the Gestapo who ask the whereabouts of a Jew.

(h)*E*   Stealing is taking, without permission, something belonging by positive law to someone else. We ought not to steal, except when our family is starving and we have no other recourse but to steal some food from someone who has plenty.

(h)*M*   Stealing is taking, without permission, something belonging by positive law to someone else, to which we have no moral right in relation to the purposes of the institution of private property. We ought not to steal. The meaning of 'stealing' does not, on reflection, exclude taking food from someone who has plenty, if one's family is starving and one has no other recourse.

Are the *E*-versions and the *M*-versions of (f), (g), and (h) exceptionless? Let us consider the *E*-versions first. The fact that an *E*-version moral rule already has universal exceptions built into it does not show that it is, or that it is not, 'exceptionless' in the sense of 'closed to any *further* universal exceptions.' An *E*-approach, by itself, does not settle the matter; additional reasons would have to be given if someone holds that an *E*-version moral rule is 'exceptionless.' At first sight, however, it seems that an *M*-approach, by itself, closes a rule to any genuine revision. No universal exception clauses are allowed. All that is permitted is a deeper understanding of the implicit meaning of 'adultery,' 'lying,' or 'stealing' in relation to new experience. Thus when Ramsey gives reasons for holding that an *M*-version of some moral rules is superior to an *E*-version, he might be interpreted as if he were thereby giving reasons for holding that these rules are exceptionless. We shall see later, however, that whether or not *M*-approach rules are *genuinely* exceptionless depends on whether or not they are interpreted narrowly or liberally; and Ramsey's interpretation tends to be liberal. Meanwhile it is important to consider the three reasons which Ramsey gives for the superiority of an *M*-approach over an *E*-approach.

First, an *M*-approach is superior in some cases because this approach has been a necessary part of civilized life as such:

Judgments within the ethico-legal system and within the ethico-political system and within the moral constitution are always of this order. For example, the whole history of Anglo-American liberties can be written as a history of the meaning of one verdict contained in Magna Carta: 'No freeman shall ...' That is, the history of our liberties can be written as the history of the deepening and broadening of the meaning of being a 'freeman,' its qualification, extension, application, the defined-features relevant to a judgment falling under it, etc. (CCE 97)

Similarly there has been agreement that murder is always wrong, and the *meaning* of the offence-term 'murder' has been gradually clarified and refined in our legal tradition. 'The wrongfulness of it does not infect or inhibit its being of a fairly definite sort. There is no circularity here, and certainly not emptiness. One is simply accumulating the feature-relevant meaning of the offense-term and out of the relevant and ruling moral principles themselves elaborating more narrowly defined discriminations of right from wrong killings' (CCE 97). If we had merely a neutral description of prohibited kinds of killing, this would not, Ramsey implies, have allowed for such a developing legal and moral code. Thus Ramsey's first reason for supporting an *M*-approach to some moral rules is an appeal to an allegedly necessary constituent in *moral tradition*.

His second reason is an appeal to what I shall call a *'moral a priori.'*[12] He says that we can and should bring to situations a moral framework rather than being totally dependent on situations in making moral judgments. He insists on the 'power of morality itself to make an imprint upon human life, the capacity of moral principle to mold and shape our lives and to specify out of its own nature the moral terrain' (CCE 90). He says that if the substantive moral relations of a covenantal morality are to survive, they 'must shape the future and not be shaped indefinitely by an expectation of future morally significant revision of our fidelities by consequences to come' (CCE 34). A further *meaning* of a moral principle 'may be brought to light by experience; it certainly "arises with" experience. But it does not "arise from" conditioning experiences. It "arises from" the implied meaning of principles as stipulations within these principles or terms' (CCE 91). Thus a new situation is an occasion for reflection concerning a moral principle, but it is viewed through the conceptual framework provided by that principle. For example, Mrs Bergmeier's problem is seen in terms of marital fidelity as a loyalty to her husband and family, and not merely in terms of an exempting condition or of a QB calculation.

Ramsey's third reason for supporting an M-approach to some moral rules is one which gives a specifically Christian backing and interpretation to his stress on moral *tradition* and moral *a priorism*. I shall consider this separately, later on. At the moment I should make some comments on his first two reasons.

My first comment is that if the M-version is liberal, if it involves a very 'elastic' meaning for the key moral terms – as it does in $(f)M$, $(g)M$, and $(h)M$ – it generally leads to exactly the same moral decisions as an E-version, and it is in practice also as open to revision as an E-version. The possible further revision is called a 'deeper understanding of the meaning' rather than an 'exception,' but if in practice the two approaches have the same openness towards revision, they equally deny that the rule is genuinely exceptionless. If an M-approach is liberal throughout, then none of its rules are genuinely exceptionless, even if the wording of the rules cannot be changed. If not only the meaning of the word, but the wording itself can be changed, than of course the approach is even more liberal. But the main point to an M-approach in contrast with an E- approach is that on an M-approach one does not change the wording by adding clauses concerning exemptions, restrictions of scope, etc; instead, on a liberal M-approach one changes (or 'interprets') the meaning of the wording.

My second comment is that although a *non*-liberal *M*-approach does propose genuinely exceptionless moral rules, it does so because it is really a disguised *E*-approach in its understanding of the rules. For example, if Mrs Bergmeier's decision is said to be morally wrong, this judgment presupposes that 'no adultery' is a verbally unrevisable rule and that 'adultery' has an *E*-version meaning ('sexual intercourse where one or both are married to another'). So we must ask whether there *should* be an unrevisable *E*-version moral rule? This is still our unresolved question. It remains for us in this form because a non-liberal *M*-approach amounts to an *E*-approach plus a denial of revisability.

My third comment does not bear so directly on the possibility of unrevisable moral rules. Rather, I shall express a reservation concerning the alleged superiority of an *M*-approach to moral rules. Consider, for example, Ramsey's claim that 'there could be no good charitable reason for saying that picking someone else's apples to save life belongs among the meanings of "theft," or for saying that mere verbal inaccuracies of speech to save life belongs among the meanings of "lying." These were extensions and explanatory principles "conditioned" by principles itself' (CCE 91–2). I agree that it would be uncharitable to use the words 'theft' and 'lying' in this way if we think that our moral (legal, religious) tradition forces us to hold that theft and lying are exceptionless (unrevisable in their wording). But if we do not think this about our tradition, or have no such tradition, if we do not hold an exceptionless rule in these matters, then charity does not require us to give such an elastic meaning to 'theft' or 'lying.' And the demands of clarity, rather than charity, would be operative – in the reverse direction. The clear and straightforward thing to say is that theft and lying are prohibited *except to save life* (*E*-approach). Nor is it plausible to claim that an exception clause 'except to save life' is best understood, not as expressing and *E*-approach exemption condition, but as an alleged extension or explanation of what the rules 'No theft' or 'No lying' *mean*. The search for alleged implicit meanings in an exceptionless moral rule can become a fantastic exercise in ingenuity, excusable only because of its charitable motivation. The real reason for the search is that a moral rule *conflicts*, in some situations, with another moral rule such as 'Preserve life' or with a *QB* humanitarian calculation concerning serious harm. Hence the real moral reasons are set forth by adding an *E*-approach exception clause or a *QB* exception clause. Ramsey's liberal *M*-approach to the rules 'No theft' and 'No lying' obscures rather than enlightens.

Ramsey's account of theft and lying may be an aberration. Certainly it is clear that he does not, in general, exclude the possibility of E-approach verbal changes, or of verbal changes which arise partly from reflection on the meaning of a rule. But we should note the dangers of a liberal M-approach if verbal changes are not allowed. A casuist may then hide the real moral reasoning not only from the masses but also from himself.

Does this force us to reject all moral reflection concerning a possible deeper meaning of traditional moral rules? Not at all. The pressure towards fantasy and self-deception comes from an initial commitment to verbal unrevisability. Once we grant the possibility of a revision of the moral rule, we are free to revise it in contexts where an alleged extension of meaning is implausible. But in some other contexts we may probe the meaning of the rule, rather than jump in with a revision. There can be rational respect for tradition and continuity, and a flexible imposition of moral concepts from that tradition, without a commitment to unrevisable moral rules. It seems to me that a great deal of moral reflection rightly starts from an accepted moral rule and involves an extension by analogy from standard cases to more problematic ones. For example, it seems to me that the interpretation of the meaning of 'No adultery' given in (e)M is illuminating, for the very rule that might seem to preclude Mrs Bergmeier's action is seen to justify it. In her case an E-approach or a quantitative-benefit approach would be less illuminating. But if her problem had been whether or not to have sexual intercourse with a guard as the price for his not killing another prisoner, it would surely be more illuminating to think of it as a problem of marital fidelity *versus* preservation of life. (Ramsey tends to interpret most moral obligations as forms of fidelity, but even if the preservation of a person's life is a form of 'fidelity' to him, this fidelity is in conflict with the *marital* form of fidelity in my hypothetical case.)

My main point is that it is possible to make considerable use of an M-approach, with its stress on traditional and *a priori* elements in morality, without being committed to exceptionless moral rules. (Indeed, as I shall show in my discussion of 'moral vocabulary and authority' in the next chapter, there need not necessarily be any reference to *rules* at all: the moral concept may merely single out a morally relevant feature which has to be given some weight in moral deliberation.) Ramsey does not explicitly deny the possibility of using an M-approach without being committed to exceptionless moral rules, and in so far as his own M-approach is liberal, it allows for what amounts to future exceptions to a rule as the meaning is reinterpreted in new situations. But his extensive discussion and defence of an M-approach seems to be part of his overall argument in favour of holding some moral rules to be exceptionless. A reader who rejects this conclusion may mistakenly think that he also has to reject all moral casuistry which focuses on the deeper meaning of traditional moral rules. There is surely a legitimate place for such reflection, especially in Christian moral thought. We may differ as to how big a place it should have, and as to which elements in a tradition should be selected for such reflection. But in so far as Ramsey reminds us that it does have a place, he is surely right.

V

In this section I shall try to clarify our basic question. 'Can there be an exceptionless moral rule?' The two key words are 'can' and 'exceptionless.' I shall examine 'exceptionless' at length, and then consider 'can.'

We have seen that it is logically impossible for there to be a singular moral exception to a moral rule, since any moral exception, like any moral judgment, must be universalizable. Any moral exception must be universal in form, though the exception clause does not have to be explicitly formulated.

We have also seen that it is logically impossible for there to be a strictly act-utilitarian 'exception' to a moral rule, since such an 'exception' changes the moral rule into a maxim. A moral rule provides an independent and distinct moral consideration alongside the calculation of benefits in a particular case; a maxim does not do this.

We have seen that an exceptionless moral rule can have some universal exceptions built into it, specifying the features of situations which constitute exempting conditions, for example, '... except to save life.' Such a moral rule is exceptionless if it is not open to any *further* feature-dependent universal exceptions. An exceptionless rule can be defined as an *unrevisable* rule. This definition, however, needs to be interpreted carefully, or it can be misleading. There are two kinds of moral rule which are held to be unrevisable in their wording, and which are nevertheless not genuinely 'exceptionless.'

One such verbally unrevisable moral rule, as we have seen, is a traditional moral rule in a liberal M-approach. The elastic meaning of the rule may allow not only for many of the exceptions already built into the rule on an E-approach but also for an openness which is in practice the same as that of an E-approach, where the E-approach allows that a rule is open to revision by future addition of further feature-dependent exception clauses. What an M-approach calls 'being open to a deeper understanding of the implicit meaning of the rule' can be the same in practice as what an E-approach calls 'being open to possible revision of the rule in which a new exception clause will be added.' Although the M-approach moral rule is not verbally revisable, it is not exceptionless, for it is open in a way which amounts to the same thing as a revisable E-approach moral rule.

Another verbally unrevisable moral rule which is not really exceptionless would be a rule with a built-in quantitative-benefit (QB) exception clause, where this rule is held to be closed to any further QB (or E-approach) revision. Consider an earlier example (b): 'Never lie except when lying, as compared with not lying, will promote at least quantity Q of benefit.' What if this rule, with its universal QB exception clause, could not be changed? It would still not be 'exceptionless' in the relevant sense of the word. The QB exception clause does not specify the *features* of $S1$ which constitute an exemption condition, and thus rule (b) provides a *qualitatively* unspecified class of exceptions. Even if rule (b) is not open to change in its QB exception clause, this clause itself already allows the moral agent to make exceptions to the rule 'Never lie' in a range of solutions which is qualitatively open. Even if it were possible to give a list of all the qualitatively specified situations which, to one's knowledge, have fulfilled the QB exception clause, such a list would be open-ended. Thus the moral rule is open in a way which, on a qualitative-exception, feature-dependent E-approach, would amount to a limitless revisability. Whether or not a QB exception clause in a moral rule is revisable, such a clause renders the moral rule open rather than exceptionless, in the relevant sense of 'exceptionless.'

Thus an 'exceptionless' moral rule is best understood as an E-approach definite-action moral rule which cannot be revised by the addition of further feature-dependent universal exceptions. Any rule which, in practice, allows what amounts to the same thing as such a further revision is not an exceptionless moral rule. Neither a liberal M-approach unrevisable moral rule nor a moral rule with an unrevisable QB exception clause is 'exceptionless.' If there is to be an exceptionless moral rule, it must fulfil three conditions: (i) it must be stated or understood without the plastic meaning of an M-approach; (ii) it must not allow any QB exception clause; and (iii) it must not be open to any further feature-dependent exception clause if it includes any such clause now, and it must not be open to any such clause at all if it includes none now. Hence if 'No adultery' is an exceptionless moral rule, it must fulfil three conditions: (i) 'Adultery' has a definite, non-plastic meaning such that what *counts* as adultery does not depend on one's moral judgment. (ii) 'No adultery' holds, whatever the *QB* calculations in particular situations; no *QB* exception clause is permitted. (iii) The rule is not open to any feature-dependent exception clause.

What about the rule 'No adultery except to save human life'? This is exceptionless if (i) and (ii) are fulfilled and if (iii) prohibits any *further* feature-dependent exception clauses.

Our question is 'Can there be an exceptionless moral rule?' Having clarified the meaning of 'exceptionless,' let us look at 'can.' At the beginning of this essay I noted two senses of 'can,' the logical and the moral. When we were considering the universalizability of moral judgments, the distinction was dissolved, for we saw that there cannot, logically, be a singular moral exception to a moral rule because there cannot, morally, in view of the very definition of the word 'moral.' This claim seemed reasonable, but it is not reasonable to define 'moral' so as to make the expression 'exceptionless moral rule' a contradiction, so the distinction between logical 'can' and moral 'can' does not dissolve here. Clearly it is logically possible for there to be an exceptionless moral rule. The question is whether there can ever be an adequate moral justification for holding that a moral rule is exceptionless. Ramsey rightly points out that the justification need not be moral, though it must be *normative*. That is, the reasons might be prudential or theological or methodological as well as moral. I agree, but I shall not try to identify the different kinds of reasons. Instead, I shall merely note here that our question is normative rather than logical or empirical.[13]

Ramsey rightly insists that the question is one of *normative meta ethics*. His opponent lays down a meta-rule concerning moral rules: 'No exceptionless moral rules.' For the opponent this is an exceptionless meta-rule which prohibits exceptionless moral rules: Ramsey presents arguments against this meta-rule. His arguments are also arguments in support of some meta-claims which have the form 'The moral rule "Never do X" is exceptionless.' To these arguments we now turn.

VI

Ramsey presents a variety of subtle and interrelated arguments, but I think it is possible to single out three main lines or argument without misrepresenting him. (In addition to these three, there are also some distinctively Christian considerations; but we will consider these separately in section VII.) All three lines of argument may converge, but we shall consider them separately, under the labels 'utilitarian,' 'deontological,' and 'fidelity-obligation.'

1 THE UTILITARIAN ARGUMENT

The main utilitarian argument depends on a rule-utilitarian approach, in which a rule is justified by noting the overall good consequences for society if the rule is usually or always observed, as compared with the overall bad consequences for society if the rule is usually or always violated. For *some* rules, this is the *only* justification (e.g. a rule against leaving a cigarette carton on a public beach); but such rules are not usually called 'moral' rules. Most moral rules are also justified in an act-utilitarian way (*usually* the prohibited kind of action produces bad effects in each particular case), and sometimes in a deontological way (the prohibited kind of action by its very nature is usually or always wrong). But the rule-utilitarian justification is relevant even though other justifications are available. And the main justification for some rules – which Ramsey calls 'rules of practice' – is rule-utilitarian. Concerning some of these rules of practice, there might be a rule-utilitarian justification for meta-rule: 'The rule prohibiting X is exceptionless.' The justification would point to the overall social utility of making the rule exceptionless, rather than leaving it open to further feature-dependent exception clauses or open by virtue of a QB exception clause.

Ramsey's view of this rule-utilitarian argument is not entirely clear. At one point he seems to give it great weight: 'I conclude, therefore, that there is no rational argument that can exclude the possibility that there are exceptionless moral rules, in some moral matters. The case for this seems especially strong in regard to *rules of practice*, whether these are warranted by *agapeic* or rule-utilitarian or other normative appeals' (CCE 112). Ramsey's conclusion, however, depends mainly on his discussion of rules of practice which are not justified solely in a rule-utilitarian way. And later on, discussing the possibility of future revision of rules, he says this:

The case for exceptions in our future is especially strong in all cases where *consequence*-features are overriding. Perhaps in regard to all *purely* societal *rules of practice*, or rule-utilitarian rules, these should never be held closed against future further morally significant exceptions. This would hold open progressive refinements and future admissible alterations in the accepted practice, and hold open also the possibility that in certain sorts of cases unforeseen consequences of the practice upon individual persons can be taken significantly into account as a reason for violating societal rules.   (CCE 118–19)

This is a neat summary of two main reasons *against* making any rule-utilitarian rules exceptionless: the fact that society changes so that rules may need to be changed accordingly, and the fact that a rule which promotes an overall balance of good over evil in society may produce grave evil to individuals in particular, often unforeseeable, cases – unless exceptions can be made. The second reason is one which must have special weight for Ramsey because, as Paul Camenisch[14] has pointed out, Ramsey's passionate concern that some moral rules are exceptionless is mainly a concern for individuals who need such rules as protection against violation of their rights by society. Ramsey explicitly contrasts his position with one which gives 'societal values' (CCE 133) priority over the individual; yet such a priority is inherent in rule-utilitarianism if its rules are exceptionless.

On balance, I do not see how a rule-utilitarian backing for exceptionlessness of a moral rule can be adequate in the case of a purely rule-utilitarian rule. Nor do I see how rule-utilitarian considerations can support exceptionlessness in the case of other rules. Note, however, that I am talking about genuinely exceptionless moral rules, which can never be open to revision or subject to a QB exception clause. I am not denying the possibility of strong arguments concerning some moral rules, similar to arguments concerning most *laws*, that any new exceptions ought not to be decided by interested parties, but rather by an authority which represents the interests of society as a whole and of individuals who may be harmed by such exceptions.

Before we leave utilitarianism, I should briefly note an act-utilitarian argument which Ramsey also considers:[15] If in this situation *S1* I regard the moral rule prohibiting *X* as a rule open to revision and act accordingly, this action will influence others to regard the rule as being open to revision in situations different from *S1*, where no revision can be justified. My revision of the rule (adding a new feature-dependent exception clause, or applying a QB exception clause) may be the thin edge of the wedge; thus even if my revision can have a rule-utilitarian justification (since the overall consequences would be good if everyone or most people were to do strictly likewise), the revision is wrong in act-utilitarian terms.

Note that this 'wedge argument' does not show that the rule in question should be exceptionless. It does not show that the rule should never be revised, for presumably there could be circumstances in which the revision would not influence anyone else, or would not influence others in a bad way. Nevertheless the wedge argument can, in some situations, reinforce other arguments in favour of not revising a moral rule.

2 THE DEONTOLOGICAL ARGUMENT

What I am calling the 'deontological' argument in support of the meta-claim ' "Don't do X" is an exceptionless moral rule' depends on the conviction that X specifies a kind of action which is wrong by its very *nature*, apart from its consequences. On one version of this argument nothing more needs to be said. If doing X is inherently wrong, then it is always wrong, regardless of consequences. And it will always be wrong. The moral rule is clearly exceptionless. Just as each biological species has its own nature, which a biological science discovers, so there are (allegedly) species of human actions which moral science discovers.

This conviction, most evident in traditional Roman Catholic moral theology,[16] requires no additional justification for the meta-rule. 'All adultery is wrong,' like 'All men are rational' or 'All swans are white,' is allegedly not open to any possible disconfirmation by future experience; and this is not because men have decided to define 'adultery,' 'men,' and 'swans' so as to make the statements analytic rather than empirical; it is because men have come to know the nature of adultery, men, and swans.

There are some indications that Ramsey is sympathetic to this conviction, especially in his zeal for what I have call the M-approach. But in so far as his M-approach is liberal, with a plastic meaning for the terms describing prohibited kinds of act, Ramsey's ethic allows in practice for what amounts to a revision of the moral rules. And in presenting his main deontological argument[17] he assumes or postulates the empirical possibility that, in a particular case, the consequence of following a rule might be so bad as to warrant breaking (or revising) the rule. He then argues that this possibility is less likely than the possibility of making a moral mistake if one regards the rule as revisable. The possibility of error is considerable, both because of one's possible ignorance of relevant facts and, more important, because one's own self-interest or passions may lead to self-deception. Such an argument would be irrelevant if the prohibited kind of action were inherently wrong, wrong whatever the consequences. The argument depends on a conviction,[18] which seems to me very reasonable, that certain species of action have an inherent moral relevance, weight, and significance, quite apart from their consequences. (This conviction has affinities with the claim that we have *prima facie* obligations, where this claim does not depend solely on rule-utilitarian considerations.) The greater the importance of the fact that what one is doing is adultery or lying or stealing, the less the weight given to beneficial consequences of the action. And perhaps, in the case of some moral rules, the weight which should be given to consequences is so relatively minimal that it does not merely verge on zero but disappears. Such, at any rate, is the general line of Ramsey's argument in so far as I understand it. He asks us to consider some very challenging examples:

(i) Never experiment medically on a human being without his informed consent.

(j) Never punish a man whom one knows to be innocent of that for which he would be punished.

(k) Never rape (i.e. force sexual intercourse on someone who is totally unwilling).

With regard to (i), (j), and (k) it is clear that we do in fact try to devise a *law* which has as few loopholes as possible, and we require that any new interpretation of the law will fulfil two conditions: first, it will be made by some socially authorized group or individual, not an interested party; and secondly, it will not involve any rejection of the fundamental moral significance of the prohibited species of action. Similarly, in so far as a *moral* rule as well as a law is involved, the same restraints on individual decision-making are reasonable. Anyone who, as an interested party, tries to revise the rule in his own case, is rightly subject to the sanction of moral disapproval from society. Yet there is surely a place for individual moral autonomy even here. A conscientious moral agent may sometimes defy a law because disobedience in a very special situation, and there only, is in his eyes justified; such a moral agent would accept the legal penalties graciously, since the particular law is just and good. Similarly he might defy a moral rule upheld by society – even (i), (j), or (k), in some very special situations, and there only – and graciously accept moral disapproval although he believes that he has acted rightly. The very special situation, though conceivable, is very, very unlikely. But, since the restriction on medical experimentation and on punishment of the innocent is stringent because of the possible pressure arising from beneficial social consequences (and not merely because of the dangers of self-interested claims), it is possible that in some situation these beneficial consequences might rightly override the rule. I personally can imagine such a situation, though it is a very unlikely one. Similarly I can imagine a situation in a concentration camp where refusal to rape might produce horrendous consequences for others and where one could not convey[19] to the unwilling victim any indications of one's reasons or intentions.

The role of individual moral autonomy in relation to (i), (j), and (k) is so minimal and so restricted in scope that I would describe the rule as 'virtually exceptionless.' That is, I think the rule should be held to be virtually closed to future exceptions, since the theoretically possible exceptional cases are virtually zero in their practical probability. Here my position seems to be very close to Ramsey's. He speaks about rules being held to be '*significantly* closed to future exceptions' or 'closed to *significant* future exceptions.' But when we consider another moral rule for which he presents a similar anti-revisability argument, the importance of moral autonomy becomes more evident. As an example[20] of an allegedly exceptionless moral rule, significantly closed to future exceptions, he proposes 'No premarital intercourse.' In support of this Ramsey legitimately stresses the way in which self-interest and passions can produce moral error and may lead to a failure to consider the responsibilities involved in the possibility of parenthood as a consequence of the intercourse. This line of argument does give some support for a moral rule prohibiting premarital intercourse, but not for making the rule exceptionless. I do not think it even shows that if, there are to be any revisions, these should be made by an authority appointed by society, though it does point to the wisdom of consulting a disinterested and wise third party in order to minimize self-deception.

In his argument Ramsey does not consider the most plausible case for breaking the rule. He assumes that the couple have not thoroughly searched their own motives and biases and possible self-deceptions and that they have not accepted in advance the responsibility for a child if contraception should fail. But what if they have? And what if they also consider good reasons for postponing marriage unless pregnancy comes – for example, there is a university regulation which would prevent the girl from completing her undergraduate studies if she married? Or consider a case where a young man has a realistic fear of impotency, is firmly committed to marry his girl friend if he is not impotent, and out of concern for both her and himself seeks intercourse with her? Unless pre-marital intercourse is, as such, inherently wrong, it seems to me quite implausible to claim that a rule prohibiting it should be exception-less. (And of course if it *is* inherently wrong no further arguments about possibilities of moral error are needed.)

In the preceding two paragraphs I have been discussing what I first took to be Ramsey's argument. I assumed that he had an *E*-approach to 'No pre-marital sex' in which the rule prohibits intercourse prior to the marriage ceremony. I was mistaken. Ramsey professes an *M*-approach, in which the meaning of 'marital' is not thus understood. In correspondence, amplified by reference to an earlier article (SROM)[21] and clarified by a rejoinder (SR), he has made it clear that the term 'pre-marital' does not for him necessarily mean 'before the marriage ceremony.' For Ramsey marriage consists primarily in a mutual pledge or covenant which may be private. Thus his rule would not necessarily prohibit intercourse in the case of the unmarried undergraduate if the couple were privately pledged in a marriage covenant. But Ramsey does reject any conditional, future-tense understanding of pre-ceremonial marriage pledges, e.g. 'I *will* take thee ... provided that I am not impotent.' His conception of pre-ceremonial marital covenant is that it is a present-tense commitment: 'I *take* thee.' In SR 186 he says that at least some conditions are for him 'beneath inclusion' in such a covenant, e.g. 'provided that I am not impotent toward thee' or 'provided that thou gettest pregnant.' It is not completely clear whether some other conditions could be included, but he does seem to rule out any condition which would shift the vow into a future-tense 'taking.'

Should we regard Ramsey's 'No pre-marital sex' as a proposal of a genuinely exceptionless rule? This depends on how elastic we understand the meaning the meaning of 'marital' to be for him. If the private or public marital pledge is 'I now take thee unconditionally as my exclusive sexual partner for life,' the meaning is so restricted that he has an *E*-approach after all and his rule is genuinely exceptionless in import. It is clear that Ramsey rejects a very liberal *M*-approach in which a 'marital' pledge is a deep commitment to the other's fundamental well-being (which could justify the impotency case). If he is to be construed as having an *M*-approach here, it is more conservative than liberal, so that he is proposing a rule which for him is very close to being genuinely exceptionless.

My own view is that 'No pre-marital sex' is unacceptable as an exceptionless rule. Only gross violations of other human beings seem to me to be even candidates for consideration – immoralities comparable to medical experimentation on involuntary patients, punishment of the innocent, and rape. (I also reject his stress on covenant-pledge rather than caring love as the crucial condition for sex.) But I do agree with Ramsey that *some* moral rules should be regarded as being what I have called 'virtually' exceptionless. Alongside the rules in (i), (j), and (k) consider another proposed by Ramsey: 'Never torture your wife to death, giving her to believe that you hate her' (CCE 101). This rule, with its reference to a combination of torture, unfaithfulness, murder, and heinous deceit, strains the imagination if one tries to conceive a situation so horrendous that an exception would be justified. If someone were to insist that even this rule is only 'virtually' exceptionless, this would seem like saying that the series '1 plus ½ plus ½^2 plus ½^3 ... ½^{1000}' is only 'virtually' 2. Yet there is a point in saying 'virtually.' Moral rules form a continuum: some are open to very extensive revision, some are much less open, and some are in varying degrees exceptionless. Some moralists such as Ramsey are concerned about 'creeping exceptionism,' which shifts rules which should be virtually exceptionless back among wide-open rules. Other moralists are concerned about 'creeping legalism,' which extends the range of allegedly exceptionless rules down to rules which should be held fairly open, and even to situations where the role of rules should be minimal. Some of the moral passion expressed in the debate arises from reasonable convictions that both creeping exceptionism and creeping legalism are, and have been, menaces to morality. Though Ramsey's article sometimes makes me worry about a tendency towards creeping legalism, it is mainly a salutary reminder of the dangers of creeping exceptionism. Concerning some moral rules, the onus is on the exceptionist to show why the rule should *not* be held as virtually exceptionless. Yet since Ramsey's argument assumes an empirical possibility that in a particular case the consequences of following the rule could be so bad as to warrant a revision of the rule, it is important to insist on the word 'virtually.' The insistence is a check on creeping legalism.

3 THE FIDELITY-OBLIGATION ARGUMENT

Ramsey's third main argument is especially illuminating because of the way in which it puts the onus on the exceptionist. He considers *fidelity-obligations* which arise from explicit or implicit promises. In so far as a moral rule sets forth a fidelity-obligation, this counts against keeping the rule open to further revision in relation to unforeseen future circumstances. For example, the point of a marriage vow is that one is making a commitment of fidelity which will be binding *in spite of* unforeseen future conditions which otherwise might justify a termination of a relation of cohabitation. If there are to be exception clauses in a promise, these should be included when the promise is made; after that, the moral obligation is not open *indefinitely* to *further* revisions, for this would destroy the point of the promise.

Some moral rules are linked with explicit promises. For example, the prohibition of adultery is linked with the marriage vows. But many other moral rules are linked with promises which are implicit. The notion of an implicit promise is a tricky one, but surely it is clear that there can be fidelity-obligations, say, of friendship, even though no one has said, 'I'll stand by you' or anything similarly explicit. And many of our institutional obligations arise because we voluntarily accept a job or a role and thereby implicitly accept responsibilities to individuals or groups. So the range of fidelity-obligations is quite wide. (As we shall see in section VII, Ramsey tends to interpret almost all obligations as fidelity-obligations.)

Fidelity can, of course, be considered in both a rule-utilitarian way and a deontological way. A rule-utilitarian can justify moral rules which depend on promises by pointing to the overall social utility of these rules. And a deontologist can justify such rules by discerning an inherent rightness in fidelity and an inherent wrongness in infidelity. Ramsey's *special* emphasis on fidelity is justified, however, because the special point to promises and to fidelity is to reduce the dependence of one's moral decisions on future circumstances and on consequences in general.

I agree with Ramsey that fidelity-obligations have this distinctive and important feature, and that in so far as an ethical view stresses the fidelity-bonds of human life it will give proportionately less weight to concern about future circumstances and beneficial or harmful consequences. But I do not think that he shows that any fidelity-rules are genuinely exceptionless, even if we add the word 'virtually' or 'significantly.' It is obvious that most promises do not create such a weighty moral obligation that the related moral rule is a serious candidate for exceptionlessness. My moral obligation to return a book today as I promised, or to prepare the minutes of the club as its secretary in time for the meeting, can be overridden by a host of other obligations. Only a few kinds of promises, especially designed for the purpose, are so worded that they apparently subordinate all other moral obligations to themselves. The range of possibly exceptionless fidelity-rules narrows to a few: fidelity to one's spouse or to one's country or to one's church. If the 'fidelity' is understood in a liberal *M*-approach way, then in each case there can be a moral rule which is verbally unrevisable. But the rule is then not genuinely exceptionless. Mrs Bergmeier can be faithful to her husband while having intercourse with the camp guard. Bonhoeffer can be faithful to Germany while plotting Hitler's death. Charles Davis can be faithful to the Roman Catholic Church while leaving it. If, on the other hand, 'fidelity' is understood in a more definite way, the possibility of its being overriden by other obligations should, it seems to me, be left open. And there should be a *QB* exception clause written into it: 'except where following the rule would cause such great harm as to outweigh the moral obligation not to break it.' Here I have merely expressed a moral conviction without argument. Support for the claim would have to take the form of a detailed description of cases where a failure to acknowledge the need for openness in a fidelity-rule has led to morally disastrous consequences. It seems to me that the likelihood of such an outcome in the future is greater than the likelihood of morally disastrous consequences if the need for openness is acknowledged. It seems to me that this is especially obvious in the case of loyalty to one's country.

I do not deny that if we keep fidelity-bonds open this can involve difficulties and dangers. For one thing there is a *psychological* problem which gives weight to a moralist's fear of morally disastrous consequences if the need for openness is acknowledged. It is difficult to grant the possibility that in some remote and undesignated circumstances a moral rule would not apply, while at the same time giving tremendous weight now to this moral rule. Certainly there is a danger that an intense preoccupation with remote contingencies can undermine one's moral commitment in the present. A person who is already wondering about what he would do if his wife were to become incurably insane or if she were to run off to another continent with a stranger might be indulging in self-fulfilling prophecies, producing the situation which he fears because of his lack of trust. The psychological problem is important in other contexts too. A soldier who concedes that torture of prisoners could possibly be justified in some remote and undesignated circumstances may be undermining his will not to torture prisoners when the issue actually arises a few hours later. It is not surprising that Ramsey talks about the claim that there is nothing men should never do as the 'most uncivilizing principle' (CCE 135). He even refers us to Auschwitz. But Auschwitz can also be cited, with as much justice, as an outcome of an ethic of exceptionless fidelity to the state (though Ramsey does not set forth such an ethic in his article). And, more generally, an exceptionless-rule approach has often involved the perversities of moral judgment against which Joseph Fletcher and other anti-legalists have rightly spoken. Ramsey's article, however, is not designed to support such an approach. He has tried to show that *some* moral rules should be held to be significantly exceptionless. And if 'significantly' means much the same as 'virtually,' I think he has succeeded.

He has also shown that we ought to give 'first place' (CCE 126) to many claims of justice or faithfulness which are embodied in rules of deontology or fidelity within a moral tradition. These claims have an intrinsic moral relevance and great moral weight, even though the rules are not genuinely exceptionless.

VII

In this final section I shall briefly outline and discuss three distinctively Christian considerations which Ramsey proposes in support of the possibility that some rules are exceptionless. Two of these considerations provide additional support for arguments considered earlier. The third introduces new considerations.

1 CHRISTIAN EMPHASIS ON SIN

The Christian conviction that all men are *sinners* reinforces the argument that a man's private self-interest and passions may lead him into moral error if he holds such-and-such a moral rule to be revisable by his own moral judgment. Christians speak of 'another law in our members' alongside our human capacity to reason as moral beings (CCE 118). The fact that sin can lead to distortions of individual moral judgment supports the need for meta-rules which are rule-strengthening.

It seems to me that even if this argument shows the need for rule-strengthening rules, it does not show that any rule should be exceptionless. And even the rule-strengthening emphasis can be challenged by another Christian conviction, concerning the work of the Holy Spirit in guiding men towards right moral judgments in difficult moral decisions, freeing them from bondage to the law. If we are talking about broad policy for Christians in general, the doctrines of sin and of the Holy Spirit cancel each other out, as it were. Christian pessimism and Christian optimism concerning human moral insight combine – in terms of broad and general expectations concerning Christians or men generally – so as to be little different from the less dramatic reasoning of realistic secular moralists. In *particular* cases, of course, the convictions concerning sin or Holy Spirit can make a great deal of difference to the individual Christian – but not, it seems to me, in general arguments as to whether human beings generally, or Christians generally, need any rules which should be exceptionless.

2 CHRISTIAN EMPHASIS ON FIDELITY

Ramsey's stress on *fidelity*-obligations is supported by the Christian conviction that fidelity, covenants, promises, loyalty, etc are at the heart of the theological basis for moral conduct. God has acted to establish a covenant with us and with all mankind. To this 'performative' action the appropriate human response is fidelity towards God and man. This is how Ramsey puts it (CCE 125):

If one *begins* in Christian *normative ethics* with some such statement as 'Look on all men as brothers for whom Christ died' or 'Be grateful to the Lord who made us His covenant people,' and if all moral reasoning is then reasoning from these 'premises,' then the ultimate warrant of them must be an appeal to what the Lord of heaven and earth is believed to have been doing and to be doing in enacting and establishing His covenant with us and all mankind, in all the estates and orders and relations of life to which we have been called.

If it is true that in Christian ethics we are mainly concerned about the requirements of loyalty to covenants among men, about the meaning of God's ordinances and mandates, about the estates and moral relations among men acknowledged to follow from His governing and righteous will, about steadfastness and faithfulness, then it follows that in Christian ethics we can and may and must be enormously disinterested in any exception, or openness to exceptions, that would have to be justified primarily by future consequences-features, and indeed, consequences imagined in extreme, fictitious cases.

Ramsey not only sees Christian faith as a source of *emphasis* on human bonds of fidelity as the main concern of ethics, but also as a reason for *extending* the understanding of fidelity so that it covers most or all our moral obligations. Consider the following passages:

Faithfulness-claims and canons of covenant loyalty may be the profoundest way to understand all our concepts of fairness and justice.   (CCE 119)

[Concerning rape] We may gain a fuller realization of the heinousness of unwilling sexual intercourse because we come to see more clearly the obligations created in relation to all men by a woman-being who, simply by being, claims at least this *faithfulness* of us.   (CCE 127, my italics)

In medical ethics there is a rule governing experimentation involving human subjects that this should be done only when an informed consent has been secured ... The *faithfulness*-claims which every man, simply by being a man, places upon the researcher are the morally relevant considerations.   (CCE 129)

[Concerning an argument by Jonathan Bennett in favour of abortion to save a mother's life] Bennett's other argument was concerning what *is* the relevant canon of loyalty and what *does* fidelity to two lives in conflict require in obstetrical cases. His argument did not crucially depend on consequences, other than those marked out by the faithfulness-claim upon us to save life rather than allow to die.   (CCE 130,n 63)

The idea of fidelity has here been extended so as to provide the basis for justice, for not raping a woman, for not experimenting on someone without his consent, an for not allowing a woman to die. It has become and 'onlook' in terms of which *all* our fundamental obligations to human beings are understood. Why? Because 'Christians look on all men as brothers for whom Christ died.' It is a *fraternal* fidelity, extended from one's literal brothers to include all men.

I agree with Ramsey to some extent concerning the special Christian emphasis on human bonds of fidelity, but I would qualify this in various ways. First, there should be no *unconditional* fidelity except to God. Christian theology may say 'Yes' to marriage, to the state, or to the religious institution called 'the church,' but it also says 'No' where any of these purports to be a loyalty 'whatever the consequences.' Secondly, Christians can experience conflicts between different fidelity-obligations, and between a fidelity-obligation and other moral obligations. We ought not to try to resolve these problems in advance by reference to unrevisable moral rules. A Christian 'onlook' which turns all moral obligations into fidelity-obligations gives a deontological colour to them all, but it leaves unresolved the problems of priorities and conflicts. Thirdly, Christians have New Testament warrant for being concerned not only about covenant-bonds between men but also about human suffering. A *QB* exception clause in covenantal moral rules has Christian, and not merely utilitarian, warrant.

When I first read Ramsey's article I had a more serious worry concerning Ramsey's application of Christian covenantal theology to ethics. When I read about 'all the estates and orders and relations of life to which we have been called' (CCE 125) and 'the estates and moral relations among men acknowledged to follow from His governing and righteous will', (CCE 125), I wondered whether Ramsey claimed to know, with certainty and precise definition, what these estates and orders and relations of life are. In correspondence, however, he vigorously rejects making any such claim. The interpretation of our various obligations to church, state, or home in terms of covenant-fidelity involves for him a *liberal M*-approach. The approach is important, for in the past a Christian covenantal theology has been used to give a spurious divine authority to precisely defined human estates, orders, and relations – often the existing social institutions and conventions of church, state, and home. Ramsey, however, is content with reinforcing some traditional and *a priori* elements in morality by pointing to their distinctively Christian versions:

Principles of faithfulness are unfolded from the elevating and directing power of divine charity. This and our intervening principles are capable of producing within Christian morality itself deeper meanings, clarifying explanations and stipulations for the 'upbuilding' of the actions and the moral agency going on ordinarily.   (CCE 91)

This passage, in its context, seems to presuppose a liberal *M*-approach – which, as we have seen, does not involve genuinely exceptionless rules.

3 CHRISTIAN HOPE AND MORALITY

Ramsey's third distinctively Christian argument as a 'defender of exceptionless rules' (CCE 133) is one which relates Christian morality to Christian *hope*:

The primary assumption or conviction is that the *ultimate* consequences cannot be such as to render his (the Christian's) performance of fidelity obligations *wrong*. This is, I suppose, a sort of Kantian 'postulate' which we Christians make when spelling out in thought and life the meaning of fidelity in all covenants. It is a postulate (not a mere supposition) that the grain of things cannot ultimately prove unsupportive of the doing of our fidelities under the moral constitution God makes known in His word-deeds towards us. But that is far and away different from supposing that the final worldly consequences of faithful deeds will show the success of the good (or that from taking account of that, one gets to know the meaning of the right and the good in any morally significant measure. (CCE 133)

Ramsey has explained in correspondence that he does not mean this to imply that we should rigidly follow fidelity-rules *regardless* of consequences which are foreseeable and subject to human control, for fidelity-rules require us to consider such consequences. Rather, he is expressing Christian confidence that the unforeseeable and uncontrollable later consequences of performing a fidelity-obligation will not be such as to render the performance wrong. Such hope and trust in divine Providence, however, do not warrant exceptionless moral rules. Some time in the future I may *foresee* that the consequences of following an existing fidelity-rule would be so harmful that I ought to revise the rule.

Where a belief in genuinely exceptionless moral rules is combined with a trust in divine Providence the approach to some moral issues is often deplorable. Supposedly we cannot be responsible for the consequences of refraining from breaking (i.e. revising) an exceptionless moral rule. Supposedly we must never bear arms or we must never disobey a commanding officer or we must never seek a divorce or we must never use artificial contraceptives or we must never have an abortion or we must never masturbate or we must never tell a lie (except with'mental reservation':), etc, etc. If anyone gets hurt because we are preserving our moral purity, that's his tough luck (or in the jargon of theological moralists 'his suffering is within the inscrutable purpose of God').

Yet Christian hope and trust in divine Providence have been a creative and renewing force. The conviction that the value and ultimate significance of our best efforts do not depend on their actual success or failure as these can be seen in history has been a conviction which inspires Christians to do their best and 'leave the rest in the hands of God.' It is not the same conviction. The second conviction does not involve rules which are strictly exceptionless, and it involves a two-sided attitude towards mundane utilitarian consequences. On the one hand, these consequences matter enormously; we must do all that we can to relieve suffering and to promote happiness. On the other hand, what matters ultimately is the honest attempt, not the success. What matters ultimately is not whether we have won or lost, and certainly not whether we have 'played the game' according to some allegedly exceptionless rules, but whether we have *loved*.

Yet the expression of love involves many things, including rules. And Ramsey has rightly reminded us that some of these rules are virtually exceptionless.

Postscript

Although I have conceded virtually exceptionless rules to Ramsey, I find his view of love inadequate as the basis for those rules and, more generally, as the basis for ethics. In CCE Ramsey understands love for people almost entirely in terms of fidelity towards them. Also, he understands faith in God almost entirely in terms of fidelity towards God. In each case the fidelity is a covenent-fidelity, dependent on explicit or implicit self-involving promises which the Christian has made in response to God's covenant-establishing actions. Ramsey has made use of my own account of biblical language in my *The Logic of Self-Involvement*, where I view divine actions as implicit 'performatives': in creating mankind, Israel, and the church God implicitly *promises* to care steadfastly for them, *gives* them existence as a good which He values positively, and authoritatively *appoints* them to various roles in relation to Himself and to one another. Faith in God is a self-involving response to these performatives in the form of correlative performatives addressed to God: 'I hereby commit myself to trust your promises, to acknowledge gratefully my indebtedness to you for your gift, and to act towards you and people in accordance with the roles assigned.' To love people, them, is to look on them in the role-accepting ways which God prescribes and to live accordingly; for example, one looks on each person as a brother for whom Christ died and acts accordingly. (As I have noted in chapter 1, I have given these ways of 'looking on x as y' the label 'onlooks'.) To love people is to be faithful to the performative covenant-relation which God has established, living according to the onlooks which have His authority.

Both before and after I worked on Ramsey's essay, I was becoming increasingly dissatisfied with my own and Ramsey's focus on covenant-fidelity, correlative performatives, and onlooks as the *primary* way of describing faith in God and love for people. By the time I wrote chapter 5 all this had become *secondary*, though still important. There are four different reasons for this shift in emphasis. I shall not try to justify these reasons, but shall simply outline them.

My first reason is philosophical. The shift in emphasis in my way of understanding faith and love is one instance of a more general shift in my philosophical method which I shall explain more fully in chapter 7.

Instead of mainly interpreting profound experiences and attitudes by reference to the language used to articulate them, I have been increasingly trying to interpret the language by reference to the experiences and attitudes. For example, instead of interpreting self-involvement mainly in terms of the logic of the language which articulates it (performatives such as explicit promises), I have focused more on the non-verbal experiences and attitudes from which the articulation originates. It is true, as J.L. Austin[22] has pointed out, that promises are not reports of inner states, experiences, or attitudes. In saying 'I promise' I perform the act of promising whether or not there is any self-involvement other than the purely linguistic act. But *verbal* self-involvement is only authentic to the extent that it originates from a *personal* self-involvement which is articulated in the verbal promise. And, most important, this personal self-involvement is ontologically (and to some extent temporally) prior to the use of language; it can be distinguished in a rudimentary, opaque, but profound form prior to its linguistic articulation. Various forms of existentialism and psychoanalysis provide accounts of this prelinguistic raw material so as to illuminate the language which authentically articulates it, including the language which creates verbal self-involvement. It is true, of course, that the language in turn sheds light on the prelinguistic material. Though the verbal without the personal is empty, the personal without the verbal is almost blind. But I stress the word 'almost,' for there are ways such as Marcel's 'secondary reflection'[23] by which the prelinguistic can be illuminated. And where deeply personal self-involvements such as those which occur in religion and morality are being studied, a study of the prelinguistic materials should be primary.

My second reason for shifting from a primarily covenantal approach can be expressed in terms of a judgment which I have come to make concerning *analogies*: of relation, of attitude, and of activity. Concerning analogy of relation, it seems to me increasingly that the most significant interhuman relation (significant both in itself and as a basis for thinking analogically about the divine-human relation) is not correlative performatives but I-Thou encounters. The mutual receptivity, confirmation, and creative presence which occur in an I-Thou encounter are more fundamental than the covenantal relations to which they may give rise; and they are certainly more fundamental than any covenants abstracted from an I-Thou context, which can be external, conventional, and superficial. Liberal personalists such as Buber, Marcel, and Baum increasingly seem to me to provide a better starting-point in their anthropology and theology than neo-orthodox theologians who focus mainly on interhuman covenants and divine-human covenants. If we think in terms of analogy of *activity*, what human act is most plausibly regarded as supremely good, as a paradigm which provides the best starting-point for thinking analogously about divine activity? Increasingly it seems to me that this is not an enacted fidelity to another person, which could be largely behavioural and external, but an inner spontaneous love, a creative caring for self and for others. Such love gives rise to various behaviour, including performatives such as promises; but it is not itself merely a performance. And if we think in terms of analogy of *attitude*, what human attitude is at the core of worship? Is it a self-committing acknowledgment of divine actions as having such-and-such performative meaning and a commitment to onlooks concerning one's relation to God and man? Increasingly it seems to me that, though these are important, the crucial ingredient in worship is an inner receptivity, a pervasive and profound prelinguistic stance of the whole personality. And this basic attitude or way-of-being-in-the-world is also the crucial condition for the I-Thou encounters and the creative love which are fundamental in morality. (In chapters 6 and 7 I shall explain more fully what I mean by 'receptivity.')

The third reason for shifting my emphasis from the covenantal approach which I largely shared with Ramsey is closely related to what I have already indicated concerning the choice of human paradigms in constructing analogies. In an extreme version of a covenantal approach there is nothing at all in human nature as such which claims or calls forth our love; rather, our love is entirely based on active acknowledgment of the role relations with God and with people which God authoritatively establishes. To my knowledge Ramsey never explicitly propounds this extreme version, but as Charles Curran has said: 'The nature of the person is not the foundation for Ramsey's insistence on the existence of exceptionless rules in Christian ethics.'[24] Rather, the foundation is a fidelity in grateful and obedient response to, and in imitation of, God's covenant-fidelity. On reflection it seems clear to me that, although I agree with Ramsey concerning virtually exceptionless rules, I do not agree with his foundation. My own main foundation is a modified natural-law conviction concerning human nature: Quite apart from the specific covenantal revelation to which the scriptures bear witness, but not apart from divine grace which liberates our hearts and minds to discern what it means to be a human being, human nature in ourselves and others claims our love. This love confronts and confirms and creates in relation to needs and aspirations which are common to all humanity. The claim of love is sometimes unconditional (cf Ian Ramsey); thus, where a *kind* of action would be contrary to love in virtually any situation, it is prohibited by a virtually exceptionless rule. Love is articulated in many different ways, including specifically Christian covenant-fidelities and onlooks, but these are not in themselves the basis of morality. (In chapter 6 I try to clarify the relation between the *love* to which divine grace calls and liberates *anyone* who is receptive, and the specifically *Christian* ethical elements: Christian moral vocabulary, Christian onlooks, and Christian focus on Jesus as moral paradigm.)

The fourth reason for shifting my emphasis away from covenant-fidelity as the central form of faith and morality has arisen from a concern about Ramsey's authoritarianism. Although Ramsey does not cite obedience to God as our only moral motive, and although he also refers to our imitation of God and our gratitude to God, the main thrust of his theology is on obedience, and he understands obedience in terms analogous to that which pertains to our (allegedly) proper stance towards civil authorities. His views concerning divine authority and civil authority seem to be closely connected. Given his theology, it is not surprising to find that his political ethics is criticized for its increasing stress on order at the expense of love and justice[25] and for its unquestioning acceptance of the ends (though not the means) decided upon by civil authorities.[26] Although Ramsey is concerned to defend the individual against the state, much of his political ethics tends to legitimate existing 'structures of domination' (to use Baum's expression) more than to undermine them. His theology thus tends to be 'ideological' rather than 'transformist.' And in general his ethical system does not ensure moral freedom in relation to God and in relation to the state. Certainly he does not advocate an extreme form of authoritarianism, but his ethics (and my own previous work in so far as it resembles his) is such as to force me to ask myself: 'Does religious faith conflict with moral freedom?' It seems to me that in order to answer with a firm and convincing 'no,' I have to provide an account of faith and morality which differs considerably both from Ramsey's and from what I had depicted in *The Logic of Self-Involvement*. In the next chapter I provide such an account. The influence on my work of Ian Ramsey, Sam Keen, and Gregory Baum will be evident.

6

Does Religious Faith Conflict with Moral Freedom?

I was assigned to the public information office so I had a good look at army propaganda. The training films, for example, were grotesque – persuading people to accept chemical and biological warfare; there was one in particular about some scientists in West Virginia who'd perfected the bubonic plague ... Breaking with the church was good, because it taught me that one can doubt a huge, powerful organization's rightness. When some hillbilly sergeant would tell me, 'You've got to have faith in your government,' I'd find myself thinking, 'If I can question the Big Bopper up there, I can certainly question you, you dingaling.' (An American deserter, quoted in *The Toronto Star*, 14 June 1969)

If religion is understood in an authoritarian way, a break away from it is necessary for moral freedom. Instead of submitting without question to the 'Big Bopper' and to other authorities such as government or church, a man begins to make up his own mind on many matters. For some people the change of consciousness called 'the death of God' is a liberating event, for God has seemed to be a threat to human dignity, maturity, and freedom. Indeed, many people would agree with the philosopher Patrick Nowell-Smith when he rejects religious morality as 'infantile' and finds maturity and freedom only in a secular morality.[1]

Does religious faith conflict with freedom in making moral decisions? Sociological evidence indicates that, in general, it does. William Eckhardt, summarizing the results of many sociological studies, says this:

Instead of teaching people the 'truth' which is supposed to make them 'free' (and therefore responsible), it would seem that religion generally teaches people to escape from freedom into the autocratic arms of whatever rules and regulations may be currently prevalent, making them into authoritarian, bureaucratic, compulsive, conformist, conservative, militarist (at least in the West), national-ist, and racialist personalities, fit to serve well the rules and regulations designed to keep them in their personal places and to maintain the social status quo.[2]

Eckhardt's conclusions need not be accepted unreservedly. He himself notes that the generalizations do not apply to all religious individuals and groups. Also, we may question his move from statistical correlations to claims concerning the influence of religion. Perhaps religion is less the cause of the various attitudes than it is the effect of some of them. Or perhaps religiosity and the other attitudes have as their main cause some unmentioned psychoanalytic factor, not easily accessible in sociological studies. Nevertheless the main tenor of Eckhardt's findings seems indis-putable. Much religion, perhaps most religion, is associated with atti-tudes which are in conflict with moral freedom. People who simply do what they're told are not free. They say: 'He knows what is best' or 'His word is law.' Sometimes 'he' is human (father, sergeant, prime minister or pope), sometimes divine. In either case submission is a form of willing slavery.

But not all religion is authoritarian; nor are an anti-authoritarian independence and autonomy the only alternative. In this essay I shall argue that some religious convictions, namely those expressed in a con-temporary Christian creed, are compatible with moral freedom, where this freedom is understood to be 'responsive' rather than 'wilful.' My focus will be on the creed and on 'responsive' freedom. The creed deserves serious philosophical scrutiny, for it expresses a broad concen-sus within a mainline denomination and within a wide range of contem-porary theology, and it differs radically from authoritarian versions of Christianity against which philosophers and others have protested in the name of freedom. The 'responsive' view of freedom which is presup-posed in the creed will gradually emerge in the course of the essay. On such a view freedom increases rather than decreases when an agent is receptive to the (non-authoritarian) influence of another agent and to the depths within himself which are beyond his direct control. I shall be contrasting this with a 'wilful' notion of freedom, in which freedom is a power to do what one wills, a power exercised over others so as to reduce their power over oneself, which reduces one's own power; or it is a power over oneself, an ability to use at will various physical and intellec-tual skills which one has acquired.

Although this is primarily a philosophical essay, it includes a great deal of theology and psychology. The theology is included because it seems obvious to me that the best way for a philosopher to consider issues of faith and freedom is to explore religious convictions in detail and in depth within their theological framework; otherwise he risks religious irrelevance. An exposition of a creed in the context of contemporary theology provides an undeniably religious focus for philosophical analysis, criticism, and reflection. The psychology is included because my thesis is that the religious convictions expressed in the creed, if properly understood, are compatible with moral freedom, and because I shall be assuming that the meaning of the statements expressing these convictions is intrinsically connected with psychological states or events in the speaker who properly understands the statements. Indeed, I shall argue that an inner receptivity is the psychological condition for the basic attitudes which are rendered explicit in the religious convictions, and for the moral impulse which is expressed in the moral convictions. Logical issues concerning connections of meaning between 'We believe in God' and 'Love and serve others' are thus inseparable from psychological issues concerning connections between psychological states or events. In some studies of relations between religion and morality, logical issues and psychological issues are considered separately. This can be a useful procedure, for it is sometimes helpful to consider logical relations between statements in abstraction from the experiential depth of understanding and strength of conviction of particular persons who make the statements. In this essay, however, we shall consider statements as they are profoundly understood and authentically affirmed, statements whose meaning is intrinsically connected with psychological states and events in speakers who are neither superficial nor inauthentic.

This chapter differs from the 1973 version of the essay[3] in two respects. First, I have inserted or added some passages which do not substantially change the thought but which either make for greater clarity or connect what is said with ideas in previous chapters. Secondly, in a postscript I interpret the essay in relation to my analysis of kinds of analogy and I also criticize the essay in ways which indicate further problems which need to be explored.

A new creed

In 1968 the General Council of the United Church of Canada approved a new creed for use in congregational worship. This creed is not a doctrinal test, setting forth a minimum of belief necessary for church membership; nor is it a denominational statement of faith or 'confession,' elaborating what most United Churchmen believe; nor is it an ecumenical creed, though it may eventually be used in many other denominations. Nevertheless it does express an important religious consensus. It is a liturgical summary of some central convictions which have a claim to be representative within the largest Protestant church in Canada, for the creed has been approved by its highest court and is actually in use in congregations. And it has a special advantage in view of the focus of this essay. Unlike an ecumenical creed such as the Apostles' Creed, it includes explicit moral convictions, and it links these with the convictions concerning God. Here it is, with the lines numbered for easy reference:

Man is not alone; he lives in God's world.   1

We believe in God: 2
   who has created and is creating,   3
   who has come in the true Man, Jesus, to reconcile and make new,   4
   who works in us and others by his Spirit.   5
We trust him.   6

He calls us to be his church: 7
   to celebrate his presence,   8
   to love and serve others,   9
   to seek justice and resist evil,   10
   to proclaim Jesus, crucified and risen, our judge and our hope.   11

In life, in death, in life beyond death, God is with us.   12
We are not alone.   13
Thanks be to God.   14

Obviously this creed is relevant to our problem concerning the relation between religious and moral convictions. I have an additional, personal reason for considering it, since I was on the committee which drafted it, I can interpret it with a fair degree of confidence. I know how a group of theologians (academics, pastors, and laymen) laboured on it for several years, working through many different versions. It was designed so as to be open to a variety of interpretations, and there were differences of interpretation within the committee itself; but I am sure that my own interpretation is not idiosyncratic. And I know many of the varied reasons and varied meanings which were pondered as the present wording gradually emerged. I should note, however, that my interpretation of the creed is influenced not only by committee discussions but also by a wide range of contemporary writings in theology and philosophy of religion.[4]

The simple beauty and brevity of the creed have been achieved at a price. Some ideas which the committee thought to be very important theologically had to be omitted. These omissions should be noted, since the ideas are part of the theological consensus which underlies the creed, and that consensus is what matters most. For example, there were two omissions from line 5. The first was the idea of liberation. Many committee members held that the main work of the Spirit is the liberation of man. Indeed, some saw in liberation a central unifying idea for the whole creed, uniting together all the various activities of God.[5] But no satisfactory wording concerning liberation could be found. The second omission in line 5 occurred when an earlier wording was changed. The line had read: 'He works within us and *among* us by his Spirit.' This suggested that God acts not only directly within each individual, deep in the psyche, but also in relations between individuals, in society. (We shall consider some of the actions 'among' men later in the essay.) The line was changed because it seemed even more important to make explicit the conviction that God is at work in non-Christians as well as Christians; so that now it reads: 'He works in us and others by his Spirit.' We shall see that the words 'and others' are of immense significance in interpreting the whole creed: the divine activity which is somehow linked with human moral activity is an activity in non-Christians as well as in Christians, in atheists and agnostics as well as in religious believers. But the words 'among us' in the earlier version will also be borne in mind.

There was also an omission in line 9. Committee members agreed that a Christian is called to love not only his neighbour but also *himself*. God helps a man to accept and to confirm himself; this is a psychologically necessary precondition for accepting and confirming others. But if line 9 had read 'to love our neighbour as ourselves,' the word 'serve' would have had to be deleted. It was thought that 'serve' was important, since 'love' by itself might connote only an attitude, whereas 'serve' clearly connotes practical activity. It also connotes an absence of concern about acquiring or maintaining social status and authoritarian power.

Another important omission is the word 'mystery.' Early drafts of the creed referred explicity to the mystery of God, suggesting that God's activities and presence transcend man's intellectual and practical grasp and evoke in man a response of awe and wonder. Unfortunately the word 'mystery' had to be left out because of necessary rearrangements in the wording and the structure of the creed. But I know from my own experience that, when the creed is used in congregational worship, it does express wonder in response to mystery; the liturgical context reinforces what many of the words of the creed already indicate.

Line 1 was vigorously debated in the committee. The present version stresses a contrast between the feeling that man is alone in a starkly impersonal cosmos (Sartrean 'forlornness') and the feeling that a trustworthy spiritual power is present everywhere in the world. There is also a suggestion that since man lives in God's world, he is responsible to God; that is, man should regard himself neither as an isolated impotent infant nor as an isolated omnipotent deity but as a passive and active responder to divine activity. Line 1 also hints at other themes which some members of the committee proposed: meaningless versus meaningful life, alienation versus at-homeness, separation versus togetherness, anxiety versus inner peace. Note that all these various themes mention alternatives to faith. Indeed, to say 'man is not alone' is to suggest an alternative conviction, namely that man *is* alone. In the committee there was some uneasiness, especially during the early discussions, about beginning a creed with a negative statement, even when it is immediately followed by 'He lives in God's world.' The uneasiness arose, I think, not so much from the grammatical form of the opening, but from the haunting allusion to the possibility of unfaith. But this realism is a merit of the creed. The Christian maintains his faith that man lives in God's world and is thus not alone *in spite of* much that goes on in the world, and *in spite of* his own tendencies to unfaith – to self-isolation, alienation, and anxiety. When he says the creed, he reaffirms his conviction and his commitment, 'Though sometimes I seem to be alone, and though sometimes I live as if I were, I am not alone. Though I sometimes live in resigned despair or strident self-assertion, responding to a world which seems indifferent or hostile, I reaffirm my trust in God.' This real tension within the typical Christian believer is implied in line 1. Indeed, for some theologians the line may suggest an aloneness which is not an alternative to Christian faith but a necessary ingredient in that faith. Some theologians, influenced by mystical, existentialist, or psychoanalytic experience and thought, hold that a man must experience the absence of God if he is to become genuinely aware of the divine presence. He must experience an utter aloneness, a nothingness within and a nothingness without, as the context in which he then comes to understand what it means to believe that God is with him. He must experience darkness, captivity, and insecurity if he is to become aware of divine light, liberation, and peace. To me it seems that there is a great deal of truth in this approach, but I do not know whether it is a universal spiritual law for all men rather than the path for some. Certainly it is at most a subordinate theme in the theology which lies behind the creed, which views aloneness mainly as an alternative to faith, not an ingredient in it. Indeed, by the time we reach line 13, aloneness has disappeared even as an alternative. 'We are not alone' is a ringing declaration, a confident way of summing up the many ways in which the creed has proclaimed the intimate relation of man to God. As we shall see, the creed sets forth divine activities and human responses. It involves an internally connected set of concepts which links the activities and the responses, a coherent overall pattern of meaning for the believer. In my interpretation of the creed I shall assume that the pattern is unreservedly held and applied by the believer, whose faith is thus an ideal faith. This assumption is, of course, unrealistic. I make it so as to reduce the obscurity and complexity of the topic. Nevertheless it is important to remember that a man who affirms the creed has a faith which falls short – often far short – of the ideal. There is a serious danger that if he is not genuinely aware of this, he will use the creed to support the self-deceptive fantasy that he has already achieved or received a final self-unifying certainty. Such a fantasy petrifies a man in his present stage of personal and spiritual development and reinforces his resistance to being changed by God. In this essay, however, we will not be considering the very real risk of bad faith in affirming a creed – using it to prevent the very receptivity to God which the creed expresses.

The rest of this essay is made up of two parts, each of which has five sections, followed by the postscript. The five sections of the first part are reflections concerning the creed, considered under the following headings: basic attitudes of trust, hope, wonder, etc as responses to divine activities; basic attitudes, explicit faith and implicit faith; receptivity to divine activity which comes *via* other men and *via* one's own inner depths; the divine call which enables and directs men to love; love, justice, and particular moral decisions. At the end of this first part one broad conclusion is that the creed does not dictate particular moral decisions, but does set them in a distinctive Christian context. In the second part of the essay five aspects of this context are discussed: responsive freedom as a directed and dependent freedom to love; the influence of the basic attitudes on particular decisions; the role of a world-view in which fact and value are inseparable; the importance of a community's common moral vocabulary; the commitment to Jesus as moral paradigm.

Creed and conduct

1 DIVINE ACTIVITY AND HUMAN RESPONSE

The creed begins and ends with man in relation to God. In between it sets forth this relation, a relation of human responses to divine activities. The creed refers to a number of different divine activities: God creates, comes, reconciles, makes new, liberates ('works'), and calls. Two further activities are implied by the words 'with us' (line 12): God accompanies men on their journey through life and beyond, and God confirms men, providing His strength, support, and backing. All these activities go on in the present, in which man responds, although they have gone on in the past and will continue into the future. God *has come* in Jesus, here and now, though of course God *came* in Jesus many years ago and *will come* in Jesus, our hope, as we move into the future. Note also that all the activities of God are activities to which the Christian believer responds. Most of the activities have men as their object; God does something directly *to* men. In the case of the activity of creation, the creed omits any explicit object-word. The believer does not say, 'who has created and is creating *the world*,' for this might suggest a cosmological theory which can be understood and accepted without any basic attitudinal responses. Instead, the creed places the creative activity of God alongside other divine activities on behalf of man ('has come,' 'reconcile,' 'make new,' 'works') as the focus for a basic human trust (line 6). The believer expresses his conviction that God acts creatively on behalf of man in the world and in his own personal existence. Some men may believe that the fundamental power or powers which dominate man's natural and social environment and which bring about human existence are impersonal, or, if personal, neutral; they are not related either positively or negatively to human fulfilment. Other men may believe that these powers are hostile to human fulfilment. The Christian believer, however, is convinced that the source of his own personal existence is also a creative, trustworthy power, everywhere active in his environment as a reliable friend of man. The Christian's pervasive, generalized attitude in life, as expressed in the creed, is thus trustful, responsive, and relaxed, rather than wary, wilful, and anxious. For a non-Christian the expression 'God the Creator' may mean an impersonal power, or a neutral personal power, or a malevolent personal power. But for the Christian believer God's creative activity, like any divine activity, is trustworthy by definition. No activity counter to human fulfilment counts as divine activity.[6]

Since Christians include human *freedom* as an element in human fulfilment, divine activity by definition cannot be contrary to human freedom. This definitional assumption of Christian theology is not, of course, in itself an answer to the critic who claims that Christian convictions conflict with moral freedom. Some religious authoritarians have an idea of freedom which is close to what everyone else, including many Christians, would call non-freedom. What matters is the content given to the idea of freedom.

In general, we shall see that there is a mutual interconnection of meaning[7] between divine activity and human attitudinal response. We cannot understand what is meant by talk about divine activity in a Christian creedal context if we try to think of it in abstraction from attitudinal responses. And the extent of our understanding depends on the extent of our responses.

Let us now consider more carefully some of the responses which are indicated in the creed. I propose that they be divided into three kinds: attitudinal, receptive, and practical. We shall consider attitudinal responses first. These include trust (line 6), joy (line 8), hope and courage (lines 11 and 12), gratitude (line 14), and wonder or awe (throughout). These are attitudes towards God, who is active wherever there is a mysterious process of creation, reconciliation, renewal, liberation, or confirmation in human life. Each attitude is of such a kind as to be connected in meaning with one or more of the activities: trust in divine creativity, joy in divine reconciliation, hope based on divine confirmation, gratitude for divine renewal, wonder at divine liberation, etc. To be convinced of divine activity involves having the specific attitude and other attitudes; having the specific attitude, if explicit, involves being convinced of the divine activity and other divine activities. The attitude is 'fitting' or 'appropriate' as a response to divine activity because of an internal connection of meaning between response and activity. Usually there is no simple one-to-one correlation between a kind of divine activity and a kind of attitudinal response. For example, divine creativity is connected with trust, gratitude, and other attitudes; trust is connected with divine creativity, divine liberation, and other activities.

The various attitudinal responses are expressed in *worship*, which the creed describes as a celebration of the divine presence (line 8). Although the main attitude indicated by the word 'celebrate' is joy, the other worshipful attitudes were meant to be included: trust, hope, gratitude, and wonder. (In each case, as we shall see later, the attitude is a 'basic' one, unrestricted and pervasive in its scope; it is a stance of the whole being in relation to the whole environment.) One reason for the choice of the word 'celebrate' was that the note of joy should be clearly evident somewhere in the creed; but there were other reasons, of course, such as the associations with both 'celebrations' of sacraments and 'celebrations' in secular life. The word 'presence' emphasizes the fact that divine activities are activities to which men respond here and now, personally and directly. God is actively present to man. The word 'presence' thus fits in well with the rest of the creed. We should note, however, the absence of an expression which is important in Christian theology: the divine 'word.' Worship is often depicted as a response to the divine 'word.' This is compatible with the creed. All the divine activities are understood by means of human language, so the activities communicate meaning to man, and are responded to in terms of their meaning. Worship, then, may be defined as the expression of such-and-such basic attitudes to God in response to the active, meaningful presence of God. And God may be defined as the active, meaningful presence to whom men fittingly respond in worship (expressions of basic attitudes).

Both definitions, however, are incomplete, for we have been considering only the first kind of response to God, the attitudinal. There are two others, the receptive and the practical. Later we shall consider practical responses, especially the moral responses as sketched in lines 9 and 10: 'to love and serve others, to seek justice and resist evil.' The receptive response, however, is the central focus of faith, the human starting-point for both Christian worship and Christian morality. Receptivity towards God is, of course, an attitude, and might therefore seem to belong among the other 'attitudinal' responses to God. It differs, however, in being the sine qua non, the precondition, of the other attitudes. For whereas for Christians the attitudinal responses to God presuppose that God is acting in a man, receptivity is what allows God to act in a man. God cannot act in a man unless the man permits it. Instead of being receptive to divine activity a man can block, impede, and resist it. Instead of allowing God to liberate him, a man can reinforce his own self-imprisoning defences. God does not help those who help themselves; he helps those who realize their own need of help. God creates new life in those who acknowledge the destructive elements in their lives and let go of them. God speaks to those who are willing to listen to him. God is present to those who are open to receive him. The activities of God, to which men respond attitudinally, are activities within men which do not occur unless there is a receptive response. This is true even in the case of divine creativity, which has to be received, allowed, welcomed by the believer if it is to be recognized for what it is, and responded to with trust and gratitude. At an unconscious level a man may reject divine creativity, not allowing it to sustain him against physical or psychical suicide.

The notion of 'unconscious resistance' is very important in any reflections concerning receptivity. For example, a man may be resisting divine liberation, not allowing God to free him from bondage to the rigidities of his present character-structure, without being conscious of anything except some anxiety and some inhibitions in his responses to other people. The notion of the unconscious here has affinities with that in modern psychoanalysis, but it is also linked with a traditional theological conception of sin as an 'ignoring' of God, a culpable 'not-knowing' of what one in some way already knows, a form of paradoxical self-deception.[8] Thus I am bringing together psychoanalysis and theology when I speak of an 'unconscious resistance' to divine activity within oneself.

2 IMPLICIT FAITH AND BASIC ATTITUDES

In so far as a man is conscious of a liberating process going on within himself, he is *not* resisting divine activity, whether consciously or unconsciously; as resistance decreases, liberation increases; as receptivity increases, liberation increases. Indeed, a reference to unconscious receptivity is involved in a theological interpretation of the phrase 'in others' (line 5). God works in non-Christians, including many who do not understand what is going on in terms of inner receptivity to divine activity. They *are* inwardly receptive to divine activity and they are conscious of much that a genuinely receptive Christian experiences: an inner freedom, basic attitudes of trust, hope, gratitude, joy, and wonder, and a relatively uninhibited love for themselves and their fellow men. They also may express their basic attitudes in art, as they create and celebrate beauty in the world – though without explicitly worshipping God. But they do not interpret any of this in terms of their own inner receptivity to divine activity. In the eyes of a Christian such men have faith, but it is implicit rather than explicit.

The creed expresses an explicit faith. For Christians the creed renders explicit the convictions which are implicit in the basic attitudes, whether these be in Christians or in non-Christians. Before we examine the notion of 'implicit' faith, I should say more about the basic attitudes. We have considered them in the chapters on Ian Ramsey and Sam Keen and I explore them much more thoroughly in my book *Struggle and Fulfilment,*[9] so a brief outline will suffice here. Reflections on my own experience and in response to a variety of thinkers[10] have led me to think of a basic attitude as an attitude of the whole human being to the whole universe, pervasive both internally and externally, affecting every element in a person in his responses and initiatives to everything he encounters in his environment.[11] Consider, for example, basic trust. It has an all-inclusive temporal scope in its influence on the life of a man and an all-inclusive spatial scope in its application to the world. Temporally, it provides continuity and inner harmony for a life as a whole; it is like a musical ground bass pervading the polyphony of man's transitory trusts and distrusts. Spatially, basic trust extends all-inclusively to whatever it is that pervades the whole cosmos, giving it some unity; often a man regards the trustworthiness of a particular person or persons as being somehow representative of the whole, in spite of the frequent untrustworthiness of this or that item in his natural and social environment. A basic attitude differs from other attitudes not only in its unrestricted, pervasive scope (internal and external) but also in its apparent lack of determinate content. Basic trust and basic hope, for example, may continue even when it seems that there is nothing in which to trust or for which to hope. Actually there *is* a content, but it can be understood only in relation to whatever goes on within a man when he is inwardly receptive. In the next section I shall try to describe this elusive and mysterious happening. Meanwhile, however, I shall add some reflections concerning basic trust and then turn to the notion of 'implicit' faith.

Concerning basic trust I have spoken of the trustworthiness of a particular person being regarded as somehow representative of the whole. I seem to be opting for the second of two alternatives considered by H. Richard Niebuhr:

It remains questionable whether the self is led more to trust in the ultimate because it finds all the finite beings about it unreliable, or more because it is led by stages from trust in the near-at-hand to trust in the ultimate. Is it because all finite powers on which we have relied for value have failed us that we turn to the ultimate? or because we have seen traces of the structure of faith in the whole realm of being that we are led to confidence in Being simply considered?[12]

But as I go on, talking about 'nothing in which to trust,' I am closer to the first alternative, which finds finite things unreliable and therefore trusts only in the ultimate. Any adequate account of faith needs to include both alternatives, just as it needs to consider 'aloneness' both as a rival to faith and as an ingredient in faith. My own reflections concerning the dialectic of trust begin with the conviction that the trustworthy God acts primarily through men. Hence he who cannot trust man cannot trust God, though he who trusts solely in men is evading human frailty and mortality. A trust in God which is not supported by a trust in men (oneself and others) is likely to be a flight from both, a self-deceptive clinging to a fantasy; but to focus an unlimited trust on limited men is both unwise and idolatrous. All this, however, is only the rudiments of a dialectic of trust; the subtleties and complexities are beyond the scope of this essay, and are explored in *Struggle and Fulfilment*.

Concerning the notion of *'implicit faith'* the first thing to recognize is that expressions of attitude usually imply beliefs. To put it more strictly, the speaker who expresses an attitude usually, in saying what he does, implies that he has such-and-such beliefs. Such implications of speech-acts, though not the same as entailments between propositions, are logical relations. In chapter 7 I shall show why speech-act implication, though initially plausible in analysis of implicit faith, and important in its stress on *expressions* of attitude, is less appropriate than propositional entailment. Here, however, I shall continue the presentation without changing the 1973 version of the essay in this respect, and with only partial revisions in other respects. As I go on I shall be interpreting the relation between basic attitudes and religious convictions in a way which seems to contradict what I have said in chapter 3. In chapter 7 I shall show how both accounts, somewhat modified, contain elements of truth which can be brought together without any contradiction.

But now I will continue my outline of speech-act implication. Expressions of attitude are not the only speech-acts which carry implications. In saying 'The cat is on the mat' I *imply* that I believe that the cat is on the mat. In saying 'I promise to come tomorrow' I *imply* that I intend to come tomorrow. Consider some expressions of attitude. In saying 'I trust John' I *imply* that I believe that John is trustworthy. In saying 'I am grateful to Mary' I *imply* that I believe Mary did something beneficial for me. In saying 'I trust whoever it is that is sending us the information' I *imply* that I believe that some person is sending us the information. In saying 'I am grateful to whoever it is who turned over my wallet to the police' I *imply* that I believe that someone turned over my wallet to the police. In all such cases the implication is clear and rigorous, since the words used to express the attitude make evident to us the belief that is implied.

If, however, the attitude under consideration is a *basic* attitude, the implication need not be clear and rigorous, for the basic attitude need not be already articulated so that the implied beliefs are explicitly set forth. Consider basic trust. Since its scope is not restricted and its focus is not any one particular, people can intelligibly and reasonably differ concerning the belief that is implied. Earlier I used the expression 'whatever it is that pervades the whole cosmos, giving it unity,' but beyond this description of the focus people may differ. A cautious believer may hold that the focus cannot be directly described further except in a strictly negative way, as *not* being any particular or aggregate of particulars. An agnostic critic may claim that having such an indeterminate belief is indistinguishable from having no belief at all. A Christian believer goes beyond both of these positions, though he concedes much truth in their *via negativa*. He understands basic trust in himself and others as implying a belief in God, 'a trustworthy spiritual power present everywhere in the world,' active within a man when he is inwardly receptive. This is an *interpretation* of basic trust, a proposed way of articulating it. Such interpretation, when it renders explicit a basic trust, promotes and sustains that trust, though it cannot by itself create that trust.

Thus if a Christian says to an agnostic who has basic trust, hope, gratitude, etc, 'You have an implicit faith in God,' he is offering an interpretation which the agnostic is logically free to reject. The interpretation is not a wily manoeuvre in a Christian apologetic specially devised for outsiders; for the Christian his own explicit faith in God is logically implied by his own basic attitudes, which resemble those of the agnostic. Indeed, he is sometimes as agnostic as the agnostic, not interpreting his own experience in terms of his explicit faith. Sometimes, however, he does so interpret it. To be a Christian is, in part, to accept a way of talking and thinking such that basic attitudes are understood in a distinctive way. It is to accept and to bear witness to an interpretative framework concerning some 'depth-experiences'[13] or 'peak-experiences'[14] common to many men, including non-Christians. The most fundamental experience is understood in terms of receptivity to divine activity. To this we now turn. (Later we shall consider basic attitudes again, in relation to moral freedom.)

3 RECEPTIVITY TO DIVINE ACTIVITY

Christians believe that there is a kind of creative or providential activity in society, as in nature, which does not depend on human receptivity, whether conscious or unconscious. But a conviction concerning this activity presupposes, both for understanding and for acceptance, a receptivity to divine activity within oneself.

The creed indicates the pattern of receptivity in lines 11 and 12:

to proclaim Jesus, crucified and risen, our judge and our hope.
In life, in death, in life beyond death, God is with us.

The believer is receptive to crucifixion-death and judgment, and to risen life and hope. First he has to expose himself to judgment, to critical scrutiny, which shows him that part of himself which is destructive and enslaving, a part which has to be abandoned, to be left to die. In this shattering crisis of judgment the Christian is enabled to acknowledge the truth about himself which has been exposed, and to let go of his old, defensive sources of security; for he allows the creative, liberating power of God to give him new life and hope. As old patterns of life are exposed and abandoned, it seems as if he were dying: he is 'giving himself away.' But the Christian finds that God confirms his sense of his own identity and reality, and gives him new creative energies.[15] God liberates men from domination by destructive and enslaving elements within themselves so that they can become creative and free. God liberates men from despair and drabness, granting hope and wonder. In a world where death has seemed to represent an ultimate cosmic untrustworthiness, God frees men from anxiety, or enables them to bear it; whatever happens, even in death, God is with us, giving new life. The condition of divine activity within a man, however, is receptivity. This is not a matter of 'earning' a divine reward, or 'doing' something by oneself to which God then responds. It is a matter of letting go, permitting, allowing, yielding, not resisting, welcoming. It is not a wilful exercise of one's existing powers or abilities. It is allowing oneself to be empowered, enabled to live creatively in basic trust, hope, gratitude, joy, and wonder.

Except for creative or providential activity in nature and in social processes and structures, divine activity is always in one sense 'within' a man, for that is where the receptive man provides an 'opening' for God. But the 'route' or 'medium' of the divine activity may be either within the man or outside him. God may inspire him, touching the unconscious depths of his personality directly; but God may also act *via* other people; God works 'in others' (line 5) in a sense which we have not yet considered: he acts in others *for us and towards us*. He acts *via* the words and deeds which others, both Christian and non-Christian, address to us.

Indeed, the way in which another man influences me when I am receptive to him is a basic analogy for the divine-human relation.

The underlying structure of the creed can now be summarized as follows: Where the believer or any man is receptive, God is active within
him, bringing about change. The change gives rise to attitudinal responses and practical responses. On the one hand, there are new attitudes which may be expressed in worship towards God. On the other
hand, there are new activities towards men. This practical, man-ward
aspect has two elements: witness and morality. The Christian bears witness to the divine activity in men – in Jesus, in fellow Christians, in other
men, and in himself. The idea of witnessing is suggested in line 11: 'We
proclaim Jesus ...' Later we shall examine the distinctive Christian witness to *Jesus*, but here we should note that the creed as a whole is meant
not only as a prayerful communication to God but also as a proclamation
to men, bearing witness to divine activity and human response. As we
have seen, a Christian explicitly accepts and proclaims a theological
interpretation of what is already going on in human beings. In this essay
I shall restrict the word 'witness' to this explicit interpretative act,
although Christians sometimes extend its meaning so as to refer to that
to which the interpretation is applied, for example, exemplary moral
activity. In this extended sense a Christian 'bears witness' to God when
his own inner receptivity to divine activity is expressed in loving actions;
but so also does a non-Christian. In the interests of clarity let us maintain
a distinction between 'witness' and 'morality.' And let us see how the
creed introduces morality.

4 MORALITY AND THE CALL TO LOVE

Lines 9 and 10 are obviously moral in content:

to love and serve others [and ourselves]
to seek justice and resist evil

My reason for adding 'and ourselves' was given earlier. The immediate
question here is 'how is moral activity related to the divine activities and
human responses, both attitudinal and receptive?' In the creed the link is
provided by the word 'calls.' God calls us to be his church, and being his
church involves not only worship (line 8) and witness (line 11) but also
moral activity (lines 9 and 10). Note that the creed does not say 'He
commands (orders, decrees, etc) ...' or 'He designs (purposes, manufac-

tures, etc) ...' The primary image of God in the creed is neither an absolute monarch, exercising unquestionable political or legal authority, nor a master craftsman, designing and making artefacts (including man) to fulfil his own purposes rather than theirs. Morality is here understood in a context of calling (*klesis*) rather than of law (*nomos*) or of purpose (*telos*).[16]

In its Christian theological setting the word 'call' has three distinguishable elements:

(a) call *together* (out of godless life into a community, an assembly, a church or *ekklesia*, which means 'the called ones')
(b) call *forth* (evoke, create, liberate, enable, empower)
(c) call *upon* (urge, exhort, appeal, challenge, ask to volunteer, direct)

Element (a), which stresses the communal nature of Christian faith and life, will be considered later, but I note two things here. One is that there is a tautology: 'He calls us to be his church (i.e. his called ones).' The other is that the called ones are those who are receptive to divine activity, whether consciously (the 'visible' church) or unconsciously (the 'invisible' church). Elements (b) and (c) are more important here. God both enables and exhorts. For example, God's calling to love others is related both to a man's ability and to a man's obligation to love others, both to 'can' and to 'ought.' But the 'ought' comes not as an order but as an exhortation, a challenge, an appeal in relation to what a man now can do, empowered by God.

Let us consider (b) first, the element of enabling, empowering by God. We have already looked at the *fundamental* Christian convictions concerning this. Divine activity liberates the receptive man from that which impedes his growth towards whole-hearted, creative living. And divine activity is itself creative, not only confirming the man in his present existence but also providing new creative energies and powers. We have seen how the attitudinal responses of trust, gratitude, hope, joy, and wonder are expressed in worship. Here, however, we should notice the relation between these attitudinal responses and moral activity. This has two aspects: self and others. We shall consider them in turn.

In some philosophies and theologies a man's way of dealing with himself is not a moral matter. Instead, it is dealt with under 'prudence' or 'self-interest' rather than under 'moral duty' or 'moral altruism.' In the Christian theology which we are considering, however, the kind of love which a man should have for himself is similar to the kind of love which

he should have for others. 'Love your neighbour as yourself.' What kind
of love should he have for himself? In one way he should *not* love himself. Receptivity to divine activity involves abandoning a false defensive
self, giving it up. But receptivity also brings a new self-regard and self-
acceptance, a new wholeheartedness in wanting and willing. Trust and
hope and gratitude and wonder as basic attitudes towards God at work
in one's natural and social environment are also basic attitudes towards
God at work within *oneself*, liberating one's own energies and desires,
creating abilities, confirming one in one's humanity. If a man is receptive
to divine activity and has these basic attitudes towards God, he is given a
new freedom to want or desire or 'wish' wholeheartedly, without inhibi-
tion or internal division, for himself. 'Doing the will of God' does not
mean that every action must conform to what God commands or plans
or wants. It does not even mean that every action must be a response to
some specific activity of God in a particular situation. In much of life
what is called 'God's will' is simply that *as receptive men we do what we
want to do,* that we become fully aware of our deepest needs and impulses
and act accordingly.[17] At the risk of being misleading we can parody
Sartre and say: '*Since* God exists, everything is permitted.' That is, since
God is active within the receptive man, enabling and encouraging him to
be wholehearted, the man can want anything and act accordingly, except where this would impair his own receptivity or contradict his love
for others. There are various alternatives to such a wholehearted self-
affirmation. A man may want and act in an alternating conformity and
defiance towards other men, rarely wanting or acting on his own. He
may do this towards an imaginary authoritarian god as well. Or he may
try to repress and inhibit his wanting, trying to isolate himself from
others and the world, trying to ignore such deep desires as the passion to
give and receive affection. ('It is better *not* to have loved and lost ...') Or
he may turn some one thing into an absolute, an obsessive, compulsive
cause to which he devotes himself, ascribing unconditional value to it,
making it his (idolatrous) ultimate concern. Or he may view himself
'objectively,' from outside, as if he were a complex machine, to be
manipulated and controlled in a detached 'value-free' way. These are all
alternatives to being receptive to God and thereby being able to want
wholeheartedly for oneself. We must remember that being receptive to
God is not necessarily a conscious state. In so far as an avowed atheist or
agnostic is able to love himself, to want wholeheartedly, accepting and
respecting himself, this is for the Christian an indication that he is
unconsciously receptive to divine activity, which comes to him *via* other

men and *via* his own psychic depths without his recognizing it as such. On the other hand, a man may be consciously, in his own eyes, a Christian, yet unconsciously resisting divine activity. He may recite the creed, agreeing with what he takes to be its meaning, while being unconsciously unreceptive, having only superficial attitudinal responses of trust, hope, gratitude, and wonder, and not allowing himself to be liberated to love himself.

God also enables a man to love *others*. We have seen that in coming to love himself a man drops a variety of defences against self-knowledge and self-acceptance: the competitive/conforming pattern, repression and self-isolation, compulsive fanaticism, and 'value-free' detachment. These are all ways by which one also keeps *others* at a distance, not being open to them as they really are. When the defences are dropped in the new security provided by the divine activity and the attitudinal responses, a man accepts and respects not only his own fundamental needs and wants, but also those of others. He becomes aware of these, forming a common humanity. And since divine activity comes to him not only from within his own psychic depths but also *via* love from others, and since divine activity also comes to others *via* his own love as well as from within themselves, there is a mutuality of human love in all this, a giving and receiving in which God acts.[18] A man cannot only be liberated by God, acting through others; he can also be the medium through which God liberates others. To love others is, in part, to desire and foster their liberation to a life of wholehearted wanting and self-affirmation. It is also, of course, to desire the satisfaction of their ordinary needs, as well as one's own – whether these be for food or health or recognition.

We have been considering the divine call as an *enabling* call, a calling-*forth* by which a man is empowered to love himself and others. But it has not been possible to keep the element of enablement distinct from the element of calling-*upon*, of exhortation or challenge. What a man now *can* do is what he *ought* to do. Sometimes the divine challenge may be to love oneself better ('Stop letting yourself down, wallowing in your despair and self-hatred') and sometimes to love others better ('Give him some of the affection which he needs as much as you do'). In each case the divine challenge is to do what the divine activity enables him to do. The new freedom is a power which includes within itself a spur in a given direction; it combines ability and obligation, 'can' and 'ought'; it comes as both a gift and a directive, an enabling and an impelling. A man can resist the divine activity, rejecting the new freedom, but in so far as he accepts it, he does not receive an independent ability, which is henceforth at his own disposal to use at will in any way he chooses; he does not then have a wilful freedom to love to not to love. The new freedom is a *responsive* freedom, which depends on continuous receptivity to God, and which is an ability with a built-in direction – to love oneself and others. Responsive freedom is dependent and directed freedom. A man who accepts the divine call allows himself to be changed, dependent on God's liberating activity within as he becomes a different person, loving people more deeply and spontaneously. A man is freed to love. This leaves many alternative options open for action, for he can love himself and others in many different ways. But some particular options – unloving ones – are ruled out. He is enabled and directed to love, but he is also disabled and diverted from non-love. The extent to which a man allows himself to be changed determines the extent to which he understands what the divine call is, and what love of self and others is. Love of self and others is not only an indication of (conscious or unconscious) love-receptivity towards God. As viewed by Christian theology the three loves grow and are understood together.

5 LOVE AND JUSTICE

How does a man best express his love towards others? It is not only a 'spiritual' matter of encouraging in others a receptivity towards God by allowing himself to be a medium of divine activity towards them. There is also, as we have seen, a desire that their ordinary 'material' human needs be satisfied. One of the reasons for including the word 'serve' in the creed was to stress this less elusive but very important expression of love for the whole person, who may be hungry or thirsty or sick or lonely. But even this addition is not enough. People exist in society, with its impersonal institutions and power-structures, where corporate injustice and corporate evil are major sources of spiritual and material destructiveness in human life. Love is rationally expressed in *political* activity as well as in the intimacy of personal or small-group activity. Obviously a change in the power-structure of society may be more effective than private charity in reducing hunger. But the elusive 'spiritual' realm is also affected by the institutional framework of society. The extent to which a man is able to 'let go' of himself and be receptive to divine activity depends in part on what the political and economic power-structure has done to him. Receptivity is deadened by the resignation and despair and self-contempt which tend to be fostered among the oppressed in an unjust society; it is also deadened in the oppressors by their arrogance and callousness.

Seeking justice is thus one way of actively expressing love for others, a love which the creed understands as arising from a gift and directive received by individual men as God acts within them. Seeking justice also has another context in the creed. I have noted a conviction that God is somehow active among men in ways which do not depend on human receptivity, whether conscious or unconscious. This activity in human society, like that in nature, is believed to be creative or providential, and the response to it is basic trust. But the activity is also believed to be God's promotion of *justice* in the institutional relations which exist among men, a justice which stresses the *liberation* of the oppressed. There is not only a divine liberation in individuals but also a divine liberation in society, in politics. When a man seeks to promote justice, he is thus participating in a divine activity which is already going on in society. This is a different way of conceiving the promotion of justice. The idea of participation in God's political activity is different from the idea of expressing in society a capacity and a challenge to love which one has received interiorly and individually from God. The two ideas are compatible, but the idea of participation is secondary in the theology which forms the background of the creed. A serious difficulty for the idea of participation is that it assumes we can somehow *identify* what God is doing politically and then join in. Such an approach can reinforce political fanaticism. On the alternative approach the decision as to how to express one's love politically is a matter to be decided alongside non-Christians by using one's political reason, which is admittedly fallible.

More generally, the theology of the creed leaves largely open the ways in which love is to be expressed, whether in personal or political contexts. This openness is encouraged, not because love is thought to be somehow by itself a way of knowing what one ought to do in each particular situation, but because love by itself is not enough. Other elements are needed, for example, moral reasoning. Indeed, whether a man has a loving or a defensive life-stance, whether he is receptive or unreceptive to divine activity within him, whatever his conscious religious or anti-religious ideas, he still has to *think* about what he ought to do in particular situations. He may make moral decisions with great deference to moral rules or with great concern to be 'situational.' The creed leaves open the issue as to the relative importance of rules and situations, an issue which faces men whether they accept the creed or reject it.[19]

Love is an inner motivating state and stance in which and from which a man affirms and accepts himself and others. Love by itself is not a self-sufficient faculty by which a man rightly perceives what he ought to do, or a sufficient criterion in accordance with which he rightly decides what he ought to do. Love may seem to be such a faculty because a man whom God has enabled and directed to love realizes in some situations that he has been rendered unable and unwilling to do such-and-such a wrong action. If the action is a *kind* of action which might recur, he may find himself committed to a virtually exceptionless moral rule, as we have seen in chapter 5 (though here the basis is responsive love rather than convenant-fidelity). Another reason why love may seem to be a self-sufficient faculty of moral perception is that such a man knows that he recognizes and responds to human needs which without love he would not perceive. And love may seem to be such a moral criterion because a loving man may summarily refer to his own right actions as being 'loving' and his own wrong actions as being 'unloving.' Since love has been a factor in many or all of his moral decisions, talk about love as a faculty or a criterion is not entirely misleading; but love is *a* faculty among others, *a* criterion among others. Other things have been involved: a man's basic attitudes, his world-view, his moral framework, his empirical knowledge, and his rational deliberation.

We have seen that the creed does not dictate particular moral decisions, but it does set moral decision-making in a distinctive context for Christians. Five aspects of this context can be distinguished, each one being important in our consideration of faith and moral freedom: responsive freedom to love; basic attitudes; world-view; moral vocabulary; and Jesus as paradigm. We shall consider each briefly in turn.

Christian context for moral decisions

1 RESPONSIVE FREEDOM TO LOVE

Earlier I have noted the Christian conviction that the activity of God comes *via* the influence of other men and *via* a man's own unconscious depths. It comes interpersonally (cf Baum's main theme in MB) and intrapersonally (cf Keen's main theme in TDG). Receptivity to God involves a receptive stance towards other men and towards one's inmost self.

Towards other men a man abandons the effort to control, to wield power and authority. The 'wilful' freedom which is appropriately exercised over his own skills, whether physical or intellectual, is not imposed on another man. Yet receptivity does not mean submissively accepting control imposed by another man. Instead one man allows another man to help him to change within, to become what he cannot wilfully *make* himself become.

Receptivity towards one's own unconscious depths also involves a 'letting go' of wilful control. A man allows himself to be changed by an upsurge of vital energies which impel him in unforeseen directions. When a man is open to the inner dynamism of the psyche and the body,[20] he loses the security of the order which he has already imposed on his life. If he empties his mind of the orderly structures which he has concocted as his defence against inner chaos and expectantly waits for something to happen, he somehow overcomes his anxiety, somehow trusts the forces within him in spite of the risk. The new freedom which then may come is a spontaneous, creative freedom. It is not like a skill which a man can methodically develop and then exercise at will. Such skills are important in human life, though I have classified them under 'wilful' freedom, which is a derogatory term; wilful freedom is not intrinsically evil. What is evil is extending a wilful-freedom approach to all aspects of life, instead of being receptive to other men and to one's unconscious drives. (As I have argued in chapters 3 and 4, skills and wilful freedom should be included but subordinated in a life where the dominant pervasive stance is receptivity and the overall life-style arises from responsive freedom.

Many kinds of receptivity to others and to one's own depths have been advocated by Christian theologians,[21] but there are three main points of agreement. The first is that the activity of God comes to the receptive man *via* the others and *via* a man's own depths. The second point is that the activity of God evokes in the receptive man some basic attitudes of trust, hope, joy, gratitude, and wonder which may be expressed in worship. (In the next section we shall consider the relation between these basic attitudes and moral decisions.) The third point is that the activity of God is a call which enables and directs a man to love, that is, to affirm and accept himself and others. This theological conviction thus includes a built-in criterion concerning what is to be acknowledged as divine activity. Whatever enables and directs a man to love comes from God; whatever disables and diverts him from love does not.

But this is an oversimplification, which may even misleadingly suggest that receptivity is redundant in religion and morality. A man does not already know what love is, and hence what divine activity is, prior to being receptive; he understands only to the degree that he is receptive. Nor is love the only criterion. If a man has the basic attitudes which we have considered, this is also a sign that he has been receptive to activity which is divine. Nor is love a *clear* criterion, for it is an elusive inner state and stance which may be expressed in a variety of ways, and it is only one factor in the moral decision-making and behaviour of the agent, as we have seen. In spite of all this, however, it is important to note that, for the Christian, love is a criterion for what counts as divine. Thus religious convictions partly depend on moral convictions (though in a dialectical and dynamic way which is remote from Kant's account of religion and morality).

In this essay, however, our main interest is in the dependence of morality on religion. Concerning this issue the notions of receptivity and of responsive freedom are crucial. Receptivity to divine activity is understood by Christians mainly in terms of an analogy with receptivity to the activity of another agent. Even divine activity within the depths of the psyche is partly understood in this way. Traditional language concerning the 'will of God' reflects this personalistic analogy. The language is easily misunderstood if the only notion of 'will' that a man has is one which is linked with wilful freedom rather than responsive freedom, for then the will of God is construed as an absolute instance of a power to use others for one's own purposes. To do the will of someone else, be he human or divine, is then to submit in what would otherwise be a power struggle. It is to evade responsibility for making up one's own mind concerning what one ought to do. Even if one believes that the other's will is wise and benevolent, one's own freedom of decision is lost. In contrast with this, if 'will of God' is understood in the context of responsive freedom, no such implications follow when a man prays 'Thy will be done.' The divine will is *like*, and acts *through*, the other person and the unconscious depths. These gratuitously free a man to love if he responds. The Christian believes that these liberating influences are the gifts of God. To respond to a man who says 'Thou' to me, and to respond to the creative *'eros'* within myself, is to respond to God. In each case there is a 'letting go' of oneself, a self-abandonment, a kind of inaction. But it is not a resigned submission to the wilful will of another. It is a discovery and a liberation and an expression of one's own true self. This occurs not when a man exercises his own wilful freedom, but when he responds to divine activity.

I have indicated how the idea of responsive freedom which is presupposed in the creed is in conflict with authoritarian interpretations of the 'will of God.' But the idea is also in conflict with some secular views, in which each man tries to become for himself an authoritarian 'god' over his own life. On these views the ideal is a maximal self-sufficiency and independence, a minimal dependence on other men for help or influence in becoming what one has decided to become. There is also an attempt to become independent of one's own unconscious urges by wilfully imposing law and order on oneself – a law which one may discover by the use of reason (Kant),[22] or invent (Sartre). The ideal is *autonomy* and the enemy is *heteronomy*. Since these are the exhaustive alternatives on this view, there is no place for responsive freedom – or it is misinterpreted and classified as a form of heteronomy. As for theology, God is either identified with one's own self-imposed law (and thus with one's own will) or rejected as a heteronomous 'Big Bopper,' a threat to freedom and dignity, a deity whose 'death' seems to provide a liberation. For the theology of the creed this is a mistake. Nevertheless God *is* a threat to human autonomy, not because He is a heteronomous authority, demanding submission to his controlling will, but because He calls each man to 'let go' of his attempt at autonomy and, instead, to become receptive to His call. The call comes in ways beyond a man's control, *via* other men and *via* his own hidden depths. Responsive freedom is a dependent and directed freedom, as we have seen. A man depends on the activity of God as he is enabled and directed to love.

As a postscript to this section I should note that, although responsive freedom abandons the wilful will, it fosters a *responsive will*, or, in Eriksonian psychoanalytic terms, an *ego-in-relation*. Although a man is *directed* to love, he also *directs* his love. Although he *receives* vital energy from others and from his own depths, this enables him to *affirm* himself. Although he is *dependent* on what is beyond his control, he is thereby strengthened to think and live *decisively*. Although he *'gives himself away'* to others, he discovers and nourishes a new *self* which deeply influences others. Other features of the responsive will might be mentioned, but here my purpose is merely to see that my contrast between wilful freedom does not give rise to the mistaken impression that responsive freedom and responsive freedom eliminates or minimizes the will and the *ego*, granting reality only to what is received from others or from the unconscious forces of the *id*. In avoiding what Keen would call the 'Apollonian' wilfulness of a Freudian ego I am not advocating a 'Dionysian' passivity and formlessness. As I have said in chapter 3: 'Instead of the ego as intellect and/or will dominating the internal passions and external chaos, Erikson's ego is the whole personality learning mutual adjustment with its environment, an adjustment which involves both giving and receiving.'

2 BASIC ATTITUDES AND MORAL DECISIONS

In my exposition of the creed I have tried to show how convictions concerning divine activity involve, as part of their meaning, various basic attitudes: trust, hope, joy, gratitude, and wonder. How are these attitudes related to the making of particular moral decisions? The relation is very complex and subtle, but I will sketch a few of its more prominent features:

(a) From a basic attitude no particular action follows in a particular situation. A basic attitude can be instantiated or expressed in a variety of ways in any one situation. 'I have basic attitude A' and 'The situation is such-and-such' do not entail 'I ought to do X.' Nor from 'He has basic attitude A' plus 'The situation is such-and-such' can I deduce that 'He will decide he ought to do X' or 'He will do X.'

(b) A basic attitude nevertheless contributes to the distinctive 'style' or 'timbre' or 'spirit' of a particular action.

(c) A basic attitude is sometimes a necessary condition psychologically for seeing what ought to be done and/or for being able to do it. For example, a man who lacks basic hope may be unable to discern and utilize a way out of a difficult human predicament.

(d) The basic attitudes expressed in the creed are contrary to a variety of alternative attitudes, each of which is appropriately expressed in a *world-view* which in turn is linked with a characteristic moral stance. I shall give three oversimplified examples of this. First, some attitudes are expressed in *conflictual* world-views, in which humanity (and sometimes also the cosmos) is divided into two roughly equal and warring camps, one side being absolutely right and the other absolutely wrong. Such world-views promote a *crusading* morality, in which the Bad Guys have no value or rights over against the fanatical, self-righteous zeal of the Good Guys. Secondly, some attitudes are expressed in *technological* world-views, in which whatever is real can only be known objectively, with a scientific detachment which enables men to control and manipulate reality; there is no reality known responsively. Such world-views are today often linked with a *quantitative utilitarianism*, a 'social engineering' approach to political morality and a 'behaviour therapy' approach to private morality. Thirdly, there are *alienated* world-views, in which an individual or a small, closely related group feels strange in an alien environment; no meaning or value or vital activity can be discerned in nature or in the institutions and historical processes of society – only within oneself or one's group does one feel at home, if at all. Such world-views encourage a *privatized,* opting-out morality, with no ecological or political dimensions.

(e) Basic Christian attitudes are expressed in a world-view which has its own link with a characteristic moral stance. The world-view is neither thoroughly conflictual nor technological nor alienated, though radically revised elements of each of these world-views can be included. First, there is a conflict between forces of good and forces of evil, but evil is always present to some extent on *both* sides of any human conflict. (When the committee included 'resist evil' in the creed, the evil envisaged was both inside and outside the individual, inside and outside his group.) The goal is not total victory for one human side, but reconciliation (cf line 4: 'to reconcile and make new'). Secondly, a scientific, technological world-view is subordinated to the awareness of realities which can only be known responsively; and a calculative form of utilitarianism, though appropriate as part of one's approach to many moral problems, is subordinated to the requirements of responsive freedom. As for an alienated world-view, it has some measure of truth, for the supreme clue to reality is to be found within intimate personal relations or within the depths of the psyche, but God is also active in nature and in society; ecology and politics have great religious and moral significance; one ought not to 'opt out.'

None of the elements in a Christian world-view dictates any particular answer to particular questions of moral decision: 'What precisely is the loving thing to do in this situation?' But all of them do affect such decisions, in two distinguishable ways. On the one hand, the world-view expresses basic attitudes, which themselves affect moral decisions, as I have noted. On the other hand, the dominant imagery in the world-view provides an important element in the way the situation of moral choice is understood. To this we now turn.

3 'ONLOOKS' AND CHOICES

Early in chapter 1 have mentioned the notion of 'onlooks,' which I first introduced in *The Logic of Self-Involvement.* One example is: 'I look on God as father (or shepherd, or judge, or liberator, or light, or breath of life, or architect and maker of the universe.' An onlook is an attitude which has the form 'I look on *x* as *y*,' or which *can* be expressed in this form. The notion covers much of what has been called 'myth,' 'world-view,' 'ideology,' 'parable,' and 'symbolic framework.' An analysis of the linguistic form is illuminating because it helps to show how 'is' and 'ought,' whom so many philosophers have put asunder, can be joined together in logical wedlock. If I look on x as y, I assume that there is some obviously appropriate way of treating y, and I judge that x is sufficiently like y to be treated in a similar way. I am judging what really *is* the case, for I judge that x really is sufficiently like y. Yet the judgment of sufficient likeness is inseparable from a decision concerning how I *ought* to be or behave towards x. Deciding-*that* and deciding-*to* are here combined. I do not first decide-*that* and then, as a separable, open decision, decide-*to*.

An onlook which is part of a world-view is focused primarily and initially on life and death and man and the state and human history and nature and, sometimes, God; only secondarily is it applied to particular situations. Often, however, an onlook is focused entirely on a particular person, for example, 'I look on you as a problem child (or an open book or a doormat).' Even in these cases, however, the onlook does not, by itself, determine precisely what ought to be done in a particular situation. What the application of the onlook does, in every case, is twofold. First, it affects the selection of facts deemed to be relevant to the choice. The agent notices some features of his situation and ignores others because of his onlook. Secondly, the onlook provides within itself a combination of 'is' and 'ought.' The onlook enables the agent (so he believes) to discern what kind of action is *fitting* or *appropriate* to reality. Such a kind of action is what he 'ought' to do – in a sense of 'ought' which is wider than what most people think of as a *moral* 'ought.' The onlook commits him to a kind of action which may be very general or fairly specific, depending on the onlook. In any case, the precise determination of what, in particular, ought to be done does not depend on the onlook alone. If, for example, a Christian looks on an alcoholic transient at his door as a brother for whom Christ died, this onlook commits him to a kind of caring for the man, but the particular action which expresses this kind of caring is not dictated by the onlook alone. A further judgment is required in which the particular facts of the situation are considered.

Christian scripture and tradition include an abundance of onlooks. A few of these are mentioned or suggested in the creed. A Christian may look on his daily life as death-and-resurrection ('crucified and risen') or as a journey ('in life, in death, in life beyond death') or as an active battle against evil ('resist evil') or as a courtroom drama culminating in a verdict ('our judge') or as a grateful offering of oneself as a gift in response to manifold gifts from God ('thanks be to God'). Many of these onlooks are also applied to the large-scale events of human history. There are also onlooks concerning nature (God's property, for which man is steward) and all other men (God's children, all in the same family with me).

Do onlooks reduce moral freedom? As Iris Murdoch has pointed out,[23] the answer to such a question depends on one's conception of moral freedom. Some philosophers hold what I shall label the 'is-then-ought' conception: for maximal moral freedom the agent should first describe the facts of his situation in neutral and literal language which does not commit him in any way concerning what he ought to do; then he makes a moral decision, 'I ought to do X,' applying or creating a (universalized) moral rule whose only value-word is 'ought.' No value-laden, non-liberal description of the situation should bias the moral decision in any particular direction; nor should it enter into the wording of the moral rule, which has the form, 'In situations of type T, anyone ought to do X.' Once the decision is made, an onlook (parable, image, symbol, myth) may legitimately have a role in inspiring a man to act on his decision, counteracting any weakness of will. But moral freedom involves making up one's own mind as to what one ought to do, while not being logically compelled to a moral conclusion because of an onlook which one has brought to the situation. On a less strict version of the 'is-then-ought' view onlooks are allowed some role in moral deliberation, deciding what to do, but they should first be selected and appraised in a purely moral judgment based on neutral literal facts.

In contrast with this 'is-then-ought' approach some philosophers propose something similar to what I call 'onlooks' and maintain that these are necessary in order to come to know what situations *really* are, and what I as an agent *really* am, and what is genuinely *fitting* or *appropriate* as a response to these realities, which are apprehended, not in a neutral, literal way, but in value-laden imagery. Moral freedom is then not a matter of making up one's own connections between what is and what ought to be, but of having an imaginative moral insight which combines 'is' and 'ought' in seeing that x is sufficiently like y to be treated like y. On this approach to decide rightly is to decide in the light of a correct apprehension of what one's situation really is. To have that apprehension one must be viewing it in terms of a particular, self-involving 'onlook.' To call for a 'moral' appraisal of all onlooks is a mistake, for the 'is-then-ought' philosopher is wrongly assuming that a non-self-involving, literalistic stance towards the world provides superior apprehension of reality, and he is wrongly assuming that moral rules accepted without onlooks are morally superior to all onlooks.

I have sketched two extreme and oversimplified positions in this controversy concerning onlooks and freedom. It seems to me that neither position in its pure form, excluding the other, is tenable; rather, a complex combination and revision of the two are needed for both secular and religious morality. But it seems to me that Christian theology has a special stake in rejecting the first position as it stands and in claiming some truth for some version of the second. Christians differ concerning which onlooks in scripture and tradition concerning God, world, and man are central and which are peripheral or discardable, but there is general agreement that some of the onlooks provide a reliable way of coming to know what *really* is the case, while also involving broad commitments to *be* and to *behave*, thus bringing 'is' and 'ought' together. A Christian may think that a neutral, non-literal description of a situation is often very helpful; indeed, one usually needs to fill in the facts of the particular situation in addition to applying the onlook, and these facts are often mostly described in a neutral, non-literal way. Sometimes, perhaps, the neutral, non-literal description of the situation is what should dominate over any onlook description. But it seems to me that an 'is-then-ought' view as an all-inclusive stance in epistemology and morality must be rejected by Christians as inadequate and misleading. It is part of Christian faith to look on situations, at least sometimes, in terms of Christian onlooks; perhaps it is part of Christian faith always to look on situations to some extent in terms of Christian onlooks. Here are some examples of onlooks which many Christians hold:

I look on human beings as brothers and sisters for whom Christ died.

I look on my life and on people whom I meet as gratuitous gifts from a generous God.

I look on God as a trustworthy Shepherd who guides me along life's way.

I look on God as a loving Father who yearns for the return of his prodigal sons.

I look on God as a righteous Ruler who liberates the poor and powerless from their oppressors.

I look on moral obligations as divine commands.

I look on human love as a manifestation of divine love.

I look on the face of suffering, oppressed, and hungry humanity as the face of Christ.

Is a man's freedom reduced by looking at a situation in terms of a Christian onlook? The answer to this question depends on one's conception of moral freedom, as we have seen. But there is an additional problem which should be mentioned. The reason for accepting a Christian onlook is partly that it has the *authority* of scripture or tradition behind it. One does not simply make a private individual judgment, though many modern theologians would allow for a 'testing' of the onlooks in one's own experience.[24] In the postscript I shall argue that the appeal to experience should be regarded as more important. Nevertheless it seems obvious that being a Christian involves responding to a call to identify oneself with a community of the called, the church, in which one acknowledges some *authority* in ways which are relevant to morality. One of the ways has to do with onlooks, another with one's basic moral vocabulary. There is no sharp line between onlooks and moral vocabulary. The former differ in being clearly non-literal and imaginative, and the latter is, more frequently, immediately and decisively relevant in the making of specific decisions in particular situations of moral choice.

4 MORAL VOCABULARY AND AUTHORITY

A number of contemporary philosophers and contemporary Christian ethicists have stressed the importance of the vocabulary of moral terms which a man brings to situations of choice. These thinkers[25] have been influenced by the later Wittgenstein or by one strand in natural-law ethics, or by both. Though they vary considerably (Eric D'Arcy differs greatly from D.Z. Phillips, and Paul Ramsey from Herbert McCabe), they unite in their rejection of the picture of moral reflection which 'is-then-ought' philosophers propose. For the moral-vocabulary theorists moral reflection is not primarily a matter of first describing the facts of a situation and the probable consequences of alternative actions in a neutral, non-moral way, and then deciding what one ought to do. Rather, it is primarily a matter of probing the *meaning* of a moral term in relation to a proposed course of action. One asks, for example, whether an action would or would not be an instance of 'adultery.' Concerning other actions one might ask whether they would or would not be instances of 'slander,' 'torture,' 'breach of confidence,' 'stealing,' 'direct killing of the innocent,' 'rudeness,' 'cowardice,' 'disloyalty to a friend,' or 'lying.' Or, to use positive moral terms, would or would not the action be an instance of 'loving action' or 'temperance' or 'justice' or 'promise-keeping' or 'honesty'? Among contemporary moral agents we hear (in addition or instead) such questions as these: Would this action be 'personally authentic' or 'counter-revolutionary' or 'racist' or 'sexist' or 'consciousness-raising' or 'authoritarian' or 'sexually repressive.' In Baum's RA some of the key terms are 'ideological,' 'de-privatizing,' 'utopian,' 'alienating,' 'consciousness-raising,' and 'structures of domination.'

Opponents of the kind of reflection which focuses on the meaning of a moral term in relation to a proposed action do not deny that such reflection actually occurs; it obviously does. As 'is-then-ought' theorists they deny that it *ought* to occur. Instead, moral reflection should have a form in which such value-laden terms are quickly replaced by neutral ones, or in which they are avoided entirely. Suppose a man takes a loaf of bread from a bakery, without permission or payment, for his starving family. Instead of asking whether this counts as 'stealing,' one asks, directly, whether the action is morally right, whether he ought to have done it. If a woman becomes pregnant by a concentration camp guard for the purpose of being discharged to return to her husband and children, don't ask, 'Was this adultery?' but ask, directly, 'Ought she to have done it?' On an 'is-then-ought' view the questions are answered by outlining the relevant facts of the situation and then applying some form of utilitarian test or universalizability test, or both. This is believed to be superior to a reflection concerning the meaning of some partly descriptive, partly evaluative term in relation to these facts.

In this controversy between moral-vocabulary theorists and 'is-then-ought' theorists, as in the controversy between onlook theorists and 'is-then-ought' theorists, I find it impossible to adopt one position to the total exclusion of the other. Indeed, my view of the moral-vocabulary approach varies in chapter 5 from case to case. For example, I criticize it in the case of the loaf of bread and I support it in the case of the concentration-camp pregnancy. But since the moral-vocabulary approach does have special relevance and importance for Christian morality, we shall consider it carefully. The first step is to note that thinkers who emphasize moral vocabulary, whether they be secular philosophers or Christian ethicists, can differ among themselves in relation to three variables, which I shall call 'stringency,' 'universality,' and 'specificity.' (My account of these variables is obviously influenced by my study of Paul Ramsey's ethics in chapter 5.)

Concerning *stringency*, three positions can be distinguished concerning what follows from, say, 'X is an instance of *lying*':

(i) X is morally wrong (there is an exceptionless moral rule prohibiting lying).
(ii) X is morally wrong unless there is a strong moral reason for overriding the fact that X is lying (there is a moral rule prohibiting lying, but it is not exceptionless).
(iii) One morally relevant consideration concerning X, a consideration which cannot, morally, be omitted, is that X is lying.

Concerning *universality*, one position is that for all men (or, alternatively, for all genuinely moral agents) there is a basic common moral vocabulary. The other position is that there is a variety of moral vocabularies, each moral framework being held and practised by a different group, even within the same society. A man can decide to identify himself with one group and its moral framework rather than another, but once he has done so he does not then decide whether or not it matters that a term within that framework applies to what he plans to do, for by identifying himself with the group he has at the very least committed himself to position (iii) concerning stringency. A middle position between universality and group-relativism would be to hold that there is a minimal basic moral vocabulary for all men (or for all genuinely moral agents) and that, in addition, there is for the individual a further moral vocabulary which belongs to the group with which he identifies himself.

Concerning *specificity*, there are differences as to whether only such broad terms as 'loving,' 'unjust,' or 'authentic' belong in the moral vocabulary or whether more specific terms such as 'lying,' 'stealing,' or 'adultery,' belong as well. We have seen in chapter 5 that if the more specific terms are included, people differ concerning the extent to which their meaning is thought to be precise and capable of definition by reference to public observables; to the extent that this is not the case the application of the term is a matter of moral reflection and judgment, requiring moral insight and sensitivity. For example, if 'adultery' means 'sexual intercourse where one or both parties are married to another' (and 'married' has a similarly precise and publicly verifiable meaning), the moral rule 'No adultery' is very different in meaning from the same rule where 'adultery' means 'act of marital infidelity.' Given the former meaning, the rule is in actual practice, as applied, very specific and stringent; and its application requires minimal exercise of moral judgment. Given the latter meaning, it is possible, for example, to deny that the woman who became pregnant by the concentration-camp guard committed adultery: one can argue that she was actually performing an act of marital fidelity, acting out of loyalty to her husband. Where, as in this case, specific moral terms are thought to have a fairly open, plastic meaning so that their application involves an exercise of sensitive and insightful moral judgment, moral rules expressed in such terms may appear to have stringency-(i), since their overt, explicit formulation is as exceptionless rules; in actual practice, however, the stringency of such rules is similar to stringency-(ii). There a rule is overtly and explicitly formulated in such a way as to allow for exceptions, while ascribing a non-open, non-plastic meaning to the key moral term, e.g. 'Don't commit adultery (i.e. don't have sexual intercourse with someone where one of you is married to another) unless there is a strong moral reason for overriding the fact that the act is adultery.' In the case of the woman who became pregnant, the strong moral reason would be that by committing adultery she could return to her husband and family. One final point concerning specificity: where broad, general terms such as 'loving' are used in expressing moral rules which are exceptionless (e.g. 'Always do the loving thing'), there is great need and scope for the exercise of sensitive and insightful moral judgment in applying the rule. Where *only* such broad and general moral terms are used, or where only such terms plus specific terms interpreted in a very plastic way are used, a moral framework is extremely different from one in which the only, or the determinative, moral terms are specific ones, interpreted in precise, publicly observable terms. Yet both frameworks have in common a rejection of a purely 'is-then-ought' morality.

I have sketched some of the issues in recent discussions of moral-vocabulary ethics since they are very relevant to the issue of religious faith and moral freedom. Some conservative forms of Christian theology have suppressed moral freedom, claiming (a) *unquestionable* divine *authority* for (b) a *traditional* set of moral terms, (c) applied in rules which are *exceptionless* even though fairly specific, and (d) applied in rules which are allegedly mandatory for *all* human agents, both inside and outside the Christian community. This eliminates the possibility of individual human decision concerning the following: (a) whether the moral framework should be tested, questioned, or even scrutinized in relation to human experience and moral insight; (b) whether new moral terms should be permitted alongside or replacing the ancient ones; (c) whether the terms, including the specific ones, should all be applied with exceptionless stringency; and (d) whether or not to identify oneself with this or that moral community. Such an inherently conservative and authoritarian morality is obviously contrary to moral freedom. That such a morality has existed and still exists is obvious. Alasdair MacIntyre[26] has even argued that theism requires some such morality for its very existence. The decline of theistic faith is as much the effect as the cause of the decline of such a morality: 'If everything is permitted, God does not exist.' It seems to me that MacIntyre is correct in so far as he is showing a logical and sociological connection between authoritarian morality and an authoritarian form of theism. Each reinforces and complements the other.

But what about the religious and moral convictions expressed in the United Church creed? To say this creed is to identify oneself with a Christian community which has a moral vocabulary: 'love,' 'serve,' 'justice,' 'evil,' 'reconcile,' 'make new.' Two other terms are suggested by the creed: 'sacrifice' and 'courage.' The phrase 'crucified and risen,' which I have interpreted in relation to the dynamics of inner receptivity, also has a moral connotation; it suggests a willingness to sacrifice, to give up what one wants, even life itself, for the sake of others. Earlier I note that courage (a traditional moral virtue) is implied in line 12. We could also add two terms which the committee reluctantly failed to include: 'forgive' and 'peace.' Some influential modern theologians would want to add 'humanize' or 'responsible' or 'revolutionary.' If we include all these terms we have a basic moral vocabulary which some non-Christians may share[27] with Christians, even if some of the Christian connotations for terms are included, for example, 'justice' as a partiality for the poor and the powerless, and 'evil' as a real power operative in institutional structures and within individuals. Is this a freedom-suppressing moral framework? Let us consider it in relation to the points considered above: (a) The moral framework is not placed beyond testing or scrutiny. (b) There is no prohibition or new moral terms to modify or replace traditional ones. (c) The terms are very broad, so that even if they are interpreted for use in exceptionless moral rules, plenty of scope for decision in application remains (what counts as 'love,' 'service,' 'justice,' 'evil,' etc?). (d) A man is free to reject the moral framework of the creed and to accept, instead, that of some other community; a common moral vocabulary for all men has yet to be created.

If a man accepts the broad moral framework, he thereby accepts a structure which will enter his moral reflections and affect his moral decisions. As we have seen, to accept the moral framework of a group is to relinquish decision-making as to whether or not it matters morally that a term within that framework applies to what one plans to do.[28] This is a restriction on freedom if a man's ideal of freedom in moral deliberation and decision is as follows: first he describes his situation in non-evaluative terms, deciding for himself what facts count as morally relevant; then he decides what he ought to do. If he is to follow this procedure, he cannot bring to the situation a moral vocabulary which, by virtue of the public meaning of the words within a group, *determines* that some of the facts are morally relevant. He himself must decide everything except the facts if he is to be free. Some critics of this position have argued that it is unintelligible: a man can only decide some moral matters if others are for him *not* open to his own decision.[29] Whether or not this criticism is correct, my own claim here is clearly warranted: an 'is-then-ought' conception of freedom in moral reflection is not the only possible position. A man may be free in that he has freely accepted a moral framework which then limits his freedom of decision as to what counts as morally relevant.

But the creed involves a further complication. Although a man who rejects all the explicit religious convictions in the creed is free to decide for or against the creed's moral framework, a man who accepts the explicit religious convictions does not regard himself as being free in this respect. The appropriate practical response to the divine activity is action in accordance with the broad moral framework. Divine activity does not direct a man to act against that framework; whatever influence seems to be so directing a man is not divine. Thus morality becomes a criterion in theology. Yet theology is not thereby made redundant to morality, for a man does not *adequately* understand by his own unaided powers what the terms mean ('love,' 'serve,' etc). He grows in understanding as he responds to the divine activity and as he interprets that activity in accord with the religious convictions of the creed. In accepting the creed he is identifying himself with a community in which the moral convictions are connected with religious convictions. Both sets of conviction have an authority for him within the Christian community, in which he says both 'We believe ...' and 'He calls us to be his church, to love and serve others ...' This is different from the situation of a man who adopts roughly the same moral framework but without the religious convictions to reinforce its authority. Nevertheless the Christian's religious convictions need not be regarded as providing additional restrictions on his moral freedom. Rather, the conscious response to divine activity within, the basic attitudes, and the onlooks of a Christian worldview all enhance his freedom – as he understands freedom.

To summarize: the relation between religious convictions and moral convictions in the creed enhances moral freedom if freedom is primarily responsive rather than wilful and if freedom is promoted more by understanding a situation in terms of onlooks and an accepted moral vocabulary than by understanding it in the strictly literal and non-evaluative terms of 'is-then-ought' philosophy. The creed's religious convictions are a threat to moral freedom only if maximal freedom means being minimally influenced by other agents – their actions towards oneself, their onlooks, and their moral vocabulary – in making moral decisions; and if it means being minimally dependent on other agents for help in becoming what one ought to become.

There remains one more element in the creed to consider: Christian convictions concerning *Jesus*.

5 JESUS, FAITH, AND MORALITY

Although the creed stresses the importance of Jesus and is very rich in its allusions to him, there is little that raises issues concerning moral freedom in addition to those we have already considered. So I shall only note very briefly some of the main convictions.

Jesus, 'the true Man,' is the paradigm of human faith and morality. His life and teaching provide the norm for the faith and morality expressed in the creed and outlined in my exposition: inner receptivity to divine activity; basic attitudes of trust, hope, joy, wonder, and gratitude; God enabling and directing man to love. Jesus is the perfect man, the ideal of responsiveness both to God and to other men.

Jesus is also divine. The creed indicates two ways in which this is so. First, Jesus is the unique locus of divine activity, unique in that there is an identity between his activities and God's. 'God ... has come in the true Man Jesus, to reconcile and make new.' This echoes 2 Corinthians 5:19: 'God was in Christ, reconciling the world to himself.' The identity continues in the present, for the Christian understands the divine activity within himself, to which he is receptive, as being identical with that of the risen Christ. Secondly, worshipful attitudes which are appropriate towards God are also appropriate towards the risen Jesus, 'our judge and our hope.' Jesus, like God, is the focus of basic hope, and also of basic trust, joy, wonder, and gratitude.

The Christian's faith is directed to Jesus in several different ways. First, the faith of Jesus as norm and example of faith is a guide and an encouragement to the Christian, whose own faith is defective and weak; Jesus not only exemplifies faith, he also evokes it. Secondly, the divine activity in Jesus is believed to be representative of all divine activity, and is thus the warrant for a Christian's basic trust, hope, etc, in spite of all that tends to challenge and undermine them. Since God is not only like Jesus but was and is uniquely active in Jesus, faith is not a blind step into total darkness, and faith is not based solely on one's own inner states, though these are necessary. Thirdly, the Christian attributes implicit faith, whether in himself or in non-Christians, to the activity of the risen Christ, which is identical with God's activity. Fourthly, the Christian finds in Jesus a focal interpretative symbol for understanding divine activity in nature, history, and society. For example, a Christian world-view takes the original event of death-and-resurrection as a symbol or onlook which is in principle applicable to everything. Some theologies speak of the 'cosmic Christ.'

How is Jesus more directly related to the making of moral decisions? There are four ways, which we have already considered without explicit reference to Jesus, in the preceding four sections of the essay. First, Jesus' love provides the test for what is to count as love. Secondly, Jesus' basic attitudes provide the paradigm for basic trust, hope, etc. Thirdly, Jesus' parables, whether taught or enacted (e.g. washing the disciples' feet) provide onlooks for situations of moral choice. Fourthly, Jesus' moral teaching provides much of the moral vocabulary for the Christian community. Of these four points it seems to me that only the first raises a further issue concerning moral freedom. In accepting Jesus as moral paradigm, accepting Jesus' love as the criterion for love and Jesus' life as the ideal life, the Christian is not merely allowing responsive freedom in relation to another man and he is not merely identifying himself with a group, its onlooks and moral vocabulary. He is modelling himself on another man. Does this reduce moral freedom? If Smith's modelling himself on Jones means trying to turn himself into a duplicate of Jones, Smith's moral freedom *is* reduced; he is no longer free to be and to become himself. But there are other ways in which Smith can model himself on Jones, other ways of 'identifying' with Jones, which can be *liberating*. Instead of slavish literal imitation, Smith adapts Jones's style of life to his own needs and capacities and situation. Indeed, identification with another person is an important and perhaps necessary step in the process of human maturation. When a Christian accepts Jesus as moral paradigm, some such liberating process occurs, or ought to occur. I am sure that is what the creed means when it expresses commitment to 'the true Man, Jesus.' Many theological and psychological subtleties would need to be explored in a thorough study of the idea of Jesus as moral paradigm. I refer the reader to J.M. Gustafson and R.S. Lee concerning this matter.[30]

Before I conclude I shall set forth the overall structure of my presentation in schematic form (see figure 1).

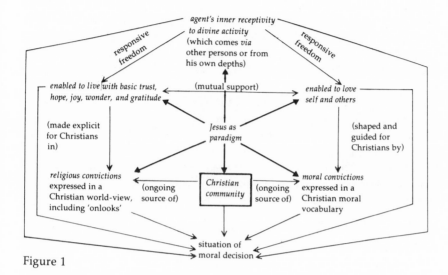

Figure 1

The main conclusion of the chapter thus far can be stated quite simply: the religious convictions of the creed are connected with the moral convictions and with the making of moral decisions in a variety of ways which enhance rather than restrict moral freedom – unless freedom is understood in a 'wilful' or an 'is-then-ought' manner.[31]

Postscript

This chapter has focused on a single question, but it has involved an exploration of many issues. By the time I conclude that religious faith need not conflict with moral freedom I have outlined a prolegomenon to a whole philosophy concerning faith and morality, drawing on material not only from previous chapters but also from many other sources. Obviously many problems arise which need further study. Only a few can be considered in this postscript. I have therefore selected four topics concerning which my present views are substantially different from what I wrote in the 1973 version of this essay. As I revised this chapter I did not change it with respect to these topics, since I prefer to explain my change of mind here in the postscript. The four topics are political involvement, analogies and epistemologies, onlooks, and the relation between religious attitudes and moral virtues. Concerning *political involvement*, my account in terms of receptivity leading to love leading to justice now seems inadequate. A different kind of receptivity is needed, one which leads directly to politicization. Concerning *analogies* and *epistemologies*, I now find tensions between the existentialist epistemology which I associate with my analogy of relation and the authoritarian epistemology which I associate with my analogy of attitude. I also want to relate my analogy of attitude to a neo-Kantian epistemology in which some basic attitudes promote human fulfilment and imply religious convictions. Concerning *onlooks*, I am now critical of an appeal to authority as the main basis for accepting them and I now stress the dangers of self-deception if one bases one's life on them. Concerning *religious attitudes and moral virtues*, I am now inclined not only to link them to receptivity as a common source but also to find some of them to be identical. For example, basic trust is not only a religious attitude but also a moral virtue.

1 POLITICAL INVOLVEMENT

In the 1973 version of this essay I held that the primary locus of divine activity is in individuals who are consciously or unconsciously receptive to divine grace. Concerning divine activity in nature or in social structures one may believe in an overall providential care, but one should be agnostic concerning specific interventions. Moreover, attempts to identify what God is doing politically so as to be able to join in with Him lead to dangerous and ruthless fanaticism. Since these are still my convictions, one of my criticisms of Baum's RA is that we should not base our decisions concerning political involvement on convictions concerning alleged divine activity in social$_3$ liberation. But I agree with Baum concerning the importance of social$_2$ liberation (faith conversion as politicization), with its recognition of the social evil in structures of domination and its identification with the powerless. In this chapter as well various elements in social$_2$ liberation are mentioned. In my discussion of moral vocabulary I describe evil as a real power in institutional structures and I define justice as a partiality to the poor and the powerless. In my section on love and justice I say that, since power structures and corporate injustice are major sources of destructiveness in human life, love is rationally expressed in political activity. Thus receptivity leads to love and love plus reason leads to a concern for justice in the structures of society. But although I thus find a place for social₂ liberation, I do not adequately convey its importance as a part of religious faith and I do not adequately explain its origins. A hint concerning what is needed is the onlook which I include in my revision of the essay for this chapter, an onlook which reminds us of Baum's vision: 'I look on the face of suffering, oppressed and hungry humanity as the face of Christ.' But what is actually needed is a separate consideration of politicization as a part of faith, grounding it in a different kind of receptivity: not only receptivity as a joyful openness to life-giving grace but receptivity as painful sensitivity to the hurts of humanity. I need not repeat here what we have learned from Baum concerning this, especially his portrayal of the charismatic prophet. What I would like to add here are some further reflections concerning this painful receptivity. It jolts people out of the narcissism which can pervert even the best kind of joyful receptivity ('Look how good God has been to *me*') and impels them into active political involvement. It moves people beyond a love which calmly seeks fulfilment for others to an outrage at the collective injustice which dehumanizes them. It moves beyond a kind of 'service' to others which involves an affirmation of one's own power over them to a kind of 'service' which means a vulnerable identification with the powerless. In my current interpretation of the creed I would say that God is calling (enabling and challenging) us not only to love self and others but also to serve the powerless against injustice.

2 ANALOGY

There are two kinds of analogy at work in this essay: analogy of relation and analogy of attitude. I am quite explicit concerning my use of analogy of *relation*: 'The way in which another man influences me when I am receptive to him is a basic analogy for the divine-human relation' (p 212). I am also explicit in my interpretation of this analogy as one in which neither divine activity nor human attitudes can be understood separately, since the meaning of each correlates with that of the other: 'Worship, then, may be defined as the expression of such-and-such basic attitudes to God in response to the active, meaningful presence of God. And God may be defined as the active, meaningful presence to whom men fittingly respond in worship (expressions of basic attitudes)' (p 206). I am less explicit concerning the content of the analogy, that is, its human starting-point. What kind of human influence is like divine influence? What I actually say is vague: 'One man allows another man to help him to change within, to become what he cannot wilfully make himself become' (p 219). What I imply in various passages, however, is more specific: the inner change involves a liberation from self-deception and self-destruction and it involves a call (enabling and challenging) to love. My use of such a content is less explicit than Baum's, but it is clear that I see the relation between God and man as being similar to a relation between man and man where the latter has elements of such a liberation and such a call. How then does the divine-human relation transcend the human starting-point, that is, what is the form of the analogy? I have said that the basic attitudes which are the human responses in the divine-human relation are pervasive attitudes, unrestricted in external scope. Hence the divine-human relation and the divine activity must be pervasive. Therefore I imply a use of the way of pervasiveness.

It is important to note that my use of analogy of relation is associated with an existentialist epistemology. That is, I hold that there are not only existential conditions for understanding meaning but also existential conditions for ascertaining truth. I not only hold that a man understands what divine activity is only to the degree that he is receptive; I also imply that he discerns that activity only if he is receptive. And I claim that such discernment, a direct awareness of the divine active presence, is possible: 'The word "presence" emphasizes the fact that divine activities are activities to which men respond here and now, personally and directly. God is actively present to man' (p 206). In this passage and others my epistemology is roughly similar to Buber's. According to Buber one is aware of an active personal presence, whether human or divine, only if one enters into a relation of personal encounter. A necessary condition for the encounter, and hence for the discernment of a reality which transcends the merely physical or psychical, is that one have an I-Thou attitude. Buber's personalism is one possible existentialist epistemology, but, as we have seen in chapter 2 there are many others. In each case a specified self-involving attitude is allegedly a necessary condition for discerning some metaphysical reality which is not accessible if one's attitude is neutral and detached. According to some philosophers the self-involving attitude is also a sufficient condition for discernment. In the case of discernment of God, however, theistic thinkers usually posit the grace of God as at least a co-condition. Whatever the alleged metaphysical discernment, there are difficulties raised by the rival claims of other seeming metaphysical discernments which occur from the vantage-point of other attitudes. Sometimes the discernments are incompatible, and even if they seem to be compatible, the issue of relative priority arises. For example, consider the discernments of God in an I-Thou attitude as a personal reality addressing us, in mystical contemplation as an impersonal reality in unity with us, and in politicized concern as a liberator of the oppressed. Are these discernments compatible? If they are compatible, which should have priority in one's theology and in one's spiritual quest?

In this chapter I deal with the problem of selecting attitudes by appeal to an epistemology which is very different from the existentialist metaphysical-discernment approach. I shall call this alternative an 'authoritarian' epistemology. According to it there are many different kinds of 'depth-experience'[32] associated with various self-involving attitudes such as trust or distrust or contemplation or *angst* or hope or despair. These depth-experiences do not of themselves bring a metaphysical discernment, even with the aid of divine grace. Rather, there is a problem of selection and interpretation, either by arbitrary choice or by appeal to some authority. A Christian selects a set of depth-experiences and correlated attitudes, setting others aside, on the basis of an appeal to the authority of Christian scripture and tradition. And he interprets the depth-experiences as revelatory of the divine on the basis of an appeal to the same authority. Thus, on this approach two people who have the same basic attitude of trust and who have the same depth-experience associated with trust might differ radically. One might remain agnostic concerning the depth-experience's significance as an indication of ultimate reality. He might even regard his own *angst* as more significant in this respect. The other might interpret the depth-experiences as revelatory. In doing so he would either arbitrarily decide to select it and to interpret it in this way, or appeal to an authority as his reason for doing so. In this chapter I implicitly appeal to authority in my selection of the basic attitudes (receptivity, trust, hope, gratitude, and wonder), for I merely note that they are the attitudes expressed in the creed. No other reason is given for choosing them. And I appeal explicitly to the authority of a Christian 'interpretative framework' in my account of the relation between basic attitudes and religious convictions in terms of an interpretation of depth-experiences: 'For the Christian his own explicit faith in God is logically implied by his own basic attitudes, which resemble those of the agnostic ... To be a Christian is, in part, to accept a way of talking and thinking such that basic attitudes are understood in a distinctive way. It is to accept and to bear witness to an interpretative framework concerning some 'depth-experiences' or 'peak-experiences' common to many men, including non-Christians. The most fundamental experience is understood in terms of receptivity to divine activity' (p 210).

The two rival epistemologies in this chapter are associated with different kinds of *analogy*. The existentialist epistemology is associated mainly with an analogy of *relation*, but the authoritarian epistemology is associated mainly with an analogy of *attitude*. This analogy is explicit in my statement that 'receptivity to divine activity is understood by Christians mainly in terms of an analogy with receptivity to the activity of another agent' (p 220). The most fundamental content for the analogy is receptivity, but there are also the basic attitudes of trust, hope, gratitude, and wonder. All of these are doubly pervasive, so the form of the analogy is provided by way of pervasiveness. As we have seen, I employ an authoritarian epistemology in answering the question, 'On what basis are the attitudes selected, and what is their relation to religious convictions?' My own position now is that this double question should be answered by reference to an existentialist epistemology and to a neo-Kantian epistemology, with its associated anthropological-logical argument. The authoritarian epistemology is largely set aside, and the attitudes are selected in two (fortunately concurring) ways: (i) the attitudes are necessary conditions for discernments of God which are then articulated in religious convictions; and (ii) the attitudes are necessary conditions for human fulfilment and they include or imply religious convictions.

Religious tradition still has a role, however. In chapter 7 I shall show how the articulation of religious convictions in both (i) and (ii) may involve implicit or explicit use of traditional religious conceptual frameworks. Moreover, in this book as a whole my own selection of attitudes as conditions for human fulfilment has depended not only on philosophical reflection (especially personalist existentialism) and depth psychology (supplemented by humanistic sociology as in Baum) but also Christian tradition.

I should note that in this chapter the appraisal of attitudes by reference to human fulfilment is not central, though there are some elements of this approach. With reference to freedom, though not to attitudes, I say that 'no activity counter to human fulfilment counts as divine activity' (p 204). And in the section on 'morality and the call to love' I depict the basic attitudes as foundations for a kind of self-love which clearly promotes self-fulfilment. But the neo-Kantian approach is not nearly as obvious or as central as it is in the chapter on Keen. For a detailed examination of attitudes with reference to human fulfilment I refer the reader to *Struggle and Fulfilment*.

It seems to me that my existentialist and neo-Kantian epistemologies are broadly compatible and mutually supplementary. The neo-Kantian approach encourages a religious-philosophical-psychological study of human fulfilment which can provide some basis for selecting basic attitudes (and also for establishing their relative priority, as we shall see in section 4 of this postscript). Thus a defect in the existentialist approach can be partly remedied. It in turn can help to remedy a defect in the neo-Kantian approach: the focus on human needs rather than on divine reality. Attitudes which promote human fulfilment can also be attitudes which foster awareness of the divine presence. But the two approaches can still conflict. For example, some of the attitudes which promote what Otto calls 'numinous' experiences of God seem to me to be obstacles to human fulfilment.[33] But in many instances the two approaches work well together. As Keen and Baum have maintained, God is *discerned* in that which promotes human *fulfilment*, for God frees us to become authentically human.

There are in this chapter allusions to a third kind of analogy, in addition to analogy of relation and analogy of attitude. For example, I say that 'the divine will is *like*, and acts through, the other person and the *unconscious depths*' (p 220, italics changed). Note that one thing I am saying here is that the relation between God and man is like the relation between a man's unconscious depths and the rest of himself. This analogy does not fit into my classification of analogies. It is not what I have called an 'analogy of relation,' for I restrict the content of such analogy to person/person relations. Yet it does have as its content a relation rather than an activity or an attitude. Its main importance, however, does not lie in the difficulty of classifying it. Rather, it is important as a counter-emphasis to an exclusively I-Thou personalism in the conception of divine grace. Divine activity is not only interpersonal, but intrapersonal. God is not only 'out there' but 'in here.' Discernment of the divine is not only extraspective but introspective. God's liberation of an individual comes not only *via* others but *via* his own inmost depths.

3 ONLOOKS

I now have two reservations concerning my account of onlooks. First, I do not think that onlooks should be justified mainly on the basis of an appeal to the authority of scripture and tradition. Secondly, I do not think I have been sufficiently aware of the dangers of self-deception which are present in a religious faith which stresses conscious onlooks. These two reservations are to some extent connected, as we shall see.

From my discussion of the three epistemologies in relation to basic attitudes what I want to say about the basis for selecting onlooks will be evident. The authoritarian epistemology should be subordinated to the existentialist and the neo-Kantian. Onlooks should be appraised primarily by reference to whether they facilitate discernments of the divine and contribute to human fulfilment. It is now my conviction that they do both if and only if they are expressions of certain basic attitudes which do both. So we need to ask what basic attitude an onlook expresses. One passage in this chapter already points in this direction. In the section on 'basic attitudes and moral decisions' I describe how various basic attitudes which are contrary to those in the creed are expressed in conflictual or technological world-views. These world-views are onlooks. If they are to be appraised by reference to the basic attitudes which they express, so too should religious onlooks. The most important alternatives are not at the level of onlooks, but at the level of basic attitudes. In my exegesis of line 1 of the creed, 'Man is not alone,' I set forth the struggle between basic trust and basic distrust as the 'real tension within the typical Christian believer' (p 202).

In recent years I have become increasingly suspicious of the conscious acceptance of onlooks on authority as an indication of genuine religious faith. All too often such an acceptance of them can foster a superficiality and a self-deception concerning what one's hidden, deeper attitudes really are towards oneself, towards others, and towards God. A person who preaches the Providence of God in moving metaphors and striking similes may be hiding from himself the hidden paranoia in his heart. The focus of my own reflections has therefore shifted from onlooks (their basis in authority and their linguistic form) to the underlying pervasive stances of the whole personality which must be there if onlooks are to be authentic expressions of how one actually views reality. Onlooks at best give shape to, and encourage, basic attitudes of trust and hope and gratitude and wonder and concern for the oppressed. It seems to me that these pervasive attitudes and the struggle against their opposites are at the core of the Christian faith as it is actually lived. I do not deny that there is an element of authority in Christian faith. To be a Christian is to share in onlooks common to the Christian community as one understands that community. But if a Christian is relatively free from self-deception, he will probably realize that he 'accepts' a particular Christian onlook not in the sense that at a deep level he as yet lives by it, but in the sense that he acknowledges this onlook as an expression of how he *ought* genuinely to view the world. And the real struggles towards authentic

Christian faith go on at a deeper level, especially in relation to the familial unconscious, which so radically affects our basic attitudes.

Baum's insights in RA concerning the social unconscious provide an additional reason for caution in our reliance on conscious acceptance of authorized onlooks. What Baum calls a 'symbol' is very similar to what I call an 'onlook.' Baum notes that symbols often reflect the interests of powerful groups in society and hence are ideological, legitimizing structures of domination, producing false consciousness in individuals. Christian onlooks may be ideological. A properly critical theology must be alert to abandon these or to reinterpret them in a socially responsible way. Onlooks should be selected and interpreted in relation to human fulfilment, both social and personal. One of the conclusions to be drawn from Baum is that some onlooks *can* contribute to the humanizing of society – he describes creative, imaginative vision as a crucial element in utopian thought. And personal growth towards a more authentic human existence *can* be encouraged by onlooks. But onlooks must be subjected to an ongoing social and therapeutic critique. Otherwise they may reinforce our self-deceptions concerning what is really going on in society and in ourselves.

Can some onlooks help us to discern metaphysical reality? I think they can. But it is mainly a matter of their encouraging basic attitudes which themselves help to bring such discernments.

4 RELIGIOUS ATTITUDES AND MORAL VIRTUES

In this chapter I find the core of the relation between religion and morality in receptivity, which is the common necessary condition for various religious attitudes on the one hand and for the central moral virtue, love, on the other. 'Receptivity is what *allows* God to act in a man' (p 206). The religious attitudes of trust, hope, gratitude, and wonder and the moral virtue of love are responses to divine activity. As responses to divine activity they presuppose that divine activity has already been allowed since the person has been receptive rather than resistant. (Although both receptivity and resistance are to a great extent unconscious, there is a possibility of choice between them.) I claim that receptivity is 'the psychological condition for the basic attitudes which are rendered explicit in the religious convictions, and for the moral impulse which is expressed in the moral convictions' (p 199). I summarize the underlying structure of the creed as follows: 'Where the believer or any man is receptive, God is active within him, bringing about change. The change gives rise to attitudinal responses and practical responses. On the one hand, there are new attitudes which may be expressed in worship towards God. On the other hand, there are new activities towards men' (p 212). Figure 2 depicts the relations between receptivity, religious attitudes, and moral virtues as conceived in this chapter (apart from the postscript, which introduces an additional kind of receptivity, painful rather than joyful).

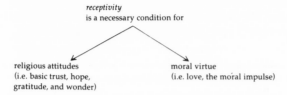

Figure 2

It now seems to me that a different set of relations, as depicted in figure 3, is more illuminating:

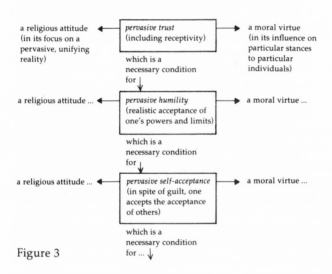

Figure 3

The series continues with five other pervasive stances: responsibility, self-commitment, love as I-Thou involvement, love as social concern, and love as contemplative detachment. The eight stances correspond roughly to those advocated by Erik Erikson for each of the successive eight crises in human life. The first three occur in infancy, the next two in childhood and adolescence, and the final three in adulthood; but all the earlier crises recur, in new forms, throughout life. Each stance I call an 'attitude-virtue,' for it is both a religious attitude and a moral virtue. As a religious attitude it is focused on God, who is the being *such that* the pervasive stance is (believed to be) appropriate; it is expressed in worship of God and articulated in religious convictions. As a moral virtue it profoundly influences the way in which one deals with people in particular situations and it is a constituent in one's own human fulfilment; it is expressed in action towards persons and articulated in moral convictions.

According to my new proposal receptivity still has a primacy in that it is the central element in pervasive trust, which is a necessary condition for *all* the other attitude-virtues. Also, divine activity within oneself is still permitted or prevented according to whether one is receptive or resistant. Each of the attitude-virtues has an opposite against which one struggles (pervasive distrust, power-preoccupation, crippling guilt, irresponsibility, etc), and each of these attitude-vices involves a resistance against life-giving forces which come from God *via* other people and *via* one's own depths. So the ongoing struggle between attitude-virtues and attitude-vices involves an ongoing choice between receptivity and resistance.

Although receptivity is still important in my new proposal, it is no longer the sole locus of unity between religion and morality. According to my earlier proposal religion and morality, while having different constituents, have a common origin in the divine activity which is at work in the receptive person. According to my new proposal, while the common origin is still affirmed, religion and morality have the same constituents, the set of attitude-virtues which are constituents of human fulfilment. My conception of individual human fulfilment is drawn not only from depth psychology but also from philosophy (moral and existential) and Christian tradition.

I have given only a cryptic sketch of a way of construing religion and morality which is explored at length in *Struggle and Fulfilment*. I shall say no more about it here, except for clarifying a few issues which now arise in relation to previous items in this chapter and this book. First, I should note that the attitudes of gratitude and hope, which have been frequently mentioned in chapter 3 and in this chapter, are so closely associated with receptivity and assurance that they all now seem to be most appropriately studied as elements in pervasive trust. Secondly, the attitude of wonder, which has also been frequently mentioned, is an element in all the attitude-virtues, for each of them involves a sense of mystery. Thirdly, I have argued in this chapter for a direct connection between receptivity and love: to the extent that we receive life we are *moved* to share it. This still seems true to me, but now I would also point out the need for the first five attitude-virtues if one is to be *able* to love in any of the adult ways. Such love requires a sense of one's own personal identity, and the first five attitude-virtues are conditions for this. If one is intensely preoccupied with discovering who one is, still immersed in intrapersonal crises, one is not free for interpersonal involvement and communal concern and cosmic contemplation.

A fourth issue which can now receive initial clarification is one which I have mentioned earlier in this postscript: the relative priority of various pervasive stances. If the stances belong to the series of attitude-virtues, we can see that they may have one or other of two different kinds of priority. Some attitude-virtues are 'prior' to others in that they are necessary conditions for the others. The first three attitude-virtues are especially 'prior' in this sense. Other attitude-virtues are 'prior' to others in that they are goals towards which we move on the basis of the others. The last three attitude-virtues are especially 'prior' in this sense. Since people vary greatly from each other as to the relative state of their struggles against each of the attitude-vices, the question of relative priority cannot be settled in general (though, as I have noted in chapter 4, a desperate social context may require intense social involvement from people whether or not they have had much success with their intrapersonal and interpersonal problems).

I have implied that the series of attitude-virtues can be seen as a movement from the mainly intrapersonal (trust, humility, self-acceptance, responsibility, self-commitment) to the fully interpersonal (I-Thou involvement) to the communal (social concern) to the cosmic (contemplative detachment). All have a cosmic reference, but the final attitude-virtue is concerned with the divine not primarily in relation to *me* or to *us-two* or to *us-humans* but for itself. Contemplation goes beyond a concern about human fulfilment to an appreciation of that which transcends the human.

In chapter 2 we have seen that contemplation is expressed in language by the way of negation. Both contemplation and the way of negation have been neglected in this book since we pondered them in relation to Ian Ramsey. In coming back to them here, at the end of this chapter, we have not simply come full circle, back to where we started. We are now in a different place altogether, for we have been involved in many studies of the human in relation to the divine and of the divine in relation to the human. But the contemplative path, in which we seek God purely for His own sake, remains open for exploration.

7

Understanding Attitudes: Language and Experience

The preceding six chapters have left many issues unresolved which can be explored elsewhere by me and by others. Two issues, however, seem to demand further study within this book. One, which will be considered in the second section of this chapter, has been repeatedly postponed and can no longer be evaded: the nature of the alleged logical connection between basic attitudes and religious convictions. The other, to which I now turn, is the justification for my shift from analysing the language of basic attitudes to investigating their phenomenology and psychology.

1 From language to experience

In chapter 1 I have noted that since 1963, when I published *The Logic of Self-Involvement*,[1] my work in philosophy of religion has gradually shifted from an analysis of secular and religious language to a phenomenological and psychological investigation of secular and religious attitudes. I have indicated one reason for this change: a purely linguistic study of analogy of attitude is inadequate; the choice of content in analogies is, on a linguistic approach, a matter of arbitrary opting or authoritarian *fiat*. But the choice can be a rational one if some attitudes can be shown to be conditions of human fulfilment. For this and other reasons I have argued that in general Ian Ramsey's linguistic approach needs to be supplemented by a philosophical anthropology such as that of Sam Keen's.

All this, however, does not reveal or justify the basic shift in philosophical method which lies behind some of the more obvious changes. I have indicated in the postscript to chapter 5 that I underwent a philosophical conversion, but here I shall set forth the stages of reasoning which gave rise to it. I shall begin with its origins in *The Logic of Self-Involvement*. (What follows is drawn largely from a recent essay.[2])

In *The Logic of Self-Involvement* I claim that a philosophical analysis of religious self-involvement requires a prior analysis of linguistic self-involvement. I concede, however, that an analysis of linguistic self-involvement is inadequate in relation to two crucial issues: sincerity and speaker-dependent meaning. What are the conditions for sincerity in utterance, when one means what one says? And what are the conditions for speaker-dependent meaning, that is, when one intends one's words to have *this* meaning rather than *that*? In *The Logic of Self-Involvement* I agree with philosophers influenced by Wittgenstein and Austin that in both cases there need not be a 'special mental event or activity concomitant with and in addition to the utterance of the words' (pp 260–1). So it is not a matter of introspecting the sincerity or the private meaning as one might introspect a pain in one's leg or an after-image in one's visual field. But how then do I know when I mean what I say rather than not mean it? And how do I know when I mean my words to have this meaning rather than that? Having ruled out introspection, linguistic philosophy can provide no alternative account:

It is true that a framework of public meaning is required if one is to say X and mean it; and it is true that where sincerity is in question, subsequent public behaviour may be relevant not only to the observer but also to the speaker. Nevertheless there is an inherently private element which is extremely puzzling. If Jones said, 'I'll return this book to-morrow,' in most cases he knew at the time whether or not he meant what he said. How did he know? What is it to mean what one says? A linguistic philosopher may object: 'Jones did not *know* whether he meant what he said; he merely was in a position to *say* whether he meant what he said.' Very well then, let us ask, 'How was he in this position?' ,Surely it was not *merely* by virtue of a convention of language,similar to a rule in a game ('Umpires are in a position to say whether a play is offside'). Another linguistic philosopher may object: 'You have missed the point; you are asking a question which ought not to be asked, for there is no possibility of an answer.' But if that is the 'point,' it may merely indicate a limitation of the particular philosophical method which has been employed.

Another problem concerning private meaning arises when we consider cases where the meaning of an utterance is, to some extent, speaker-dependent. On what basis does one say, afterward, 'That's what I meant?' Indeed, what is it, at the time, to say such-and-such, *intending* the words to have one meaning rather than another meaning? Here too we presuppose the existence of a framework of public meaning; here too the speaker as well as the observer may find that his subsequent public behaviour is relevant; but here too there is an inherently private element which cannot be dismissed by reference to a convention of a language, or by a dogmatic claim that one has asked an unanswerable question.

Both 'meaning what one says' and 'intending one's words to have this meaning rather than that' are matters of great importance in religion. Indeed, they are both crucial in my attempt to analyse the biblical conception of Creation. If someone says, in the biblical context, 'God is my Creator,' the mere utterance has religious value only if he means what he says. What is it to 'mean what one says'? And what is it to intend that the utterance have its meaning in the biblical context rather than some other context? These are questions which I have not answered. (Pp 261–2)

In this passage I note that linguistic philosophy cannot cope with sincerity and speaker-dependent meaning, but I do not directly challenge the assumption that private psychological states can be and should be ignored in a study of the meaning of language. Elsewhere in the book, however, there is a line of thought which is relevant to speaker-dependent meaning (though I did not then make the connection), and which is already the beginning of such a challenge. I claim that there is a personal or existential prerequisite for *understanding* biblical language correctly. One must have a *rapport* or affinity with the divine if one is to understand talk about the divine. Since *intending* words to have a biblical meaning presupposes *understanding* them in that way, one would need rapport with the divine in order to intend successfully that one's words have meaning in the biblical context. I focus, however, on rapport as a condition for *understanding* rather than for *intended meaning*. In *The Logic of Self-Involvement* I am concerned to show that biblical language concerning God as Creator is not only self-involving but also what I call 'rapportive' (see pp 110–13). Rapport with the divine involves an openness and a kind of likeness. It depends on the influence of divine grace on the depths of one's whole personal being. There are thus personal, existential conditions for understanding talk about God in the biblical context. In particular, in so far as the transcendence of God is understood *via* analogy of attitude, one needs to have the attitude oneself in order to understand the transcendence. Just as one understands what Buber means by 'person' only to the extent that one has an I-Thou attitude towards human beings, one can understand what the Bible means by 'God' only to the extent that one has an attitude of worship, for example, unlimited trust.

In later essays[3] I move from concern about a *biblical* context to concern about a (broader) *religious* context, but I continue to stress the personal or existential conditions for understanding. Gradually I have realized how much this stress undermines a purely linguistic approach in philosophy of religion. In 'Faith and Belief' I write as follows:

By an 'existential' belief I mean a belief where what is believed can only be understood to the extent that one has fulfilled certain existential conditions – that is, conditions which existentialist philosophers emphasise, conditions having to do with the personal depth and authenticity of one's commitments, attitudes and general life-experience. A non-existential belief is one which has no such conditions for understanding (though it is often a belief concerning what exists).

An existential belief is not purely intentional or attitudinal. There is a 'belief-that' concerning reality. But *what* one believes can only be understood to the extent that one's basic commitments and attitudes – and the life-experience arising out of these – have been both authentic and appropriate. For example, what Buber means by the 'Eternal Thou' can only be understood to the extent that one has had I-Thou attitudes of commitment and openness to other human persons. Or what Tillich means by God as the 'Power of Being' can only be understood to the extent that one has resolutely faced the abyss of meaninglessness on the edge of human life. Or what Otto means by God as the 'numinous' can only be understood to the extent that one has had profound experiences of awe and wonder and exultation. And in each case it is not only the jargon of the religious philosopher that has special existential conditions for understanding, but also – and much more important – the basic language about God within the religious tradition.

And in each case since what one believes can only be understood in *relation* to the existential states, and since these vary considerably among men, we cannot be assured of a straightforward common meaning or family of meanings for the words used to express the belief. What I understand by 'God is love' is likely to be different from what Buber and Tillich and Otto each meant, and also from what you understand. Statements of doctrine will mean different things to different people within the same tradition and within different traditions, and these meanings will vary greatly. So we cannot ask of a proposition, divorced from who it is that understands the proposition, whether it is closer to the truth about God than some other proposition. 'God is merciful' as understood by me is likely to be less close to the truth than 'God is a consuming fire' as understood by Martin Buber, even though we may agree that the meaning of the latter statement as understood by most people usually makes it farther from the truth. And what I believe when I believe that God is merciful may differ greatly from what you believe, or disbelieve. What a man believes, as expressed in statements about God, depends on what his basic commitments and attitudes have been, and on their relative authenticity or sincerity, since his understanding of statements about God depends on these. So Buber's faith could be more 'true' than my faith in two ways: in the sense of being more authentic than mine and in the sense that what he believed was closer to the truth concerning God, since he had a deeper understanding of statements concerning God whose words I also accept. (Pp 199–200)

From what I say in this essay it follows that any philosopher who seeks a deep understanding of religious language must move beyond a purely intellectual analysis of its common public meaning to a concern about fulfilling existential conditions for religious understanding, for example, a growth in authenticity and in I-Thou openness. His philosophizing is then part of a personal pilgrimage which may involve radical personal change. But since the pilgrimage involves the whole person, including the intellect, it can include philosophical reflection.

My initial queries in *The Logic of Self-Involvement* concerning sincerity and speaker-dependent meaning thus lead, *via* the doctrine of 'rapportive' language, to a challenge of a crucial assumption in much analytic philosophy of religion. I conclude that one cannot get at the genuinely religious meaning which a religious utterance has for a genuinely religious individual merely or mainly by studying the public meaning of his language. One must also consider the authenticity and the other existential elements in his personality which he brings to an understanding of the language, elements which vary in degree and in kind from person to person. Moreover, one's own degree of understanding will depend less on one's analytic skills than on one's most basic life-commitments, attitudes, and experiences. In 'Faith and Belief' I do not entirely reject a place for public meaning of religious language, which I refer to as 'the obvious or surface meanings of the words' (p 201). Some words are more appropriate than others in talking about God, 'namely the words which harmonise most readily with the view of God implicit in the conviction as to what is the requisite existential condition for understanding' (p 201). But this public meaning is a bare framework. The actual meaning is a largely private and variable matter. So the assumption which I challenge is that one can give an adequate analysis of religious language by studying public meaning. On the contrary, private meaning is what mainly matters.

Private meaning can, however, be broadly shared by people who fulfil the requisite existentialist conditions for understanding. And the conditions are usually accessible, though in varying degrees, to all human beings. Furthermore, as I argue later, the conditions are allegedly necessary for human fulfilment. So issues concerning religion need not be removed from intersubjective scrutiny, as if each man's religious understanding were utterly idiosyncratic to him. There can be shared meaning, which is necessary not only for successful communication but also for philosophical discussion and for common action in the world. But this shared existential meaning is not the least-common-denominator public meaning of religious language which non-existentialist philosophers like to analyse.

A second, related assumption which I began to challenge is one which I strongly held when I wrote *The Logic of Self-Involvement*, especially when I argued that Buber's self-involvement has to be elucidated by reference to linguistic self-involvement. I assumed that one can only get at primary experience and attitudes *via* language. By this I did not mean the platitude that one can only *talk* about *anything* by means of language. I meant, rather, that there is no way of elucidating what self-involvement is except by reference to the linguistic acts (such as promises or expressions of attitude) in which self-involvement publicly takes place or could take place. Thus to be *devoted* to someone, for example, is to have an attitude which is expressed or could be expressed in certain kinds of *vow*. At the time I thought that there is no way of getting at *prelinguistic* experiences of human states so as to compare them with language and so come to understand the meaning of words in relation to the states, for example, the meaning of 'vow' in relation to devotion. I now reject that assumption, for three different reasons. First, I have myself during psychotherapy relived experiences prior to my learning of language and I have been with dozens of people who have also done so; moreover, I know what it is to be aware of the same experience in one's present daily life, saturated though that life now is with language. As I have written concerning trust and distrust earlier in this volume and also in *Struggle and Fulfilment*,[4] I am aware of this dimension of adult experience. Secondly, other philosophers have shown that it is possible to philosophize in an intelligible and illuminating way concerning experience which is epistemologically prior to language and reflection. Marcel's 'secondary reflection' is an example of this. He argues convincingly that – to take only one of his many claims – an understanding of the expression '*my* body' by reference to the meaning of 'my' in '*my* possessions' or '*my* tools' is useless, for all three depend on a primary, prelinguistic awareness which Marcel somehow conveys through language.[5]

Thirdly, contemplative writers also successfully write about prelinguistic experience – or perhaps we should also refer to it as 'postlinguistic' experience – somehow choosing appropriate (though at times paradoxical) language to fit what they intuit. And in reflections concerning my own limited contemplative experience I have found the same process going on.

In general, then, it seems to me that personal self-involvement is epistemologically (and to some extent temporally) prior to linguistic self-involvement. It is true, of course, that the language sheds light on the prelinguistic material, as well as vice versa. Though the verbal without the personal is empty, the personal without the verbal is almost blind – almost, but not entirely. And though opaque, it is basic. Where deeply personal self-involvements such as those which occur in religion are being studied, an investigation of prelinguistic material should be primary. Indeed, it seems to me that all the important existential conditions for religious understanding which have been alleged are prelinguistic. I do not wish to minimize the problems in trying to use language to get at that which is prior to language. But the alternative is superficiality.

The possibility of using language to get at what is prior to language will eventually emerge in the next section as the crucial item in understanding the connection between basic attitudes and religious convictions. But before I thus bring together the two sections of this chapter, a great deal of patient exploration will be necessary.

2 Basic attitudes and religious convictions

In an important article George Nakhnikian has criticized attempts to move from cosmic stances to belief in God:[6]

The conceptual point about gratitude and thankfulness is this: they presuppose a belief that someone has done us a favor, a kindness, a good turn, while cosmic gratitude and thankfulness may arise in the absence of such a belief. An atheist cannot (logically) be grateful if he does not believe that someone has done him a good turn, but the same atheist can have a feeling of cosmic thankfulness. The feeling of cosmic thankfulness is like the feeling of thankfulness minus the belief that someone has done us a good turn. In place of that belief there is an inclination to grant that if anything existed to bring about this (the starry heavens, my birth) in a providential way, it would be majestic enough to be the fitting recipient of my cosmic gratitude and thankfulness. Psychologically, it is quite possible that a man who feels cosmic thankfulness may entertain the hypothesis that there is something, a superhuman personality, toward whom this thankfulness is properly directed. But the fact that I feel cosmic thankfulness does not imply that such a superhuman personality exists.

But does his feeling of cosmic thankfulness imply that he *believes* that such a superhuman personality exists? In my anthropological-logical argument the conclusion is not that God exists but that a person *believes* that God exists. This is the crucial issue arising from Nakhnikian's argument as well, for he holds that someone can have the attitude without the belief. He says that the feeling of cosmic thankfulness is 'like the feeling of thankfulness minus the belief that someone has done us a good turn.' But this is not an intelligible notion. Any attitude – and any feeling which includes an attitude – implies a belief that a focus of the attitude exists. Words which are used to refer to attitudes describe directional states which focus on some X which is believed to exist. If I am thankful, I must believe that an X exists towards which I am thankful. Otherwise I may be correctly described as 'joyful' or 'elated,' but not as 'thankful.' Moods such as joy and sorrow, elation and depression, have no believed-in focus; I can be joyful without being joyful *about* anything or *in relation to* anything. But the very meaning of such words as 'thankfulness' and 'trust' is such that they are incorrectly applied if the person using them does not focus them on an X which he believes to exist. He may be mistaken in this belief, of course; but that is a different matter.

The logical relation between attitude and belief can be expressed as an entailment-relation between propositions, in two steps: 'Nakhnikian is thankful' entails 'Nakhnikian is thankful towards X' which entails 'Nakhnikian believes that X exists.' This entailment depends on the meaning of the word 'thankful' as this is universally understood. It is a matter of universal definition. To be thankful without being thankful towards some X is not merely irrational; it is logically impossible. And the same impossibility applies to being thankful towards X while not believing that X exists. This latter point does not hold, of course, if the general context is one of make-believe, so that one is not really thankful towards X, but only pretending to be. In such a context, however, many other entailments of belief are suspended; for example, neither 'Jones trusts X' nor 'Jones hates X' nor 'Jones admires X' entails 'Jones believes that X exists.' A context of make-believe is precisely one in which such entailments are suspended. According to Nakhnikian 'an atheist cannot (logically) be grateful if he does not believe that someone has done him a good turn'; but he fails to show how this logical impossibility can disappear when thankfulness is cosmic. He interprets the logical connection as if it were changed to the following form: 'Attitude A entails the belief that *if A* has an object or focus, it must have such-and-such characteristics.' But the conditional clause 'if A has an object or focus' is only plausible if attitude A occurs in a context of make-believe, which is clearly not the context for Nakhnikian in his article. I see no way by which Nakhnikian can evade the conclusion that he must believe that some X exists towards which he is thankful.

I have not shown, however, that he must believe anything more concerning this X, for example, that X is a superhuman personality who has done him a good turn. What additional entailments, if any, does *cosmic* thankfulness have beyond the entailments which *any* thankfulness has? Obviously the answer to this question depends on what Nakhnikian means by 'cosmic.' He seems to mean that he is thankful for the sheer existence of himself and the starry heavens. But whatever it is that he is thankful *for*, from what he says it is clear that he is thankful *to* an X which, he believes, brings this about in a providential way. Hence, *as he describes the attitude*, a religious belief is entailed. But since he does not acknowledge any such religious belief, he finds himself in a self-contradictory position. One way of avoiding this would have been to have said: 'If I were to try to articulate an attitude of thankfulness in which I sometimes find myself, I would do so in the following way ... ; but this description entails belief in God, which on other grounds I reject, so I do not endorse the description.' I am not sure whether this would be an accurate exposition of Nakhnikian's position. I am sure, however, that in general we need to contrast two questions: (a) Does such-and-such an attitude, as described, entail a religious belief? (b) Is such-and-such a description of an attitude an appropriate articulation of the attitude? Later I shall say more about the contrast and the connection between these two questions, but first we need to examine entailments of descriptions more thoroughly. Then we shall look at how the descriptions can originate in reflections on the attitudes.

Nakhnikian considers thankfulness, but in this book I have given far more attention to basic trust, so we shall here consider entailments of descriptions of basic trust. In chapter 3 I have defined a 'basic' attitude as one which is doubly pervasive and doubly unifying. So if an attitude of trust lacks any of these features, it is not basic trust. Because of this definition 'Jones has basic trust' entails 'Jones has a cosmic conviction.' This can easily be shown by considering the way in which the external pervasiveness and external unification of a basic attitude are defined. The external pervasiveness of basic trust means that it is not focused on any particular or set of particulars in *contrast* with other particulars but rather on all particulars as an aggregate. The external unification of basic trust means that this aggregate is dealt with in a unified way, for the trust is focused on an X which is somehow common to all the particulars in spite of their differences. This X, a unifying constant in the cosmos, can be called a 'cosmic' focus. So basic trust entails a belief in a cosmic focus. 'Jones has basic trust' entails 'Jones has a cosmic conviction.'

We have seen in chapter 3 that basic trust, as defined thus far, might entail only a minimal cosmic conviction. Where the trust is minimal – only what is needed to function in the world at all – the cosmic conviction could merely assure us a minimal order or regularity. We have also seen that if a trust is not correctly described as 'basic,' then no cosmic conviction at all is entailed. If someone's trust as articulated by him is not basic trust, then, unless we presume to articulate it for him as an instance of basic trust, there is no entailment of cosmic conviction.

In this book I have defined basic trust in ways which go beyond double pervasiveness and double unification. The cosmic focus has been further characterized in a way which involves setting aside alternative possibilities. Three kinds of cosmic focus could be proposed:

(a) a *characteristic* common to all particulars;
(b) a *reality* which, though immanent in all particulars, is not reducible to them, but somehow transcends them;
(c) *existence* or being, which can be construed as somehow combining (a) and (b), that is, as resembling a category (universal characteristic) and an immanent-transcendent reality.

The kind of focus depends on the kind of basic attitude, and in this book I have so defined basic trust that the focus comes under (b). Hence the cosmic conviction can be appropriately labelled 'religious,' for it is similar to what traditional religious people have believed concerning God. Perhaps the most striking example of this is the way in which I have set forth the core of basic trust as a *receptivity* to a pervasive, unifying *activity* which liberates us to authentic, loving existence. I have defined basic trust in such a way that it includes a central religious conviction. To accept the definition and deny the conviction would be comparable to denying that man is rational after having defined man as a rational animal. But of course anyone can reject my definition of basic trust. And obviously I could have proposed a different definition, equating it with cosmic (pervasive and unifying) trust. Then I could have said that *some instances* of basic trust involve the receptivity which is described above; these would be religious instances of basic trust, but basic trust as such would not entail religious belief. I could then ascribe basic trust to someone without thereby ascribing religious belief. In this book, however, since I have defined basic trust as a religious species of cosmic trust, religious belief is entailed.

My account of basic trust can be contested in two quite different ways. First, someone may question my account of the character of the logical connection between a proposition ascribing basic trust to a person and a proposition ascribing religious belief to that person. My analysis has been in terms of entailment-relations. I argue that there is a universally accepted definition of 'trust' such that 'Jones trusts' entails 'Jones believes that X exists as focus of trust.' Then I propose a stipulative definition of 'basic trust' as not only cosmic (doubly pervasive and unifying) but also religious (receptive to a cosmic activity which liberates us to authentic, loving existence). Obviously someone may find flaws in the various steps of my argument concerning entailment-relations. Secondly, someone may question my claim that there is a kind of trust which is (i) a constituent of human fulfilment and (ii) articulated appropriately in a way similar to my description of basic trust. In chapter 3 I have considered (i) to some extent and in *Struggle and Fulfilment* much more thoroughly. In this chapter I am more interested in (ii). Even where someone's normative anthropology is fairly close to mine, so that there is an agreement that something *roughly* like what I have described as basic trust is a constituent of human fulfilment, there may be important differences in articulation. Two somewhat different descriptions could be articulations of roughly the same attitude, for the attitude is at its core a prelinguistic way of being in the world which begins in infancy and matures in adult life. Since trust is essentially prelinguistic, the selection of combinations of words which seem most appropriate to it involves judgment. Such reflection concerning trust is a matter of using language to try to get at what lies behind language. One is somehow comparing experience and language so as to get the language which best 'fits' the experience. This is very different from logical analysis where one compares two linguistic structures to see whether they are logically consistent. In what I am calling 'reflection' one structure is prelinguistic. And the structure of this way of being in the world is not simply mirrored in the structure of the language one uses to articulate it, for when one gives a linguistic form to the way of being in the world, one to some extent changes it: one starts trusting in such-and-such a linguistically articulated way.

Indeed, reflection involves a combination of decision-*that* and decision-*to*. The decision-*that* is a judgment that one's prelinguistic experience of trust as a way of being in the world is best articulated in such-and-such words. The decision-*to* is a commitment to be in the world in this linguistically articulated way. This combination of decision-*that* and decision-*to* in the process which I am calling 'reflection' makes it similar to an expression of an onlook where one says 'I look on x as y': I judge that x sufficiently resembles y to be treated in a similar way. Reflection differs, however, in that its x is prelinguistic, whereas in an onlook x is already articulated. Later I shall refer again to the element of decision-*to* in reflection on trust, but here I want to emphasize the element of decision-*that*. It is because of the presence of this element that there can be two rather different articulations of what we can assume to be roughly the same trust.

A further feature of trust as a prelinguistic way of being in the world is that it includes in indissoluble unity what is later distinguished through articulation into two elements: a cosmic or religious *stance*, which includes behaviour, emotion, and will, and a cosmic or religious *conviction*, which is a state of intellect. If trust is considered in an objectivist way, the convictional element is not only distinguished from the stance-element, but also *detached* from it. The convictional element is then understood in abstraction from the stance-element and from the original unity of stance and conviction. This abstraction involves a change in the meaning of the conviction, but for an objectivist it has the advantage that a cosmic or religious conviction (for example, a belief in Providence) can be understood in the same way by everyone, regardless of differences in private stance. Whether or not one's private stance is trust, the meaning which the conviction has is then the same. In contrast with such an objectivist approach, existentialist reflection concerning trust probes trust as a prelinguistic way of being in the world. In its articulation of trust such reflection tries to indicate the original unity of stance-element and conviction-element by setting forth entailment-relations between the two elements as linguistically characterized. On an objectivist approach, however, a cosmic conviction is construed as existing and having meaning separately and independently from trust as a stance. Hence no entailment-relations between stance and conviction are possible. Furthermore, the cosmic conviction is actually understood from within a way of being in the world which is a rival to trust, namely *detachment.* So when an objectivist affirms or denies that he believes in God as providential activity, he means something very different from an existentialist who affirms such a belief as part of his articulation of trust.

Thus it is easy to see why an objectivist would reject my existentialist description of trust which entails a religious conviction. He has separated the conviction from trust as a stance and he understands the conviction from an objectivist stance of detachment. In doing this he is not involved in any logical inconsistency. Rather, he is refusing to reflect existentially. But someone who does reflect existentially concerning trust may come up with a somewhat different account. This is because the structure of trust as a way of being in the world is not merely reflected but also to some extent *interpreted* by the language we use to articulate it, and because the language we bring to the prelinguistic experience varies according to our differing cultural and religious backgrounds. Also, the prelinguistic experiences of any two trusting persons differ somewhat, for we each have our own distinctive way of being in the world. In chapter 3 and elsewhere I have indicated my assumption that the more deeply one probes personally into such matters the more likely it is that one will discover universal truths concerning human beings, but this assumption is open to challenge. Thus each reader has to decide the extent to which my articulation of trust rings true to his or her own awareness of trust as an overall way of being in the world. As I have noted at the end of *Struggle and Fulfilment,* the reader's own reflection is othe test to which I submit my account.

In chapter 6 I have said that a Christian offers an interpretation of basic trust which an agnostic is logically free to reject. We can now see that this is true whether the agnostic is objectivist or existentialist in approach, for the interpretation is an invitation to existentialist reflection, not to logical analysis, though of course the interpretation can also be criticized in terms of its logical consistency. To accept a Christian interpretation involves both a decision-*that* and a decision-*to*: a decision that the articulation 'fits' one's own experience of trust as a way of being in the world and a decision to live this trust henceforth in this articulated way.

But if an agnostic is logically free to reject an interpretation of his own trust which would involve him in religious belief, how can I deny Keen that freedom in chapter 3? My point there is that if someone has *already articulated* his own basic trust in a way which includes or entails religious convictions, he is not logically free to reject those convictions. Keen's description of basic trust is clearly not religiously agnostic, and in a similar way neither is Nakhnikian's description of cosmic thankfulness. Since any trust or any thankfulness entails a belief in the existence of some X as focus of the stance, descriptions of the stance which involve further characterizations of that X entail the belief that X has those characteristics. It is true that the description of X may be 'agnostic' in the sense that it employs a negative way in analogy and conveys a sense of a mystery beyond the grasp of human minds; but there is still a *belief* in this mysterious X.

Now that I am trying to reconcile apparent contradictions which have appeared in this book I should take some time to examine the contrast between my earlier analysis of the logical relations between stance and conviction in terms of speech-act implications and my current analysis in terms of entailments between propositions. Compare the following:

(a) The proposition 'Jones trusts X' entails the proposition 'Jones believes that X exists.'
(b) In saying 'I trust X' I imply that I believe that X exists.

Both (a) and (b) are correct, but (b) involves a weaker claim than (a). This can be seen if we consider another example of speech-act implication. In saying 'I promise to do K' I imply that I intend to do K. In speech-act implication there is an asymmetry between a first-person performance of a speech-act and a third-person report, for in saying '*He* promises to do K' I do not imply that he intends to do K. But there is no analogous asymmetry in entailments between propositions, for these hold regardless of whether the subject is 'I' or 'he.' For example, the proposition '*He* trusts X' entails the proposition '*He* believes that X exists.' There is another difference between speech-act implications and propositional entailments. In a speech-act implication although the speaker is logically committed to having the state which is implied, he may as a matter of fact not have it at all, for example, if he promises insincerely.[7] In an entailment if the first proposition is true, the second must also be true: if Jones or I or anyone is correctly described as 'trusting' X then each of us must believe that X exists; we are not only logically committed to believing this, but also do believe this.

Thus a speech-act analysis of the logical relations between trust as stance and trust as conviction could be misleading, if the relation is actually one of entailment, for two reasons. First, it suggests that the relation holds only in first-person cases and not in third-person cases. Secondly, it suggests that someone who has the stance is merely logically committed to having the conviction and may nevertheless not have it. Both suggestions are false when the relation is one between trusting X and believing that X exists.

If, however, we look at more complex stance-conviction relations, speech-act analysis can be an illuminating reminder of two facts which might otherwise be ignored in entailment-analysis. First, once anyone moves beyond the bare description of a stance as 'trust' and tries to articulate it further, for example, as a cosmic stance (doubly pervasive and unifying), his *own* reflective articulation has a special priority. As I have pointed out, this articulation involves a combination of judgment and commitment on the part of whoever is reflecting on his own trust. The reflection is expressed in an articulate speech-act which combines a decision-*that* and a decision-*to*. I can propose an articulation to him, but he is logically free to reject it. I can question his judgment or his commitment, but I am not in a position to assert that he is logically committed to a cosmic conviction or that he must actually have a cosmic conviction unless his own description of his stance warrants such entailments. There is thus an asymmetry between first-person and third-person articulations. Secondly, in the actual process of reflection the distinction between discovering that I logically *should* have a conviction and discovering that I logically *must* have a conviction is blurred. In some contexts there is a clear distinction between being logically committed to a conviction which one may or may not have and being logically committed to a conviction which one must actually have. During reflection on trust as a way of being in the world, however, the articulation of the conviction is tested both by reference to the words already used in describing the stance and by reference to trust as prelinguistically experienced. What one believes involves both a decision-*to* articulate trust in a particular way which gives rise to various entailment-relations which one should acknowledge and a decision-*that* this articulation fits the trust which one actually has. And if the person who is reflecting has not as yet noticed a specific entailment-relation, then an outsider can say only that he is logically committed to the entailed conviction, not that he also *has* the conviction. In general, from 'Jones believes S' and 'S entails P' we cannot deduce 'Jones believes P.' Nevertheless, if both belief S and belief P eventually emerge as interconnected parts in an articulation of Jones's prelinguistic way of being in the world, then there is a sense in which Jones *did* believe P even before he articulated it; P is an articulation of an element in the prelinguistic conviction.[8]

Thus the priority of first-person articulation and the difference between prelinguistic and articulated modes of 'having' trust suggest why a speech-act analysis of the logical relation between stance and con-

viction appealed to me before I clearly grasped the significance of reflective articulation as the context for understanding that logical relation.
Speech-act analysis is a way of groping towards a way of using language
to get at what lies behind language in one's own most profound personal
experience. It is now clear to me that reflective articulation is the key to
understanding both contentions in the anthropological-logical argument. Let us now have another look at the structure of that argument,
setting aside the issue concerning speech-act implication versus propositional entailment.

As I have presented the argument, it is closely linked with analogy of
attitude and it has two distinct contentions. First, we describe an attitude
such as trust and propose it as a constituent of human fulfilment. Secondly, we claim that the attitude as described is logically linked to a
religious conviction. In the initial description we deal with the attitude
primarily as a stance. Even if we understand the stance existentially, the
reality of its metaphysical focus is, as it were, bracketed so that we can go
on to ask what *would be* the appropriate focus of the attitude and what
religious conviction the person who holds it is accordingly *committed* to.
The assumption is that the person does not already *have* the conviction in
some form and that he has no *awareness* of the focus as a basis for having
the conviction. But this assumption is open to challenge if my account of
reflection on trust is correct. If trust is a prelinguistic way of being in the
world which can be *experienced* and then articulated so as to display the
indissoluble *unity* of stance-element and conviction-element, there is a
sense in which anyone who has trust '*has*' the conviction, and also has
experienced the focus to which he is related in trust. He has the conviction
and experiences the focus at a prelinguistic level. Reflection on trust as a
prelinguistic way of being in the world is the basis not only for analogy
of attitude and the anthropological-logical argument but also for existentialist analogy of relation. Earlier I noted that in the latter analogy the
attitude of trust is a condition for discerning the divine. Now we see that
the reflective articulation of trust in terms of religious convictions arises
from a discernment of the divine reality which the individual prelinguistically experiences as that with which he is in relation. I would now
contend that to the extent that anyone has basic trust he has such a
discernment. The discernment can be denied, however, in three ways: (i)
in so far as we are dominated by distrust as a fundamental way of being
in the world, our distrustful metaphysical discernments overshadow our
discernments of the divine; (ii) in so far as we do not reflect at all, but
ignore or repress our prelinguistic experience, perhaps on objectivist

grounds, we are split off from both kinds of metaphysical discernment; (iii) in so far as our articulated world-view makes any attempt to articulate the religious discernment seem irrational, we tend to deny the discernment rather than modify our world-view.

Since many people deny any discernment of the divine, the neo-Kantian anthropological-logical argument provides an important approach to religious belief: it is rational to believe in God if this belief is entailed by an attitude which is necessary for human fulfilment, especially if we seem to have no experiential access to metaphysical truth, whether theistic or atheistic. One major reason for such a lack of experiential access is an objectivist approach. So if a neo-Kantian argument is explored by means of an existentialist reflection on trust as prelinguistically experienced, the metaphysical focus of trust is likely to come to be experienced rather than merely postulated. In other words, a genuinely existentialist approach in analogy of attitude is likely to lead to analogy of relation. This is because trust as a way of being in the world is a way of relating to a cosmic focus.

What I have just said is the outcome of my own reflection. The reader must test its truth by reference to his or her own reflection. The reader may also find that reflection on one's own prelinguistic experience is important, not only as a way of testing claims such as mine, but also – and more importantly – as a way of reducing a split which is present in most of us. This split is between our fundamental ways of being in the world and our explicit beliefs. Some people who are professed theists are dominated by distrust at a prelinguistic level, and others who are professed atheists are profoundly trustful at that level. Reflection can help us to uncover this split and to gain access to the fundamental level on which our human fulfilment and our relation to God mainly depend. Explicit religious belief may reinforce our basic trust but it may also hide our basic distrust. The most crucial struggle in our lives goes on below the level of language.

Notes

INTRODUCTION

1 Donald Evans, 'Love, Situations and Rules,' in Paul Ramsey and Gene
Outka, eds, *Norm and Context in Christian Ethics* (New York: Scribner's,
1968).
2 Donald Evans, *The Logic of Self-Involvement* (London: SCM, 1963;
New York: Herder, 1969); 'Religious Language and Divine Transcendence,' unpublished lectures, University of Chicago, 1967, including brief
studies of Aquinas, Barth, Ramsey, and Evans; 'Differences Between Scientific and Religious Assertions,' in Ian Barbour, ed, *Religion and Science*
(New York: Harper, 1968); 'Barth on Talk about God,' *Canadian Journal of
Theology*, 16 (1970); 'Victor Preller's Analogy of "Being",' *The New
Scholasticism*, 45 (1971).
3 Gregory Baum, MB 134.
4 Donald Evans, 'Faith and Belief,' *Religious Studies*, 10:2,3 (March and June
1974); 'Philosophical Analysis and Religious Faith: Some Retrospective
Reflections,' in F. Duchesneau, ed, *Faith and the Contemporary Epistemologies*
(Ottawa: University of Ottawa Press, 1977).
5 See ch 5 n 2.
6 Donald Evans, *Struggle and Fulfilment: The Inner Dynamics of Religion and
Morality* (London/New York/Toronto: Collins, 1979).

CHAPTER ONE

1 Donald Evans, *The Logic of Self-Involvement* (London: SCM, 1963;
New York: Herder, 1969).
2 Donald Evans, 'Barth on Talk about God,' *Canadian Journal of Theology*, 16
(1970).

3 Donald Evans, 'Victor Preller's Analogy of "Being",' *The New Scholasticism*, 45 (1971).

4 Donald Evans, 'Philosophical Analysis and Religious Faith: Some Retrospective Reflections,' in F. Duchesneau, ed, *Faith and the Contemporary Epistemologies* (Ottawa: University of Ottawa Press, 1977).

5 Evans, *The Logic of Self-Involvement*, pp 134–5. There may also be particular characteristics which all people, or most people, share, which make an attitude of respect appropriate and which are describable and discernible 'objectively,' independently of respect. If someone wishes to define 'person' in terms of such characteristics, he may well be getting at an indispensable basis for a rudimentary public morality. But for a more profound understanding of 'personal' and of morality I would add to the definition 'that to which *agapé* is the appropriate response.'

6 Austin Farrer, *Finite and Infinite* (Westminster: Dacre Press, 1943).

7 Frederich Schleiermacher, *The Christian Faith* (Edinburgh: Clark, 1928), pp 1–26.

8 Paul Tillich, *Dynamics of Faith* (New York: Harper, 1958) ch 1.

9 Rudolph Otto, *The Idea of the Holy* (Oxford: Oxford University Press, 1923), pp 1–40.

10 Martin Buber, *I and Thou*, tr W. Kaufmann (New York: Scribner's, 1970), Parts I and III.

11 Sam Keen, *Apology for Wonder* (New York: Harper, 1969), ch 7.

12 Buber, *I and Thou*, p 151; 'real simile' is from the translation by Ronald Gregor Smith (Edinburgh: Clark, 1937), p 103.

13 In an earlier study of analogy I did not include analogy of relation. See Donald Evans, 'Faith and Belief,' *Religious Studies*, 10:2 (June 1974), 205–12.

14 Concerning analogy of attitude and 'worship' I said this in 'Faith and Belief,' p 206: 'I should note two possible sources of confusion in my use of the word "worship" when I introduce analogy of attitude. First, when I speak of worship as an attitude rather than an *expression* of attitude, I am deviating from the usual meaning of "worship." My reason for doing this is that I want to allow for the possibility of *unexpressed* worship, *implicit* faith. Secondly, I am focusing on worship as an unexpressed or expressed attitude of an *individual*, whether or not he is taking part in the communal activity which the word "worship" usually connotes. My reason for doing this is that analogy of attitude is best understood by reference to attitudes in an individual.'

15 Victor Preller, *Divine Science and Science of God* (Princeton: Princeton University Press, 1967).

16 Evans, 'Faith and Belief,' pp 206–8.
17 This account is heavily influenced by Austin Farrer.
18 Evans, 'Faith and Belief,' pp 209–11.
19 Otto, *The Idea of the Holy*, pp 1–40.
20 Ludwig Wittgenstein, 'A Lecture on Ethics,' *Philosophical Review*, 74 (1965), 8.
21 Gabriel Marcel, *Homo Viator* (New York: Harper, 1951), pp 46–7.
22 Paul Tillich, *The Courage to Be* (London: Nisbet, 1952) ch 6. At first sight Schleiermacher might also seem to be using a *via causalitatis* in his application of analogy of attitude to the feeling of absolute dependence. But God is believed to be the 'Whence,' not of the feeling itself, but of our 'receptive and active existence' (*The Christian Faith*, p 16).
23 Evans, 'Faith and Belief,' pp 206–7.
24 For a more extensive discussion of 'existentialist' conditions of understanding see Evans, 'Faith and Belief.' For a distinction between scientific and religious assertions which is somewhat similar to the objectivist/ existentialist distinction see Donald Evans, 'Differences between Scientific and Religious Assertions,' in Ian Barbour, ed, *Science and Religion* (New York: Harper, 1968).

CHAPTER TWO

1 Useful bibliographies of Ramsey's writings can be found in several places: 1 / Ramsey, MDA; 2 / Pierre Lucier, *Empirisme logique et langage religieux* (Montreal/Tournai: Bellarmin/Désclée, 1976); 3 / Jerry H. Gill, ed, *Christian Empiricism* (London: Sheldon, 1974); 4 / Jerry H. Gill, *Ian Ramsey: To Speak Responsibly of God* (London: Allen & Unwin, 1976). Gill's first book is a collection of Ramsey's essays, including BP, PR, SEI, TG, and TL. His second book is an outline of Ramsey's thought.
2 One reason for this was his involvement in so many diverse matters of intellectual, ecclesiastical, and social concern at the same time. For a biographical sketch of Ramsey see David L. Edwards, *Ian Ramsey, Bishop of Durham: A Memoir* (Oxford: Oxford University Press, 1973).
3 Ramsey's reply to a request for comments on the 1971 essay arrived too late for me to revise the essay for publication in *Religious Studies*. Ramsey referred me to MDA and to BPEM.
4 I have rewritten this paragraph in response to LR, where Ramsey notes that the kind of 'objectivity' which the 'more' has might possibly be given in dreams, and in response to MDA 61–2, which clarifies Ramsey's position concerning three kinds of objectivity.

5 Martin Buber, *I and Thou*, tr W. Kaufmann (New York: Scribner's, 1970), pp 57–9.
6 Peter Berger, *A Rumour of Angels* (New York: Doubleday, 1969), pp 67–70.
7 LR: 'I am sure this difficulty arises partly because of confusion on my part, but partly also because I don't want to use the word "God" without being able to give a full justification for the introduction of the word. In other words, I want to keep away from the word "God" for as long as possible. I do not always succeed, but I always try to be ultra-cautious in moving towards deism, with an awareness of the down-to-earth empiricists breathing down my neck!'
8 It is interesting to compare and contrast Ramsey here with Gordon Kaufman in *God the Problem* (Cambridge, Mass.: Harvard University Press, 1972), especially ch 3. Kaufman starts from an awareness of finitude, an awareness of being limited in various ways – by physical restrictions, organic deficiencies, other people, and norms or ideals. The various experiences of being limited indicate for Kaufman an ultimate Limiter which unifies all the various experiences of being limited. Kaufman says that it is possible to use any of the four kinds of limitation – physical, organic, personal, or normative – as the basis for an analogy concerning the Limiter, but the third is the most satisfactory: 'the experience of *personal limiting* as known in the interaction of personal wills' (p 60). When another person actively impinges on me, I understand him to be a self whose active centre is beyond what I directly experience. He transcends his behaviour and reveals himself *via* it. God, analogously, transcends the world but acts and reveals Himself through it. Kaufman claims it is reasonable to believe in His reality even though He is – as Ramsey would say – 'more' than what is directly experienced.
9 William Temple, *Nature, Man and God* (London: Macmillan, 1934), Lecture XI.
10 William van Orman Quine, *From a Logical Point of View* (New York: Harper, 1963).
11 Ibid, p 41.
12 Ibid, p 44.
13 Ibid, pp 12–19.
14 Concerning the question of the relation between God and non-observables, Ramsey said in LR: 1 / 'Justifiably or not, I have not been too bothered about the question.' 2 / 'You are of course perfectly right in what you say about the attraction I find in Quine.' 3 / 'I am very Berkleian on this matter and would have to begin to understand this relation in terms of the observables ... God's activity and mine always meet each other

through the mediation of observables.' Concerning 3, my comment is that Ramsey failed to see how very weak Berkeley himself is concerning the relation between God and non-observables. Berkeley's 'notion' of the activity of his own *I* in relation to ideas provides a basis for analogical thought concerning the relation between God and observables; but Berkeley does not have a basis for analogical thought concerning the relation between God and Berkeley's *I* or the *I* of other people.

15 LR: 'I like very much the further distinction you made amongst qualifiers.' In ch 1 I have further developed this distinction as a tool in my own analysis of kinds of analogy. Incidentally, it seems to me that Kaufman in *God the Problem* talks about God by analogical extension from human activity in a way which is closest to Ramsey's use of universalizing qualifiers rather than other qualifiers. The same is true of my account of pervasive divine activity in relation to pervasive human attitudes as presented in ch 6.

16 Ramsey tentatively denies the entailment in some lecture notes (mimeographed but unpublished) on the problem of evil. A somewhat similar position is taken in RL 88.

17 James Collins, *God in Modern Philosophy* (Chicago: Regnery, 1959), p 3.

18 Austin Farrer, *Finite and Infinite* (Westminster: Dacre Press, 1943). There are many other important similarities between Ramsey and Farrer, in spite of their very different philosophical styles. For example, both meet the challenge of empiricism by pointing to decisive, free moral action as the paradigm instance of a reality which makes an experienceable difference while transcending sense experience. Farrer talks about this as an 'apprehension of substance,' Ramsey as a 'discernment of a disclosed "more".'

19 Ibid, p 51.

20 Brian Hebblethwaite criticizes what I say here in 'The Philosophical Theology of I.T. Ramsey, Some Further Reflections,' *Theology*, December 1973, pp 639–40: 'Donald Evans compares Ramsey's use of "qualifiers," by which one so refines a "model" that it succeeds in bringing about a disclosure, with meditative techniques. But the practice of meditation has a role *within* an already possessed religion. Christians may well find the technique very helpful, as expounded, for example, in Ramsey's pamphlet, *Our Understanding of Prayer*, prepared for the Archbishops' Commission on Christian Doctrine. But the unbeliever is not likely to be particularly impressed by the story of C.E. Raven finding a cosmic disclosure in a fish and chip shop.' To this I would reply that some elementary meditative techniques, including Ramsey's use of qualifiers, involve minimal prior

religious assumptions; an unbeliever can try them out. But I suspect that
Ramsey's proposal concerning models and qualifiers, which is made in a
dominantly intellectual context, is far less likely to 'work' than techniques
devised primarily as aids to the alteration of consciousness.

21 LR: 'I have changed my views on *activity*, which I do not see as a model,
even a "super model," but as a word which unites God and ourselves in a
literal sense.' Ramsey referred me to MDA, which was not then published,
where he claimed (p 61) that we use 'activity' concerning God 'univocally'
and 'literally.' He also referred me to his work on Berkeley, especially
BPEM. There I find Ramsey hovering between finding an analogy ('something of the same ...') and finding a parallel ('just as ...') between talk
about *I* and talk about God (p 26). But he leans towards the latter and at
p 26, n 21, he speaks of 'logical parallels.' In LR Ramsey explained why his
change of views seemed necessary. He said he needed to be able to use
'activity' literally of God 'if I am to give any answer whatever to those
who would question whether I can really argue that I am saying anything
reliable about what is objectively disclosed. For me, activity provides the
one firm link in fact and language.'

It seems to me that Ramsey could not consistently change his view concerning 'activity' in this way. At the beginning of section 5 I noted various
ways in which the transcendence of *I* and the transcendence of God are
very similar. But the rest of the section outlines the many ways in which,
according to Ramsey himself, the transcendence of God is radically different, so much so that when 'activity' is shifted from talk about people to
talk about God it needs qualifiers. Indeed, the need for universalizing
qualifiers is something which by itself rules out any univocal or literal
understanding of 'activity' as applied to God. Activity which pervades the
whole universe, somehow active in all the particular activities of all the
distinct entities which comprise the universe, cannot be 'activity' in the
same literal, univocal sense that these activities are. (Note that the issue
here is related to the one mentioned in n 14 concerning God's relation to
non-observables.)

But 'activity' does have a unique role in Ramsey's thought. It is the one
model which is *presupposed* in the application of all other models (MDA
11). Also, the word refers to God in terms of that which for Ramsey gives
disclosures their objectivity and reality as initiatives to which we respond.
Nevertheless the objectivity and reality and initiative in divine activity are
only analogous to that in human activity. The unique role of 'activity'
does not mean that it can be used univocally and literally of man and
God. If it can't, does this mean that the *reliability* of discourse concerning

God is destroyed, as Ramsey seems to assume? I do not think so. Certainly it means that discourse concerning human activity is considerably more reliable (i.e. clearer and less subject to possible error) than qualified-model discourse concerning divine activity. But this is to be expected if divine transcendence transcends human transcendence.

22 In MDA 23 Ramsey describes the relation of subordinate to dominant models in terms of logical presupposition: the model 'economy' presupposes 'purpose' which presupposes 'activity.' LR is also relevant: 'I would say that the "dominant models" were presupposed by the "lower" models in so far as a one-sided relation of entailment could be established between discourse originating from the one model and discourse originating from the other.' That is, I take it, 'God is purposeful' entails 'God is active,' but not vice versa; and 'God is wise' entails 'God is personal,' though not vice versa. But although the relation of presupposition may hold in some of the cases I have mentioned, it does not seem to hold in all, unless we prescribe special restricted meanings for one or more terms. For example, it is not true, unless we prescribe special meanings, that 'power' presupposes 'person,' that 'protection' presupposes 'love,' or that 'king' presupposes 'protection.' Think of hydro power, Mafia protection, and tyrannous kings.

23 In MDA 23 Ramsey says that the more detailed the model and the closer it is to the perimeter of an array of models which centres on activity, the less reliable the model is as discourse about God.

24 For an interesting elaboration and defence of Ramsey on 'empirical fit,' see Terrence W. Tilley, 'Ian Ramsey and Empirical Fit,' *Journal of American Academy of Religion*, 45:3 Supplement (September 1977), G:963–88. Tilley's defence depends on a questionable interpretation of Ramsey in which an ultimate claim should 'fit' not only the facts but also the *character* of the person making the claim. He also, more plausibly, finds implicit in Ramsey what he calls a 'pragmatic' criterion: an *appraisal* of the character of the person authentically making the claim. Tilley's version of Ramsey makes Ramsey less open to my criticisms, but I still give less emphasis to fitting the facts, and I insist that the appraisal of character should be made on the basis of a philosophical anthropology. A different defence of 'empirical fit' is given by Gill, *Ian Ramsey: To Speak Responsibly of God* pp 13–23, 148–50. Gill's defence of 'empirical fit' in relation to *ultimate* claims is to me vague and unconvincing, but in relation to Christian *historical* claims (which are beyond the scope of my investigation) he is illuminating.

25 One personalistic writer whose influence seems more definite is H.H. Farmer (PG 65).

26 Does this awareness of the subject in Berkeley require a self-involving (existentialist) stance different from the stance in which one is aware of sense impressions and images? And is the latter stance objectivist? I find that I cannot give a clear and definite answer to these questions (which is not surprising, since Berkeley lived before Kierkegaarde!). In so far as Ramsey follows Berkeley the same difficulty arises if one asks these questions; but there are also passages in Ramsey where he does seem to be using an existentialist/objectivist contrast in distinguishing awareness of the subject from any other awareness.

27 Would Ramsey have been wise to replace his empiricism by something like Strawson's late-Wittgensteinean approach rather than, as I am suggesting, an existentialist personalism? Strawson has argued, against empiricists such as Ayer, that we can only apply personal predicates (as distinct from material ones) to ourselves if we also already understand how to apply them to other human beings; so there is no place for alleged inferences to other minds. This Strawsonian claim is compatible with contention (a) but it is remote from (b). And in Ramsey's thought (a) is most clearly and consistently interpreted in relation to (b), which needs a personalistic existentialist framework. See P.F. Strawson, *Individuals* (London: Methuen, 1959), ch 3; for Ayer's criticism of Strawson see A.J. Ayer, *The Concept of a Person* (London: Macmillan, 1963), ch 4.

28 Donald Evans, *The Logic of Self-Involvement* (London: SCM, 1963; New York: Herder, 1969). My account of 'self-involving language' and 'onlooks' involved a revision, not a replacement, of an empiricism in which the more fundamental epistemology depended on what I have called 'flat Constatives,' which are I-It uses of language in science and in quasi-scientific common sense.

29 R.D. Laing, *The Politics of Experience and the Bird of Paradise* (London: Pelican, 1967), ch 7.

30 Ibid, pp 134–5.

31 Erik Erikson, *Childhood and Society*, 2nd ed (New York: Norton, 1963), chs 2, 7; *Identity, Youth and Crisis* (New York: Norton, 1968), ch 4; *Young Man Luther* (New York: Norton, 1962), chs 4, 8.

32 Gabriel Marcel, *Homo Viator* (New York: Harper, 1951), ch 2.

33 Søren Kierkegaard, *The Sickness unto Death* (New York: Doubleday, 1954).

34 H. Richard Niebuhr, *The Responsible Self* (New York: Harper, 1963). Subsequent quotations in this paragraph are from pp 118–19.

35 Ramsey's treatment of attitudes would have been more satisfactory if he had also provided a more careful discussion of *idolatry*. Ramsey seems to

me to be open to the same sort of criticism as the one Martin Buber directed at Scheler and, indirectly, at Tillich (Buber, *I and Thou*, pp 153–5). Idolatry is not avoided simply by making sure that any positively or negatively all-inclusive attitude which one has is focused on God rather than on a particular in the universe. It is not enough for Ramsey to require that universalizing and/or negating qualifiers be used, so that the focus of one's attitude pervades and/or transcends the universe. What is crucial is the nature of the attitude itself. The attitude expressed by 'You are the whole world to me' (i.e. nothing else matters to me except my devotion to you) is often very possessive and self-centred: another person is used to fill a void within oneself. A subtle self-idolatry is at work. Similarly against Tillich it is not enough to shift an avaricious ultimate concern from money to God; the quality of the concern needs to be changed. In general, the *content* of attitudes used in analogy of attitude requires more attention than it receives from Ramsey.

36 Hebblethwaite, 'The Philosophical Theology of I.T. Ramsey,' p 644.
37 Concerning this kind of implication see Evans, *The Logic of Self-Involvement*, ch 1.
38 Immanuel Kant, *Religion within the Limits of Reason Alone*, tr R.M. Greene and H.H. Hudson (New York: Harper, 1960), pp 22–3, italics mine.
39 In this sentence I am following the interpretation of Kant given by John R. Silber in an introductory essay for the work of Kant cited in the previous n. See especially pp lxxxvii, xci, xciii, xciv, and cxxxi.
40 Frederich Schleiermacher *The Christian Faith* (Edinburgh: Clark, 1928), pp 18, 26.
41 Immanuel Kant, *Critique of Practical Reason*, tr L.W. Beck (New York: Liberal Arts, 1956), Bk II, ch 2. According to Kant we have a moral duty to bring about a universal proportioning of happiness to virtue, a duty which is impossible to fulfil unless we postulate God as Proportioner. Kant's logical contention would have been closer in form to the one concerning pervasive trust if he had said that respect for the moral law as categorical imperative implies belief in God as Lawgiver. I have not found any such argument, though it is present in some thinkers influenced by Kant, e.g. John Baillie. What Kant does say is that all religion consists in looking on our duties as divine commands and God as the Lawgiver universally to be honoured (*Religion within the Limits of Reason Alone*, pp 90n, 95). For Baillie see *Our Knowledge of God* (London: Oxford University Press, 1939), sec 20; for the form of his argument Baillie explicitly acknowledges his debt to John Cook Wilson.

42 Schleiermacher, *The Christian Faith*, p 12.
43 John Cook Wilson, *Statement and Inference I* (Oxford: Clarendon, 1926), pp 858–65. Wilson does insist (p 859) that reverence is 'not confined to the lowest or least intellectual but reaches its completed development in the highest and most cultivated.'
44 The approach is not 'pragmatic,' if we mean by that term an approach in which religious beliefs are appraised in terms of their usefulness or non-usefulness in promoting various human purposes. In the neo-Kantian approach it is not the useful function of the beliefs which is appraised, but rather the fulfilling character of the attitudes which imply the beliefs.
45 Donald Evans, 'Philosophical Analysis and Religious Faith: Some Retrospective Reflections,' in F. Duchesneau, ed, *Faith and the Contemporary Epistemologies* (Ottawa: University of Ottawa Press, 1977).

CHAPTER THREE

1 In the 1973 version of this essay I said that Keen provides 'the most important recent answer' to the fundamental questions concerning man. As I have studied some of the thinkers on whom he draws, working towards my own creative synthesis, I have been more stimulated and enlightened by them than by him. His attempt at a comprehensive view, however, is still a heartening and helpful example for me in my work, and I still regard it as an important contribution to philosophical anthropology and theology.
2 I found BWE very uneven in quality, but the best parts are superb: 'Loneliness and Solitude,' 'The Tyranny Game,' and 'Godsong.'
3 Rudolph Otto, *The Idea of the Holy* (Oxford: Oxford University Press, 1923), chs 4–6.
4 It seems to me that Rollo May sheds a great deal of light on this distinction in his discussion of 'eros' as 'daimon' in *Love and Will* (New York: Norton, 1969).
5 Keen's opposition to perfectionism may help to explain his not using a way of perfection in any of the different kinds of analogy. It is true that worship of God as perfection need not foster perfectionism in human life, but it often does.
6 It would be misleading, however, to depict Keen as if he were utterly remote from Castaneda's preoccupation with death. In VV Keen's own increased preoccupation with death is evident (VV 5, 20). In TYS 89–91 and VV 188 he finds consolation by seeing that the 'ego-death' which occurs in radical transformation of personality is a means to a fuller life. But in VV

20 he insists that this does not solve the problem of physical death, where no subsequent life of any kind is known for the individual. In BWE fear of death looms larger for Keen: 'One of my favorite strategies for avoiding D---- is to focus on the fear that my woman will abandon me' (BWE 8). The whole Tyranny Game (dominating or being dominated) which he brilliantly portrays in BWE is explained as a desperate illusion to divert us from our impotence in dealing with death (BWE 32). Even Keen's new awareness of his body is only partly a 'joyful homecoming'; it is also a 'primal sorrow,' a 'heavy trip downward into the humus,' for 'all flesh does decay' (BWE 79).

7 This link is not surprising, for Keen's first book was an excellent semi-popular exposition of Marcel: *Gabriel Marcel* (London: Kingsgate Press, 1966).

8 Thomas Oden argues that the basic trust fostered by intensive group experiences implies religious conviction; see *The Intensive Group Experience* (Philadelphia: Westminster, 1972), ch 3. Schubert Ogden argues from our universal human need for 'basic confidence' (similar to what I call 'minimal basic trust') to our implicit faith in God; see *The Reality of God and Other Essays* (New York: Harper, 1963), pp 27–43. I think Ogden's argument shows at the most a belief in a minimal 'god.'

9 See Keen's comments on the bio-energetics of Stanley Keleman (vv 18–19).

10 Alexander Lowen, *Depression and the Body* (Baltimore: Penguin, 1973). What Lowen calls 'faith' is the opposite of depression; both have an intimate connection with the body.

11 Sigmund Freud, *The Future of an Illusion* (New York: Doubleday, 1957).

12 A.J. Ayer, *Language, Truth and Logic* (London: Gollancz, 1936).

13 For this reference and subsequent references to Erikson, see Erik Erikson, *Childhood and Society*, 2nd ed (New York: Norton, 1963), chs 2, 7: *Identity, Youth and Crisis* (New York: Norton, 1968), ch 4. See also Don Browning, *Generative Man: Psychoanalytic Perspectives* (Philadelphia: Westminster, 1973), chs 1, 6, 7.

14 Keen gives a brilliant account of this issue in 'The Tyranny Game' (BWE 25–41).

15 For an interesting defence of a kind of 'technological man' who is in many respects compatible with Keen's 'graceful man' see Victor Ferkiss, *Technological Man* (New York: Braziller, 1969).

16 Cf BWE 100: 'When we are healed we are baptized into the body politic. Rebirth is moving from isolation to community. We turn away from our private suffering to confront public tragedy. Or: United we stand. Divided I fall.'

17 Cf BWE 102–3: 'A major problem of the moral life: how to combine private satisfaction and public dis-ease, the contentment with which the body must be nourished with the prophetic outrage which is the only appropriate reaction to the public world we have created through technology?' Cf also BWE 92: 'I taste the delight of the world and of myself but what of the pain and conflict? *War and famine!* One face of the world is tragic. If I ignore it I become a shallow optimist. If I see it exclusively I become a dour presbyterian prophet tinged with grey self-righteousness. The trick seems to be to combine the sense of life as a task with the sense of life as a game, to remain playful in a world that is always haunted by the specter of evil.'

18 Gregory Baum, RA 292.

CHAPTER FOUR

1 I quote from a letter which Baum wrote on 20 July 1970 in response to an early draft of my 1971 essay: 'My ontic analysis of human life is wider and more universal than the experience of Communication Therapy. The idea of *summons* I have learnt from Rahner, who got it from Heidegger. It is found in Bultmann. It is common to the existentialists. But while the existentialists usually neglect the history of man, his childhood past, etc., I tried to integrate the Freudian thing into this perspective. This is possible because of Freud's notion of resistance. How can the resistance be broken? Only through the therapeutic word. In the idea of summons, then, two important modern streams of thought meet ... The same is true of the *gift*. The caughtness of man and his will is widely acknowledged today. Man cannot do what he wants to do; he cannot want what he wants. This is found among the existentialists and among the Freudians. They never analyse what really happens in man when he does affirm himself, leave the inauthentic mode of existence and assume a more authentic one, when he does abandon his defences, takes the leap, and trusts that the new, the healthy, the reliable will grow in him. But the stress on the unfreedom of man suggests that when the conversion does take place, it is a gift.'

2 Roughly similar distinctions have been made by Gabriel Marcel and Martin Buber. For Marcel, see *Homo Viator* (New York: Harper, 1962), pp 13–25, 50, 63, 67. For Buber, see *I and Thou*, tr W. Kaufmann (New York: Scribner's, 1970), pp 106–10, 144.

3 In RA Baum does not mention a death impulse, and in his discussion of original sin (RA 199–200) he seems to identify it with communal and familial structures of evil which distort the consciousness of every individual from the moment of birth.

4 Wilhelm Reich, *Character Analysis* (New York: Noonday Press, 1949), chs 11, 13).

5 Buber would not disagree with Baum here, but Buber *also* works an analogy of relation, way of pervasiveness and way of perfection.

6 Alexander Lowen, *Love and Orgasm* (New York: Signet, 1967), pp 312, 318–19.

7 Although my criticism of Baum for neglecting the political is dealt with in RA, Baum sheds little further light in RA concerning the realm of the 'natural' or concerning christological norms; but he does drop the demonic.

8 Baum is consciously influenced here by H. Richard Niebuhr, who has distinguished five kinds of ways in which Christian believers have responded to their socio-cultural environment. The fifth is 'Christ, Transformer of Culture.' See RA 178–80.

9 The logical-anthropological argument outlined in the postscript of ch 2 and in ch 3 is *not* pragmatic; see ch 2, n 44.

10 Baum notes that apocalyptic religion is often a revolutionary form of utopian religion, and that it is a major influence on western secular revolutionary thought (RA 105–7).

11 Abraham H. Maslow, *Toward a Psychology of Being*, 2nd ed, (New York: Van Nostrand, 1968), chs 3, 4.

12 My line of thought here leaves one crucial question unanswered: What counts as the social context for my life? If I restrict the scope to people with whom I have direct dealings in Toronto, my decision will be very different from what it would be if my social context were all mankind, which includes many millions of physiologically needy people.

13 Baum's position may turn out to be not very different from mine, as this statement from LB indicates: 'You have great difficulty in accepting God's redemptive presence in historical movements except as the sum of God's presence in the hearts of the people involved freeing them from the fetters of the past and enabling them to act. But to speak of movements of social change, collective events, transformation of structures as place of God's presence you find difficult if not impossible. Here I find that I must defend God's presence in history. I suppose that the exodus of the people of Israel remains the model for me, even though I admit that this event is unique and as such has no parallel in human history except the liberation offered by Christ. When I speak of movements in history in which God is present, I do not refer necessarily to the concrete, existing party or group struggling in my city or my country: the movement is wider and deeper, it can be detected, analysed, understood, but the relationship of the single parties and groups that constitute it is by no means clear. Alexis de

Tocqueville, in his introduction to *Democracy in America*, writes, "In running over the pages of our history, we shall scarcely find a single great event of the last seven hundred years that has not promoted equality of condition." And a little later, "The gradual development of the principle of equality is, therefore, a providential fact. It has all the chief characteristics of such a fact: it is universal, it is lasting, it constantly eludes all human interference, and all events and all men contribute to its progress." And later, "To attempt to check democracy would be in that case to resist the will of God." When Tocqueville here speaks of democracy, he does not mean this or that concrete form which the democratic movement has taken: he means the historical movement toward equality and brotherhood (sisterhood) in Western society. It is possible to be fully identified with this movement, without knowing at all times what this means strategically. By God's presence in historical movements I do not mean this or that women's liberation caucus: what I mean is that in and through the various organized efforts of women to redefine their position in society and find human equality with men there is a vector, a movement, an orientation which is due to God's presence to the world. Such a movement is more than the sum of the people involved in it: hence God's presence to it is not simply the sum of the individual liberations experienced by these people. A movement is people and their interrelations, a movement has structure and affects people through these structures. In this sense, then, it seems to me possible to speak of God's presence in historical movements – without being obliged to say that God was acting in the French Revolution as it actually took place. Admittedly, this deserves more reflection on my part.'

CHAPTER FIVE

1 Donald Evans, 'Love, Situations and Rules,' in Paul Ramsey and Gene H. Outka, eds, *Norm and Context in Christian Ethics* (New York: Scribner's, 1968).
2 A bibliography of Ramsey's astoundingly voluminous writings is available in James Johnson and David Smith, eds, *Love and Society: Essays in the Ethics of Paul Ramsey* (Missoula, Montana: Scholars Press, 1974). This book also contains discussions of his theoretical framework by Curran, Camenish, Little, and Smith which I find very illuminating. Another useful secondary source on Ramsey is Charles Curran, *Politics, Medicine and Christian Ethics: A Dialogue with Paul Ramsey* (Philadelphia: Fortress Press, 1973).
3 Donald Evans, *The Logic of Self-Involvement* (London: SCM, 1963; New York: Herder, 1969).

4 Donald Evans, 'Paul Ramsey on Exceptionless Moral Rules,' *The American Journal of Jurisprudence*, 16 (1971); reprinted in Johnson and Smith, eds, *Love and Society*. I am indebted to Paul Ramsey for extensive comments on a first draft. This does not mean that he endorsed all the exegesis and criticism in the essay.

5 Following Ramsey, we shall be focusing attention on moral rules which are *prohibitions*.

6 I shall not go on repeating this qualification. Henceforth we shall assume that what is called a 'similar situation' involves morally relevant similarity of agents as well.

7 Ramsey concedes this at one point (CCE 85).

8 Cf Evans, 'Love, Situations and Rules.'

9 Iris Murdoch, *The Bell* (London: Penguin, 1962). The novel illustrates some of the ideas she expresses in 'Vision and Choice in Morality,' in Ian Ramsey, ed, *Christian Ethics and Contemporary Philosophy* (London: SCM, 1966), which is a reply to Ronald Hepburn. (Ramsey quotes Hepburn in support of his case.)

10 David Lyons, *Forms and Limits of Utilitarianism* (Oxford: Clarendon, 1965), passim; Jan Narveson, *Morality and Utility* (Baltimore: Johns Hopkins University Press, 1967), ch 5.

11 Joseph Fletcher, *Situation Ethics* (Philadelphia: Westminster, 1966), pp 164–5.

12 Ramsey does not use the term '*a priori*,' but he refers explicitly to Kant. Although he is not endorsing Kant's own moral *a priori* (for Ramsey's *a priori* is part of a developing *tradition*), his main point is broadly Kantian: that we can bring moral concepts *to* experience, and not merely derive them *from* experience.

13 Ramsey, at one point, seems to forget this (CCE 113–14, 118). He insists that it is impossible to prove the universal negative proposition that there can be no exceptionless moral rules. But this is to confuse the issue with that which arises concerning *empirical* propositions which are universal and negative. The claim that there can be no exceptionless moral rules, like the claim that 'No adultery' *is* an exceptionless moral rule, is a universal negative *normative* claim.

14 Paul Camenisch, 'Paul Ramsey's Task,' in Johnson and Smith, eds, *Love and Society*, pp 67–9.

15 See CCE 108. On CCE 114 his second exception to the meta-rule against exceptionless moral rules may also be a form of act-utilitarian wedge argument. See also CCE 131.

16 E.G. Charles J. McFadden, *Medical Ethics*, 6th ed (Philadelphia: F.A. Davis, 1967), pp 73–7.

17 CCE 108–9, 114–18. See also CCE 126, where he grants that bad consequences can sometimes *override* a fidelity-obligation; but he insists that we look *first* to the fidelity-obligation, which is morally relevant in itself, apart from consequences.
18 Cf also Eric D'Arcy, *Human Acts* (Oxford: Clarendon, 1963), pp 1–39.
19 Ramsey seems to hold that the act could only be justified if one could somehow convey to the victim what one was really doing; see CCE 128.
20 CCE 116–17; the context for the example is set on CCE 115–16.
21 See especially pp 112–13.
22 J.L. Austin, *How to Do Things with Words* (Oxford: Clarendon, 1962), Lectures I and IV.
23 Gabriel Marcel, *The Mystery of Being*, vol I (Chicago: Regnery, 1966), chs 5 and 6.
24 Charles Curran, 'Paul Ramsey and Traditional Roman Catholic Natural Law Theory,' in Johnson and Smith, eds, *Love and Society*, p 58.
25 Ibid, pp 54–5. Cf Curran, *Politics, Medicine and Christian Ethics*, pp 11–17, 36. According to Curran Ramsey increasingly emphasizes the Lutheran concept of the state as originating not in human nature but in human sinfulness, and hence as having mainly a negative function, that of preserving order.
26 David Little, 'The Structures of Justification in the Political Ethics of Paul Ramsey,' in Johnson and Smith, eds, *Love and Society*, pp 144–5, 151–3, 159–60.

CHAPTER SIX

1 Patrick Nowell-Smith, 'Morality: Religious and Secular,' in Ian T. Ramsey, ed, *Christian Ethics and Contemporary Philosophy* (London: SCM, 1966).
2 William Eckhardt, *Peace Research*, Canadian Peace Research Institute, 2:9 (September 1970).
3 Donald Evans, 'Does Religious Faith Conflict with Moral Freedom?' in Gene Outka and John Reeder, eds, *Religion and Morality* (New York: Doubleday, 1973).
4 Theological works which especially influenced me include the following: Gregory Baum, MB; Martin Buber, *I and Thou*, tr W. Kaufmann (New York: Scribner's, 1970); James Gustafson, *Christ and the Moral Life* (New York: Harper, 1968), esp chs 1, 2, 7); Sam Keen, AW and TDG; H. Richard Niebuhr, *The Responsible Self* (New York: Harper, 1963); Paul Tillich, *The Courage to Be* (London: Nisbet, 1952), *Dynamics of Faith* (New York: Harper, 1957), *Morality and Beyond* (London: Routledge, 1964).

5 The word 'liberation' includes much of the meaning of two other traditional words which have previously been more popular: 'salvation' and 'redemption.' Liberation is not only a central theme in contemporary Christian theology, for example, in Gregory Baum's MB and RA; it is also proposed by William Nicholls as a central concept for comparative religion. See Nicholls's 'Understanding Religion after the "Death of God",' *Theoria to Theory* 2:3 (1968), and 'Liberation as a Religious Theme,' *Canadian Journal of Theology*, 16:3,4 (1970).

6 Cf Niebuhr, *The Responsible Self*, p 119.

7 For a more technical discussion of this interconnection see Donald Evans, *The Logic of Self-Involvement* (London: SCM, 1963; New York: Herder, 1969), esp pp 74–8, 106–14, 145–60, 174–88. See also Niebuhr, *The Responsible Self*, pp 57, 65.

8 Cf Reinhold Niebuhr, *The Nature and Destiny of Man*, vol I (London: Nisbet, 1941), chs 7–9. Cf Evans, *The Logic of Self-Involvement*, pp 197–204. I realize that my essay here presupposes that there is some truth in psychoanalytic and theological ideas concerning unconscious states (or, at least, degrees of awareness receding from that which is fully explicit and acknowledged). If a critic rejects this presupposition, he will also be rejecting much of the essay.

9 Donald Evans, *Struggle and Fulfilment* (Cleveland/London/Toronto: Collins, 1979).

10 Works which especially influenced me when I wrote the 1973 version of the essays included the following:
Gregory Baum, 'The Baptism of Desire,' *The Ecumenist*, May–June 1964
Peter Berger, *A Rumour of Angels* (New York: Doubleday, 1969), pp 61–71
Martin Buber, *I and Thou*, tr W. Kaufmann (New York: Scribner's, 1970)
Erik Erikson, *Childhood and Society*, 2nd ed (New York: Norton, 1963), chs 2, 7
James Gustafson, *Christ and the Moral Life* (New York: Harper, 1968); 'The Conditions for Hope; Reflections on Human Experience,' *Continuum*, 7:4 (Winter 1970)
Sam Keen, AW and TDG
Gabriel Marcel, *Homo Viator* (New York: Harper, 1962), pp 767
Schubert Ogden, *The Reality of God and Other Essays* (New York: Harper, 1964), pp 27–43; 'The Task of Philosophical Theology,' in Robert A. Evans, ed, *The Future of Philosophical Theology* (Philadelphia: Westminster, 1971)
Frederich Schleiermacher, *The Christian Faith* (Edinburgh: Clark, 1928), sections 3–5, 15–17, 29–30
Paul Tillich, *The Courage to Be* (London: Nisbet, 1952), chs 2, 6; *Dynamics of Faith* (New York: Harper, 1957)

J. Cook Wilson, *Statement and Inference* (Oxford: Clarendon, 1926), vol I,
sections 565–81; also in Ninian Smart, ed, *Historical Selections in the Philosophy of Religion* (London: SCM, 1962). Wilson influenced John Baillie, *Our
Knowledge of God* (London: Oxford University Press, 1939), sections 5, 6, 20
Ludwig Wittgenstein, 'A Lecture on Ethics,' *Philosophical Review*, 74 (1965)

11 In the 1973 version of the essay I say, 'By a "basic" attitude I do *not* mean
an attitude which is, in the psychological history of an individual, the
main *origin* of other attitudes; a child's trust in his parents would be
"basic" in this genetic sense of the word, but not in mine.' I still recognize
a difference between such a genetic definition and a phenomenological
one (where 'basic' means 'doubly pervasive and doubly unifying'); but I
am no longer concerned to emphasize the difference, for I now think that
an adult basic attitude (such as basic trust or distrust) is doubly pervasive
mainly because it is an adult version of doubly pervasive attitudes which
first occurred in infancy.

12 H. Richard Niebuhr, *The Responsible Self*, p 120.

13 Concerning 'depth-experiences' see Donald Evans, 'Differences between
Scientific and Religious Assertions,' in Ian Barbour, ed, *Science and
Religion* (New York: Harper, 1967); cf Gregory Baum, *Faith and Doctrine*
(New York: Newman, 1969), ch 2.

14 Concerning 'peak-experiences' see Abraham H. Maslow, *Religions, Values
and Peak-Experiences* (New York: Viking, 1970).

15 In this interpretation of judgment and death-and-resurrection I am obviously influenced by Baum's MB.

16 The notion of '*telos*' here, with its stress on the artisan-artefact analogy, is
rather narrow – as it is in H. Richard Niebuhr, who has influenced me.
Such a narrow notion is useful in typologies of moral views. But as I proceed, the reader will observe that *klesis* can be interpreted as a species of
telos, in a less narrow sense of '*telos*': men are called to a mode of existence which *optimally fulfils* them, a life of responsive freedom, being
liberated to love.

17 This is a central theme in William Lynch, *Images of Hope* (Baltimore:
Helcon, 1965), esp pp 155–7; cf Robert Johann, *Building the Human*
(New York: Herder, 1968), pp 145–7; also cf Dorothy Emmet, 'On "doing
what is right" and "doing the will of God",' *Religious Studies*, 3:1 (October
1967) and 'Religion and the Social Anthropology of Religion,' *Theoria to
Theory*, 3:1 (October 1968).

18 Works which specially influenced me concerning receptivity to other persons include Baum, MB; H.H. Farmer *The World and God* (London: Nisbet,
1935), ch 1; and works previously cited by Buber, Lynch, Marcel, and
H. Richard Niebuhr.

19 For a further discussion of rules and situations and love see Donald Evans, 'Love, Situations and Rules,' in Paul Ramsey and Gene Outka, eds, *Norm and Context in Christian Ethics* (New York: Scribner's, 1968).

20 I add 'and the body' here to the 1973 version of the essay to remind us of what I have said in chs 2 and 3 concerning the importance of the bodily dimension of faith, which is not indicated in the creed.

21 Tillich has been perhaps the most prominent. In this book I have studied Keen and Baum. We should acknowledge the pervasive influence of Martin Buber's personalism on contemporary Christian theology. Another influence has come from existential psychoanalysis as exemplified by Rollo May, *Love and Will* (New York: Norton, 1969), chs 5–8; and Leslie H. Farber, *The Ways of the Will* (New York: Harper, 1968), chs 1, 2, 5. See also James Lapsley, ed, *The Concept of Willing* (New York: Abindgon, 1967), pp 195–206 (which are by Lapsley). In my own experience existentialist and psychoanalytic forms of receptivity have tended to converge with mystical versions, and this discovery has heavily influenced my account of receptivity in this chapter. For a mystical version see Evelyn Underhill, *Mysticism*, rev ed (London: Methuen, 1930), ch 7.

22 See Immanuel Kant, *Religion Within the Limits of Reason Alone*, tr R.M. Greene and H.H. Hudson (New York: Harper, 1960). In general it seems to me that Kant's conception of moral freedom in that book is in fundamental conflict with Christian faith and life. His conception renders the core of Christian theology either unintelligible or repugnant. Convictions concerning a divine grace which enables and inspires and directs a man if he is responsive either make no sense to Kant or present threats to human autonomy and dignity.

23 Iris Murdoch, 'Vision and Choice in Morality,' *Aristotelian Society Supplementary Volume*, 1956; also reprinted in Ian Ramsey, ed, *Christian Ethics and Contemporary Philosophy* (London: SCM, 1966).

24 See John Baillie, *The Idea of Revelation in Recent Thought* (New York: Columbia University Press, 1956), pp 36–40, criticizing Austin Farrer, *The Glass of Vision* (London: Westminister, 1948).

25 In addition to Paul Ramsey (CCE) the following are especially important:
Eric D'Arcy, *Human Acts* (Oxford: Clarendon, 1963), ch 1
Philippa Foot, 'Moral Beliefs,' *Proceedings of the Aristotelian Society*, 59 (1958), and 'Goodness and Choice,' *Aristotelian Society Supplementary Volume*, 35 (1961)
Julius Kovesi, *Moral Notions* (London: Routledge, 1967)
Herbert McCabe, *What is Ethics All About?* (Washington: Corpus, 1969), ch 3, 6
D.Z. Phillips and H.O. Mounce, *Moral Practices* (London: Routledge, 1969)

26 Alasdair MacIntyre, 'Atheism and Moral,' in Alasdair MacIntyre and Paul Ricoeur, *The Religious Significance of Atheism* (New York: Columbia University Press, 1969); also *Secularization and Moral Change* (London: Oxford University Press, 1967), pp 50–3.

27 Elsewhere I have explored one possibility of working towards a common moral vocabulary, namely a common set of very general moral principles for decisions in international relations. See Donald Evans, ed, *Peace, Power and Protest* (Toronto: Ryerson, 1967), chs 1, 2.

28 If changes of moral vocabulary are allowed by the group, a man's thought and action may gradually contribute to gradual changes in the moral framework; I am ignoring this complication here.

29 Phillips and Mounce, *Moral Practices*, pp 12, 17, 18.

30 For Gustafson see works already cited in notes for this chapter. For R.S. Lee see *Freud and Christianity* (London: Allen & Unwin, 1970), chs 5–6, 9–13. Other books relevant to christological issues discussed in this section include Donald M. Baillie, *God was in Christ* (New York: Scribner's, 1948), chs 1, 2, 3, 5; Van A. Harvey, *The Historian and the Believer* (New York: Macmillan, 1966), chs 6, 7, 8; Norman Perrin, *Rediscovering the Teaching of Jesus* (New York: Harper, 1967), ch 3; H. Richard Niebuhr, *The Responsible Self*, pp 149–78; Keith Ward, *Ethics and Christianity* (London: Allen & Unwin, 1970), chs 5–6, 9–13.

31 Earlier drafts of this essay were revised in response to illuminating criticisms by Howard Adelman, James Beckman, David Burrell, James Gustafson, Stan Hauervas, Phillip McKenna, Graeme Nicholson, Millard Schumaker, and Wilfred Cantwell Smith. Where the essay has a psycho-analytic dimension, it depends largely on my experience of therapy in Therafields, a Toronto community.

32 Cf n 13. In my 1967 essay I speak of faith as an interpretation of depth-experiences as revelations of God. I do not appeal to religious authority as my basis for interpreting them in this way. I could give no reasons; it was a matter of individual decision. In this essay, however, the authoritarian alternative emerges more clearly.

33 For example, it seems to me that the kind of self-depreciation and self-loathing which Otto commends is contrary to the self-love which is advocated in this essay. See Rudolph Otto, *The Idea of the Holy*, tr J. Harvey, 2nd ed (London: Oxford University Press, 1923), pp 21, 55.

CHAPTER SEVEN

1 Donald Evans, *The Logic of Self-Involvement* (London: SCM, 1963; New York: Herder, 1969).

2 Donald Evans, 'Philosophical Analysis and Religious Faith: Some Retrospective Reflections,' in F. Duchesneau, ed, *Faith and the Contemporary Epistemologies* (Ottawa: University of Ottawa Press, 1977).

3 Donald Evans, 'Differences between Scientific and Religious Assertions,' in Ian Barbour, ed, *Science and Religion* (New York: Harper, 1968); Donald Evans, 'Faith and Belief,' *Religious Studies,* 10:2 (March and June 1974), section 7.

4 Donald Evans, *Struggle and Fulfilment* (Cleveland/London/Toronto: Collins, 1970).

5 Gabriel Marcel, *The Mystery of Being,* vol I (Chicago: Regnery, 1960), chs 5, 6.

6 George Nakhnikian, 'On the Cognitive Import of Certain Conscious States,' in Sidney Hook, ed, *Religious Experience and Truth* (London: Oliver and Boyd, 1962), p 159.

7 Speech-act implications vary in the strength of their logical commitment. Some are what in *The Logic of Self-Involvement* I called 'indefeasible' implications, for example, the implication of intention when one makes a promise. To say 'I promise to do X but I do not intend to do X' is self-stultifying and in some way self-contradictory. Some implications, however, are merely *'prima facie.'* In saying 'I trust X' I imply that I believe that X is trustworthy, but I can disclaim what I imply. It is part of the meaning of 'trust' that I do imply such a belief, yet in such a way that I can disclaim what is implied: 'I trust X, *but* I do not believe that X is trustworthy.' The word 'but' is both necessary and permissible. It is necessary because the meaning of 'trust' is such that anyone who hears that Jones trusts X is entitled to believe that Jones believes that X is trustworthy unless there is an explicit disclaimer of this implication. It is permissible because the meaning of the word 'trust' does not make it self-contradictory to say 'Jones trusts X and Jones does not believe that X is trustworthy.'
We should note that I have given a *third*-person example here, which indicates that the logical connection is not confined to contexts of first-person speech-acts. I shall return to this point in a moment. But first we should also note that there *is* a logical connection. Trusting X while not believing that X is trustworthy is a kind of irrationality which is radically different from the irrationality of lending money to someone whom one does not believe to be trustworthy. The latter is imprudent unless one has some hidden purpose in mind, but it is not inherently irrational. Trusting someone whom one does not believe to be trustworthy is inherently irrational in the sense that it involves a split between the behavioural-volitional-emotive components of trust and the intellectual components.

Such a split is not ruled out by the meaning of the word 'trust,' as is the case where someone allegedly 'trusts' but does not trust any X, or 'trusts' X but does not believe that X exists. The attitude is still correctly called 'trust,' but an intellectual component is missing which the meaning of the word 'trust' leads us to expect to be present unless it is disclaimed.

It is clear that the example of *prima facie* implication which we have been considering does not have a first-person/third-person asymmetry. In saying 'Jones trusts X' I imply that Jones believes that X is trustworthy. So it is tempting to try to divide entailments into indefeasible and *prima facie* types. Then one could say that 'Jones trusts X' *prima facie* entails 'Jones believes that X is trustworthy.' But since the notion of a *prima facie* entailment is initially anomalous, I have here another reason for regarding speech-act analysis as more appropriate in exploring the varieties of logical connection between stances and convictions.

8 In all this I am setting aside a contrast between logical connections and empirical connections which I have made in chapter 2. There I note, on the one hand, the claim that a person who has a cosmic stance is logically committed to a cosmic connection. On the other hand, there is the claim that, since there is an empirical correlation between such stances and such convictions (cf 'where there's smoke there's fire'), a person who has such a stance probably also has such a conviction, though perhaps unconsciously. In this chapter I am not considering an alleged empirical correlation but instead an alleged original unity of stance and conviction at the prelinguistic level; out of this unity empirical correlations might arise once stance and conviction are separated and one or both are articulated. In this chapter I have contrasted two kinds of logical contention: (i) that a person is logically committed to having a cosmic conviction but may or may not have it; (ii) that a person is logically committed to having a cosmic conviction and must actually have it. I then note that in the actual process of reflective articulation both (i) and (ii) are in different ways applicable.

Index of Authors

Index of Subjects

analogy
- kinds of: activity 4, 10, 14, 16–18, 23, 47, 58, 61, 71–2, 75, 94–5, 194–5; attitude 4, 10, 12, 14, 18–19, 23, 49–50, 61, 69, 75, 91, 123, 195, 237, 240, 262–3; relation 4, 13–14, 20, 23, 61, 63, 71–2, 119–23, 194–5, 237, 240, 263; unconscious depths 241
- ways of: negation 16, 17, 18, 20, 54–6, 96; origination 16, 17, 19, 20, 71–2, 94–5, 111, 122–3, 147; perfection 16–17, 18, 20, 49–51, 52–3; pervasiveness 13, 16, 17, 19, 20, 48–9, 51, 91–2, 121, 123, 238
- and choice of form 12–13, 16–20
- and choice of content 12–13, 15–16, 59–60, 194–5
- and shift of meaning 13, 49, 57
- and qualifiers 49–50
- empiricist argument from 62
- *See also* eternity; models; qualifiers; transcendence
anthropological-logical argument: outlined 5–6, 67; varieties of 67–8; and logical/psychological distinction 68, 260–1, 286; and analogy of attitude 69, 262; and neo-Kantian

epistemology 69–70, 240, 262–3; and cosmic or religious convictions 92, 255–6; Keen's implicit version of 93–4, 101; Nakhnikian's criticism of 254–7; and entailment relations 255–7; and reflection on pre-linguistic experience 257–8, 262–3. *See also* anthropology, normative; authenticity; implication; trust, basic
anthropology, philosophical or normative: and ethics of being 5, 159; and authenticity or fulfilment 59–60, 68–9, 73, 106–7, 110–14, 247; and theology 59–61, 73, 110–11, 142–3, 159; as supplement to linguistic analysis 61, 239–40; generalizing from personal case 68–79, 99–101, 251–2, 259, 261; and analogy of attitude 69; and death instinct 118; and Jesus as norm 130–2; and sociology 134; and historical consciousness 145–6; and deficiency- and growth-needs 152–3; and natural-law love 195; and variable interpretations 257. *See also* attitude, religious; authen-